SOCIAL RIGHTS AND MARKET FREEDOM IN THE EUROPEAN CONSTITUTION: A LABOUR LAW PERSPECTIVE

This is a timely and innovative account of the development of European labour and social security law as it interrelates with the evolution of market integration in the European Union. Giubboni presents, from a labour law perspective, a case study of the changes the European Community/European Union has undergone from its origins to the present day and of the ways these changes have affected the regulation of European Welfare States at national level. Drawing on the idea of 'embedded liberalism', Giubboni analyses the infiltration of EC competition and market law into national systems of labour and social security law, and provides a normative framework for conceptualising the transformation of regulatory techniques implemented at the EU level. This important, interdisciplinary contribution to research in EU social law illustrates how the vision of social protection and solidarity is changing.

STEFANO GIUBBONI is Professor of Labour Law in the Law Faculty, University of Florence.

CAMBRIDGE STUDIES IN EUROPEAN LAW AND POLICY

This series aims to produce original works which contain a critical analysis of the state of the law in particular areas of European Law and set out different perspectives and suggestions for its future development. It also aims to encourage a range of work on law, legal institutions and legal phenomena in Europe, including 'law in context' approaches. The titles in the series will be of interest to academics; policymakers; policy formers who are interested in European legal, commercial and political affairs; practising lawyers including the judiciary; and advanced law students and researchers.

Joint Editors

Professor Dr Laurence Gormley
Rijksuniversiteit Groningen, The Netherlands

Professor Jo Shaw
University of Edinburgh

Editorial advisory board

Professor Richard Bellamy, University of Reading; Ms Catherine Barnard, University of Cambridge; Professor Marise Cremona, Queen Mary College, University of London; Professor Alan Dashwood, University of Cambridge; Professor Dr Jacqueline Dutheil de la Rochère, Université de Paris II, Director of the Centre de Droit Européen, France; Dr Andrew Drzemczewski, Council of Europe, Strasbourg, France; Sir David Edward KCMG, QC, former Judge, Court of Justice of the European Communities, Luxembourg; Professor Dr Walter Baron van Gerven, Emeritus Professor, Leuven and Maastricht and former Advocate General, Court of Justice of the European Communities; Professor Daniel Halberstam, University of Michigan, USA; Professor Dr Ingolf Pernice, Director of the Walter Hallstein Institut, Humboldt Universität, Berlin; Michel Petite, Director General of the Legal Service, Commission of the European Communities, Brussels; Professor Dr Sinisa Rodin, University of Zagreb; Professor Neil Walker, University of Aberdeen and EUI, Fiesole.

Books in the series

EU Enlargement and the Constitutions of Central and Eastern Europe
by Anneli Albi
Social Rights and Market Freedom in the European Constitution: A Labour Law Perspective
by Stefano Giubboni
The Constitution for Europe: A Legal Analysis
by Jean-Claude Piris

SOCIAL RIGHTS AND MARKET FREEDOM IN THE EUROPEAN CONSTITUTION

A Labour Law Perspective

STEFANO GIUBBONI

Translated by
RITA INSTON

CAMBRIDGE
UNIVERSITY PRESS

CAMBRIDGE UNIVERSITY PRESS
Cambridge, New York, Melbourne, Madrid, Cape Town, Singapore, Sao Paulo

Cambridge University Press
The Edinburgh Building, Cambridge CB2 2RU, UK

Published in the United States of America by Cambridge University Press, New York

www.cambridge.org
Information on this title: www.cambridge.org/9780521841269

Originally published in Italian as *Diritti Sociali e Mercato. La Dimensione Sociale dell'Integrazione Europea* by Il Mulino, Bologna, 2003 and © Società editrice il Mulino, Bologna, 2003

First published in English by Cambridge University Press 2006 as *Social Rights and Market Freedom in the European Constitution: A Labour Law Perspective*
English translation © Stefano Giubboni 2006

First published 2006

Printed in the United Kingdom at the University Press, Cambridge

A catalogue record for this book is available from the British Library

ISBN-13   978-0-521-84126-9 hardback
ISBN-10   0-521-84126-7 hardback

To Leonardo

'Raising his son [Hector] kissed him,
tossed him in his arms and
lifted a prayer to Zeus . . .'

Iliad Book VI, 474–5

CONTENTS

SERIES EDITORS' PREFACE

This timely book addresses a number of enduring debates regarding the political and legal trajectory of the European Union's evolving constitutional framework, namely the role and nature of social policy. On the one hand, the purse strings of the national welfare states are still firmly guarded by the Member States, which retain the power to tax and grant benefits. On the other, the logic of the liberalisation of markets has placed a number of competitive pressures upon welfare states, upon national systems of labour law, and upon labour markets, which remain largely national in character. Such national systems are, by their very nature, diverse, notwithstanding the competitive pressures coming from intra-EU market liberalisation and, more recently, globalisation and the effects of the WTO. Many have therefore asked the question about the possible nature and character of any putative 'European social model', and the position of such a model under the EU's evolving constitutional settlement, in which market integration has played such a central role.

The book takes the story from the beginnings of the European integration process, with the ECSC Treaty, the work of the ILO, and other precursors to the initially minimalist social provisions of the EEC Treaty, right through to the present day. It charts the ongoing pressures for change, and the reactions of various key actors, including the political institutions of the European Union, the European Court of Justice, and the national governments. Different styles of regulation have evolved, with a decisive shift towards soft regulation. Yet, at the same time, there has been proposed an important strengthening of the social rights-basis of the EU, in the form of the proposed embedding of the 2000 Charter of Fundamental Rights as Part II of the Constitutional Treaty, agreed by the Member States in June 2004, and undergoing a painful process of ratification at the present time. This paradox constitutes a key theme of the book. Interestingly, many of the underlying themes of the book were canvassed, albeit in more emotive terms, during the French referendum debate in May 2005. However, the troubles of the EU's Constitutional Treaty do not in any way detract from the importance of a work which is located in a much longer timeline of history.

This is the second book in the new CUP series *Cambridge Studies in European Law and Policy*, edited by Laurence Gormley and Jo Shaw, and represents an important contribution to the discussion of the future direction of European social policy.

LAURENCE GORMLEY AND JO SHAW
Series Editors

FOREWORD

SILVANA SCIARRA

A foreword written by an older academic who followed and supervised a younger colleague's work conceals a very subtle dilemma. Praising too much or too little may reveal differing degrees of involvement in someone else's work and even a concern not to interfere with a distinct and separate intellectual enhancement. And yet, sharing the doubts, the aspirations and the fears of the lengthy enterprise leading to the publication of a book means, in a sense, becoming part of that journey, while at the same time maintaining a sufficiently detached critical eye.

When the final result – as in the present case – follows a rigorous, well-balanced and deeply investigated line of research, self-restraint must give way to enthusiasm and joy. A wide community of readers now becomes the addressee of what the author delivers. The circulation of ideas thus starts to follow an unpredictable route, since this book challenges the curiosities of scholars in both labour law and European law.

Stefano Giubboni is a member of a very special generation of European labour lawyers, whose interests spread well beyond the boundaries of domestic law. The stimulating environment of the European University Institute contributed, in expanding the research questions and adding new dimensions to both national and European legal research.

However, Stefano Giubboni's writing is characterized by an inborn personal instinct to seek out the historical and social reasons behind the law. This enables him to shake up some convention-ridden versions of historical events and to throw new light on significant documents which paved the way to the birth of European social policies. One move in this direction is represented by the original analysis of the interrelation between the Ohlin and the Spaak Reports, both of them relevant to an understanding of the Common Market's social and economic foundations. Similarly inspiring is the analysis of the European Court of Justice's case-law dealing with the delicate balance between social values and competition rules.

In the updated, albeit as yet tentative, interpretation of the social rights enshrined in the Treaty establishing a Constitution for Europe one can very clearly feel how Stefano Giubboni's scrupulous historical reconstruction is still the best companion for an understanding of current events.

A highly personal touch added by the author of the present book has to do with the attention he pays to the language of labour law. Although this singularity owes much to the exceptional skills of the translator, it must be underlined how such a language returns on the scene as a protagonist, showing its remarkable power. Linguistic metaphors assist the author throughout his work, as if he were seeking to express a new centrality of this legal discipline which also coincides with the construction of its new identity. Indeed, in the light of the new centrality of labour law it is greatly to be hoped that the present Cambridge University Press series will, given its aims, host other future contributions in the same field.

This foreword is therefore an opportunity to voice a sense of trust in scholarship – such as that achieved by Stefano Giubboni – which succeeds in keeping alive the discussion in European labour and social law and in strengthening the role of critical legal thinking. This invigorates the hope that social justice may remain both an aim and a methodology in the evolution of European law and enhance European integration even farther.

ACKNOWLEDGEMENTS

The book here presented to an English-speaking readership was originally published in Italian in 2003 by Il Mulino of Bologna under the title *Diritti sociali e mercato. La dimensione sociale dell'integrazione europea.*

However, the research that forms its basis was begun and almost entirely carried out, starting from an unforgettable late summer in 1996, at the European University Institute, Florence. And whereas the course of any research includes (above and beyond the essential solipsistic process of writing it up) a close interpersonal and collective dimension, the path that led to this book was from the very outset marked more than ever by the community dimension which is so typical of and, I may venture to say, so magically special to the European University Institute.

I find it hard to imagine any environment more conducive to the circulation and free exchange of ideas than the Renaissance humanistic ambience, nurtured by harmony, of the Villa Schifanoia and the Badia Fiesolana. The spirit of intellectual freedom and intimacy that imbued the small community of European labour lawyers who experienced personal development together during those intense years spent at the Villa Schifanoia constituted, for me, an enduring and highly prized source of inspiration and ideas.

Of the numerous individuals to whom I owe so much, I wish to express public acknowledgement here of my gratitude to at least Giovanni Orlandini, Sabrina Régent, Diamond Ashiagbor, Eeva Kolehmainen and Samuel Engblom for the friendship and generosity with which, on so many occasions, they shared with me the starting assumptions and results of their personal and original paths of research.

Alan Milward, Maurizio Ferrera and Maximilian Fuchs all contributed equally, albeit at different stages and in different ways, to the development of many of the ideas contained in this book, not only with their suggestions but even more so through the example of their own writings.

Silvana Sciarra exercised her *ars maieutica* on me with grace and affection, offering me the continual example of her irrepressible curiosity and intellectual rigour. This study, so different from what I had imagined when I first arrived at the Institute, is in large measure an endeavour to respond to the inspiration she gave me.

Last, but by no means least, my warmest thanks go to Rita Inston, who in preparing the English version, revised and updated, of the book originally published in 2003 has made me realize how great a part of our intellectual experience lies in the activity known as 'translating'.

STEFANO GIUBBONI,
Florence/Perugia, December 2004

CASES

European Court of Justice

Court of First Instance

National Cases

France

Germany

Italy

United Kingdom

LEGISLATION

European Community Legislation, Treaties and Charters

Regulations

Directives

Treaties

International sources

National Legislation

Austria

Germany

Italy

United States

INTRODUCTION

This book presents a study of the complex and changing relations that have successively prevailed – in the magmatic development of European integration – between the construction of the Common Market and social rights and policies. In essence, it examines the nature of the space and role that have been, are and are likely to be allocated, in the construction of the Community, to social rights and policies at national and supranational level.

The focus of the analysis is centred on the constitutional dimension of the relations in question. This is reconstructed both (and primarily) from the dynamic perspective offered by an examination of the changes that have effectively remoulded the Community's economic constitution since its beginnings up to the present day, and from the static perspective ensuing from a comparison of the various ideal – or, more accurately, ideal-type – models of that constitution which, although obviously not claiming to explain the historical realities of the changes, nonetheless help to categorize them from a normative point of view.

The book develops a research perspective that could be described as intrinsically interdisciplinary.

Labour law – perhaps more than other legal disciplines – has in fact always found in the interdisciplinary and comparative method one of the features that best connote and specify its identity and its cognitive status, immersed as they are in the reality of more deep-seated social dynamics.

As one author (Collins) has written recently, labour law congenitally represents 'a contextual field of study rather than a rigid doctrinal category'. It has always not merely allowed but axiomatically demanded and, as it were, imposed a fundamental freedom of method and research. The very plurality of sources and heterogeneity of levels and dimensions that define its underlying identity have always made it fertile ground for disseminating and experimenting with new approaches and methods of analysis and regulation.

The Community dimension adds yet another element of complexity to what has always been the composite, multitiered and extraordinarily dynamic framework of labour law and means that, now more than ever, the original multidisciplinary nature of the subject is necessarily extended still farther.

The present study follows in the path of this methodological tradition, in full awareness that, for a proper understanding of the profound changes that Community integration has brought and is bringing about in the field of labour and social-security law, there needs to be continual comparison with other disciplines, both legal and non-legal.

The historical research and political theory of European integration constitute the natural hinterland of any study of Community law in context. They have been decisive factors in defining the keys to an interpretation of those changes in the Community's economic constitution in whose light European social law is analysed and 'contextualized' here. From the same point of view, comparison with constitutional doctrines of European integration and also with the disciplines – legal and economic – dealing more specifically with the form and content of the construction of a single market proved equally necessary.

Albeit in new forms, the language of labour law appears to have regained, in today's scientific and political debate on Europe, a centrality that seemed irrevocably lost.

This is being evidenced in a number of different contexts, variously linked with the requirements, opportunities and restraints deriving from economic integration.

It is happening, in particular, in the context of the open method of co-ordination for national employment and social policies and also the laborious process of Community-level constitutionalization of fundamental social rights. Both cases involve processes which are open and fluid and, as things stand, similarly characterized by a predominance of Community soft law, and yet which are capable of reactivating virtuous mechanisms converging towards the necessary new balance between negative integration and positive integration.

They prefigure, in point of fact, a competitive market firmly based on a common constitutional space in which economic freedoms and social rights, the values of efficiency and solidarity, are able to find a more evenly balanced position within the construction of the Community. However ambiguous, the formula of a 'highly competitive social market economy' introduced by Article I-3 of the Treaty establishing a Constitution for

Europe is in a way expressive of this tendency, in so far as it seeks to distil such a 'rebalancing'.

This recovery of the necessary autonomy of the fundamental principles of labour law as against the dictates of purely negative integration denotes a reaffirmation of the very identity of the European social model. It also reaffirms the notion – on which the original compromise of embedded liberalism devised by the founding fathers was itself manifestly based – that strong social rights, in addition to being an expression of the insuppressible calls for fairness and solidarity embodied by the various traditions of the European welfare state, also constitute one of the most important institutional preconditions of the long-term competitiveness of European economies.

Be that as it may, the processes in question are still weak and very much stamped by 'experimentation'. If the 'reformist' heritage of European labour law is to be safeguarded and enriched, they need to find a more solid anchorage in the full constitutionalization of a strong and comprehensive catalogue of fundamental social rights at EU level and the definition of effective policies supporting their translation into practice.

The book is divided into two parts (and four chapters) which are, as it were, connected in form and substance in that Part II examines more closely – in both analytical and theoretical terms – concepts treated in Part I from a mainly historical perspective.

Chapter 1 sets out to recount the evolving nature of the relationship between construction of the market and social rights in general terms, seeking to trace the thread that links the profound changes undergone by the Community's economic constitution since its beginnings up to the present day. It explains at length the content of the original compromises represented by embedded liberalism and the reasons for its crisis.

Chapter 2 starts out from the conclusions of Chapter 1 in an attempt to re-establish the guiding thread of the present phase of the Community integration process, which appears to be characterized by the quest, from outlines that are still uncertain and very fluid, for a new balance between the negative and positive integration of national welfare states. This guiding thread is investigated with particular reference to the need to reaffirm – albeit in new forms adapted to the extraordinary changes of our era – the centrality of the values of labour law and welfare institutions, as the common heritage of European democracies, which was at the very basis of the construction of the Community. The innovations introduced starting from the Treaty of Amsterdam, and in particular the new elements recently contained in the constitutional Treaty signed in Rome on 29 October 2004, are examined analytically here from this perspective.

Chapter 3 focuses attention on what might be considered the field of choice for identifying possible tensions between the construction of the integrated market and national social rights. It broaches the subject of the 'infiltration' of Community competition law into national systems of labour and social-security law, using the perspective of the recasting and necessary rebalancing of potentially conflicting but equally essential and fundamental values in the process of European integration.

Chapter 4 first dwells on the changes that have taken place, from the start to the present day, in the forms and techniques of supranational regulatory intervention in social matters, and then goes on to present a systematic comparison between the various ideal models of a Community economic constitution as viewed in the abstract. This is because the differing relations between the market and social rights as respectively envisaged by the ideal-type constitutional models of 'competitive', 'solidaristic' and 'co-operative' federalism inevitably give rise to differing issues regarding the legitimacy of Community law that need to be analysed systematically.

The book ends with a set of Conclusions presenting a number of deliberations that sum up the underlying trends of the European social model.

PART I

Social policies and market principles. European
social integration revisited

Embedded liberalism: the original constitutional compromise and its crisis

1. A preliminary review of the historical background

Two fundamental processes, at once simultaneous and symbiotic, mark the history of Western Europe from the immediate post-war period onwards and more particularly the years during which the European Community was formed: first, what has been called the 'rescue',[1] the genuine rebirth, on democratic foundations, of the nation-state as a welfare state; and second, (participation in) the reconstruction, conclusively overcoming the blinkered nationalistic attitudes that had cast a pall over the inter-war years, of the international economic order.[2] The two processes come together, or perhaps rather find their moment of synthesis, in the establishment of first the European Coal and Steel Community (ECSC) and later the European Economic Community (EEC).[3]

They are identifiable as two separate 'movements' only by virtue of the apparent contrasts and contradictions between them; they actually, at least in the extraordinary and probably unique and unrepeatable phase in European economic history coinciding with the hectic thirty-year period of economic recovery in the aftermath of the Second World War known as the *Trente Glorieuses*, followed a mutually complementary course of development, with each supporting and reinforcing the other.

'At the end of the period of reconstruction of the national economies shattered by the war' – as one author has tellingly put it[4] – 'income redistribution and discretionary macroeconomic management emerged as the top policy priorities of most Western European governments.

[1] A. S. Milward, *The European Rescue of the Nation-State*, London 2000 (2nd edn revised and enlarged with the assistance of G. Brennan and F. Romero).

[2] J. G. Ruggie, 'International Regimes, Transactions and Change: Embedded Liberalism in the Postwar Economic Order', *International Organization* 1982, vol. 36 no. 2, pp. 379ff.

[3] Cf. A. S. Milward and V. Sørensen, 'Interdependence or Integration? A National Choice', in A. S. Milward *et al.* (eds.), *The Frontier of National Sovereignty: History and Theory 1945–1992*, London 1993, pp. 1ff.

[4] G. Majone *et al.*, *Regulating Europe*, London-New York 1996, p. 1.

The market was relegated to the ancillary role of providing the resources to pay for this government largesse, and any evidence of market failures was deemed sufficient to justify state intervention, often in the intrusive forms of centralized capital allocation and the nationalization of key sectors of the economy.'[5]

European states embarked on an enterprise, unprecedented in terms of scale and government commitment, of systematic intervention in economic and social life with, for the first time, 'the express purpose of shaping and controlling their national destinies'.[6] An enterprise which was beyond all comparison with the embryonic and somewhat confused and approximative forms of pre-Keynesian state intervention that had also occurred in Europe before the war[7] in that, apart from being based on a new political ideology,[8] it differed from them in (and was characterized by) its use of the more refined instruments of intervention made available in the meantime by the 'empirical-Keynesian synthesis'[9] and in the more pronounced slant towards 'social engineering', or the 'technology of social design', that constitutes one of the most authentic keynotes of the period.[10]

Above and beyond any manifest national differences in the various technical forms in which its prescriptions on the political economy of the state were actually put into effect, it may be said that in placing the nation in the centre of its intellectual map Keynesianism offered the politicians of the time a strong theoretical basis to justify intensive intervention in every sphere of economic and social life. It created – as Alan Milward has put it – 'a mental world in which the political machinery of the nation could be used to improve the lot of mankind and helped to give post-war national politicians the justificatory ideology they needed.'[11]

---

[5] The reader need only consult R. Vernon (ed.), *Big Business and the State*, Cambridge, Mass. 1974.

[6] Milward and Sørensen, 'Interdependence', p. 4.

[7] See the account of them presented by J.-P. Thomas, *Les politiques économiques au XXe siècle*, Paris 1994.

[8] Cf. L. Magnusson and B. Stråth, 'From Werner Plan to EMU: In Search of a European Political Economy. Historical Perspectives and Future Prospects', in Magnusson and Stråth (eds.), *From Werner Plan to EMU: In Search of a Political Economy for Europe*, Brussels 2001, especially p. 27.

[9] Thomas, *Les politiques*. Here as elsewhere, unless otherwise stated the translation from non-English sources is by Rita Inston.

[10] C. S. Maier, 'I fundamenti politici del dopoguerra', in P. Anderson *et al.* (eds.), *Storia d'Europa*, vol. I, *L'Europa oggi*, Turin 1993, especially pp. 320 and 333.

[11] Milward, *The European Rescue*, pp. 42–3.

Throughout Western Europe – in both the countries that emerged from the Second World War as victors and those that emerged as the vanquished – social and welfare policies rose to become the mainstay of the reassertion of the nation-state as the 'basic unit of political organization'[12] and acted as a decisive factor in its democratic (re)legitimation.[13]

The state now no longer confined itself to what had already been the case after the First World War, i.e. 'providing assistance in situations of social emergency and financial hardship', or even 'safeguarding the elementary vital needs of the population', but went so far as to shoulder 'the burden of comprehensive responsibility for the subsistence and development of society in cultural, economic and social terms'.[14]

Without exception, albeit in forms and with degrees of emphasis differing from one country to another, the promise offered by Keynesian policies of full employment and a system of guaranteed social security for all citizens 'from the cradle to the grave', as echoed in the famous slogan that quickly gained widespread currency as the motto of the epoch following the extraordinary international success of the Beveridge Report,[15] constituted a central element of the constitutional agreements drawn up during the immediate post-war period: official 'acts of political appeasement, subscribed to by governments under the looming threat of internal civil war in a world divided into ideological and power blocs',[16] and at the same time the genuine expression of an entirely new notion of social solidarity and cohesion.[17]

All of the post-Second World War constitutions in Western Europe – and more especially those of the major founding countries of the EEC – espoused, even if in diverse forms, the welfare-state model.

Compared with what had been the case in the past, and in particular with the short-lived Weimar experiment usually remembered for the

---

[12] A. S. Milward, 'L'Europa in formazione', in Anderson *et al.* (eds.), *Storia d'Europa*, vol. I, p. 163.

[13] M. D'Antona, 'Diritto del lavoro di fine secolo: una crisi d'identità?', *Rivista Giuridica del Lavoro e della Previdenza Sociale* 1998, vol. I, pp. 311ff.; now also in D'Antona, *Contrattazione, rappresentatività, conflitto. Scritti sul diritto sindacale*, edited and with an introductory essay by G. Ghezzi and a foreword by S. Cofferati, Rome 2000, p. 273, on which the above statement is based.

[14] D. Grimm, 'Il futuro della costituzione', in G. Zagrebelsky, P. P. Portinaro and J. Luther (eds.), *Il futuro della costituzione*, Turin 1996, pp. 129ff., here p. 143.

[15] *Social Insurance and Allied Services. Report by Sir William Beveridge*, London 1942. But see also the other and equally famous report by the same author: *Full Employment in a Free Society*, London 1944, which in a sense constituted the natural continuation and complement of the earlier one.

[16] D'Antona, 'Diritto del lavoro', p. 273.   [17] Cf. also Maier, 'I fondamenti', pp. 313ff.

partial provision for anticipated future developments it contained, the inherent defining element of this welfare-state model lay in the constitutionalization of the function of social protection as made explicit in the form of social rights, which, in conjunction with the guarantee of fundamental rights to liberty, complete 'the material legitimation criterion of a state governed by the rule of law'.[18]

Leaving aside the difference in the constitutionalization techniques used – which were based in some cases on the insertion into the basic law of a catalogue of social rights of varying extent and detail, and in others on the provision of a general welfare-state clause[19] – the new constitutional principles fulfilled the priority function of a normative guarantee of the process of political and social integration realized by the 'multi-class' state.[20]

So – and this is the main point of discontinuity with respect to the European experiences of the first half of the twentieth century – 'In welfare-state mass democracies, highly productive capitalist economies were socially domesticated [*sozialgebändigt*] for the first time, and were thus brought more or less in line with the normative self-understanding of democratic constitutional states.'[21]

The social bond imposed in this way by the European constituents of the post-Second World War period defines an economic constitution based on the pre-eminence of politics.[22] This is a fundamentally important aspect of post-war European constitutionalism that should be given maximum emphasis. It may, indeed, be said that it is only with the provision of so penetrating a social bond that the programme which characterizes twentieth-century constitutionalism as '*the age of political constitutions*' was accomplished.[23]

[18] L. Mengoni, 'I diritti sociali', *Argomenti di Diritto del Lavoro 1998*, no. 1, pp. 1ff., here p. 3; more recently, in the same vein, G. Maestro Buelga, 'Constitución económica y derechos sociales en la Unión europa', *Revista de Derecho Comunitario Europeo 2000*, pp. 123ff.

[19] See again Mengoni, 'I diritti sociali', pp. 3ff. and also, at more length, A. Baldassarre, 'Diritti sociali', in *Enciclopedia Giuridica Treccani*, vol. XI, Rome 1989, *ad vocem* (now also in Baldassarre, *Diritti della persona e valori costituzionali*, Turin 1997, pp. 123ff.); M. Luciani, 'Sui diritti sociali', *Democrazia e Diritto 1995*, pp. 545ff.; L. M. Díez-Picazo and M.-C. Ponthoreau, 'The Constitutional Protection of Social Rights: Some Comparative Remarks', *EUI Working Papers in Law* No. 91/20.

[20] M. S. Giannini, *Il pubblico potere. Stati e amministrazioni pubbliche*, Bologna 1986.

[21] J. Habermas, *The Postnational Constellation. Political Essays* (translated, edited and with an introduction by M. Pensky), Cambridge 2001, p. 48.

[22] See Maestro Buelga, 'Constitución', p. 127.

[23] M. Fioravanti, 'Costituzione e politica: bilancio di fine secolo', in L. Ornaghi (ed.), *La nuova età delle costituzioni. Da una concezione nazionale della democrazia a una prospettiva europea*, Bologna 2000, pp. 49ff., here p. 56 (the emphasis is in the original).

The constitutionalization (with varying degrees of strength and explicitness) of the welfare-state principle contributed decisively to making the constitution – fuller in both form and extent – the legitimation criterion and 'founding instrument' of the power of the democratic state that rose again from the ruins of the war; and it was predominantly in this context, in specifically indicating the priority direction of the transformation of society, that the constitutions of post-Second World War Europe demonstrated all their 'political *origin*' and their propensity for '*producing* politics'.[24] Thus, the post-war constitutions gave practical implementation to the premisses (and promises) contained *in nuce* in the tragic Weimar experiment: 'economic power went from being the active subject of revolutionary constitutional transformation to becoming the object of the rules and limits of welfare-state government . . . which from then on imposed *Ergreifung*, the constitutional control and domestication of the economic sphere. A new conception of relations between economic power and political power consequently became the characterizing feature of democratic constitutions.'[25]

For over thirty years national welfare-state systems witnessed, on this basis, an almost continuous process of impetuous development, driven by an economic growth that was uninterrupted and on a scale unprecedented in the continent's history.[26] This development was in some respects broadly convergent in having as its final outcome a guarantee of the unequalled levels of social cohesion and equality that even to this day are particular to European societies,[27] as enshrined in the unifying metaphor of the 'European social model'. A model which exhibits unquestionable features of underlying sameness that justify representing it as a single model, even if within itself it is differentiated, broken down into elements

[24] *Ibid.* (the emphasis is in the original).

[25] C. Pinelli, 'La dicotomia fra democrazia e mercato e i costi dell' incertezza', in Ornaghi, *La nuova età*, pp. 195ff., here p. 197, who in turn quotes M. Luciani, 'L'antisovrano e la crisi delle costituzioni', in *Scritti in onore di Giuseppe Guarino*, Padua 1998, vol. II, pp. 731ff., especially p. 775.

[26] Of the copious literature on the subject, the most distinguished account is still to be found in P. Flora (ed.), *Growth to Limits. The European Welfare States since World War II*, Berlin-New York 1986–7 (in four volumes), in addition to which there are the likewise well-reputed summaries by: P. Flora and A. J. Heidenheimer (eds.), *The Development of Welfare States in Europe and America*, New Brunswick-London 1981; J. Alber, *Vom Armenhaus zum Wohlfartsstaat: Analysen zur Entwicklung der Sozialversicherung in Westeuropa*, Frankfurt am Main-New York 1982; and G. A. Ritter, *Storia dello Stato sociale* (Italian translation), Rome-Bari 1996 (with a final chapter on Italy by L. Gaeta and A. Viscomi and a foreword by P. Pombeni).

[27] Cf. L. Gallino (ed.), *Diseguaglianze ed equità in Europa*, Rome-Bari 1993; C. Crouch, *Social Change in Western Europe*, Oxford 1999.

and in certain respects equally profoundly split along historical, political and institutional divides which vary greatly from one national experience to another and can at most, again only by making a somewhat forced generalization, serve to categorize 'worlds'[28] or 'families'[29] of 'welfare capitalism', or 'solidarity models',[30] which are far removed from each other and are themselves continually shifting and escaping from the confines of their defining boundaries.

The construction of a powerful structure of social policies which functioned as the primary factor in the reassertion and re-legitimation of the nation-state that emerged in ruins from the war simultaneously provided the basis for the rebuilding of an international economic order.[31]

This second fundamental 'movement' in post-war Western economic history is linked to the first by an indissoluble connection which makes the international economic order that proceeded to be rebuilt in the name of free trade and the opening-up of markets a radically different phenomenon not only from, obviously, the nationalistic protectionism of the inter-war years but also from the *laissez-faire* system which had predominated up to the outbreak of the First World War and which was in its turn dominated by the dictates of neoclassical liberalist orthodoxy.[32]

Each movement enabled and at the same time strengthened the other: in protecting society from the disruptive force of capitalism newly released 'in the outside world', the social cohesion and stability guaranteed by the rebirth of the nation-state in the form of the democratic welfare state made the opening-up of national economies to free trade socially possible and were in their turn reinvigorated and reinforced by the latter, in a virtuous circle fed by the fruits of the imperious economic growth thus

---

[28] As in the title of G. Esping-Andersen's well-known book *The Three Worlds of Welfare Capitalism*, Cambridge 1990, which reopened and to some degree inspired the most recent spate of comparative welfare research. For a critical re-examination of this vast body of literature, which nowadays tends to be increasingly linked to the equally protean literature on the 'worlds of industrial capitalism', see R. E. Goodin *et al.*, *The Real Worlds of Welfare Capitalism*, Cambridge 1999.

[29] F. G. Castles (ed.), *Families of Nations. Patterns of Public Policies in Western Democracies*, Aldershot, Hants 1993.

[30] M. Ferrera, *Modelli di solidarietà*, Bologna 1993.

[31] See Ruggie, 'International Regimes'; Ruggie, 'Trade, Protectionism and the Future of Welfare Capitalism', *Journal of International Affairs* 1994, vol. 48 no. 1, pp. 1ff.; Ruggie, 'Globalization and the Embedded Liberalism Compromise: The End Of an Era?', *Max Planck Institut für Gesellschaftsforschung Working Paper* No. 97/1.

[32] K. Polanyi, *The Great Transformation. The Political and Economic Origins of Our Time*, Boston 1957 (orig. edn 1944).

ensured.[33] Both the mixed economy and the welfare state facilitated 'the process of internationalization and European integration by enabling governments to smooth out and, sometimes, even slow down the necessary adjustment arising from the increased openness of national economies'.[34]

The Keynesian national welfare state does not, however, confine itself to fulfilling a basic function of stabilizing the internal economic cycle in providing 'the linking mechanism between output and mass consumption'.[35] It also performs a concurrent and contributory essential function of integrating national economies into the world market.[36]

The system conceived at Bretton Woods in 1944 fixed the optimum conditions, in this sense, for a controlled and steered reopening of national economies to international trade. An opening-up that was harmoniously adapted to the convergent requirements for an expansion of social and economic intervention by the state within the confines of its own borders and supported by the deliberate intention 'to strike a balance between a liberal world market and the domestic responsibility of states'.[37] A balance in which the internal dimension of a progressive extension of welfare-state functions accompanied and supported the external dimension of a process of economic liberalization.[38]

The essence of 'embedded liberalism' – the name suggested by John Ruggie, using a metaphor explicitly originating from Polanyi, for the new and complex post-Second World War institutional economic order – was therefore as follows: 'unlike the economic nationalism of the thirties, it would be multilateral in character; unlike the liberalism of the gold standard and free trade, its multilateralism would be predicated upon domestic interventionism'.[39] And, more briefly, it was a 'symbiosis

---

[33] See Thomas, *Les politiques*.

[34] L. Tsoukalis, *The New European Economy Revisited* (3rd edn), Oxford 1997, p. 22.

[35] A. Perulli, 'Postfordismo, forma dello Stato e diritto del lavoro', *Lavoro e Diritto* 1998, pp. 251ff., here p. 259.

[36] See E. Rieger and S. Leibfried, 'Welfare State Limits to Globalization', *Politics & Society* 1998, vol. 26 no. 3, pp. 363ff., especially p. 377.

[37] R. W. Cox, 'Global Restructuring: Making Sense of the Changing International Political Economy', in R. Stubbs and G. R. D. Underhill (eds.), *Political Economy and the Changing Global Order*, London 1994, p. 45; also, in the same vein, A. Martin, 'Labour, the Keynesian Welfare State and the Changing International Political Economy', in Stubbs and Underhill, *Political Economy*, pp. 60ff.

[38] Also R. O. Keohane, 'The World Political Economy and the Crisis of Embedded Liberalism', in J. H. Goldthorpe (ed.), *Order and Conflict in Contemporary Capitalism. Studies in the Political Economy of Western European Nations*, Oxford 1984, pp. 15ff., especially p. 18.

[39] Ruggie, 'International Regimes', p. 393.

between external liberalization and the strengthening of the economic role of the state at the domestic level'.[40]

The creation of the ECSC in 1951 and the EEC (and Euratom) in 1957, in the name of the ideal of peacemaking and political and economic union in Western Europe, directly reflected the compromise inherent in this new order, of which the European Community came to form an essential component.

The integration – at first sectoral and later general – of the economies of the original six members of the Community into a common transnational market answered the priority need for the rebuilding of the participating states and remained fundamentally functional to the delicate and difficult process of rebirth[41] within a restored framework of peace, flourishing democratic stability and progressive reopening at international level. As the most thoughtful historical account of the process of Community integration has shown, the latter was therefore originally an essentially national choice.[42] It was 'an agreement between weak states . . . to guide the processes of economic opening-up, steering their social and political effects by identifying a path of progressive adjustment',[43] in which although it was based on the construction of a new type of supranational institution the surrender of albeit significant and gradually increasing shares of sovereignty was, in actuality, instrumental in reaffirming the decisive economic and political role of the state and the national interest.

And there can be no real doubt that at the centre of this national interest there was, no less strongly than the impelling necessity of creating an institutional framework that would ensure the stable opening up of the

---

[40] Tsoukalis, *New European*, p. 22; and see also M. Rhodes, 'Defending the Social Contract: The EU Between Global Constraints and Domestic Imperatives', in D. Hine and H. Kassim (eds.), *Beyond the Market. The EU and National Social Policy*, London-New York 1998, pp. 36ff., especially p. 49.

[41] See also in this sense M. D'Antona, 'Sistema giuridico comunitario', in A. Baylos Grau *et al.* (eds.), *Dizionario di Diritto del Lavoro Comunitario*, Bologna 1996, pp. 3ff., especially p. 8; S. Sciarra, 'From Strasbourg to Amsterdam: Prospects for the Convergence of European Social Rights Policy', in P. Alston (ed.), *The EU and Human Rights*, Oxford 1999, pp. 473ff.

[42] Milward and Sørensen, 'Interdependence', and Milward, *European Rescue*, p. 18, who talks of 'an act of national will'. And also cf., albeit in a context of significant reconstructional and methodological differences, A. Moravcsik, *The Choice for Europe. Social Purpose and State Power from Messina to Maastricht*, Ithaca, N.Y. 1998 (and London 1999).

[43] P. Bianchi, 'Europa smarrita ed Europa ritrovata: decisione politica e gap democratico', in L. Paganetto (ed.), *Oltre l'Euro. Istituzioni, occupazione e crescita*, Bologna 1999, p. 52.

European economies to each other and thereby allow the rapid expansion of intra-Community trade, the will and the need to extend the state's capacity for economic and social intervention.

2. Metamorphoses of the European economic constitution and their impact on national social policies and rights

The idea underlying this study is therefore that the European Community's original 'economic constitution' (i.e. all the fundamental principles relating to the organization of and the course followed by economic processes[44] as directly or indirectly enshrined in the founding Treaties of 1951 and 1957) was a full and conscious expression of, and indeed totally reflected, what has been described above as the post-war institutional compromise of embedded liberalism. And, conversely, that its successive profound metamorphoses represent, in their turn, a reflection of or response to – in certain instances more direct and explicit and in others more indirect and even unconscious, and in the case of some aspects a manifestation of the declared will and choices of (to borrow the German

[44] The expression 'economic constitution' is therefore interpreted here in a broad and non-technical sense as meaning all the fundamental principles that govern the nature and form of the process of socio-economic co-operation, particularly through the definition of the content and limits of the economic role of the state with respect to the market. And in this context, therefore, through the actual determination of the breadth and relevance of social policies as the main instruments for correcting 'spontaneous' market processes and outcomes, in Marshall's classic definition of such state intervention as the use of 'political power to supersede, supplement or modify operations of the economic system in order to achieve results which the economic system would not achieve on its own' (T. H. Marshall, *Social Policy*, London 1975, p. 15). It should be stressed that the use of the expression 'economic constitution' with reference to the Community order dates back almost as far as the start of the integration process and in fact figures in the Spaak Report itself: cf. Comité Intergouvernemental Créé par la Conférence de Messine, *Rapport des Chefs de Délégation aux Ministres des Affaires Etrangères*, Brussels 1956, widely known and hereinafter referred to simply as the Spaak Report (summarized in English in *PEP [Political and Economic Planning] Planning* 1956, vol. 22 no. 405); and see L.-J. Constantinesco, 'La constitution économique de la CEE', *Revue Trimestrielle de Droit Européen* 1977, pp. 244ff. The definition adopted here echoes in large measure the classical one developed by the German ordoliberal school (on which cf. D. J. Gerber, 'Constitutionalizing the Economy: German Neoliberalism, Competition Law and the "New" Europe', *American Journal of Comparative Law* 1994, vol. 42, pp. 25ff., especially p. 44, and also R. Miccù, '"Economia e costituzione": una lettura della cultura giuspubblicistica tedesca', *Quaderni del Pluralismo* 1996, pp. 243ff.). Compared with the latter, however, it is characterized by the emphasis it places on the essential and substantively equal importance of social policies in general. A similar meaning is used in A. Predieri, *Euro. Poliarchie democratiche e mercati monetari*, Turin 1998, pp. 190ff.

Federal Constitutional Court's expression) the '*Herren der Verträge*' but in the case of other no less decisive aspects more an expression of the 'self-driven' dynamics of the integration process – the radical changes that have occurred, from the mid-1960s to the present day, in the institutional and economic order planned in the years immediately following the end of the Second World War.

In particular, it will be argued here that the apparent flimsiness of the social provisions of the Treaty of Rome (and of the slightly less meagre ones of the Treaty of Paris) was in reality consistent with the intention, imbued with the embedded liberalism compromise, not only to preserve intact but hopefully to expand and strengthen the Member States' powers of economic intervention and social governance: i.e. their ability to keep the promises of protection underlying the new social contract signed with their own citizens at the end of the war.

In the scheme of things as viewed by the founding fathers, the construction of a strong transnational market in Europe would open up and integrate the member countries' economies *without* creating any threat to their respective national sovereignty in social matters, which would in fact be able to count on the beneficial effects of the spontaneous and progressive harmonization of their social systems or, at least, on the greater fiscal *dividend* deriving from the creation of the common market. The EEC would, therefore, have no need – except in a few well-defined areas and at most only where the theory of international trade had identified real risks of dumping – of social powers of its own.

From this perspective, it is easy to understand why the only social rights to be expressly guaranteed at supranational level, marginal to – or perhaps more accurately as a corollary of and as it were 'in the service of' – effective enjoyment of the economic freedoms guaranteed by the Treaty of Rome, were those strictly functional to the creation of an integrated market (in labour and services) as envisaged in Articles 48–66 (now Articles 39–55).[45] As the most shrewd historical research has demonstrated, however, even those few social rights did not compromise but actually confirmed 'the essential nature of national economic strategies',[46] based as they were – at least up to the end of the transitional period – on continued statal control of migratory flows and the complete independence of labour-market policies.

---

[45] As was already the case with Article 69 of the ECSC Treaty, although this provision was more 'timid' than those contained in the EEC Treaty.

[46] F. Romero, *Emigrazione e integrazione europea 1945–1973*, Rome 1991, p. 129.

And this observation, when we look closely, is true of more than just social rights, although in their case it is undeniably apparent. More generally, the original absence of any kind of Community catalogue of fundamental rights cannot be explained solely, and perhaps so much, by the conviction (which was certainly present) that because economic integration was only sectoral it would not really create any likelihood of violation and, consequently, any need for protection that was not already adequately provided for by the Member States' own national constitutions and above all, as far as the transnational level was concerned, by the 1950 European Convention on Human Rights, to which all the Community founding members were committed. The more deep-seated explanation probably lay in the conviction that the entire construction of the Community was, as such, actually aimed at rebuilding – in a new internal and international order – the economic preconditions for the full and effective enjoyment, within each individual national legal order, of fundamental (civil, political and social) rights. In this sense there was no need for a Community catalogue, because the objective of protecting fundamental rights – and particularly social rights – formed part of the very founding mission itself of the European Communities and was embodied in the actual 'genetic code' of Community economic integration.

The institutional framework conceived by the founding fathers was therefore totally in line with the cornerstones of embedded liberalism: the gradual institutionalization and later, through the effect of the case-law of the European Court of Justice, out-and-out constitutionalization of free-market principles at *transnational* level would be based on the guarantee, no less secure for being implicit, of the preservation of strong and deeply rooted *national* welfare-state systems. Meaning that the 'destructive' potential in abstract terms – again *à la* Polanyi – of the forces of a common market would, with the latter actually far from merely resembling a 'self-regulating'[47] or 'self-organizing'[48] system, be adequately counterbalanced by, and find an insuperable 'defence of society' in, national institutions of social and industrial citizenship. Without any external constraints and conditioning factors other than those of the virtuous type already mentioned, these would be able to continue performing their function of social cohesion and, therefore, political and material legitimation of the reborn nation-state.

---

[47] Still in the sense used by Polanyi, *The Great Transformation*, pp. 3 and 68ff.

[48] *Contra* M. E. Streit and W. Mussler, 'The Economic Constitution of the European Community: From "Rome" to "Maastricht"', *European Law Journal* 1955, vol. 1 no. 1, pp. 5–30, especially p. 14.

As one author has put it succinctly, 'however reinvigorated it may have been in the 1980s, particularly with a view to 1992, the liberalist vision of the integration process is therefore historically untenable in relation to the first thirty years of the post-war period'.[49]

But embedded liberalism – at least in the historical form envisaged by the architects of the Treaties of Paris and Rome, which is often described with the somewhat crude but effective slogan 'Keynes at home and Smith abroad'[50] – was by its very nature an 'unstable chemical compound'.[51] It was one which found it increasingly difficult to keep itself in equilibrium as changes progressively occurred in the economic and political environment in which it had been conceived and generated; and one which in fact went into acknowledged crisis once that environment changed too much and became extraneous and unrecognizable to it.

The signs of irreversible change emerged with explosively dramatic force with the collapse of the system of fixed exchange rates conceived at Bretton Woods and the first oil shock, and became more pressing after the mid-1970s. Stagflation, an entirely new phenomenon simply inconceivable in the light of the analytical categories on which macroeconomic management had up till then been based,[52] revealed the illusory nature of the virtuous effects of the Keynesian multiplier in an international economy that found itself increasingly exposed to the erratic circulation of capital in a regime of fluctuating exchange rates, pitilessly highlighting its adverse effects.

The second oil crisis of the late 1970s and the failure of the attempt at traditional expansive policy implemented by the socialist government in France in the early 1980s – the last (unhappy) experiment in (explicit) Keynesianism 'in one country alone'[53] – already conveyed the entire sense of the end of an era and also symbolically marked its closure.[54]

---

[49] Romero, *Emigrazione*, p. 145.

[50] See, for example, R. Gilpin, *The Political Economy of International Relations*, Princeton 1987, p. 355; Tsoukalis, *New European*, p. 22; R. Santaniello, *Il mercato unico europeo*, Bologna 1998, p. 28.

[51] To repeat the colourful image used by S. Veca (in *Cittadinanza. Riflessioni filosofiche sull' idea di emancipazione*, Milan 1990, p. 42) with regard to (social) citizenship: a restless mix that is constantly changing in the vain search for a permanent balance 'between the ideals of liberal emancipation and those of socialist emancipation'.

[52] See Tsoukalis, *New European*, p. 26.   [53] Thomas, *Les politiques*.

[54] As observed by W. Sandholtz, 'Choosing Union: Monetary Politics and Maastricht', *International Organization* 1993, vol. 47, pp. 1ff., especially pp. 6–7, the resounding failure of the reflationary strategy in stimulating growth and employment acted as the decisive

The Keynesian compromise of the post-war period plunged into a structural crisis. In the Bretton Woods system, the autonomy of monetary and macroeconomic policies – itself functional, in its turn, to the necessary total availability of the political levers of growth and full employment – could, from a Mundellian perspective,[55] exist in a system of fixed exchange rates only on condition that the circulation of capital was *effectively* limited and contained.

In Mundellian terms, the Bretton Woods system comprised a harmonious trio of autonomous monetary policies, fixed exchange rates and increasing liberalization of international trade in a perfectly consistent manner thanks to a low level of capital mobility.[56] The 'trio' (or, if preferred, 'quartet') became 'irreconcilable' or 'inconsistent'[57] when – driven by the globalization of financial markets and the rapid spread of new information technologies – the flow of capital in circulation 'became simply too high to continue to coexist with a regime of fixed exchange rates and monetary sovereignty'.[58] The entire history of European monetary

incentive for the 'turnaround' by France's socialist government from 1983 onwards in favour of fiscal austerity and monetary rigour and was a pre-eminent factor in convincing the country's policy-makers of the need to relaunch European integration in the direction subsequently opened up effectively with the Single European Act and the Maastricht Treaty. In a similar vein, see Moravcsik, *Choice*, pp. 269–70.

[55] This obvious reference is to R. Mundell, 'The Monetary Dynamics of International Adjustment Under Fixed and Flexible Exchange Rates', *Quarterly Journal of Economics* 1960, vol. 74, pp. 227ff., and also to Mundell, 'A Theory of Optimum Currency Areas', *American Economic Review* 1961, vol. 51 no. 4, pp. 657ff.

[56] See K. R. McNamara, 'Consensus and Constraint: Ideas and Capital Mobility in European Monetary Integration', *Journal of Common Market Studies* 1999, pp. 455ff., especially p. 459. This was because the liberalization of the post-war years was essentially confined to trade in goods and affected capital movements only to a limited extent: cf. N. Crafts and G. Toniolo, 'Postwar Growth: An Overview', in Crafts and Toniolo (eds.), *Economic Growth in Europe since 1945*, Cambridge 1996. The freeing-up of trade itself was, in any case, achieved gradually and not without important limitations, as noted by G. R. D. Underhill, 'Introduction: Conceptualizing the Changing Global Order', in Stubbs and Underhill (eds.), *Political Economy*, p. 30. Above all, non-tariff barriers – although an essential component in a context of exponential growth of economic and social regulation within Member States – were to remain in place. That is why Milward, *European Rescue*, pp. 130–1, describes the political economy of the (partial) liberalization of the 1950s as 'a form of internationalized neo-mercantilism', a 'peculiar mixture of liberalism and protectionism'.

[57] To use the well-known words of T. Padoa-Schioppa, *L'Europa verso l'unione monetaria. Dallo SME al trattato di Maastricht*, Turin 1992, p. 70; Padoa-Schioppa, 'The Genesis of EMU: A Retrospective View', *Jean Monnet Chair Papers, Robert Schuman Centre – European University Institute* No. 96/40.

[58] McNamara, 'Consensus', p. 460.

integration, from the Snake to the European Monetary System and on to the euro, can be read retrospectively as an attempt to restore a minimum of consistency to the system[59] around the central fact of the by then unstoppable worldwide mobility of capital. And this 'consistency' was in fact progressively pursued and restored, within the Community, through the gradual sacrifice of monetary sovereignty, a sacrifice viewed as almost inevitable in order to recover, at least within the Community context, the public good of stable exchange rates (and prices).

This new context brought a radical change in the relationship between social policies and the laws of economics. The order of political values and priorities was reversed. The market emerged, perforce, from its previously designated ancillary role as a docile instrument for producing resources to be redistributed for the purposes of general emancipation and social equalization, and (re)assumed a position at the top of the list of objectives.

Economic theory accompanied and to some extent anticipated this profound transformation. There was a radical change in the predominant scientific paradigm, symbolized by the award of the Nobel Prize in economics to Milton Friedman in 1976.

A country's politico-economic virtues were now measured more and more by the strength and stability (both internal and external) of its currency and the effectiveness of its supply-side economy, and less and less by its employment levels.[60] In the context of the new paradigm, discourse on labour flexibility likewise came to assume – albeit with widely differing slants even within the European Community itself – the centrality until only recently reserved to interventionist policies of full employment.[61]

However much its real effects may often have been overestimated and in some cases deliberately dramatized,[62] there is no doubt that the process

---

[59] See again Padoa-Schioppa, *L'Europa* and, lastly, T. Padoa-Schioppa, *Europa forza gentile*, Bologna 2001, especially pp. 49ff. and also Moravcsik, *Choice*, pp. 205ff.

[60] See again McNamara, 'Consensus', pp. 462–3.

[61] See the historical summing-up by B. Ström, 'After Full Employment and the Breakdown of Conventions of Social Responsibility', in Ström (ed.), *After Full Employment. European Discourses on Work and Flexibility*, Brussels 2000, pp. 11ff. Of the enormous body of legal literature, mention should at least be made of the now classic studies by S. Simitis ('La giuridificazione dei rapporti di lavoro'), J. Clark and Lord Wedderburn of Charlton ('La giuridificazione nel diritto del lavoro britannico') and G. Giugni ('Giuridificazione e deregolazione nel diritto del lavoro italiano'), *Giornale di Diritto del Lavoro e di Relazioni Industriali* 1986, respectively pp. 215ff., 277ff. and 317ff.

[62] As rightly remarked by L. Tsoukalis, 'The European Agenda: Issues of Globalization, Equity and Legitimacy', *Jean Monnet Chair Papers, Robert Schuman Centre – European University Institute* No. 98/49, pp. 9ff.

of globalization tends, more generally, to displace the traditional forms of nation-state economic and social intervention and create a growing lack of phase between production circuits, based on increasingly nomadic resources, and citizenship circuits, still today largely anchored to rights that are by definition 'non-migratory', as national rights.[63] That is, it tends to generate a basic asymmetry between market processes – increasingly global – and what are still essentially national forms of democratic control and government and the redistribution of resources for solidarity purposes.[64]

In an age of overwhelming globalization of financial markets and increasing internationalization of production processes, in which nation-states saw themselves as inexorably losing control over their own economies, the embedded liberalism metaphor therefore seemed destined to have to give way to its opposite:[65] to disembedded or, even, subversive liberalism.[66]

The European Community's economic constitution (both formal and substantive) did not, and obviously could not, remain indifferent to this genuine passing of an era. The basic postulates of the new international economic order that was emerging eventually had an impact on it and profoundly remoulded the Community's *Wirtschaftsverfassung*.

Naturally, this was not a causally simple and linear process driven by improbable dynamisms of a deterministic or mechanistic type. Nor was it a process which, in all its extraordinary complexity, could be encapsulated by explanations of a mono-causal type, or from the specific point of view of prevailing (whether more or less classical or merely current) 'general' theories of Community integration.[67]

Likewise from the most recent and here most relevant perspective, the transformation of the European economic constitution is portrayed

---

[63] V. E. Parsi, 'La costituzione come mappa: sovranità e cittadinanza tra risorse nomadi e diritti stanziali', in Ornaghi, *La nuova età*, pp. 145ff., here pp. 167.

[64] As examples of what is by now a flood of literature, see the noteworthy papers collected together in W. Streeck (ed.), *Internationale Wirtschaft, nationale Demokratie. Herausforderungen für die Demokratietheorie*, Frankfurt am Main-New York, 1998.

[65] See Ruggie, 'Globalization'.

[66] M. Rhodes, '"Subversive Liberalism": Market Integration, Globalisation and the European Welfare State', *EUI Working Papers, Robert Schuman Centre – European University Institute* No. 95/10 (also in *Journal of European Public Policy* 1995, pp. 384ff.).

[67] An up-to-date and meticulous review of these theories is given by F. Morata, *La Unión Europea*, Barcelona 1998, chapter 3, and by B. Rosamond, *Theories of European Integration*, Basingstoke-New York 2000.

as the outcome of a heterogeneous, plural, discontinuous and still open process.[68] This perspective reveals a particularly varied and multifaceted panorama which cannot be depicted in its entirety by using one single colour but needs to be represented in a manner that is mindful of the countless nuances and necessarily polychrome.[69]

Nowadays, the heuristic validity of the ingenious metaphor of the blind man and the elephant – used in the early 1970s by Donald Puchala to indicate the fruitlessness of any attempt at a *reductio ad unum* of the plurality and intrinsic complexity of the various logics underlying the process of Community integration[70] – not only remains intact but is in fact reinforced more than ever.[71] An inevitable degree of eclecticism and cultural syncretism in applying the various 'competing' theories of Community integration[72] therefore seems adequately justified by the awareness that, today more than ever, we 'simply do not know of any grand theory that would enable us to fully understand the present course of European integration and provide us with a coherent and normatively attractive model of the future shape of a European republic'.[73]

The neo-functionalist logic of spillover – albeit expediently revised and corrected in the light of the most sophisticated versions of

---

[68] Similarly, *ex multis*, M. Barbera, *Dopo Amsterdam. I nuovi confini del diritto sociale comunitario*, Brescia 2000, especially pp. 88 and 107, where European integration is stated to be a fundamentally 'open-ended process' which constitutes 'more than a single, however complex, phenomenon' and as such cannot be defined in terms of a single, all-encompassing interpretative model.

[69] H. Wallace, 'Piecing the Integration Jigsaw Together', *Journal of European Public Policy* 1999, pp. 155ff., especially p. 158.

[70] D. J. Puchala, 'Of Blind Men, Elephants and International Integration', *Journal of Common Market Studies* 1972, pp. 267ff.

[71] A meaningful confirmation of this is given by the same author: see D. J. Puchala, 'Institutionalism, Intergovernmentalism and European Integration: A Review Article', *Journal of Common Market Studies* 1999, pp. 329ff.

[72] A similar approach, with specific regard to evolving models of the European economic constitution, is to be found in the study by M. Poiares Maduro, *We, The Court. The European Court of Justice and the European Economic Constitution*, Oxford 1998, here especially p. 12.

[73] C. Joerges, 'European Economic Law, the Nation-State and the Maastricht Treaty', in R. Dehousse (ed.), *Europe after Maastricht. An Ever Closer Union?*, Munich 1994, pp. 29–62, here p. 30. F. W. Scharpf, 'Notes toward a Theory of Multilevel Governing in Europe', *Max Planck Institut für Gesellschaftsforschung Discussion Paper* No. 00/5, proposes the combined and complementary use of theoretical approaches which in abstract terms compete with each other, as a way of gaining a better understanding – in all the complex variability of their dynamics – of the logics characterizing the various interaction subsystems of the European polity.

neo-institutionalism[74] – constitutes an undoubtedly indispensable ingredient of any realistic explanation of the process of metamorphosis of the European economic constitution. To give just one example, the dynamics of judicial integration under the aegis of the extraordinary instrument for moving the European Community along the path to becoming a 'community based on law' which Article 177 of the Treaty of Rome (now Article 234) has proved to be[75] illustrate quite decisively the striking process of spillover of the economic freedoms guaranteed by the Treaty into potentially any area of public regulation within the Member States which, as we shall see, marks one of the clearest aspects of the transformation of the European economic constitution.

It is, however, equally apparent that in such a multitiered and plural context realistic consideration of all the persistent weight of Member States' interests and preferences, primarily of an economic nature, cannot plausibly be omitted, particularly when the changes in question were the fruit of, or at least formed the subject of, fundamental amendments to the Treaties wanted or at least accepted by their '*Herren*', who would inevitably have been taking respective national interests into account.[76] And also because in many instances they can perhaps be better represented as the combined product of the interaction of diverse factors, as the outcome of a complex game in which national and supranational actors reciprocally

---

[74] Cf. W. Sandholtz and A. Stone Sweet (eds.), *European Integration and Supranational Governance*, Oxford 1998 (and especially the contribution by the two editors, 'Integration, Supranational Governance and the Institutionalization of the European Polity', pp. 1ff., and that by P. Pierson, 'The Path to European Integration: A Historical-Institutionalist Analysis', pp. 27ff.).

[75] The actual 'constitutionalization' of the Treaties represents the most important outcome of this fundamental and complex dynamic. At least retrospective reference should be made here to the now classic contributions by: E. Stein, 'Lawyers, Judges and the Making of a Transnational Constitution', *American Journal of International Law* 1981, pp. 1ff.; M. Cappelletti, *The Judicial Process in Comparative Perspective*, Oxford 1989, pp. 350ff.; G. F. Mancini, 'The Making of a Constitution for Europe', *Common Market Law Review* 1989, vol. 26, pp. 595–614, now also in his *Democracy & Constitutionalism in the European Union. Collected Essays*, Oxford-Portland 2000, pp. 1ff.; and J. H. H. Weiler, 'The Transformation of Europe', *Yale Law Journal* 1991, vol. 100, pp. 2403ff. (now republished with an afterword on '1992 and Beyond' in Weiler, *The Constitution of Europe. 'Do the New Clothes Have an Emperor?' and Other Essays on European Integration*, Cambridge 1999, pp. 10–101: subsequent references are to this text).

[76] The merits of Moravcsik's book, *The Choice for Europe*, are undeniable from this perspective, although in other respects it fails to capture the complexity of the integration process. The Member States remain decisive actors in the Community arena and the relative weight of their interests (principally economic) and their positions of influence and bargaining power seem essential elements of a proper understanding at least of European 'high politics'.

enter into commitments and accept conditions in a system of increasingly diffuse and shared sovereignty in which the prevalent form of discourse is ultimately and inevitably 'dialogue',[77] albeit often with marked disparities and asymmetries in the 'conversational rights'[78] of the parties involved.

At all events, a turning-point (at least in symbolic terms) in this patently non-linear process of constitutional metamorphosis can be identified in the relaunching of Community integration around the programme for a single large market, without internal frontiers, as confirmed by the ratification of the Single European Act (SEA) of 1986. And then in the creation of economic and monetary union in the form devised by the Maastricht Treaty of 1992, as the final completion and crowning step of that programme.[79]

According to some observers, these fundamental moments of Community constitutional revision actually marked the culmination of a genuine 'revolution'[80] which signified the total (and only apparently painless) overthrow of the relationship between the political and economic spheres in the terms that had stamped twentieth-century European constitutionalism: a kind of historical nemesis with respect to the Promethean will to affirm national economic sovereignty that fanned the European constitutions of the second half of the century.[81] Both in the 'programme for

---

[77] Once again the allusion is manifestly to the fundamental importance, already emphasized above, of 'judicial dialogues' in the evolution of the Community legal order, but intended here to assume a broader validity with reference to the process of European decision-making and integration in general. Be that as it may, on the decisive role of European judicial dialogues from the point of view of labour law see the articles collected together in the special issue of *Lavoro e Diritto* nos. 3/4, 1998 entitled *Sul diritto sociale comunitario: la Corte di giustizia e i suoi interlocutori*, and now also, in particular, S. Sciarra (ed.), *Labour Law in the Courts. National Judges and the European Court of Justice*, Oxford-Portland 2001 (and especially the introductory chapter by the editor, 'Integration through Courts: Article 177 as a Pre-federal Device', pp. 1ff.). From a more general perspective, see also A.-M. Slaughter, A. Stone Sweet and J. H. H. Weiler (eds.), *The European Court and National Courts: Doctrine and Jurisprudence. Legal Change in its Social Context*, Oxford 1998; G. De Búrca and J. H. H. Weiler (eds.), *The European Court of Justice*, Oxford 2001.

[78] To repeat, with a certain degree of freedom, the telling expression used by A. Lo Faro, 'La Corte di giustizia e i suoi interlocutori giudiziari nell'ordinamento giuslavoristico italiano', *Lavoro e Diritto* 1998, no. 3, pp. 621ff., here p. 622.

[79] In the words of Pinelli, 'La dicotomia', pp. 197–8.

[80] This is the thesis strongly defended by G. Guarino, 'La grande Rivoluzione: l'Unione europea e la rinuncia alla sovranità', *Rivista di Diritto Pubblico e di Scienze Politiche* 1998, no. 2, pp. 193ff. See also, by the same author, *Verso l'Europa ovvero la fine della politica*, Milan 1997.

[81] See M. De Cecco, 'Trionfo e nemesi della sovranità economica', in P. Ciocca (ed.), *L'economia mondiale nel Novecento*, Bologna 1998, p. 75.

1992' and in the – complementary from this viewpoint – programme for a single currency, the concern to overcome stagnation and Eurosclerosis linked the Community integration process, for the first time, to a precise 'planned deregulation'[82] of national welfare states, obviously antithetic to the aspirations of the founding fathers.

Whatever the various paths followed by this process and its various excursions or real or presumed turning-points, the basic direction and outcome of the metamorphosis of the European economic constitution seem, overall, fairly clear: the new laws of the transnational economy have become direct and explicit constraints that – aided by the supremacy of Community law – prevail over (formerly protected) national sovereignty in social policy.[83]

The eclipse of national sovereignty in social matters does, it is true, reflect the substantial reduction of the Member States' *de facto* autonomy, their effective capacity freely to decide the destinies of their economies.[84] However – and this is what most interests us here – it is in the new Community *Ordnungspolitik* that it finds its actual, and more penetrating and imperative, *legal* sanction.[85]

The main factors of this genuine overturning of the original constitutional balance – for which the colourful image of 'converse pyramids', suggested by one author for different purposes,[86] is probably very appropriate – will be analysed at more length in the course of the present study. They will largely be found in the effects of (purely) negative integration deriving from the progressive 'infiltration' of supranational market and competition rules into national labour and social-security law; in the rigorous economic and financial constraints that govern monetary union, as constitutionalized by the Treaty on European Union (TEU) under the primacy of the objective of monetary stability; in the increased

---

[82] W. Streeck, 'La dimensione sociale del mercato unico europeo: verso un'economia non regolata?', *Stato e Mercato* 1990, pp. 29ff., here p. 38.

[83] See W. Streeck, 'Public Power Beyond the Nation State: The Case of the EC', in R. Boyer and D. Drache (eds.), *States against Markets. The Limits of Globalisation*, London 1996, pp. 299ff.

[84] As regards the distinction alluded to in the text between statal 'autonomy' and 'sovereignty' – respectively indicating *de facto* and *de jure* independence of decision-making capacity in economic and, consequently, social matters – see, albeit in partly different terms, D. Hine, 'Introduction: The European Union, State Autonomy and National Social Policy', in Hine and Kassim (eds.), *Beyond the Market*, pp. 1ff.

[85] See F. W. Scharpf, *Governing in Europe. Effective and Democratic?*, Oxford 1999, pp. 28 and 47ff.

[86] B. Fitzpatrick, 'Converse Pyramids and the EU Social Constitution', in J. Shaw (ed.), *Social Law and Policy in an Evolving European Union*, Oxford-Portland 2000, pp. 303ff.

importance acquired, directly or indirectly, by the dynamics of 'regulatory competition' between national socio-economic systems; and in the associated weakening of the principle of territoriality of national systems of social protection. All of them, in fact, elements extraneous to (and from many aspects in open contrast to) what has been described as the original embedded-liberalism compromise.

The image of a multitiered system[87] that became increasingly widely used during the 1990s to indicate the new institutional order of Community action in social matters, in which Member States had inevitably lost a significant part of their sovereignty *without* its having been replaced at supranational governance level to fulfil equally efficiently the functions of positive integration formerly performed by them, illustrates very well the potential effects of disembedding produced by the joint operation of the above-mentioned factors on national welfare-state arrangements.

The European social dimension remains a prisoner of the 'joint-sovereignty trap',[88] and Community social policies do not (are unable or not equipped to) counterbalance the varyingly marked effects of deregulation produced – directly and semi-automatically – by negative integration in the internal market, particularly given the increased potential for the latter after monetary unification. Political solutions blocked at national level by negative-integration spillover operating vertically through the direct effect and supremacy of Community law, and now also by the macroeconomic constraints ratified at Maastricht, are not made up for at supranational governance level, given the political and institutional impasse encountered by possible positive-integration options, subjected as they are to the blocks and bottlenecks of the 'intergovernmental method'.[89]

---

[87] Cf., among others, P. Pierson and S. Leibfried, 'Multitiered Institutions and the Making of Social Policy' and again Leibfried and Pierson, 'Semisovereign Welfare States: Social Policy in a Multitiered Europe', both in Leibfried and Pierson (eds.), *European Social Policy between Fragmentation and Integration*, Washington D.C. 1995, respectively pp. 1ff. and 43ff., and also S. Sciarra, 'Collective Agreements in the Hierarchy of European Community Sources', in P. Davies *et al.* (eds.), *European Community Labour Law: Principles and Perspectives. Liber Amicorum Lord Wedderburn*, Oxford 1996, pp. 189–212; and more generally, G. Marks, L. Hooghe and K. Blank, 'European Integration from the 1980s: State-Centric vs. Multi-Level Governance', *Journal of Common Market Studies* 1996, pp. 341ff.

[88] S. Leibfried, 'The Social Dimension of the European Union. En Route to Positively Joint Sovereignty?', *ZeS-Arbeitspapier* No. 11/94, University of Bremen, p. 16, who readapts the famous wording of F. W. Scharpf, 'The Joint Decision Trap: Lessons from German Federalism and European Integration', *Public Administration* 1988, vol. 66, pp. 239–78.

[89] Cf. in particular the contributions of F. W. Scharpf: 'Negative and Positive Integration in the Political Economy of European Welfare States', *Jean Monnet Chair Papers, Robert*

The result is a twofold weakening – adversely affecting both levels of the multitiered system – of what Fritz Scharpf describes as 'output-oriented' democratic legitimacy,[90] i.e. democratic legitimacy that is based on the capacity to offer effective political solutions in the common interest. A weakening which is in any event dangerous but which in the long run threatens to damage – still in a negative-sum game – the Community level more than the national level, since the latter can count on input-oriented legitimacy resources (i.e. resources based on the sense of belonging and collective identity) which, at least as things stand, the former almost entirely lacks.

The deep-seated cause of this dangerous institutional gap between negative integration and positive integration of national welfare-state systems[91] is beginning to be more and more insistently imputed to what Massimo D'Antona called the 'genetic anomaly'[92] of Community social law compared with the constitutional traditions of national welfare states (at least those of continental and Mediterranean Europe): the absence, particularly in the economic constitution of the post-Maastricht European Union, of a counterbalance to the unconditional principle of an open economy and free and competitive market in the shape of 'the principle of the welfare state or at least of labour protection'.[93]

Thus, in definitively breaking away from the 'functionalist compromise'[94] underlying the process of European integration, the Maastricht Treaty poses the question of the Community's economic constitution afresh, in entirely new and explosive terms.

Schuman Centre – European University Institute No. 95/28 (also in Marks et al., Governance in the European Union, London 1996, pp. 15–39); 'Introduction: The Problem-Solving Capacity of Multi-Level Governance', Journal of European Public Policy 1997, pp. 520 ff; 'Economic Integration, Democracy and the Welfare State', Journal of European Public Policy 1997, pp. 18ff.; 'Integrazione negativa e integrazione positiva: i dilemmi della costruzione europea', Stato e Mercato 1998, no. 1, pp. 21ff. In the legal literature see, more recently, Barbera, Dopo Amsterdam, pp. 49ff.

[90] Scharpf, Governing in Europe, p. 11.

[91] Which reproduces the more general democratic gap 'between a systemic economic and administrative integration taking place at supranational level and a political integration achieved only at nation-state level': J. Habermas, Morale, diritto, politica (Italian translation), Turin 1992, p. 118.

[92] M. D'Antona, 'Armonizzazione del diritto del lavoro e federalismo nell'Unione europea', Rivista Trimestrale di Diritto e Procedura Civile 1994, pp. 695ff., here p. 704 (now also in D'Antona, Opere, vol. I, Scritti sul metodo e sulla evoluzione del diritto del lavoro. Scritti sul diritto del lavoro comparato e comunitario, eds. B. Caruso and S. Sciarra, Milan 2000, pp. 325ff.).

[93] Ibid., p. 697.   [94] Ibid., p. 695.

This is a question whose solution crucially affects the very essence of the material legitimacy of Community law and public policies. Many of the reasons for the present-day public disaffection with the European Union, and for the phase of acute malaise in which the latter has increasingly and worryingly found itself since 1992,[95] are actually rooted in this problematic issue.[96]

It is therefore not surprising that attempts to tackle this question are at the centre of the most recent drives to relaunch the process of Community integration.

If we set aside – as closer analysis prompts us to do – at least the attitudes of more radical and negative scepticism surrounding the negotiation and ratification of the Treaty of Amsterdam, it has to be seen as incorporating a concrete initiative, albeit partial and incomplete, to re-establish the threads of a possible positive answer to the 'problems of legitimacy and effectiveness of Community action'[97] in the social dimension.

From this viewpoint, the phase in the integration process opened up by the Treaty of Amsterdam appears objectively to embody the attempt to find a new balance between the laws of the economy and social policies. It offers a balance less biased in favour of purely negative integration of markets and more concerned to accelerate at supranational level a mainly positive role in favouring the necessary processes of a restructuring and reform of national welfare-state arrangements, marrying economic competitiveness with social solidarity. Thus, the question of establishing a new balance between social policies and the laws of the economy at supranational level – or, to use the widely used metaphor, re-embedding the new unified European market – seems to have regained all the centrality it merits.

The Treaty of Amsterdam not only reinforces the objective importance of social values in the Community's constitution but also, especially with its new Title on Employment, redirects what had been depicted as a 'neo-voluntarist'[98] approach intended to be, or at least having the effect of being, essentially deregulatory, towards a more positive function of achieving the convergence of national systems of employment policy and

---

[95] Cf. the lucid reflections of Weiler, *The Constitution*, pp. 329ff.

[96] See G. Amato, *Europe Needs Europeans*, talk given at Humboldt University, Berlin on 7 May 2001 (typescript).

[97] Barbera, *Dopo Amsterdam*, p. 172.

[98] W. Streeck, 'From Market Making to State Building? Reflections on the Political Economy of European Social Policy', in Leibfried and Pierson, *European Social Policy*, pp. 389ff., especially pp. 423ff.

social protection around European best practices. Although the significance and real import of these innovations will be made more apparent later in this study, it is useful to note at this point that they have in fact proved to be more incisive and promising than could have been imagined when they first appeared.

The Treaty of Nice – certainly disappointing in important respects, *in primis* for not having completely overcome the difficulties associated with the definition of an institutional arrangement adequate to meet all the challenges posed by the enlargement of the Union – has the merit, at least, of having consolidated the social *acquis* of the Treaty of Amsterdam and in fact created new opportunities for expanding and strengthening it. Above all, however, it is the Charter of Fundamental Rights of the European Union as solemnly proclaimed at Nice which confirms with great symbolic resonance the centrality of the shared commitment to seeking precisely in the founding values of the European social model the most deeply rooted and solid bases for legitimation of the Community polity. It is no accident that the incorporation of the Nice Charter into Part II of the Treaty establishing a Constitution for Europe represents – in the social field – the most important and promising aspect of the process of profound constitutional reform which is still in progress in the European Union.

Be that as it may, this is a very open quest in terms of its methods and possible final outcomes which has nothing of the flavour of a return to the past or any contemplation of an improbable resurrection of the social compromise and constitutional balances of the post-war period. It has all the marks of a profoundly fresh appraisal of the European social model and the forms (and perhaps the very notion itself) of solidarity in which it has hitherto found concrete expression.

3. 'Embedded liberalism': the original compromise in the ECSC Treaty . . .

However much it may hitherto have been assumed, Federico Mancini's felicitous image of the 'social frigidity'[99] of the Community's founding fathers does not do full justice to the composite nature of the compromise reflected in the European economic constitution of the early days.

---

[99] G. F. Mancini, 'Principi fondamentali di diritto del lavoro nell'ordinamento delle Comunità europee', in *Il lavoro nel diritto comunitario e l'ordinamento italiano*, Atti del Convegno di Parma 30–31 ottobre 1985, Padua 1988, pp. 23ff., here p. 33.

It is not just that, when viewed overall, the rules of the common market do not express the model of unfettered liberalism[100] that has been repeatedly imputed to them when they are viewed solely in terms of the unquestionable modesty, if not downright poverty, of the purely formal social provisions of the Treaty of Rome, which was even 'colder' in this respect than the Treaty of Paris. If, as is suggested here, they are viewed from the (unprejudiced) standpoint of the respect for the Member States' social autonomy and sovereignty that they guarantee, these provisions can in a way actually suggest the opposite or, more accurately, reverse image of a strong 'social empathy' on the part of the founding fathers.[101]

Particularly eloquent confirmation of the soundness of this proposition will be obtained, in subsections 4 and 5 below, from a re-reading (methodologically oriented in the direction argued here) of the document which was used as a basis for drafting the Treaty of Rome and can be said to have mapped out its 'guidelines': the Spaak Report.[102] And before that, from an analysis of the report on the social aspects of European economic integration produced on behalf of the ILO by a prestigious group of experts chaired by the Swedish politician Bertil Ohlin.[103] The Ohlin Report had developed the ideas, then adopted and summarized by the Spaak Committee, more fully and widely on a systematic and theoretical

---

[100] In a similar sense, with clear emphasis on the 'mixed' nature of the European economic constitution in the early days in particular, F. Snyder, *New Directions in European Community Law*, London 1990, pp. 63ff.; W. Sauter, 'The Economic Constitution of the European Union', *Columbia Journal of European Law* 1998, no. 4, pp. 27ff.

[101] For an approach and conclusions that are materially not dissimilar, cf. S. Deakin, 'Labour Law as Market Regulation: The Economic Foundations of European Social Policy', in Davies *et al.*, *European Community Labour Law*, pp. 63–93. Nor must it be forgotten that, although belonging to different political families and traditions (essentially Christian Democrat and Socialist), the national politicians who were protagonists of the start of European integration shared to a varying degree a strong awareness of the issues of social and labour protection (see Milward, *European Rescue*, pp. 318ff., especially p. 337). Monnet himself, the inventor of the 'Community method', was during more or less the same years in which he was formally engaged in the supranational project, in charge, within his own country, of public plans for the modernization of the French economy. It was he who invented 'both the term for, and the very concept of, a concerted economy' (Thomas, *Les politiques*).

[102] A kind of 'White Paper' of the EEC Treaty, as it is incisively described by P. Davies, 'The Emergence of European Labour Law', in W. E. J. McCarthy (ed.), *Legal Intervention in Industrial Relations: Gains and Losses*, Oxford 1992, pp. 313ff., here p. 319.

[103] See *Social Aspects of European Economic Co-operation. Report by a Group of Experts*, ILO, Geneva 1956. An official summary of the Ohlin Report was published in *International Labour Review* 1956, vol. 74 no. 2, pp. 99–123, and it is to this text that reference is made in subsection 4 below where the Report is examined in detail.

level and therefore seems particularly useful and relevant to our present purposes.

It is, however, appropriate – if for no other reason, because of the proper need to follow the exact historical sequence of events – to start here with the Treaty of Paris. For it was this which, in 1951, formed the basis of the construction of the Community: the foundation stone on which Jean Monnet had set out, with passion and reason, to put in motion a process which in accordance with his intentions (and the confident convictions of neofunctionalism theorists)[104] was meant to lead, through its progressive, natural and incremental extension to functionally linked sectors, to a more general and far-reaching outcome of integration: European political unity.

There is a widely held view that, in its delineation of the complex legal and institutional framework that was to guide economic integration in the two sectors which at the time were the most important for the recovery and development of the European economy, the ECSC Treaty exhibited a far more marked sensitivity than the EEC Treaty to social issues.

Gérard and Antoine Lyon-Caen have spoken tellingly, in this connection, of a 'less dogmatic' liberalism[105] than that which inspired – six years later – the drafting of the EEC Treaty. Brian Bercusson goes farther, and sees in the ECSC Treaty the adoption of a social-intervention model directly contrasting with that acknowledged by the EEC Treaty. In his view, the former embraced the innovative idea of an active labour policy and involvement of the social partners in the regulation of related profiles, while the latter supported – a few years afterwards – a strategy of pure 'neoliberal *laissez-faire*', clearly perceptible in the almost total absence in it of provisions relating to social policy and labour law.[106]

We shall see more clearly below that this radically dichotomous view of the opposing strategies on social and labour matters alleged to have been incorporated by the two Treaties unduly encourages a cliché which is broadly refuted by the convergence of the assumptions and normative options adopted in these two cases by their negotiators. Nor does it seem plausibly tenable from a historical point of view.[107]

As Gérard and Antoine Lyon-Caen also make clear,[108] the difference with regard to social matters displayed by the Treaty of Paris as compared with the Treaty of Rome is more one of degree and quantity than one

---

[104] See the classic work by E. B. Haas, *The Uniting of Europe: Political, Social and Economic Forces, 1950–1957*, Stanford 1958.
[105] As stated in the 8th edn of their *Droit social international et européen*, Paris 1993, p. 160.
[106] B. Bercusson, *European Labour Law*, London 1996, pp. 44–5.
[107] Cf. Milward, *European Rescue*, pp. 46ff.   [108] *Droit social*, pp. 161ff.

of substance and quality. The underlying ideas and strategies had not, and could not have, really changed that much in the six years separating the signing of the two Treaties. The only (partial) difference lay in the instruments provided for their implementation.

The major element of continuity which links the two Treaties along the narrow and slippery contours of embedded liberalism is to be found in the attitude adopted in both to the relations between competition in a common market (sectoral and then general) and national social policies. This is, obviously, a central issue to which we shall return repeatedly in the course of this study and which will be examined in systematic detail in Part II in particular, but which also needs some explanation at this point.

The key provision in this sense (wrongly ignored because it was not applied in practice)[109] is represented by Article 68 of the ECSC Treaty.[110] The EEC Treaty did not contain a general provision of the same tenor; but this does nothing to detract from the fact that its basic creation reflected the same principles and – as we shall see – was inspired by the same philosophy as that professed *ore rotundo* by the founding fathers in the form of Article 68 of the Treaty of Paris.

The Article in question, which included a number of paragraphs and was complex in structure, opened Chapter VIII of Title III entitled Wages and Movement of Workers. It was directly and naturally linked to the provisions on competition in the common market for coal and steel, because it immediately followed the single Article comprising Chapter VII which specified the rules governing interference with the conditions of competition ensuing from 'any action by a Member State'.[111]

The first paragraph of the provision established its cardinal principle and basic objective: 'The methods used for fixing wages and welfare benefits in the several Member States shall not, in the case of the coal and steel industries, be affected' by the Treaty. The intention was that the Member States – and primarily the national trade-union and employers'

---

[109] Given that Article 68 was essentially a penalty provision – or, in the language of legal theory, a 'secondary rule' – the fact that it was never applied in practice manifestly does not signify per se that it was without effect. On the contrary, it may be seen as evidence of the full effectiveness of the primary precept to which it was instrumental, and hence that it is this reading which is the correct one.

[110] On this point see, in addition to G. and A. Lyon-Caen, *Droit social*, pp. 162–3, A. Meric, 'Aspects sociaux de la CECA', *Droit Social* 1954, pp. 552ff., and in particular L. Riva Sanseverino, 'Commento all'articolo 68', in *Trattato istitutivo della Comunità Europea del Carbone e dell'Acciaio. Commentario*, under the editorship of R. Quadri, R. Monaco and A. Trabucchi, Padua 1970, vol. II, pp. 959ff.

[111] See G. Olivier, 'Commento all'articolo 67', in *Trattato istitutivo della CECA*, pp. 944ff.

organizations – should retain their full autonomy as regards the methods, forms and content of pay determination and the regulation of their respective welfare systems. The Member States' competence in the matter was therefore preserved intact and the social partners likewise retained their autonomy within the limits to which it was recognized in individual national systems. In short, the full 'social sovereignty of the Member States'[112] was preserved.

The new competition rules on which the Treaty based the common market for coal and steel were therefore not to interfere in any way with this fundamental principle. However, the fact – to be confirmed more circumstantially in the Treaty of Rome – that a general system of harmonization of working conditions and social-protection regimes was therefore not, at least in principle, necessary or useful (one reason being that it inevitably represented a second-best solution compared with the principle of full Member State autonomy) did not mean that the Community could not and would not intervene when the opening-up of the common market led to practices which distorted competition and were likely to threaten the viability of the *de facto* preconditions of that autonomy.

This much was expressly stipulated in paragraphs 2 onwards of Article 68 in that they made a 'reservation', i.e. stated exceptions to the principle of full Member State social autonomy/sovereignty as laid down in the first paragraph. The fact is, however, that the reservation in question was only apparent, since what it actually did was to contain and confirm 'the essence of the provision under examination'.[113]

As we shall see shortly, in actuality the exceptions in question imposed limits on the Member States' autonomy solely for the purpose of better protecting and defending the essence of that autonomy. They were intended to prevent the common market – and the new, harsher dynamics of competition potentially fostered by it – from giving rise to distortional forms of social dumping and forcing even the most virtuous parties, i.e. the Member States with the highest levels of pay and welfare protection, to engage in a ruinous 'race to the bottom' inevitably damaging to their autonomy (and also, obviously, to the living and working conditions of the employed labour force concerned).

Competition was lawful provided it did not lead to forms of social dumping, i.e. provided it was not aimed – save in specified and quite exceptional circumstances – at conditions relating to direct or indirect

[112] G. and A. Lyon-Caen, *Droit social*, p. 162.
[113] Riva Sanseverino, 'Commento all'articolo 68', p. 961.

labour costs disadvantageous to workers.[114] The creation of the common market for coal and steel was intended, in point of fact, to establish common bases for economic development that would make an effective contribution to raising the standard of living of European workers.[115]

The increase in the dynamics of competition was therefore to be accompanied by specific measures of a kind aimed at the *upward* levelling and equalization of conditions of competition as far as the cost of the labour force was concerned. To that end, the social provisions contained in the ECSC Treaty started with a rule on the 'regulation of competition in the coal and steel sector from the point of view of the cost of labour'.[116]

The first of the 'reservations' envisaged by Article 68 was intended to operate in the event that one or more undertakings were charging abnormally low prices because they were 'paying abnormally low wages compared with the wage level in the same area'. If in such a case the High Authority found a direct correlation between abnormally low prices and wages, after consulting the Consultative Committee it was to make 'appropriate recommendations'[117] to the undertakings concerned. The High Authority had the same power and duty to intervene if abnormally low prices and wages were the result of governmental decisions, an eventuality obviously intended to relate to the case of public or nationalized undertakings in the coal and steel sector. The only difference was that in this case the supranational body first had to confer with the national Government concerned and attempt to reach agreement with it – but still retained the final power to make a 'recommendation'.

The Authority's powers of intervention were therefore very broad, covering everything it might consider necessary in order to restore fair conditions of competition through a return to normal wages, i.e. wages in line with the level regularly paid in the area.

This clearly demonstrates the 'decisive importance'[118] indirectly attributed by the provision to the function of limiting and fixing fair

---

[114] F. Durante, 'Introduzione agli articoli 68–69', in *Trattato istitutivo della CECA*, pp. 952ff., especially p. 957.

[115] Cf. D. Del Bo, 'Natura ed esercizio del potere supranationale nel Trattato CECA', R. Monaco, 'Commento al Preambolo del Trattato' and G. Olivier, 'Commento all'articolo 2', in *Trattato istitutivo della CECA*, respectively pp. 3ff., 30ff. and 70ff.

[116] Riva Sanseverino, 'Commento all'articolo 68', p. 960.

[117] It should be noted that, unlike the measures of the same name provided for under the present Article 249 of the EC Treaty (formerly Article 189), 'recommendations' in the context of the ECSC system were legally binding on those to whom they were addressed as to the aims to be pursued, although leaving them free to choose the appropriate methods for achieving these aims.

[118] Riva Sanseverino, 'Commento all'articolo 68', p. 961.

conditions of competition as performed by collective bargaining. In essence, 'the hypothetical case of abnormally low prices being charged because of abnormally low wages paid by one or more undertakings can occur only where those undertakings are not covered by norms on pay and working conditions collectively agreed between trade unions and employers' organizations; in other words, the presence of collectively agreed norms that are applicable and applied . . . is already enough in itself to ensure that wages do not fall below a specified level.'[119]

It therefore does not seem inappropriate to see in the provision not only an indirect recognition of the necessary role of collective bargaining but also an implicit preference for mechanisms supporting and extending the effects of collective agreements, in the terms envisaged at the time by all the legal systems of the ECSC founding States, albeit on the basis of different preconditions and in different forms.

Another hypothetical case of intervention by the High Authority was defined by the third paragraph of Article 68 in relation not to individual situations of one or more undertakings (private or public) but to events connected with the general economic situation. What it envisaged was the far more relevant eventuality in which, following the establishment of the common market for the sector, 'wage reduction entails a lowering of the standard of living of workers and at the same time is being used as a means for the permanent economic adjustment of undertakings or as a means of competition between them.'

In that event, after consulting the Consultative Committee the High Authority was to 'make a recommendation to the undertaking or Government concerned with a view to securing, at the expense of the undertakings, benefits for the workers in order to compensate for the reductions'.

In a sense, this provision epitomized the essence of the philosophy that inspired the construction of the common market for coal and steel: observance of the new supranational rules on competition and free movement of the factors of production should not entail, and in any event could not in principle justify, a permanent economic adjustment of the reciprocal competitive position of national undertakings based on a lowering of labour costs and wage reductions. There should be no adverse effects on workers and – in the event of any such circumstance – they were to enjoy at the expense of the undertakings compensatory benefits which cancelled out the effects of the reduction in wages and resultant lowering of their standard of living and at the same time represented a fair counterpart to the competitive advantage gained by the undertakings employing them.

[119] *Ibid.*

The only cases in which this rule did not apply were those also expressly spelled out as exceptions in the third paragraph of Article 68. These included, first of all, any case where the economic adjustment in question resulted from overall measures taken by a Member State to restore its external equilibrium, albeit without prejudice in such case to the possible enforcement of Article 67 of the Treaty.

This latter Article endowed the High Authority with major powers of intervention in general when any action by a Member State was liable to have 'appreciable repercussions on conditions of competition in the coal or the steel industry' and began by establishing an obligation on the Government concerned to bring the action to the knowledge of the High Authority.

It then went on to stipulate more specifically that if the action in question was having harmful effects on undertakings in the sector the High Authority could authorize the Member State to grant aid to them, the amount, conditions and duration of which were to be determined in agreement with itself. The Article further added that these provisions were also to apply in the case of any change in wages and working conditions which would have the same effects, even if not resulting from any action by the State concerned.[120]

Lastly, the other exceptions (this time wholly physiological) to the rule laid down in the third paragraph of Article 68 related to potential wage reductions resulting from a general fall in the cost of living or correcting abnormal increases that had occurred previously in exceptional circumstances which no longer obtained.

The fifth paragraph of Article 68 then specified the practical content and scope of application of the rule, and in so doing once again expressly stated a link with the preceding Article 67. It established that if a Member State changed its national arrangements for the financing of social security or for dealing with unemployment and its effects – both of these hypothetical cases being equated with a change in wages[121] – the High Authority would then be empowered to take the steps already provided for in Article 67. That is, it could authorize the payment of subsidies by individual States in accordance with terms and methods agreed with it and also make all such recommendations as it considered necessary in order to restore fair conditions of competition that were not damaging to the levels of protection guaranteed to the workers concerned.

[120] See in more detail on all these points Olivier, 'Commento all'articolo 67', pp. 955ff.
[121] See Riva Sanseverinao, 'Commento all'articolo 68', p. 964.

In all cases, the recommendations that the High Authority was empowered to make to undertakings were backed by a heavy sanction consisting in the ability to impose fines and periodic penalty payments of up to twice the amount of the saving in labour costs improperly effected (sixth paragraph of Article 68).

As will become more apparent in the subsections below, the ECSC Treaty – no differently from the Treaty of Rome that followed it – therefore already conceived supranational social policy in restrictive terms and essentially as instrumental to the correct regulation of market processes.

Article 68 had, in fact, a clear anti-dumping thrust and did not envisage authentic social competences for the ECSC. On the contrary, these were jealously guarded within the perimeter of the Member States' social sovereignty.

From this point of view, the instruments offered by Article 68 of the ECSC Treaty were less invasive than those potentially provided by the EEC Treaty. Both Treaties excluded the necessity, as such, of preventive harmonization of social-protection mechanisms in the interests of *ex ante* equalization of the costs (mainly indirect) of labour utilization. However, the Treaty of Rome was decidedly more open than the Treaty of Paris to the possibility – albeit by way of exception – of intervention in the form of harmonizing measures in the social field to correct distortional or negative dynamics of the transnational competitive process (Articles 117 and 100). The Treaty of Paris, by contrast, almost entirely excluded the instrument of harmonization and envisaged a general mechanism for restoring fair conditions of competition in terms of labour costs which was intended, instead, to operate within individual national systems and took as its reference the level of social protection regarded as normal for them.[122]

---

[122] There was no general mechanism of this kind in the EEC Treaty, although it did contain – in more restricted contexts – instruments that could be considered functionally equivalent or at least comparable. One such example may be seen in its 'Protocol on Certain Provisions Relating to France', the second part of which related to payment for overtime. This Protocol – in the same vein as Article 68 of the ECSC Treaty but spelled out in concrete terms – provided that if by the end of the first stage of the common market the basic number of working hours beyond which overtime rates were paid and the average rate of additional payment for overtime did not equal those obtaining in French industry in 1956, the Commission could authorize France to take, in respect of the sectors of industry adversely affected, protective measures for which the conditions and details were to be determined by the Commission. On the other hand, the hypothetical case of social or wage dumping was omitted from the scope of Article 91 of the Treaty of Rome, which provided that if, during the transitional period, the Commission, on application by a Member State or by any other interested party, found that dumping was being practised within

Be that as it may, the fundamental feature shared by the two Treaties consisted in the definite affirmation of the principle of the Member States' social autonomy/sovereignty and the certainty that in all national systems the latter was driven by upward and acquisitive dynamics – moving towards harmonization while maintaining improvement, as was to be stated expressly in Article 117 of the EEC Treaty – whose effects would be favoured and magnified by the construction of the common market (first sectoral, and then general).

On the other hand, the fact that one of the main objectives of the Treaty of Paris was to strengthen national welfare-state institutions was also revealed by the illustrative example of its set of provisions aimed at softening and rendering painless – from the social point of view – the effects of inevitable processes of industrial restructuring in the coal and steel sector. Unlike those examined above, these provisions had an effective role of paramount importance. For example, they enabled a country such as Belgium to carry out – in the face of the unstoppable decline of the coal industry from the end of the 1950s – policies of social intervention and protection which would otherwise have been difficult to sustain at individual level, at least as regards the scale and generosity that characterized them.[123]

The provisions concerned are the ECSC's best known and most frequently mentioned instruments of social intervention.

Emphasis has rightly been placed on the striking modernity and 'newness'[124] of the approach exemplified by the principle of continuity of employment on which the provisions set out in Article 56 of the Treaty (in the 1960 amended text) were based. This adapted and modernized at transnational level one of the most fundamental objectives of protective labour-law rules, namely job security, by translating it into the different – but not opposing[125] – objective of continuity of income and resources in

---

the common market, it was to address recommendations to the persons with whom such practices originated and, should the practices continue, authorize protective measures on the part of the injured Member States. See A. Pappalardo, 'Commento all'articolo 91', in *Trattato istitutivo della Comunità economica europea. Commentario*, under the editorship of R. Quadri, R. Monaco and A. Trabucchi, Milan 1965, vol. II, pp. 702ff., especially p. 704.

[123] See Milward, *European Rescue*, pp. 113ff.

[124] G. and A. Lyon-Caen, *Droit social*, p. 161.

[125] As would, however, appear to be suggested by Bercusson, *European Labour Law*, p. 45. On the other hand, Article 58 of the ECSC Treaty envisaged a kind of intervention directly in line with the principle of job security or 'job continuity' within the *same* undertaking (Olivier, 'Commento all'articolo 2', p. 48).

making the move (guaranteed and assisted) from one job to another, or indeed to a different occupation.

If within the framework of the general objectives of the ECSC the introduction of new technical processes or equipment should lead to an exceptionally large reduction in labour requirements in the coal or steel industry, making it particularly difficult in one or more areas to re-employ redundant workers, the High Authority, on application by the governments concerned, was in the first place to be empowered to facilitate – with investment and financial aid – programmes aimed at the 'creation of new and economically sound activities capable of reabsorbing the redundant workers into productive employment' (paragraph 1(b) of Article 56). And next – at a more immediate social-policy level – it was to be empowered to provide non-repayable aid towards: 'the payment of tideover allowances to workers; the payment of resettlement allowances to workers; the financing of vocational retraining for workers having to change their employment' (paragraph 1(c) of Article 56).

All this manifestly amounted to a fairly broad range of social benefits including tideover, resettlement and vocational-retraining allowances[126] towards which national governments were to receive generous aid mainly (but not solely) over the lengthy period during which the coal extraction and processing industry was dismantled.

The concern to maintain employment levels and adequate social guarantees for workers who found themselves temporarily unemployed as a result of industrial restructuring processes in the common market for coal and steel was, however, a constant feature of the ECSC Treaty and inspired numerous other measures, representing in one way or another a general limit on and tempering of the rules relating to competition and, in particular, the provisions prohibiting the grant of aid or subsidies to their national undertakings by individual Member States.[127]

More generally, all the rules on free movement of the factors of production and competition – unquestionably central to the creation of the common market for coal and steel – were subject to the considerations of an accentuated interventionist culture which found extensive manifestations

---

[126] Cf. E. Reuter, 'Commento all'articolo 56', in *Trattato istitutivo della CECA*, vol. I, pp. 730ff., who gives a detailed illustration of the different types and content of the various benefits provided for under Article 56 of the Treaty.

[127] The main exemptions from the prohibition on the grant of aid by individual States included those already mentioned as set out in Article 67 of the Treaty: see G. Olivier, 'Commento all'articolo 4', in *Trattato istitutivo della CECA*, vol. I, pp. 77ff., especially p. 84.

in the Treaty as particularly evidenced by the breadth of the discretionary powers in the matter conferred on the High Authority.[128]

The competition regime devised by the Treaty of Paris therefore cannot but seem, particularly in view of the significant powers for controlling and administering current prices in the common market vested in the High Authority,[129] a system of wholly 'imperfect'[130] competition instrumental and adaptable to the attainment of differing industrial-policy objectives.[131]

In short, the entire framework of the ECSC was one which oscillated between competition and *dirigisme* and is therefore best represented in terms of a mixed economic type, an experiment in welfare economics on a regional scale.[132]

4. . . . in the Ohlin Report . . .

'The public commitment of the Treaties of Rome to improve the level of welfare provision to that of the most generous provider' – Alan Milward has written – 'repeated that of the Treaty of Paris for the same reasons . . . The Treaties of Rome had to be also an external buttress to the welfare state.'[133]

These are words which highlight an essential dimension of the Treaty establishing the EEC, a dimension wrongly underestimated by commentators who see in it no more than a neoliberal programme for the progressive opening-up of national markets with few and, if anything, accessory and purely ancillary social guarantees in favour (only) of those participating in the process.

---

[128] A breadth of powers which exhibited traits of real dirigisme, as was often lamented at the time in some economic circles: see Milward, *European Rescue*, p. 80. The High Authority's powers included – as stated pithily by Tsoukalis, *New European*, p. 11 – the right to 'levy taxes, influence investment decisions and also impose minimum prices and production quotas in times of "imminent" and "manifest" crisis respectively. Walter Hallstein referred to the economic system set up by the Paris Treaty as one of "regulated competition", and this was clearly very different from the liberal order dreamt of by postwar US administrations.'

[129] See in general paragraph (c) of Article 3 of the ECSC Treaty.

[130] Olivier, 'Commento all' articolo 2', here pp. 46–7.

[131] See Del Bo, 'Natura ed esercizio', pp. 20ff.

[132] Cf. Olivier, 'Commento all' articolo 2', pp. 43ff., and also Olivier, 'Commento all' articolo 3', again in *Trattato istitutivo della CECA*, pp. 52ff., especially p. 67, where the author specifically talks of 'welfare economics' in referring to paragraph (c) of Article 3 of the ECSC Treaty.

[133] *European Rescue*, p. 216.

The protection of national welfare-state systems constituted a by no means minor concern of the EEC's founding fathers. The report officially presented to the foreign ministers of the Six in Venice on 29–30 May 1956 by the Committee chaired by Paul-Henri Spaak demonstrates very clearly this concern and this basic goal of the future EEC Treaty.[134]

But the same concern emerges no less clearly from the report drawn up by the group of ILO experts formally entrusted by the United Nations, in a sense to lend technical support to the essentially political work of the Spaak Committee, with the task of making a systematic study of the social implications of European economic integration. It is therefore this influential report which seems better taken as a starting-point in giving a more detailed content to the meaning of the quotation chosen to open this section.

The Ohlin Report[135] was inspired by a suffusively neoliberal view – moderate and not at all dogmatic – of the theory of international trade, the first proponent of which was, as is well-known, one of the leading figures of the age.[136] This view took Ricardo's theory of comparative advantage (which still underlies the justification of the principle of free international trade) and tempered and remodelled it in accordance with the prerequisites for a process of regional integration clearly conceived as a form of co-operation between national welfare states which – while autonomous in pursuing their macroeconomic welfare policies – opened themselves up again, with a view to their fundamental advantage, to foreign trade.[137]

It is common for authors to highlight the marginal and manifestly instrumental role, compared with the demands imposed by the creation and efficient functioning of the common market, which the Ohlin Report (like the Spaak Report) assigned *to the supranational level* of social policies in general and the regulation of employment relationships in particular.[138] On the other hand, not enough emphasis tends to be placed on the recognition – mostly implicit but no less clear for all that – which it reserved to the *national level* in securing high standards of social protection.

---

[134] *Ibid.*, pp. 211ff.   [135] See note 103 above.

[136] Ohlin's contribution to the theory of international trade remains fundamental to this day: see E. F. Hecksher and B. Ohlin, *Hecksher-Ohlin Trade Theory*, edited and with an introduction by H. Flam and M. J. Flanders, Cambridge, Mass. 1991.

[137] Cf. J. Pelkmans, *The Process of Economic Integration*, Tilburg 1975.

[138] See, for example: A. Sapir, 'Trade Liberalization and the Harmonization of Social Policies: Lessons from European Integration', in J. Bhagwati and R. E. Hude (eds.), *Fair Trade and Harmonization. Prerequisite for Free Trade*, vol. 1, *Economic Analysis*, Cambridge, Mass. 1996, pp. 543ff.; C. Barnard, 'EC "Social" Policy', in P. Craig and G. De Búrca (eds.), *The Evolution of EU Law*, Oxford 1999, here pp. 479ff.

Yet the main concern of the Ohlin Report was precisely that of guaranteeing the maintenance (and progressive expansion) of highly developed and autonomous systems of social protection *within individual Member States*, as an indispensable condition of European economic integration.

This is evidenced by the fact that, as is well known, the Report fairly plainly rejected the notion – save in relatively exceptional and minor cases – that the creation of a common market required prior harmonization of the Member States' national social and labour legislation. Differences, even large ones, in the '*general level* of wages and social charges between different countries', so states the Report,[139] 'broadly reflect differences in productivity'. And so 'where productivity is high because a country has rich natural resources, abundant capital, efficient entrepreneurs and well-trained managers and workers, the general level of wages, as of other incomes, will tend also to be high'.[140] Free movement of the factors of production as ensured by the creation of the common market would, so the thinking went, tend to promote better allocation of resources and foster a spontaneous catching-up process in the countries lagging behind in this respect.

In adopting this stance the Report exhibited total adherence to the postulates of the so-called 'convergence school', to which Ohlin himself had made major contributions. Within the paradigm of neoclassical theory, the convergence school – predominant at the time[141] – generally attributed to free international trade the capacity to bring about a gradual removal of economic and social disparities between the different regions or areas affected by it. This, it held, was because the free movement of capital and labour would tend almost automatically to reduce differentials in wages or investment yield between different countries or regions.

From this viewpoint, according to the Report, the widely perceived danger of unfair competition based on low labour costs (direct or indirect)

---

[139] Ohlin Report, p. 104.   [140] *Ibid.*

[141] It was only later that convergence theory became the target of strong criticisms backed by studies aimed at demonstrating that the creation of economies of scale or the construction of centres or poles of growth and development could, on the contrary, trigger processes of divergence between the different areas involved and so increase regional disparities (cf. P. Krugman, *Geography and Trade*, Cambridge, Mass. 1991). In a sense, the regional development policy inaugurated by the Community in the mid-1970s and, even more systematically, the policy on economic and social cohesion launched by the Single European Act constituted official awareness of such situations in making an attempt (only partly successful) to prepare the financial and institutional resources needed to remedy them: cf. R. Leonardi, *Convergence, Cohesion and Integration in the European Union*, London 1995.

needing to be removed through harmonization of the different systems of legislation involved actually lacked – at least in principle – any real substance. On the contrary, 'there is a mechanism ensuring that differences in levels of wages and other incomes in the various countries remain in line with international differences in productivity. When countries engage in foreign trade the value of each partner's receipts from abroad must in the long run roughly equal its foreign payments. This equilibrium in the balance of payments depends, *inter alia*, on the choice of an appropriate rate of exchange. If a country finds that its costs of production for most commodities are too high to enable the country to pay its way, equilibrium could (and should) be restored, for example, by letting the price level fall as productivity increases, by fresh investment in export industries, or by revision of the rate of exchange.'[142]

The result would then be the virtuous circle primed to mutual advantage by closer economic co-operation to guarantee a natural upward realignment of the productivity levels and hence incomes of the trading partners concerned, with a spontaneous – *ex post* – effect of harmonization of their social systems as well.[143] Wage and welfare levels, and therefore the relative burden of overall labour costs, would favour a natural tendency towards levelling-up because of the generalized gains in productivity, movement of labour and advantages in general deriving from the co-operative division of labour within the common market.

Other than this, the rejection of the need for preventive harmonization shown in the Report and, correlatively, its confidence in the automatic incremental and equalizing qualities of the common market being instituted were by no means absolute.

As regards the first of these two aspects, although stating that 'such cases are not numerous in Europe'[144] the Report acknowledged the existence of a (potentially broader) category of situations in which harmonizing intervention at supranational level was justified by the need to eliminate practices that constituted unfair competition. This related to instances where 'the foreign competition to which a particular group of producers is exposed arises not because the *general level* of labour costs in the competing country is low but because foreign producers in the same line of business pay wages, or have to bear social charges, that are exceptionally low in comparison with the general level of wages and social charges in the *same country*.'[145]

---

[142] Ohlin Report, p. 104.   [143] *Ibid.*, especially pp. 101 and 111–12.
[144] *Ibid.*, p. 105.   [145] *Ibid.*

In such cases – and the examples given in the Ohlin Report (subsequently repeated and amplified by the Spaak Report) particularly concerned wage differentials between women and men and differences in overtime premium rates arising from the various laws in force in individual Member States[146] – preventive upward harmonization of this national legislation was considered essential.

It was, however, in relation to the second of the two aspects mentioned that the Report more clearly revealed its adherence to the basic postulates of embedded liberalism, in proving fairly categorical in its assertion of the principle whereby the liberalization of trade had to be accompanied by compensatory measures, or certainly restricted, whenever it constituted an effective threat to the social balances and welfare arrangements of the participating States.

Any trade liberalization programme would, first of all, necessarily have to be gradual, in order to 'mitigate the hardships and losses to the employers and workers affected to the greatest possible extent, without however, preventing progress towards a better allocation of resources'.[147] To cope with the need to carry out substantial restructuring it would, nonetheless, be necessary to ensure special state assistance at national level, given the difficulty of reproducing on a general scale the same model of common intervention already effectively tested by the ECSC High Authority on a sectoral level.[148] In a context of mutual collaboration between national authorities, capital movements would remain largely confined to instances in which they were effectively aimed at fostering long-term economic growth. And in any event – the Report reads – 'Should it appear that differences in social policies did give rise to undesirable capital movements, measures might be taken to correct this situation.'[149]

Lastly, as the key sector of national economies from the point of view of social-policy balances, and the subject ever since the inter-war years of increasingly penetrating protective intervention by national governments, agriculture would need to be extensively sheltered from the process of liberalization.[150]

As Simon Deakin has put it clearly,[151] all this 'meant that transnational institutions could be largely confined to the role of ensuring freedom of movement for economic resources; but it equally followed that the Community's policy of "neoliberalism" at the transnational level should not necessarily be translated into similar policies at national level. On the

---

[146] *Ibid.*, pp. 106–10.   [147] *Ibid.*, pp. 114–15.   [148] *Ibid.*, pp. 116 and 117.
[149] *Ibid.*, p. 121.   [150] *Ibid.*, p. 117.   [151] 'Labour Law as Market Regulation', p. 67.

contrary, Ohlin assumed that active economic policy-making and government intervention at the level of the nation state would not only continue, but would provide an essential mechanism of adjustment as international barriers to mobility were removed. In particular, the realization of economic gains from freer trade was seen as dependent on the preservation of strong labour standards *within* states.'

Similar considerations apply in the case of the Spaak Report, which as regards these aspects even goes beyond the pointers indicated by Ohlin and his colleagues, notably in prefiguring – *ceteris paribus* – a more incisive role for the supranational authorities.

5. ... in the Spaak Report ...

Likewise in the Spaak Report, as well as in the Treaty of Rome itself, 'the gradual assimilation of social and labor legislation and administration is intended to serve two related but distinct purposes: the removal of obstacles to migration of labor, and the removal of what are called "distortions" of competition.'[152] There too, 'a "gradual coalescence of social policies" appears ... not perhaps as an indispensable condition for the functioning of a common market, but as one of the elements which may greatly assist in giving it firm foundations'.[153] The Spaak Report was certainly pervaded by the same spirit of liberal optimism about the equalizing qualities of a common market as had underlain the Ohlin Report: it was similarly strongly influenced by the expectation that, because labour demand would grow where labour costs were lowest, wages there would tend to rise and that, furthermore, the free movement of labour would gradually facilitate the levelling-up of working conditions.[154]

But it was also permeated, no less and in fact more than the Ohlin Report, by the idea that the common market would strengthen the individual Member States' capacity for intervention in the social field and thereby ensure the maintenance *within them* of high levels of protection, and that the Community would need to prepare the appropriate guarantees – whether by fixing common rules or by taking direct action – for all

---

[152] O. Kahn-Freund, 'Labor Law and Social Security', in E. Stein and T. L. Nicholson (eds.), *American Enterprise in the European Common Market. A Legal Profile*, Ann Arbor, Mich. 1960, vol. I, pp. 297–458, here p. 299.

[153] *Ibid.*

[154] *Ibid.*, p. 300. In the Spaak Report (see note 44 above, here p. 234) it was stated: 'In addition, wage and interest rates tend to level up in a common market a process which is hastened by free circulation of the factors of production. This is a consequence rather than a condition of the common market's operation.'

instances where the functioning of the market might (exceptionally) put that capacity in a critical position. In this respect, as already mentioned, the Spaak Report seems in fact to have been based on an approach that could be described as more 'constructivist'[155] than that inherent in the Ohlin Report.

In the first place, the specified instances in which the preventive harmonization of national systems of legislation was considered appropriate were considerably more extensive than those taken into consideration in the Ohlin Report.[156] The main difference concerned the very sensitive matter of harmonization of the various systems for financing social security, on the subject of which France protested, as is well known, that compared in particular with its neighbour Germany it was at a considerable competitive disadvantage owing to the high level of social-security contributions paid by its undertakings.

The start made in the Spaak Report on confronting this sensitive issue, which furthermore was shelved when it finally came to drafting the Treaty, was rather timid and in some respects ambiguous, but nonetheless significant. The case where in a given country social security was financed from percentage-based contributions levied on wages with the burden therefore falling essentially on industries which used a large labour force was expressly included among the hypothetical instances of specific distortion of competition whenever, in the same branches of economic activity, in another country social security was financed essentially from the national budget, that is, from taxes affecting the entire economy, with the result that industries which used a large labour force were relatively less heavily burdened than those in the first-mentioned country.[157]

The ambiguity of the example suggested by the authors of the Report clearly lay in the fact that, in reality, at the time all the original members of the Community had social-security systems essentially based on the insurance principle and financed mainly from the levy of contributions.[158] Nonetheless, it is impossible to ignore – especially when viewed from a modern-day perspective – the importance of the Report's reference to so crucial an element of national systems of social protection as a factor potentially representing a specific distortion of competition to be corrected through the use of powers of harmonization.

---

[155] To use the Hayekian adjective in the sense in which it has recently been adopted by L. Nogler, 'Individui, istituzioni e scelte pubbliche nel diritto del lavoro', *Lavoro e Diritto* 1998, pp. 271ff., especially p. 274.

[156] See Spaak Report, p. 234.   [157] *Ibid.*, pp. 233–4.

[158] Cf. Kahn-Freund, 'Labor Law', pp. 442ff.

An even larger dose of 'constructivism' informed those pages of the Report dedicated, in its Title III, to the growth of the common market and the full use of European resources. Here, the functions of what was intended to be (but only partly became) a future EEC investment fund were outlined broadly and incisively as being to ensure 'the smooth and steady growth of the common market'.[159]

The fund's prime tasks were to be in connection with participation in the financing of major projects of a European nature and interest and a collective thrust towards the development of backward areas.[160] However, what is more striking and more relevant to our present purposes is the prominence of the tasks prefigured for the fund as regards industrial reconversion and readaptation.

'Reconversion in industry', so stated the Report,[161] 'is an essential consequence of the introduction of the common market' inasmuch as it would ensure a continuity of employment in steadily more productive forms, facilitate progressive adjustment to the common market, make better use of existing resources and achieve the maximum reduction in the cost of inevitable changes. According to the Report, not only was this policy the most humane because it would avoid company closures, the discontinuation of economic activity or dismissals as far as possible and would tend to ensure re-employment *in loco*. It was also the most economic because it would make it possible to utilize the existing means of production and all the housing, communication and transport facilities that gravitate around industries.

The Report saw as a mission of equally fundamental social utility[162] that of entrusting a fund, where it should prove necessary, with the total readaptation of labour.

In this case the direct influence of the approach already tested by the Six in the context of the ECSC was even more marked. During the intervening years, the provisions of the Treaty of Paris had in fact already started to provide the ECSC High Authority with an extraordinarily effective instrument for dealing with the crisis in Belgium's coal industry, making it possible in practice, as mentioned earlier, fully to 'absorb' the social effects deriving from its progressive dismantling.

Modelling itself on the provisions of the ECSC Treaty, the Spaak Report suggested the establishment of a 'readaptation fund contributed by member countries as a proportion of their total wage bill plus social services'.[163]

---

[159] Spaak Report, p. 238.   [160] *Ibid.*
[161] *Ibid.*, p. 239.   [162] *Ibid.*   [163] *Ibid.*, p. 240.

No proof was to be needed that the cases of unemployment to be covered by assistance from the fund were a direct consequence of the creation of the common market, and it was to offer intervention amounting to up to half of the expenditure involved, in cases and for purposes previously agreed and, generally speaking, whenever it was in the interests of the Community as a whole and also of the State in question, in order to achieve enhanced productivity and raise the standard of living, to effect progressive structural changes within industries, national reorganization within companies and better utilization of labour.[164]

In particular, the Community was to bear part of the social cost of these changes in cases of the total or partial closure of a company or establishment, or redundancies involving 'a cut in personnel of 10% or over, or of at least 10 people'.[165] In such cases, in which the fund was to intervene with different kinds of aid comprising immediate coverage of expenditure on resettlement and retraining and, thereafter, possible combination with the grant of unemployment benefits by Member States themselves, the Report prefigured the progressive delineation of a real system of assistance for the unemployed[166] which in the course of time would foster a natural process of harmonization of the regimes prevailing in the countries participating in the common market.

In the event that a company in process of adaptation were to reduce or temporarily lay off all or part of its workforce, the Report even went so far as to conceive of a kind of Community wage integration whereby the fund was to provide other forms of aid such as 'temporary grants to workers suspended during the reconversion of enterprises, and grants to firms to enable them to close down bit by bit instead of all at once'.[167]

As intended by the Report the prefiguring of such incisive powers to take action at supranational level would not, however, erode the principle of total autonomy of 'social governance' on the part of the Member States. In this connection it emphasized that however much it may be extended, the economic integration that will be achieved by the 'free movement of goods, services, workers and capital is only partial economic integration, since the common market does not involve interference with national budgetary, financial or social policies, nor the establishment of a single monetary system'.[168]

In the embedded-liberalism philosophy, of which the Spaak Report was still an expression, the macroeconomic and social autonomy of nation-states constitutes both the fundamental empirical starting-point and the

---

[164] *Ibid.*   [165] *Ibid.*   [166] *Ibid.*   [167] *Ibid.*   [168] *Ibid.*, p. 242.

indisputable basic normative principle.[169] The provisions shortly afterwards dedicated in the Treaty of Rome to the co-ordination of the Member States' economic policies were to prove little more than 'symbolic'[170] and to confirm the postulate of the total macroeconomic autonomy of the Member States as consistently maintained in the Spaak Report itself. The goal of full employment – not stated explicitly as such in the text of the Treaty – was in reality the *a priori* assumption of the entire construction of the Community and for that reason the latter was not intended to erode in any way the panoply of instruments of fiscal, monetary and trade policy available to Member States in pursuing that goal.[171]

6. . . . and in the Treaty of Rome

In a sense, the approaches actually adopted by the Treaty of Rome fell halfway between the more moderate ones suggested by the Ohlin Report and those of a more 'constructivist' stamp indicated by the Spaak Report.

On the subject of the Common Agricultural policy (CAP) the Treaty opted fairly radically for a system embodying strong regimentation and control of the market and substantial elimination of the scope left for free competition,[172] one of the explicit objectives being 'to ensure a fair standard of living for the agricultural community, in particular by increasing the individual earnings of persons engaged in agriculture' (as stated in Article 39(1)(b), now Article 33(1)(b) of the EC Treaty).

Despite all the vicissitudes that increasingly marked its development and to this day call for a profound restructuring that was not set in motion until the reforms of the early 1990s, the CAP largely functioned as a real sector-based Community welfare-state system[173] aimed at providing shelter from the vagaries of the market and a subsidiary network of instruments of income protection and redistribution (albeit often 'the wrong

---

[169] See P. Kosonen, *European Integration: A Welfare State Perspective*, Helsinki 1994, pp. 24ff.

[170] Moravcsik, *Choice for Europe*, here p. 149.

[171] See G. Dawson, 'Governing the European Macroeconomy', in G. Thompson (ed.), *Governing the European Economy*, London 2001, pp. 98ff., especially pp. 102 and 111.

[172] See, by way of example, F. Snyder, *Law of the Common Agricultural Policy*, London 1985.

[173] Cf. S. Leibfried and P. Pierson, 'Le prospettive dell'Europa sociale', *Stato e Mercato* 1993, no. 1, pp. 43ff., especially p. 55; and, in more detail, E. Rieger, 'Protective Shelter or Straightjacket. An Institutional Analysis of the Common Agricultural Policy in the European Union', in Leibfried and Pierson (eds.), *European Social Policy*, pp. 194ff., especially p. 223.

way round')[174] in favour of a class in society whose consensus was seen as decisive for the democratic reconstruction of the nation-state in the EEC's formative years.

Perhaps more clearly in this context than in others, the Community institutions – through the massive protection of national agriculture – rather manifested their nature as 'devices intended to reinforce national economic policies'[175] characterized, at the time, by a genuine explosion of state intervention and support for agricultural incomes. And the fact that this 'farmers' welfare'[176] was from the start structured as an objective mechanism of positive integration in which individual beneficiaries did not hold rights directly enforceable with respect to the Community[177] (as has, by contrast, typically happened in the case of the various national welfare systems) simply serves as a further demonstration of the strict functional complementarity intended by the founding fathers in this respect between the two levels of protective intervention, i.e. the supranational and the national.

On the other hand, the European Social Fund – the other instrument of potential Community redistribution of economic resources for social purposes *sensu lato* – was conceived at the start by the Treaty of Rome in more restrictive terms than those prefigured by the Spaak Report. The task assigned to it by ex Article 123, mostly instrumental to the creation of a common labour market, was that 'of rendering the employment of workers easier and of increasing their geographical and occupational mobility within the Community'. During the first phase of its history (1960–72) it was, in addition, confined by its very rules of operation to intervening 'blindly and automatically at a necessarily late stage, as a passive mechanism that had no impact on working life' and did no more than 'pay back to Member States what had been received from them'.[178]

In fixing the regulatory bases and objectives of Community social policy the Treaty then followed what was more or less a middle line between the indications of the Ohlin Report and those of the Spaak Report and one which in any event clearly represented a compromise between the German and French positions.

The idea of at least partial harmonization of the forms of financing of Member States' social-security systems, strongly urged by France and – as seen above – ambiguously foreshadowed in the Spaak Report

---

[174] Rhodes, 'Defending the Social Contract', p. 41, talks in this connection of 'a perverted and distorted form of distribution'.
[175] Milward, 'L'Europa in formazione', pp. 194–5.
[176] Leibfried and Pierson, 'Le prospettive', p. 55.
[177] Rieger, 'Protective Shelter', p. 227.   [178] G. and A. Lyon-Caen, *Droit social*, p. 267.

itself, was given no explicit recognition in the text of the Treaty, which with its Articles 117 and 118 appeared instead to adopt the opposing position preferred by Germany. In other words, the thesis that social charges and labour costs in general (including direct costs) constituted only one element of the broader range of factors, all of them closely connected and interdependent, likely to determine a productive system's competitiveness in a market of open competition. Meaning that it would not be possible – nor, obviously, correct – to single out this one factor and make it the subject of measures imposing forced and artificial harmonization which would therefore deviate from the logic of the market and distort competition.

On the other hand, the generous pensions reform introduced in Germany in 1955 had already established the regulatory premises for the gap in protection, and hence costs, between the two national systems to begin to close 'spontaneously' and so disappear within the space of a few years.[179]

Even in a field as crucial as this one it was therefore to be left to the natural dynamics of the common market to activate a process of spontaneous and automatic harmonization (of the results)[180] of the competing national social systems without, on the whole, any need for heteronomous intervention.

Accordingly, ex Article 117 of the Treaty explicitly envisaged what was primarily perceived as the intrinsic tendency of close integration between European economies 'to promote improved working conditions and an improved standard of living for workers, so as to make possible their harmonization while the improvement is being maintained', i.e. upward harmonization. And this was presented as a natural development that 'will ensue not only from the functioning of the common market, which will favour the harmonization of social systems, but also from the procedures provided for in this Treaty and from the approximation of provisions laid down by law, regulation or administrative action'.

Hence, the programme[181] conceived by Article 117 was not accompanied by an explanation of *specific* regulatory bases and instruments of intervention in social matters. Ex Article 118 did not constitute 'a legal basis for attaining the objectives stated in Article 117, but an

---

[179] The importance of this circumstance is underlined by Milward, *European Rescue*, pp. 212–13.

[180] Cf. S. Simitis and A. Lyon-Caen, 'Community Labour Law: A Critical Introduction to Its History', in Davies *et al.* (eds.), *European Community Labour Law*, pp. 1–22, especially p. 4.

[181] On the programmatic nature of Article 117 of the Treaty, at least in its original wording, see *ex plurimis* G. Arrigo, *Il diritto del lavoro dell'Unione europea*, Milan 1998, vol. I, p. 111.

organizational rule on the work of the Commission, which, in conformity with the Treaty's general objectives . . ., was to have the task of promoting the mutual collaboration of Member States in the "social field" in general and, in particular, in a number of matters including "labour law and working conditions" . . .'[182] Any potential approximation of provisions laid down by law or regulation was to take place – as indeed happened as far as the (partial) implementation of the first Social Action Programme of 1974 was concerned but subsequently proved increasingly difficult – by virtue of the general basis constituted by Article 100 of the Treaty.

On the other hand, Articles 119 and 120 of the Treaty, as also its Third Protocol containing provisions on *inter alia* the payment of overtime in France, clearly reflected transalpine concerns, albeit in terms in line with the indications given by both the Ohlin Report and the Spaak Report.

Article 120, like the Third Protocol annexed to the Treaty, confined itself in a sense to 'freezing'[183] the situation in the matters concerned as it existed when the common market was being created. In committing Member States to endeavour 'to maintain the existing equivalence between paid holiday schemes' Article 120 configured a bland and somewhat indeterminate reciprocal obligation between the Member States but did not in itself, like the Protocol, provide any legal basis for Community regulatory intervention. The most that was done was that the Protocol, despite the relative vagueness of its provisions (themselves more akin to a 'prediction' than a real 'prescription'),[184] gave some substance to the content of this obligation by, in particular, charging the Commission with the duty to authorize a Member State affected by potential unfair competition to take measures to protect its own interests, where necessary in the form of imposing quantitative restrictions on imports.[185]

Consequently, the sole 'social' provision that conferred on the EEC a specific competence to carry out regulatory harmonization was Article 119 of the Treaty. Worded 'rather cautiously', it was not in fact intended to confer rights on individuals or 'to become an integral part of the Member States' national legal orders'[186] but was directed solely at establishing a legal basis for action at supranational level on the assumption that differences between national laws on the matter constituted (particularly to the disadvantage of France) a form of specific distortion of competition.[187]

---

[182] *Ibid.*, p. 112.   [183] Kahn-Freund, 'Labor Law', p. 332.
[184] *Ibid.*, p. 333.   [185] *Ibid.*, p. 335.   [186] *Ibid.*, p. 329.
[187] In this sense see, by way of example, C. Barnard, 'The Economic Objectives of Article 119', in T. Hervey and D. O'Keefe (eds.), *Sex Equality Law and the European Union*, Chichester 1996, pp. 321ff.

Rediscovery of the provision in question as the source of a fundamental social right to equal treatment between men and women in terms of pay, directly actionable within the legal systems of individual Member States independently of specific implementing measures, has therefore brought about, in the case-law of the European Court of Justice (ECJ), a kind of heterogenesis of the objectives which the founding fathers had in mind and has endowed the Article with a function and meaning very different from those originally intended for it.[188]

So the only social rights which emanated directly from or could at least be extrapolated from the Treaty of Rome were, as mentioned earlier, those recognized by Articles 48–66 (now Articles 39–55) in the context of their general guarantee of freedom of movement for workers and freedom of establishment within the common market.

They therefore consisted in – and despite the institution of Community citizenship still largely consist in[189] – social rights strictly functional to the establishment of an integrated market. Social rights, which, although considerably enriching the European citizen-worker's patrimony of rights and in that sense very quickly manifesting an autonomous expansive attitude, i.e. one to some extent independent of their clear market slant,[190] nevertheless remained a corollary, albeit essential, of the measures taken to remove obstacles to free movement of the factors of production within the common market and therefore formed part of a logic of predominantly 'negative integration' of national systems.[191]

Such is, typically, the function of the rules on the co-ordination of national social-security schemes for migrant workers:[192] the EEC's most

---

[188] See also B. Hepple, 'Equality and Discrimination', in Davies *et al.* (eds.), *European Community Labour Law*, pp. 237–59, and M. Barbera, *Discriminazioni ed eguaglianza nel rapporto di lavoro*, Milan 1991, pp. 103ff.

[189] See S. Giubboni, 'Cittadinanza comunitaria e sicurezza sociale: un profilo critico', *Argomenti di Diritto del Lavoro* 1997, no. 6, pp. 67ff., especially pp. 79 and 102, and Giubboni, 'Libertà di circolazione e protezione sociale nell'Unione europea', *Giornale di Diritto del Lavoro e di Relazioni Industriali* 1998, pp. 81ff.

[190] See C. A. Ball, 'The Making of a Transnational Capitalist Society: The Court of Justice, Social Policy and Individual Rights under the European Community's Legal Order', *Harvard International Law Journal* 1996, vol. 37, pp. 307ff.

[191] In the interpretation first developed and examined in detail by J. Tinbergen, *International Economic Integration*, 2nd edn, Amsterdam-London-New York 1965, p. 77.

[192] Cf. also L. Nogler, 'Quale sicurezza sociale nell' Unione europea?', *Rivista Giuridica del Lavoro e della Previdenza Sociale* 1994, vol. I, pp. 49ff., especially pp. 52ff.; A. Andreoni, 'Sicurezza sociale, 1, Sistemi nazionali e armonizzazione', in Baylos Grau *et al.*, *Dizionario*, pp. 527ff.; B. Schulte, 'The Welfare State and European Integration', *European Journal of Social Security* 1999, no. 1, pp. 7ff. especially p. 18.

conspicuous achievement in the social field, at least throughout the transitional period.[193]

In implementation of Article 51 of the Treaty of Rome (now Article 42), Regulation 3/58[194] confined itself to establishing 'communication' between systems that were closed to each other,[195] while jealously preserving their autonomy and diversity,[196] in order to remove what was a key obstacle for the purposes of the free movement of labour.

In this sense, the rules on the co-ordination of national social-security schemes can be seen as a metaphor more generally reflecting the role assigned to law and to Community social policy by the founding fathers.

'The Treaty thus presumes that social policy basically remains "within" the national state and is unaffected by the EC mantle. National differences are to be respected and only "co-ordinated" in case of need.'[197] The 'abstentionist'[198] option as codified in this sense by Article 51 of the Treaty was in line with the idea that the creation of a transnational market, including a transnational labour market, should proceed in step with the preservation of national foundations of social citizenship rights, the principal guarantee of integrity and stability of the domestic democratic political systems that had been rebuilt.

It must also be remembered, in the same connection, how much weight was carried in the negotiations attending the drafting of the Treaty by the concern not to encroach on the sphere of the original autonomy of the trade unions and employers' organizations as recognized in the several national systems. The need to defend the strong constitutional principle of *Tarifautonomie* had a significant influence on the position of the German government[199] and was one of the factors that accounted for this philosophy of supranational abstentionism adopted by the Treaty of Rome.

---

[193] R. Nielsen and E. Szyszczak, *The Social Dimension of the European Community*, Copenhagen 1993, pp. 37ff.

[194] But the same obviously applies to Regulation 1408/71, which replaced it and is currently in force.

[195] M. Roccella and T. Treu, *Diritto del lavoro della Comunità europea*, 2nd edn, Padua 1995, p. 135.

[196] See Simitis and Lyon-Caen, 'Community Labour Law', p. 5; Deakin, 'Labour Law', p. 73.

[197] S. Leibfried, 'Social Europe. Welfare State Trajectories of the European Community', *ZeS-Arbeitspapier* No. 10/91, University of Bremen, p. 9.

[198] F. Corso, 'Comunitarizzazione del diritto del lavoro italiano', in Baylos Grau *et al.*, *Dizionario*, pp. 139ff., here p. 158.

[199] See Milward, *European Rescue*, pp. 212–13.

Along the red line linking the creation of a common market to the preservation of national social sovereignty the Treaty of Rome therefore accommodated and incorporated within itself diverse and potentially even contradictory instances. The abstentionist option epitomized in Article 51 and the associated neoclassical and unquestionably neoliberal trust in the equalizing qualities of a common market were accompanied by a guarantee of Community intervention in terms of necessary upward harmonization in the event of the latter's potential failures and jealous preservation of the Member States' Keynesian competence in macroeconomic governance in the interests of full employment.

Thus the conviction was certainly present that, à la Smith, 'the propulsive force of the market on its own generates rights and, more importantly, on its own redistributes them among the subjects who operate in the market;'[200] that the spontaneous process of levelling-up driven *naturaliter* by the common market required heteronomous correction through intervention only in the presence of factors of specific distortion of the conditions of competition; and that therefore the social-policy functions appropriate to the supranational level were ones that were in a sense atypical and in any event of a different kind from those performed by national governments, i.e. ones 'concerned with market-making rather than market-correcting, aimed at creating an integrated European labour market and enabling it to function efficiently, rather than correcting its outcomes in line with political standards of social justice.'[201]

At the same time, however, the idea was also clearly present that the functioning of the common market should not erode the autonomous capacity of national systems to ensure higher levels of welfare for their own citizens. That in particular national governments should retain 'direct control over fiscal and monetary policies to be used for the attainment of the objective of full employment at home',[202] with inevitable resultant pressures on the free movement of capital, the real attainment of which was left, not inadvertently, until the internal market had been established. That maintenance of the Member States' competitive position in the integrated market should never be to the detriment of their full autonomy of

---

[200] S. Sciarra. 'Diritti sociali fondamentali', in Baylos Grau *et al.*, *Dizionario*, pp. 71ff., here p. 72.

[201] W. Streeck. 'Neo-voluntarism: A New European Social Policy Regime?', in Marks *et al.*, *Governance*, p. 72. Also in *European Law Journal* 1995, no. 1, pp. 31–59.

[202] Tsoukalis, *New European*, p. 14.

social governance.[203] That community integration should therefore leave their spheres of social sovereignty intact. And that whenever the abstentionist option given preference by the Treaty as the one best serving that sovereignty failed, Community heteronomous intervention should, by way of exception, correct the distortions generated by the common market by imposing the upward harmonization of national social systems.

7. Crisis and 'overthrow' of the original model

Notwithstanding the apparent soundness of the rational basis offered for it by the Ohlin and Spaak Reports and its effectiveness, 'the balance struck in the Treaty of Rome between State action and Community competence in the conduct of economic and social policy' soon revealed its inherent precariousness and 'has become increasingly difficult to maintain as the push for economic integration has intensified'.[204]

A prime reason for its crisis or rather, at least from a certain point onwards, 'impasse', as Spiros Simitis and Antoine Lyon-Caen prefer to call it,[205] arose from the very rationale itself justifying potential regulatory action by the Community and concerned in particular the *harmonization model* implied and adopted by the Treaty of Rome.[206] There were certainly other factors, some in any case inherent in the model, such as the intrinsic ambiguity, quite apart from the objective meagreness or inadequacy of the legal basis for action in social matters; the inefficiency of the political decision-making process, hinged on the unanimity rule and afflicted in general by the defects typical of the intergovernmental method;[207] and, obviously, the irreducible heterogeneity of the several national systems, enough in itself to render any attempt at their rigid harmonization fruitless, especially one stamped by the idea of forcibly transplanting solutions typical only of some into the others as well.[208]

The ingenuously illuminist notion of a natural and progressive tendency towards the upward harmonization of national systems quickly showed itself to be a fatal illusion. In particular, the basic assumption that direct harmonizing intervention by the Community should be confined

---

[203] Clearly, when faced with a deterioration in its competitive position a Member State was to be free 'to adjust its exchange rate accordingly' (Tinbergen, *International Economic Integration*, p. 78) *without* having to restrict its wage or social policies.
[204] Deakin, 'Labour Law', p. 70.   [205] See note 180 above, p. 7.
[206] See *amplius* subsection 2 of chapter 4 below.
[207] Cf. in particular Scharpf, 'Joint Decision Trap'.
[208] See Roccella and Treu, *Diritto del lavoro*, pp. 29ff.

to responding to specific episodes of distortion of competition in the common market proved to be inadequate.

Actually, the two major 'success stories' of Community regulatory intervention – those which Streeck has identified as the two spheres of 'encapsulated federalism'[209] in what is otherwise deemed the vanishing body of social Europe – have extended far beyond this logic of action. Although as such fundamentally 'compatible . . . with the principles of a liberal economic order',[210] the vast areas of social regulation on the subjects of equality/equal opportunities between men and women and health and safety protection at work are in no way reducible to a strict anti-dumping logic as viewed in economic terms.[211] With respect to sex equality in particular, the decisive thrust of ECJ case-law has demonstrated the distancing of Community rules from a strict functionalist-economics rationale of that kind and established a perspective of outright fundamental-rights protection,[212] whose strong innovative impact on the actual elaboration of the Member States' constitutional principles quickly became clear.[213]

By contrast, that logic was certainly the basis of the three famous enterprise-restructuring Directives of the second half of the 1970s. The latter nonetheless essentially marked the end of the brief cycle of 'functionalist harmonization'. As the belated fruit of the final remnants of the 'social-democratic consensus' underlying the Community's first Social Action Programme of 1974,[214] the three Directives respectively on collective redundancies (Directive 75/129/EEC), transfers of undertakings (Directive 77/187/EEC) and the protection of employees in the event of their employer's insolvency (Directive 80/987/EEC) saw the light of day at the precise moment when the harmonization model adopted by the Treaty of Rome began its rapid decline, first in the official rhetoric of the Commission and shortly afterwards in concrete regulatory decisions themselves and the evolution of the European Community's primary sources.[215]

---

[209] Streeck, 'Neo-voluntarism', p. 76.

[210] G. Majone, 'The European Community Between Social Policy and Social Regulation', *Journal of Common Market Studies* 1993, vol. 31 no. 2, pp. 153–70, here p. 156.

[211] D'Antona, 'Sistema', p. 22, talks in this connection of forms of 'cohesive harmonization' i.e. ones which, unlike the forms of 'functionalist harmonization' devised by the founding fathers, are directed towards 'adapting the Member States' legislation to essential Community standards and [promoting] the definition of common social values'.

[212] See, e.g., ECJ Case C-50/96 *Schröder* [2000] ECR I-743; also Joined Cases C-270/97 and C-271/97 *Sievers and Schrage* [2000] ECR I-929.

[213] Cf. S. Sciarra, 'Integrazione dinamica tra fonti nazionali e comunitarie: il caso del lavoro notturno delle donne', *Diritto del Lavoro* 1995, vol. 1, p. 153.

[214] Streeck, 'Neo-voluntarism', pp. 74–5.

[215] This argument will be examined in more detail in chapter 4 below.

As early as in its 1975 Green Paper on employee participation within companies, the Commission candidly acknowledged that 'a sufficient convergence of social and economic policies and structures in these areas will not happen automatically as a consequence of the integration of Community markets',[216] although it contextually renewed a commitment to reducing (only) 'degrees of divergence that were *unacceptable*, without being able to specify in any detail what measures would be useful to that end'.[217]

It was only later, from the early 1990s onwards, that the rhetoric of (horizontal) convergence of national systems was officially to replace that of their (vertical) harmonization, in explicit homage to the principle of subsidiarity now adopted by the Treaties.[218] In the meantime, however, it was the Single European Act that was entrusted with the task of removing from the body of the Community's economic constitution the supporting elements of the original model:[219] alongside the principle of mutual recognition it codified as a guiding criterion for establishing the internal market (albeit initially only for health and safety protection at work) a new rule on the adoption of (only) 'minimum requirements for gradual implementation, having regard to the conditions and technical rules obtaining in each of the Member States' (ex Article 118a, now Article 138 of the EC Treaty).[220]

This did not, however, leave the alternative to the original social-harmonization model clearly delineated. There remained an underlying uncertainty as to the rationale justifying Community regulatory intervention in social matters. At times the Commission continued to voice the idea of such intervention serving the purpose of achieving a '"parity of costs" between undertakings in different States',[221] a 'level playing field'

---

[216] Quotation from the Green Paper taken from Simitis and Lyon-Caen, 'Community Labour Law', p. 7.

[217] *Ibid.* (the emphasis has been added).

[218] See, for example, Y. Chassard and O. Quintin, 'Social Protection in the European Community: Towards a Convergence of Policies', *International Social Security Review* 1992, vol. 45 nos. 1–2, pp. 91ff.; Schulte, 'Welfare State', pp. 38ff.

[219] See Simitis and Lyon-Caen, 'Community Labour Law', p. 8.

[220] That rule, ontologically different from the notion of (spontaneous) upward harmonization although still lexically bound up with it but without any further operative impact, Article 117 (now Article 136 of the EC Treaty), was then extended to all social matters by the Agreement on Social Policy annexed to the Maastricht Treaty and therefore incorporated in this broader version into the text of the EC Treaty following the Amsterdam revision.

[221] Deakin, 'Labour Law', p. 78.

capable of reducing or at least smoothing-out the competitive disadvantage arising from high labour costs.

Besides, the notion of 'minimum requirements for gradual implementation' was still far from the notion of a common floor of standards as proposed by Wedderburn,[222] which refers more to a strategy of constitutionalization of the fundamental social rights of European workers whose emergence was even more uncertain, at least until fairly recently.

The progressive institutionalization of European social dialogue from the Single European Act onwards and the subsequent inclusion of Community collective bargaining among the sources of the Community's legal order,[223] on the other hand, forms part of the plan to move beyond and abandon the original social-harmonization model. Community collective agreements represent a new type of 'regulatory resource' of the supranational order intended to provide new instruments and techniques capable of making good the 'regulatory deficit' due to the crisis of the old harmonization model.[224] They are therefore a regulatory technique alternative to that model, but endowed – at supranational level – with a weak constitutional and material base.[225]

A second (and here more relevant) factor in the crisis of the original constitutional model lies in the above-mentioned erosion of the Member States' autonomy of social governance. Here again the issue appears to be one of a latent contradiction of the model adopted by the Treaty of Rome, under which it became increasingly difficult to link the strong push towards economic integration through the legal construction of a common market with an equally rigorous defence of national prerogatives in the social field. The founding fathers had, in essence, believed it possible to make the economic element a common one while leaving the social element within the sphere reserved to the nation-state. The facts have shown that it was not possible to keep the two separate.[226]

A quick outline has been given above[227] of the profound changes in the political economy of the Community integration process which took place

---

[222] Lord Wedderburn, 'European Community Law and Workers' Rights after 1992: Fact or Fake?', in Wedderburn, *Labour Law and Freedom. Further Essays in Labour Law*, London 1995, pp. 247ff., here p. 273.

[223] See recently R. Nunin, *Il dialogo sociale europeo. Attori, procedure, prospective*, Milan 2001.

[224] In this sense, A. Lo Faro, *Regulating Social Europe. Reality and Myth of Collective Bargaining in the EC Legal Order* (English translation), Oxford 2000, pp. 123ff.

[225] *Ibid.*, pp. 155ff.; see subsection 5 of chapter 4 below.

[226] Cf. A. Supiot (ed.), *Au-delà de l'emploi. Transformations du travail et devenir du droit du travail en Europe. Rapport pour la Commission européenne*, Paris 1999, p. 11.

[227] See subsection 2 above.

from the mid-1970s onwards and which underlie this metamorphosis of the original constitutional balance. In the remaining subsections of the present chapter, this second occasion of radical transformation or outright 'overthrow' of the original constitutional arrangements will be illustrated in more detail, from the point of view of its various component profiles.

However, the image of 'semisovereign welfare states' suggested by Leibfried and Pierson[228] effectively restores an overall sense of this metamorphosis and makes it easier to perceive, above and beyond the individual aspects that can be singled out analytically, the reality of its profoundly unitary nature.

The principles of Community *lex mercatoria* – interpreted by the European Court of Justice in the same way as a constitutional court would apply a rigid Constitution – were progressively imposed as 'outer limits' to the degree of Member State discretion as regards forms of social policy and regulation previously recognized during the phase in which the liberalization implemented with the institution of a common market left the arsenal of neo-mercantilist development policies that were the distinctive features of the resurrected nation-state[229] still largely intact.

In determining the structure of economic and monetary union (EMU) the Maastricht Treaty then confirmed, directly within the body of the new European economic constitution, the end of the Keynesian welfare state based on total discretion as regards deficit spending policies. By setting in advance the upper limits on government deficit, national debt and rate of inflation permitted to Member States for the purposes of participating in (and lawfully staying within) EMU, the Treaty essentially fixed the boundaries of their macroeconomic governance in indirectly imposing precise restrictions on their actual fiscal and social policies.

At the same time, by taking away the participating States' monetary powers it forced them to turn to measures for 'flexibilizing' their labour-market and social-protection regulatory systems as the main means of maintaining their position in the case of increased intra-Community and international competition. Thus, in the EMU context the dynamics of regulatory competition between the several national systems – as institutionalized with the creation of the internal market – have been given new blood and are reflected, in forms again totally new as compared with the original arrangements, in a weakening of the very principle of territoriality of national systems of labour and social-security law.

---

[228] 'Semisovereign Welfare States', pp. 44–5.   [229] Milward, *European Rescue.*

8. Infiltration of Community competition and market law into national systems of labour and social-security law

That the rules on competition and the market contained in the Treaty of Rome were *not* intended to interfere in any way with the Member States' social and labour policies[230] is a fact which emerges fairly readily from the outlines of the original institutional compromise of embedded liberalism in the terms in which it has been reconstructed above. And which – to give only a single but particularly eloquent example – seems clearly illustrated by the long history of mutual indifference and non-interference between national rules on labour law and social security and Community rules on state aid, afflicted as it was until relatively recently by a more general form of highly symptomatic 'lethargy'.[231]

The progressive 'infiltration'[232] of the principles of a free market (and freedom within the market) into the formerly jealously protected national systems of labour and social-security law from the second half of the 1980s onwards, through the effect of Community case-law, therefore represents an obvious reason for the 'breakdown' of the initial constitutional balance.

However, the indisputable supremacy acquired in this way by the values of a market economy constitutionally based on a system of 'undistorted' competition was interpreted at an early stage by German ordoliberals as 'the cunning of reason' (*List der Vernunft*),[233] somehow written into the Community's economic constitution, meaning that the latter was almost 'deliberately' left without an equally explicit and cogent recognition of 'social countervalues'.[234] Viewed from this perspective, the primacy

---

[230] In this sense, A. Jeammaud, 'Lessons from Some Secondary Areas of Dialogue', in Sciarra, *Labour*, pp. 229–90, here p. 233, according to whom the problem raised by preliminary-ruling references to the ECJ posing the question of 'the compatibility of certain emblematic provisions of national labour-law systems . . . with rules of Community law on the free movement of goods and competition' 'was certainly not envisaged by those who drafted the original Treaty and had been considered by very few experts in European law until it struck imaginative lawyers . . .' .

[231] See Tsoukalis, *New European*, p. 125.

[232] To repeat the graphic expression, now entered into general usage, first employed by G. Lyon-Caen, 'L'Infiltration du Droit du travail par le Droit de la concurrence', *Droit Ouvrier* 1992, p. 313.

[233] Joerges, 'European Economic Law', p. 38, who quotes A. Müller-Armack, 'Die Wirtschaftsordnung des Gemeinsamen Marktes', in Müller-Armack, *Wirtschaftsordnung und Wirtschaftspolitik. Studien und Konzepte zur sozialen Marktwirtschaft und zur europäischen Integration*, Freiburg-im-Breisgau 1966, pp. 401ff., especially p. 405.

[234] From this point of view it could be said that the institutional compromise of embedded liberalism suffered, in the Treaty of Rome, from an actual normative or institutional asymmetry but that this did not give rise to a lack of equilibrium until primary

progressively acquired by common competition and market law – conceived as the undisputed core of the European economic constitution and the cornerstone of its material legitimacy – could usefully be conceptualized as the almost inevitable and in a sense preordained outcome of the normative dialectic triggered by the Treaty of Rome.

In this view of things, the negative-integration effect deriving from spillover of the principles of total freedom of movement of the factors of production and undistorted competition has thus been effectively conceptualized as the preordained reflection of the Treaty's specific founding mission and the most authentic legitimacy base of the Community order.[235] 'The market is conceived as the best source of legitimation of the European Economic Constitution', from a perspective in which the latter is read as preordained to protect 'market freedom and individual rights against public power',[236] i.e. against state interference in the economic sphere.

As will be confirmed in more detail in chapter 3 below, the changing interpretation of Article 30 (now Article 28) of the EC Treaty has a clear paradigmatic significance in this connection. Essentially, this provision – a real cornerstone of the European economic constitution – was progressively read by the European Court of Justice (at least until its more recent decision in *Keck and Mithouard*)[237] predominantly as an 'economic due

---

supranational *law* on economic integration – fundamentally directed towards the creation of an open and competitive market – was balanced by the primacy attributed *politically* to the principles of a mixed economy and the welfare state by Member States in the Community context as well. In other words, equilibrium was in fact maintained until – to use well-known terminology – normative supranationalism, which is essentially characteristic of competition and market law, was balanced by a decision-making supranationalism directed towards the jealous preservation of Member States' effective autonomy in the social field. It therefore would not seem rash to find a certain parallel with the disruption, not as yet made good, of the mutual balance that formerly existed between what Joseph Weiler has called the supranationalism of the legal system and intergovernmentalism of the political decision-making process of the European Community. Cf. J. H. H. Weiler, *Il sistema comunitario europeo. Struttura giuridica e processo politico*, Bologna 1985, pp. 39ff., and also, more recently, Weiler, 'Transformation of Europe', pp. 16ff.

[235] See, for example, as long ago as W. Röpke, *International Order and Economic Integration*, Dordrecht 1959 and, more recently, E.-J. Mestmäcker, 'On the Legitimacy of European Law', *Rabels Zeitschrift für ausländisches und internationales Privatrecht* 1994, no. 58, pp. 615ff. For further information and considerations on the subject, see chapter 4, subsection 10 below.

[236] Poiares Maduro, *We, The Court*, p. 109.

[237] ECJ Joined Cases C-267 and C-268/91 [1993] ECR I-6097, on which see, among many, N. Reich, 'The "November Revolution" of the European Court of Justice: *Keck, Meng* and *Audi* Revisited', *Common Market Law Review* 1994, pp. 459ff. But the reading of the judgment is controversial and according to some commentators it is not really revolutionary compared with the stances previously adopted by the Court but rather a matter of mild 'reform'.

process clause'.[238] Thus, although not *a priori* oriented in a neoliberal direction but guided, rather, by an approach which Poiares Maduro has described as 'majoritarian activism',[239] or one programmatically aimed at giving prevalence to the Community polity perspective, in practice the Court ultimately interpreted Article 30 as a means of controlling and reviewing the level of government regulation allowed to the several Member States in their respective economies.

Thus, the broad notion of 'measures having equivalent effect' to quantitative restrictions as covering 'all trading rules enacted by Member States which are capable of hindering, directly or indirectly, actually or potentially, intra-Community trade' adopted as far back as the Court's famous decision in *Dassonville*,[240] fostered the 'overflow of market integration law into political and social spheres.'[241] The fact that the function of eliminating trade barriers and freeing-up the internal market as envisaged by Article 30 endowed it with powers to interfere in the sphere of Member States' sovereign authority on a scale unknown even to the American experience[242] meant, simultaneously, that the Court became 'the arbiter of the Community's federalist disputes'.[243]

Even if not from the Community-level viewpoint adopted by the Court, at the national level of governance and social intervention the 'majoritarian' approach followed by the judges in Luxembourg has certainly quite often led to 'deregulatory effects'[244] of varying intensity and scope.

The filter offered by Article 36 (now Article 30) of the EC Treaty or by rigorous assessment of 'mandatory requirements' has not always afforded (and still does not always afford) the Court adequate protection of social rights and values that are often deeply rooted in national contexts. The same limitation applies to its ability to guarantee sufficient and certain space to strike the right balance between the preconditions for the opening-up and proper functioning of the internal market and those for the protection of social rights in some cases recognized as fundamental in Member States' constitutional traditions.

---

[238] M. Egan, *Constructing a European Market*, Oxford 2001, p. 99; cf. also the comments made by Poiares Maduro, *We, The Court*, pp. 74 and 173.

[239] Poiares Maduro, *We, The Court*, p. 68.   [240] ECJ Case 8/74 [1974] ECR 837.

[241] Poiares Maduro, *We, The Court*, p. 23.   [242] See Egan, *Constructing*, p. 8.

[243] A. McGee and S. Weatherill, 'The Evolution of the Single Market – Harmonisation or Liberalisation', *Modern Law Review* 1990, vol. 53, pp. 578ff., here pp. 592–3.

[244] M. Poiares Maduro, 'Striking the Elusive Balance between Economic Freedom and Social Rights in the EU', in Alston, *EU*, pp. 449ff., here p. 455; see also S. Weatherill, 'Recent Case Law Concerning the Free Movement of Goods: Mapping the Frontiers of Market Deregulation', *Common Market Law Review* 1999, pp. 51ff., especially p. 54.

At least the beginnings, if not the final outcome, of the famous Sunday Trading Saga[245] had already clearly revealed this inadequacy or, perhaps more accurately, basic uncertainty. It received further and significant confirmation from the more recent development occasioned by strike action on the part of French farmers and road haulage contractors which led, after proceedings before the European Court of Justice, to the adoption of Regulation 2679/98. In this latter case, the free movement of goods was imposed vertically as a new Community limit on taking industrial action within national borders. A limit which is attuned to economic freedom and which poses obvious and new problems of balance with the right to strike, still formally excluded from the sphere of Community competence (Article 137(6) of the EC Treaty).[246]

On the other hand, the problems of (im)balance – and purely negative-integration effects – thus briefly exemplified with respect to Article 30 of the Treaty are no less important when it comes directly to common competition rules in the strict sense (Articles 81 et seq. of the EC Treaty) infiltrating into national systems of labour and social-security law.

These are topics that will be dealt with in more detail and at greater length in chapter 3 below.

In this account of the main aspects of the transformation of the Community's economic constitution it should, however, be noted that – in all the cases mentioned – what emerges clearly is the fact that, essentially from the late 1980s onwards, national social policies and labour-law systems had to start contending with (and move towards adapting to) market-compatibility requirements[247] imposed, through the Court's case-law, by supranational competition and market rules, bringing problems of co-existence and, more often, actual contrast and conflict that had formerly been entirely unknown. The significant narrowing or limitation of 'the degree of freedom of the individual member states to act in the social policy field'[248] thereby entailed in the name of market-integration requirements

---

[245] M. Poiares Maduro, 'Never on a Sunday – What Has (EU) Law Got To Do With It?', in Sciarra, *Labour Law*, p. 273, describes it as 'one of the most high-profile examples of both the strategic use of Community law and the conflict between the rules of market integration and national systems of social regulation.'

[246] Both developments will be examined more closely in chapter 3, subsection 4 below.

[247] Leibfried and Pierson, 'Semisovereign Welfare States', p. 44.

[248] C. Barnard and S. Deakin, 'European Community Social Law and Policy: Evolution or Regression?', *Industrial Relations Journal – European Annual Review* 1997, pp. 131–53, here p. 145.

and the principles of free competition would therefore seem to be the most obvious element of change to the original framework.

The constitutional imbalance caused by this intrusion of supranational competition and market law into national systems of labour law has been equally obvious.[249] The dangerous difference in level thus created between negative integration and positive integration, between economic requirements and social values, has added to the Community democratic deficit – to use once again the words of Poiares Maduro – a specific and equally serious constitutional deficit: 'the spill-over of market integration rules into virtually all areas of the law has remained "prisoner" of formal reasoning and the constitutional limits of the Treaties; the functional use of market integration rules and the associated litigation have been the object of a limited community of interests and actors; there has been no political discourse developed at the supra-national level; the logic of market integration dominates the European Economic Constitution and its supremacy over national law.'[250]

9. End of monetary sovereignty and curbing of macroeconomic sovereignty in the EMU constitution

The principles that govern EMU have, in a different way, contributed to deepening this deficit and indeed appear to involve an even sharper transformation 'of the relationship between public power and the economy that has typified the twentieth century state'.[251]

The question put forward some years ago by Francis Snyder as to whether EMU can be regarded as a 'metaphor for European Union',[252] i.e. a metaphor for the entire process of Community integration and Europeanization of national political, economic and legal systems, is inevitably still an open one.[253] What is less doubtful is that it can be regarded as the metaphor which, more than any other, embodies the overall direction of the transformations of the Community's economic constitution in

---

[249] Cf. also Scharpf, *Governing in Europe*, pp. 27 and 62ff., and W. Däubler, 'Verso un diritto del lavoro europeo?' in *Scritti in onore di Giuseppe Federico Mancini*, vol. I, *Diritto del lavoro*, Milan 1998, pp. 201ff., especially pp. 215–16.

[250] Poiares Maduro, *We, The Court*, p. 30.

[251] I. Harden, 'The Constitution of the European Union', *Public Law* 1994, pp. 609ff., here p. 610.

[252] F. Snyder, 'EMU – Metaphor for European Union? Institutions, Rules and Types of Regulation', in Dehousse, *Europe After Maastricht*, pp. 63–99.

[253] See also K. Dyson, 'EMU As Europeanization: Convergence, Diversity and Contingency', *Journal of Common Market Studies* 2000, pp. 645ff.

having become – together with the single market – its underlying framework following the Maastricht Treaty. And it is no accident that in popular usage EMU is the term now taken synedochically to mean the European economic constitution, even though it is obvious that in this case the 'part' can in no way correctly represent the 'whole', if only because of the internal differentiation arising from the fact that at present some Member States are not participating in the final stage of monetary unification.

The Maastricht Treaty marked the completion of a lengthy process of transformation of the political economy of European integration in which changes in economic ideas and the Western 'economic world' itself,[254] changes in the Member States' political and institutional models and constellations of national interests and preferences, all gelled around the need to ensure the primacy of monetary stability[255] as the very pivot of the notion of the European Community as a 'community based on stability' (*Stabilitätsgemeinschaft*).[256]

The institutional asymmetry between the monetary pole and economic pole of EMU reflects the undisputed priority accorded to keeping the value of money (internal and external) stable and is consequently the aspect in which the constitutional transformation of the economic role of the state in the new Community *Wirtschaftsverfassung* is more apparent.

In the final stage of EMU responsibility for monetary policy lies exclusively, within the framework of the European System of Central Banks (ESCB), with the European Central Bank (ECB), which carries out its tasks and duties in absolute autonomy and independence (Articles 108 and 109 of the EC Treaty) and has as its primary objective 'to maintain price stability' (Article 105(1)).

It is only without prejudice to this priority objective that the ECSB, which is required to 'act in accordance with the principle of an open market economy with free competition', can 'support the general economic policies in the Community' (Article 105(1) of the EC Treaty) with

---

[254] To use Braudel's expression: F. Braudel, *La dinamica del capitalismo*, Italian translation, Bologna 1981, pp. 90ff.

[255] Cf. B. Eichengreen and J. A. Frieden, 'The Political Economy of European Monetary Unification: An Analytical Introduction', in Eichengreen and Frieden (eds.), *The Political Economy of European Monetary Unification*, Boulder 2001, pp. 1ff.

[256] This is the well-known expression used by the German Constitutional Court in its equally famous 'Maastricht' decision of 12 October 1993; the text is available in English translation in *International Legal Materials* 1994, vol. 33, pp. 388ff., and *Common Market Law Reports* 1994, vol. 69 no. 1, pp. 57–108.

a view to contributing to the achievement of the objectives laid down in Article 2 of the Treaty.[257]

The ECB is, therefore, as far as monetary policy is concerned, a true 'federal decision-maker which has price stability as its objective'.[258] The Member States (participating in the final stage of EMU) wholly and irrevocably surrender their monetary sovereignty to the ECB, which in this respect acts absolutely independently with the full powers of a federal central bank: a 'federal island'[259] in a system which is not federal nor, probably, destined to become (wholly) federal.

This competence and sphere of power of an outright federal nature,[260] with price stability as its inflexible objective, is contrasted by the decentralized competence of Member States in the field of economic policy. This is a general and yet limited competence inasmuch as it is bound by the parameters that fix the limits of fiscal rectitude and degree of discretion in macroeconomic management, mainly through the rules on excessive government deficit.

The conduct of economic policy thus remains within the competence of the Member States, who are merely committed to acting 'in accordance with the principle of an open market economy with free competition, favouring an efficient allocation of resources' (Article 98 of the EC Treaty). They are required to regard their economic policies as a matter of common concern and co-ordinate them within the Council (Article 99(1)), which

---

[257] I.e. the general objectives consisting in a commitment to promoting, through a common market and policies and a monetary union, 'a harmonious, balanced and sustainable development of economic activities, a high level of employment and of social protection, equality between men and women, sustainable and non-inflationary growth, a high degree of competitiveness and convergence of economic performance, a high level of protection and improvement of the quality of the environment, the raising of the standard of living and quality of life, and economic and social cohesion and solidarity among Member States.'

[258] Predieri, *Euro*, p. 238.

[259] S. Mantovani, 'La moneta europea tra economia e politica', *Stato e Mercato* 2000, pp. 53ff., here p. 82.

[260] See again Predieri, *Euro*, pp. 35, 319 and 337, who talks in particular of the 'clear federal nature of the monetary subsystem'. Cf., however, the differing interpretation of S. Cafaro, *Unione monetaria e coordinamento delle politiche economiche. Il difficile equilibrio tra modelli antagonisti di integrazione europea*, Milan 2001, pp. 150ff., and of C. Zilioli and M. Selmayr, 'The European Central Bank: An Independent Specialized Organization of Community Law', *Common Market Law Review* 2000, vol. 37, pp. 591–644, who both emphasize, from different perspectives, that it is incorrect to refer to the notions of 'federation/federalization' (albeit only partial and/or only of monetary policies) and demonstrate the wholly atypical and original nature of a stateless monetary sovereignty, in the manner in which it is realized within EMU with the ECB at the helm.

has the task of issuing broad guidelines for these policies and is responsible for the multilateral surveillance procedure provided to ensure proper compliance with those guidelines.[261]

The co-ordination of Member States' economic policies takes place according to a multilateral procedure with markedly intergovernmental features.[262] The instruments available to the Council within this context are essentially types of soft law.

In accordance with a model which the Treaty of Amsterdam was to add to and also extend to employment policies, the broad guidelines drafted annually by the Council acting on a recommendation from the Commission are of an eminently programmatic nature and do not produce legally binding effects. Very broad in content and progressively extending over the years to the entire spectrum of Member States' economic policies, including those relating to the internal market and social matters, these guidelines have, technically speaking, the legal status of recommendations.

However, as it draws nearer to the nucleus of economic policies more closely interrelated with attaining the objective of monetary stability assigned to the ESCB and the ECB, the procedure tends to become more stringent, the instruments available to the Council adapt to the 'hardness' of the system's priority objective and soft law gradually but decisively gives way to hard law. The fundamental constitutional principle of stability here exerts all its attractive force on the procedure for co-ordinating economic policies, equipping itself with instruments adopted to ensure the maximum effectiveness and binding nature of the parameters relating to Member States' sound government finances.

Essentially in order to enable the ECB better to achieve its primary institutional objective,[263] the Treaty itself in general, and more specifically the

---

[261] From the vast body of literature, arguing in general from a legal angle: F. Snyder, 'EMU Revisited: Are We Making a Constitution? What Constitution Are We Making?', *EUI Working Papers in Law* No. 98/6; J.-V. Louis, 'A Legal and Institutional Approach for the Building of a Monetary Union', *Common Market Law Review* 1998, pp. 33ff.; Louis, 'La politique économique', in *Commentaire Megret. Le droit de la CEE*, Brussels 1998, vol. VI, pp. 27ff.; from an economic point of view, M. Buti and A. Sapir (eds.), *Economic Policy in EMU. A Study by the European Commission Services*, Oxford 1998; G. Montani and D. Velo (eds.), *Il governo dell'economia in Europa e in Italia*, Milan 2000.

[262] Cf. Cafaro, *Unione monetaria*, pp. 67ff.

[263] J. Fayolle, 'L'ordinamento economico e sociale dell'Unione monetaria: un'analisi dei problemi', in Montani and Velo, *Il governo*, p. 99, describes the Stability Pact as 'an anti-inflationary insurance granted to the European Central Bank'. The function of the Pact is, on the other hand, to reinforce the institutionally endowed credibility of the new supranational monetary authority and thereby reduce the risk – a real one (M. De Cecco, 'La Banca Centrale Europea e i rischi della deflazione', *Stato e Mercato* 1998,

Stability and Growth Pact, directly impose – in terms entirely new in the constitutional panorama offered by existing economic federations[264] – far-reaching obligations and constraints on Member States' macroeconomic management.

The rules on sound management, which are functional to guaranteeing the principle of price stability and to that end backed by an effective apparatus of preventive controls and *ex post* sanctions, represent the fulcrum of the system. They set mandatory reference values as upper limits for government deficits and national debt,[265] lay down procedures for the monitoring and surveillance of developments in Member States' government finances with a view to convergence around the medium-term objective of a 'budgetary position of close to balance or in surplus' (Article 3(2)(a) of Regulation 1466/97), define in detail the conditions under which the excess of a government deficit over the permitted reference value is accepted as being exceptional and establish, as a last resort, sanctions for failure to comply with the relevant parameters.

The specific function of the Stability Pact is to make obligations regarding budgetary positions permanent and to clarify and speed up the system for monitoring and imposing sanctions in the event of failure by Member States to meet those obligations, mainly by spelling out a procedure whose

---

pp. 339ff.) – of the ECB being forced into restrictive or deflationary policies going beyond what is appropriate in order to obtain from markets recognition of such credibility. On this point see also G. Amato, 'Come fronteggiare gli shock asimmetrici', *Europa Europe* 1998, no. 3, pp. 59ff., and J.-P. Fitoussi, 'Una politica economica restrittiva è l'unica strada per l'EMU?', in Paganetto, *Oltre l'Euro*, pp. 105ff.

[264] Cf. Padoa-Schioppa, 'Genesis of EMU', p. 19, and – in highly critical terms – J. Grahl, *European Monetary Union: Problems of Legitimacy, Development and Stability*, London 2001, pp. 26ff.

[265] In this connection the Stability and Growth Pact includes only the upper limit (a reference value of 3 per cent of GDP) for excessive government deficit and not that (equal to 60 per cent of GDP) for (potential) national debt. This latter parameter is therefore left subject to control and correction solely in the terms provided for by Article 104 of the EC Treaty and by the two Protocols on the subject annexed to the Treaty; see H. J. Hahn, 'The Stability Pact for European Monetary Union: Compliance with Deficit Limit as a Constant Legal Duty', *Common Market Law Review* 1998, vol. 35, pp. 77ff. As is well known, in the proposals on modifying the Stability Pact currently under discussion renewed and greater attention is, on the other hand, paid to national debt and structural deficit (which takes account of cyclical effects), in order to make the Pact's obligations more flexible and relax their pressure in periods of stagnation or recession. The most significant changes envisaged by these proposals concern explicit accommodation of deficit adjustment in relation to a country's cyclical position and the differentiation of obligations according to the level of national debt; cf. F. Amtenbrink and J. De Haan, 'Economic Governance in the European Union: Fiscal Policy Discipline versus Flexibility', *Common Market Law Review* 2003, vol. 40, pp. 1075–106.

principal aim is precisely that of reducing as far as possible the margins
for freedom of judgment and political discretion, which in this respect
actually rest with the Council.[266] The lively debate of the past few years
on the need for a 'political flexibilization' of the Stability Pact, and indeed
the well-known annulment by the European Court of Justice of the Ecofin
Council's conclusions of 25 November 2003 adopted in respect of France
and Germany,[267] actually serve to demonstrate that the Pact has essentially
performed the normative function assigned to it.

As has been pointed out to great effect, 'The economic and monetary
regime of Maastricht is characterized by three interrelated components
which oppose economic soundness to democratic governance: the canon-
ization of price stability as the overriding objective, budgetary discipline
and a central bank system splendidly insulated from political bargaining.'[268] As key elements of the European economic constitution, these
components touch the deepest foundations of the Union itself and simultaneously transform Member States' constitutional framework.

Price stability emerges as a 'new *Grundnorm*'[269] of the Community with
a force unknown even to Germany's constitutional tradition, although the
latter has obviously had considerable influence on the actual framing of
EMU rules.[270] In the interests of EMU, the total autonomy and independence of the ECB are guaranteed and Member States' budgetary policies
are made subject to strict limits and obligations. In pursuit of the mandate
to secure 'freedom from inflation within the European Union',[271] the ECB

---

[266] Cf. Hahn, 'Stability Pact', pp. 89ff.; F. Amtenbrink, J. de Haan and O. C. H. M. Sleijpen,
'Stability and Growth Pact: Placebo or Panacea?', *European Business Law Review* 1997,
pp. 202ff.; L. Bini Smaghi and C. Casini. 'Monetary and Fiscal Policy Co-operation:
Institutions and Procedures in EMU', *Journal of Common Market Studies* 2000, pp. 375ff.,
especially p. 384.

[267] See ECJ Case C-27/04 *Commission v Council* (judgment of 13 July 2004, not yet reported),
whereby the controversial conclusions adopted by the Council in respect of France and
Germany were annulled, in so far as they contained a decision to hold the excessive
deficit procedure in abeyance and a decision modifying the recommendations previously
adopted by the Council under Article 104(7) of the EC Treaty. However, the Court declared
the Commission's action inadmissible in so far as it sought annulment of the Council's
failure to adopt the formal instruments contained in the Commission's recommendations
pursuant to Article 104(8) and (9) of the EC Treaty.

[268] M. J. Herdegen, 'Price Stability and Budgetary Restraints in the Economic and Monetary
Union: The Law as Guardian of Economic Wisdom', *Common Market Law Review* 1998,
vol. 35, pp. 9–32, here p. 10.

[269] *Ibid.*, p. 21.

[270] Cf. Snyder, 'EMU – Metaphor for European Union?', p. 68; Herdegen, 'Price Stability',
p. 16; Predieri, *Euro*, pp. 283ff.

[271] Zilioli and Selmayr, 'European Central Bank', p. 629.

is only indirectly and secondarily bound by Article 2 of the EC Treaty. The *lex specialis* envisaged by Article 151(1) obliges it to pursue the general objectives set out in Article 2 only if and when these are not contrary to the objective of price stability.[272]

However, the creation of a supranational institution endowed – as a result of the total surrender to it of state monetary sovereignty – with powers completely analogous to those of a federal central bank was not accompanied at Maastricht 'by the establishment of institutions for making decisions about political priorities and choices among competing social values'.[273] The development of albeit fragile and as yet only embryonic elements of European economic governance is – as we shall see later – essentially a post-Amsterdam phenomenon extraneous to the financial and monetary dogmatism applied to primary Community law by the Maastricht Treaty.[274]

The ECB remains, in actuality, the system's sole genuinely sovereign policy decision-maker. It is not (as yet) confronted with authentic European governance of the economy,[275] nor does there (as yet) exist at supranational level a network of social and institutional relations even broadly comparable to those in which the national central banks, and first and foremost the *Bundesbank* itself, were immersed.[276] The presumption is that this 'splendid isolation' enables it to pursue the fundamental objective of price stability more effectively and with greater credibility

---

[272] *Ibid.*, pp. 629ff., underlining the clear difference that exists, in this respect as well, between the ECB and the US Federal Reserve Bank, since the latter has a 'dual mandate', i.e. the obligation to promote full employment *and* stable prices, striking a delicate balance between the two goals. See also Grahl, *European Monetary Union*, pp. 19–20.

[273] Snyder, 'EMU Revisited', p. 75, who believes that this situation heralds 'a serious risk of a major institutional gap at the heart of European integration'.

[274] J.-P. Fitoussi, *Le Débat interdit. Monnaie, Europe, Pauvreté*, Paris 1995, talks of dogmatism and even 'financial tyranny'; see also, in similar terms, Dawson, 'Governing', p. 117.

[275] As is well known, this is the aspect on which neo-Keynesian criticisms of the EMU order are mostly focused. Proposals for transforming the Euro 11 Committee (Euro 12, after Greece's entry) into a genuine governance of the European economy – variously voiced in scientific debate and increasingly present in political debate, mainly at the instigation of France – aim to provide an answer of a neo-Keynesian type *sensu lato* to this gap. See, for example, the suggestion in this direction put forward by G. La Malfa, *L'Europa legata. I rischi dell'Euro*, Milan 2000, pp. 116ff., and cf., more generally, R. Boyer, 'The Unanticipated Fallout of European Monetary Union: The Political and Institutional Deficits of the Euro', in C. Crouch (ed.), *After the Euro. Shaping Institutions for Governance in the Wake of European Monetary Union*, Oxford 2000, pp. 24ff., especially pp. 77ff.

[276] See C. Crouch, 'Introduction: The Political and Institutional Deficits of European Monetary Union', in Crouch, *After the Euro*, especially pp. 10ff.

and hence thereby ensure and substantiate its own source of technocratic and non-majority legitimation.[277]

But this introduces an undeniable element of asymmetry and confusion, inasmuch as it disrupts – in the name of the system's stability – 'the balances of power characteristic of the organized polyarchic economy that underlies modern-day constitutionalism'.[278] The total monetary sovereignty of the ECB, 'which is the decision-maker in following whatever course it chooses to adopt, signifies as its corollary a constraint on the freedom of Member States, who are bound by the system of rigid thresholds . . . imposed by the rules on budgetary discipline'.[279]

In tying the key elements of economic policy to what is prescribed in the Treaties, the EMU constitution sanctions in explicit legal terms the reduction of Member States' 'Keynesian capacity'.[280] It gives legal expression, with the utmost rigour, to the principle of 'permanent austerity' of the welfare state[281] that is regarded as intrinsic to the actual operational logic of mature welfare regimes in the era of the globalization of markets and post-industrial transformation of their socio-economic foundations.[282]

Primary supranational law thus sets itself up as guardian of the dominant models of economic rationality and prudence,[283] transforming at its very roots the political and institutional architecture constructed in Western Europe immediately after the end of the Second World War.[284]

If the twentieth century was 'the century of the attempt . . . on the part of the political to appropriate (or reappropriate) the economic',[285] it can safely be said that, vice versa, 'the entire monetary union project is an ambitious political programme designed to seek such an economic determinism over politics'.[286] This is the fruit, as has been stated, of a twofold political mistrust: 'the lack of trust in politics which became widespread among social scientists and in public opinion following the failures of Keynesian policies and many forms of state intervention in the economy and the national lack of trust between the countries which were signatories to the Treaty, driven by differing preferences as regards

---

[277] As it is described by, for example, Predieri, *Euro*, p. 271, and Majone *et al.*, *Regulating Europe*, pp. 284ff.

[278] Predieri, *Euro*, p. 334.   [279] *Ibid.*, p. 335.

[280] Streeck, 'Neo-voluntarism', p. 86.

[281] P. Pierson, 'Lo Stato sociale nell'era dell' austerità permanente', *Rivista Italiana di Scienza Politica* 1999, no. 3, p. 393.

[282] G. Esping-Andersen, *Social Foundations of Postindustrial Economies*, Oxford 1999.

[283] Herdegen, 'Price Stability', p. 9.   [284] Boyer, 'Unanticipated Fallout', pp. 27 and 35.

[285] G. Zagrebelsky, *Il diritto mite. Legge, diritto, giustizia*, Turin 1992, p. 135.

[286] Crouch, 'Introduction', p. 5.

the objectives of economic policy and fearful of opportunistic behaviour on the part of their co-signatories.'[287]

All the more reason, therefore, to repeat what Claus-Dieter Ehlermann said, not without an element of congratulation, as early as on the eve of the symbolic starting-date for the internal-market project: that 'the Community has the most strongly free-market oriented constitution in the world'.[288]

10. Regulatory competition between national systems within the internal market

While they impose strong obligations and restrictions on the budgetary and, indirectly, fiscal policies[289] of the EMU Member States,[290] neither the EC Treaty nor the Stability and Growth Pact makes up for the limits on action thus specified at national macroeconomic governance level by instituting Community stabilization and/or redistribution mechanisms, automatically activated, against the eventuality – by no means remote, at least in theory[291] – of asymmetric shocks in the euro area.

---

[287] Mantovani, 'La moneta', p. 54.

[288] C.-D. Ehlermann, 'The Contribution of EC Competition Policy to the Single Market', *Common Market Law Review* 1992, vol. 29, pp. 257–82, here p. 273. It is these aspects of the post-Maastricht European economic constitution which prompted G. Guarino ('La grande Rivoluzione', p. 203) to state equally emphatically that 'the state is not a sovereign but *has* a sovereign. Its sovereign is, through the Treaty, the market.' An equally critical view is expressed by J.-P. Fitoussi, *La règle et le choix. De la souveraineté économique en Europe*, Paris, 2002, according to whom 'the logic of the European economic constitution induces a "natural" evolution towards an increasingly liberalist economy presented to European institutions which cannot choose other directions.'

[289] The margins for manoeuvre are obviously dictated in that they reflect the budgetary balance levels provided for; see, by way of example, C. Secchi, *Verso l'Euro. L'Unione Economica e Monetaria motore dell' Europa unita*, Venice 1998, p. 121; L. Bini Smaghi, *L'euro*, Bologna 1998, pp. 30ff.

[290] La Malfa, *L'Europa*, p. 103, talks of a trend towards 'sterilization' of Member States' budgetary policies, in so far as these policies are required to aim at balance or surplus in the medium term. This rigorous budgetary discipline is in fact closely correlated to the absence of European automatic stabilizers and turns *inter alia* to pushing Member States into creating for themselves 'in favourable phases of the cycle, room for manoeuvre that will then enable them to make full use of [their] stabilization mechanisms in phases of economic slowdown' (Bini Smaghi, *L'euro*, p. 38).

[291] It is well known that EMU is not generally regarded, at least in its entirety, as an optimum currency area in Mundellian terms, mainly because of low labour mobility, relative wage inflexibility and the absence of a completely unified financial market, at least as compared with that in the USA. It is therefore seen as more easily exposed to possible asymmetric shocks or, more accurately, as less equipped to absorb them efficiently. Apart from this,

The centralization of monetary policy is therefore matched with budgetary policies which are essentially decentralized to national level and merely co-ordinated at European level. The limits that the Treaty and the Stability Pact impose in this way on stabilizers and redistribution instruments operating at national level are not offset by an adequate strengthening of the Community budget, which is set – and probably destined to remain – well below what is usually indicated as the threshold of an appropriate budget even for an entity that is only pre-federal. Its very small size, and the terms in which it is configured, mean that the Community budget is inherently incapable of guaranteeing this stabilization function.[292]

The Structural Funds, on the other hand, are by definition designed as forms of permanent income redistribution between Member States (or, more accurately, between their regions) and therefore do not lend themselves, even within the limits of their financial resources which are in fact 'inelastic as regards temporary disturbances',[293] to operating as automatic stabilizers in the event of episodes of recession affecting one or more Member States asymmetrically.

Nor can the weak solidaristic mechanism envisaged by Article 100 of the Treaty be regarded in this connection as a valid surrogate. Designed for the extreme hypothetical case where a Member State is in difficulties (or is 'seriously threatened with severe difficulties') caused by exceptional occurrences beyond its control, the 'Community financial assistance' mechanism it provides for has no element whatever of being automatic. The decision to grant financial assistance relies upon the political discretion

going by recent analyses and surveys, the experience of the first two years of the euro's life shows that 'a certain increase in economic integration has been accompanied by the re-emergence of asymmetries that had in fact been lessening in the period immediately preceding the creation of EMU' (as stated in ISAE (Istituto di Studi e Analisi Economica), *Rapporto sullo stato dell'Unione europea*, edited by F. Kostoris Padoa Schioppa, Bologna 2001, p. 127). This clearly points to potentially significant problems in the (necessarily unitary) management of monetary policy by the ECB. Opinions on assessing the actual importance of the risk of asymmetric shocks and the difficulty of managing them effectively are, however, very divided; see, by way of example, albeit in the context of critically revisiting Robert Mundell's now classic analysis, P. De Grauwe, *The Economics of Monetary Integration*, 3rd rev. edn, Oxford 1997, pp. 20ff., and G. Thompson, 'Governing the European Economy: A Framework Analysis', in Thompson, *Governing*, pp. 11–13.

[292] Cf. Tsoukalis, 'European Agenda', pp. 26–7; G. Tondl, 'Fiscal Federalism and the Reality of the European Union Budget', in Crouch, *After the Euro*, pp. 227ff.

[293] B. Eichengreen, 'Politica fiscale e Unione Monetaria Europea', *Stato e Mercato* 1993, pp. 121ff., here p. 140.

of the Council, acting unanimously[294] on a proposal from the Commission, and – even more relevantly – does not imply any enlargement of the Community budget and the associated functions but, rather, presupposes that they are to be conserved in the existing terms.[295]

Consequently, in the system established by the Treaty and the Stability Pact serious recession suffered by a Member State, far from activating significant solidaristic interventions on the part of the *Stabilitätsgemeinschaft*, tends to lead to no more than 'release from the responsibility to avoid excessive deficit'.[296]

It is no accident that the smallness of the Community budget and the almost total absence of elements of fiscal federalism constitute the aspect in which the present-day EMU structure differs most markedly from the initial plans for monetary unification and, in particular, from the Werner Report of 1970. According to the latter, monetary union was to be the culmination of three transitional stages aimed at the preventive harmonization of budgetary and fiscal policies and the provision of a substantially enlarged budget for the Community to enable it to perform the tasks of a common conjunctural policy.[297] By shifting the emphasis to the primary objective of price stability the Maastricht Treaty followed, in a way, the opposite course:[298] instead of Community intervention instruments, a rigorous system of preventive checks and controls was introduced with the aim of pushing Member States into pursuing sound budgetary policies in the medium term as a way of establishing in advance the margins for manoeuvre needed in negative periods in the cycle without failing to meet the parameters regarding excessive deficit.[299]

Thus, in 'creating a kind of permanent emergency'[300] supranational budgetary constraints ultimately amount to a directive constantly to contain and/or re-dimension social (and especially welfare) expenditure, as

---

[294] By a qualified majority, following the entry into force of the Treaty of Nice.

[295] This can be seen clearly from the tenor of the Declaration on Article 100 adopted by the Nice Conference. Apart from confirming that decisions on financial assistance must observe the 'no bailout' principle enshrined in Article 103 of the EC Treaty, the Declaration specifies that they must also conform to the (restrictive) 2000–6 financial forecasts.

[296] Cafaro, *Unione monetaria*, p. 61.

[297] See Moravcsik, *Choice for Europe*, pp. 292ff.

[298] See A. S. Milward, 'L'impossibile fuga dalla storia', *Europa Europe* 1999, no. 5, pp. 57ff. especially p. 64.

[299] See C. M. Dent, 'Governing the EU Economy as a Whole', in Thompson, *Governing*, pp. 231ff., especially pp. 250–1.

[300] Cafaro, *Unione monetaria*, p. 119.

being the main component of government spending in the European Community.[301] They have in several cases already functioned in practice – during the phase of striving to meet the convergence criteria for access to the final stage of EMU – as effective 'external constraints' (*vincoli esterni*) in bringing about major reforms of national social-protection systems and will continue to exert constant pressure in this direction on Member States' governments and Parliaments.[302]

Although serving within certain limits as useful incentives for introducing reforms that are often objectively required by the profound transformations of the economic, demographic and social bases of European welfare systems, these constraints insinuate into them a potential element of structural change. This is because, as has been pointed out,[303] they cause an objective break in the link between social policy and economic policy and so make it particularly problematic to maintain the relationship of congruence between control over resources and regulatory power which seems necessary in order to give effective substance to the recognition of social rights, especially in practical terms.

Within the macroeconomic regime inaugurated at Maastricht these same constraints also contribute – from a different but similar aspect – to concentrating the main burden of adjustment in the event of asymmetric shocks more and more on the labour market.[304] The reason for this is that the EMU constitution makes it impossible to use exchange-rate policies,

[301] Cf. Observatoire Social Européen, *Economic and Monetary Union and Social Protection*, *Working Paper* No. 95/1, Brussels; I. Begg and F. Nectoux, 'Social Protection and Economic Union', *Journal of European Social Policy* 1995, no. 4, p. 285; P. Pochet and B. Vanhercke (eds.), *Les enjeux sociaux de l'Union économique et monétaire*, Brussels 1998; B. Vanhercke, 'Protection Sociale et Union économique et monétaire', *Revue Belge de Sécurité Sociale* 1999, no. 1, p. 5; E. Guild, 'How Can Social Protection Survive EMU? A United Kingdom Perspective', *European Law Review* 1999, p. 2; E. Traversa, 'The Consequences of European Monetary Union on Collective Bargaining and the National Social Security Systems', *International Journal of Comparative Labour Law and Industrial Relations* 2000, vol. 16 no. 1, p. 47; K. Michelet, 'Protection sociale et contraintes économiques et monétaires européennes', *Droit Social* 2001, p. 292.

[302] The case of Italy is one of the most emblematic from this point of view: see M. Ferrera and E. Gualmini, *Salvati dall' Europa? Welfare e lavoro in Italia fra gli anni '70 e gli anni '90: le riforme fatte e quelle che restano da fare*, Bologna 1999; and cf. also, very significantly, R. Prodi, *Un'idea dell' Europa. Il valore Europa per modernizzare l'Italia*, Bologna 1999, pp. 59ff.

[303] See M. Luciani, 'Diritti sociali e integrazione europea', in Associazione Italiana dei Costituzionalisti, *Annuario 1999. La Costituzione europea*, Atti del XIV Convegno annuale Perugia 7–9 ottobre 1999, Padua 2000, pp. 507ff., especially pp. 537–8.

[304] Cf., for example, T. Peters, 'European Monetary Union and Labour Markets: What to Expect?', *International Labour Review* 1995, no. 3, p. 315; G. Miller, 'Economic and Monetary Union: The Continuing Neglect of the Social Dimension', in Observatoire

and greatly limits the use of (common) monetary policy and (national) fiscal policies, to deal with such eventualities.

With less possibility, by definition, of varying the exchange rate within EMU and the reduced scope for fiscal and budgetary manoeuvre available to Member States, adjustment to shocks – in the presence of low intra-Community labour mobility[305] – inevitably has to take place predominantly in terms of wage and/or employment flexibility.[306]

From this aspect as well, there are signs of a constant pressure towards structural reform and the 'flexibilization' of labour-market regulation which extends beyond negative economic trends.[307] EMU permanently raises the incentives for labour-market reform, since 'In simple terms, once a country has lost the "easy option" of devaluation, it has no alternative but to tackle unemployment through supply-side measures'.[308]

The management of aggregate demand remains the dark side of the macroeconomic regime prefigured at Maastricht:[309] growth and employment are promoted, in this logic, almost exclusively with supply-side measures and structural market reforms, including reform of the labour market.

In this new context, there is an obvious incentive to compete with fellow Member States by reducing labour costs and lightening the 'regulatory burden' weighing on employment relationships more generally.

Social Européen, *Economic and Monetary Union*, p. 11; P. Teague, 'Monetary Union and Social Europe', *Journal of European Social Policy* 1998, no. 2, p. 117; G. Bertola, 'Moneta unica e mercati del lavoro', *Biblioteca della Libertà* 1999, no. 152, p. 11.

[305] Labour mobility within the Community is – for structural reasons largely independent even of the highly developed normative framework – fairly low, and certainly far lower than that in the USA. On the other hand, the hypothetical case of massive migratory flows to compensate for possible (severe) asymmetric shocks would, in all probability, create more problems than they could theoretically solve. See Buti and Sapir, *Economic Policy*, pp. 287ff.

[306] Cf. Peters, 'European Monetary Union', p. 319; L. Bordogna, 'Unione monetaria e relazioni industriali in Europa', *Stato e Mercato* 1996, pp. 467ff., especially pp. 475ff.; G. Ross and A. Martin, 'European Integration and the Europeanization of Labor', *Instituto Juan March de Estudios y Investigaciones – Centro de Estudios Avanzados en Ciencias Sociales, Working Paper* No. 98/26, pp. 29ff.; J. Visser, 'Bargaining in Euros: What Should Unions Do?', in C. Engels and M. Weiss (eds.), *Labour Law and Industrial Relations at the Turn of the Century. Liber Amicorum in Honour of Roger Blanpain*, The Hague-London-Boston 1998, pp. 461–88, especially p. 463.

[307] See also D. Ashiagbor, 'EMU and the Shift in the European Labour Agenda: From "Social Policy" to "Employment Policy"', *European Law Journal* 2001, pp. 311ff.

[308] CEPR – Centre for Economic Policy Research, *Social Europe: One for All?*, Report compiled by C. Bean, S. Bentolila, G. Bertola and J. Dolado, London 1998, p. 85.

[309] Cf. A. Martin, 'Social Pacts, Unemployment and EMU Macroeconomic Policy', *Robert Schuman Centre – European University Institute Working Papers* No. 2000/32, pp. 4–5.

The dynamics of regulatory competition between national socio-economic systems are in this sense given definite fresh impetus by the EMU constitution.[310]

Regulatory competition has for some time been incorporated into the patrimony of Community legal-integration technology as the 'operative reverse face'[311] of the principle of mutual recognition famously affirmed in full for the first time by the European Court of Justice in its historic *Cassis de Dijon* judgment[312] and then institutionalized by the Single European Act, for the purposes of constructing the internal market, as a more general alternative to the old harmonization model.[313]

In theoretical terms at least, albeit far more qualified and toned down in practice,[314] mutual recognition actually constitutes an essentially alternative regulatory technique to harmonization,[315] since it means that the optimum level of regulation is not fixed by a political decision made by the Community legislators but becomes established by the market, which will give preference – among competing regulatory systems – to those deemed

---

[310] Cf. Scharpf, *Governing in Europe*, pp. 84ff.; Boyer, 'Unanticipated Fallout', pp. 58ff.; Eichengreen and Frieden, 'Political Economy', p. 7.

[311] Lo Faro, *Regulating Social Europe*, p. 41.

[312] ECJ Case 120/78 *Rewe-Zentral AG* v *Bundesmonopolverwaltung für Branntwein* [1979] ECR 649.

[313] This is a development now so well known that not even a summary account is needed here: see, among the numerous publications on the subject, R. Dehousse, '1992 and Beyond: The Institutional Dimension of the Internal Market Programme', *Legal Issues of European Integration* 1989, no. 1, pp. 109ff.; S. Woolcock, 'Competition Among Rules in the Single Market', in W. Bratton *et al.* (eds.), *International Regulatory Competition and Coordination. Perspectives on Economic Regulation in Europe and the United States*, Oxford 1997, pp. 289ff.

[314] The fact that products lawfully manufactured in one Member State can circulate freely in any other – as the principle of mutual recognition prescribes, in essence – means that a minimum degree of initial homogeneity between the several systems, or a minimum degree of their harmonization, is necessary. This is expressly envisaged by the Single European Act itself (with ex Article 100a et seq. of the EC Treaty), which – in line with the White Paper of 1985 on Completing the Internal Market – does not exclude harmonization *tout court* but stipulates that it should be confined to fundamental safety requirements to be established through Directives adopted by a qualified majority, leaving the 'technical specifications' of these requirements to be fixed by the European standardization organizations. Moreover, in the absence of minimum harmonization measures of this kind the Court of Justice can always verify the existence of an essential functional equivalence between the protection systems in force in the several Member States. See Woolcock, 'Competition', pp. 294ff.

[315] See again Lo Faro, *Regulating Social Europe*, pp. 39–40.

more efficient or simply 'advantageous'.[316] The competition between the various national regulatory systems which it triggers gives the market precedence in deciding the level of regulation and common standards: 'It is the market that becomes the decision-making institution which decides the regulatory framework.'[317]

In abstract terms, mutual recognition makes economic integration possible without replacement of national regulations at the supranational level and without the creation of supranational political institutions. It therefore 'represents a sophisticated version of "negative integration"': that is, economic integration through the mere removal of national trade barriers', which advances through the separation of market-making from state-building.[318]

The deregulatory potential of this markedly neoliberal integration strategy is therefore very obvious, at least in the abstract.[319] Nonetheless, the undoubted move towards deregulation underlying the 1992 project did not lead to an unconditional freeing up of market forces.

Thanks to the introduction of qualified-majority voting, implementation of the internal market gave rise to a huge process of re-regulation, albeit of a new generation and essentially devoted to broadening the scope for market allocation efficiency.[320] This was then accompanied by the production of a great deal of Community social regulation in the fields of health and safety at work and consumer protection, in some cases exceeding the standards guaranteed by the most advanced countries. In short, rather than a relationship of mutual exclusion and drastic alternatives

---

[316] Or at least so the supporters of regulatory competition confidently believe. As they see it, precisely because it is directly guided by the rational preferences of economic actors, regulatory competition not only favours the most efficient regulatory options by limiting government interference but also, through the mechanism of institutional competition, helps to 'tame the Leviathan', i.e. force the political elite to promote general welfare rather than their own interests. See in this sense, by way of example, S. Sinn, 'Taming the Leviathan: Competition Among Governments', *Constitutional Political Economy* 1992, vol. 3 no. 2, p. 177; H. Siebert and M. J. Koop, 'Institutional Competition Versus Centralizatrion: Quo Vadis Europe?', *Oxford Review of Economic Policy* 1993, vol. 9 no. 1, p. 15. In a critical sense on the basis of concrete experience of the internal market see, among others, J.-M. Sun and J. Pelkmans, 'Regulatory Competition in the Single Market', *Journal of Common Market Studies* 1995, pp. 67ff.

[317] Poiares Maduro, *We, The Court*, p. 132.   [318] Streeck, 'From Market Making', p. 394.

[319] Here too there is particular significance in what is said by Ehlermann, 'Contribution', p. 259: 'The internal market is a gigantic deregulation programme', aimed at increasing the opportunities for companies to compete in the markets of other Member States

[320] See Joerges, 'European Economic Law', pp. 42ff.

concrete experience has demonstrated the link of complementarity between harmonization (of minimum safety conditions) and mutual recognition highlighted by theories which see the European Union as an incipient, modern-day (supranational) form of 'regulatory state'.[321]

Even if social policy has remained 'the dark side'[322] of the integration process in the unified market and as such dangerously exposed to a deregulatory push towards a common race to the bottom, the empirical evidence has not as yet revealed *systematic* social-dumping and social-devaluation practices,[323] although there have certainly been very significant episodes and examples.

Nowadays, however, in strengthening the transnational flow of resources the single currency is making the internal market a potentially far more competitive environment, at the very least because it eliminates or reduces the ability to use the lever of exchange-rate or fiscal policies to alleviate, albeit only in the short term, the negative consequences of any deficits or losses of national systems' relative competitiveness. Any such developments are, at the same time, made more immediately obvious by the more transparent comparison of prices and costs which the introduction of the euro allows.

Any accentuation of inflation differentials is translated into an abrupt loss of competitiveness of the national systems affected, which from now on has to be remedied essentially through supply-side measures. National collective bargaining – in the absence of any positive Community regulatory competence with regard to pay – thus acquires direct macroeconomic relevance and is under constant pressure to contain wage dynamics,[324] which will on the whole have to be strictly commensurate with trends in productivity.

---

[321] Cf. G. Majone, 'The European Community as a Regulatory State', *Collected Courses of the Academy of European Law* 1996, vol. V no. 1, pp. 321ff.; A. La Spina and G. Majone, *Lo Stato regolatore*, Bologna 2000, pp. 227ff.

[322] A. Lo Faro, 'EC Social Policy and 1993: The Dark Side of European Integration?', *Comparative Labor Law and Policy Journal* 1992, vol. 14 no. 1, pp. 1ff.

[323] Cf. in this sense D. Goodhart, 'Social Dumping within the EU', in Hine and Kassim, *Beyond the Market*, pp. 79 ff,; C. Barnard, 'Social Dumping and Race to the Bottom: Some Lessons for the European Union from Delaware?', *European Law Journal* 2000, pp. 57ff., who attributes the relative modesty – so far – of competitive social-deregulation practices on the part of Member States, in the absence of a real supranational social policy, at least partly to the compensatory performance achieved by the Structural Funds in favour of the poorer Community countries.

[324] See A. Lo Faro, 'Europei, comunitari e comunitarizzati: i contratti collettivi nell'era della sovranazionalità', *Rivista Giuridica del Lavoro e della Previdenza Sociale* 2000, pp. 860ff., especially p. 864.

In this context, differences in social protection (and costs) become potentially direct instruments of competition. The crucial departure from the model originally adopted by the Treaties of Paris and Rome lies in the fact that the Maastricht Treaty does not set against this eventuality strong harmonizing intervention at Community level to restore equilibrium. The model becomes, instead, one of market-based harmonization.

The dividing line 'between the Europeanization of monetary policy and the subsidiarity of budgetary policy brings a structural disequilibrium and potential political conflict, and exacerbates the heterogeneity of national industrial relations and *regulation* modes'.[325]

The fact that there are no effective co-ordination instruments at supranational level greatly increases the risk of a strong push towards deregulatory economic competition *tout court* between national social-policy regimes,[326] especially in view of the extension of Community borders towards the East.[327] And thus also increases the risk of entrenched fiscal competition in which Member States can likewise find themselves trapped in a situation resembling that typical of the 'prisoner's dilemma',[328] where the non-co-operative actions of the actors involved tend to produce suboptimal results potentially damaging for all of them.

So the framework that here too seems to emerge is again one – as the reverse of the main thrust of the embedded-liberalism compromise – in which the ability to regulate the labour market and tax mobile factors of production autonomously and to the degree desirable at national level is greatly reduced, if not blocked, by increased regulatory competition between Member States without being adequately replaced at supranational level.[329]

11. Weakening of the principle of territoriality of national systems of social protection

The competitive pressures indirectly unleashed by the new monetary and macroeconomic regime inaugurated at Maastricht are accompanied by other pressures more directly based on regulatory competition which

---

[325] Boyer, 'Unanticipated Fallout', p. 58.
[326] See Streeck, 'From Market Making', p. 420; Deakin, 'Labour Law as Market Regulation', p. 82; S. Deakin and F. Wilkinson, 'Rights vs Efficiency? The Economic Case for Transnational Labour Standards', *Industrial Law Journal* 1994, pp. 289ff., especially p. 296.
[327] See CEPR, *Social Europe*, p. 144.
[328] Scharpf, *Governing in Europe*, pp. 104ff.   [329] *Ibid.*, pp. 82–3.

laps at the very borders of national systems of labour and social-security law and verges on insinuating itself into their respective territories.

In the Single European Act (SEA) system, the principle of mutual recognition has no direct application to the (common) labour market and, save for minor exceptions, concerns only the areas relating to free movement of goods and services. National systems of labour and social-security law accordingly remain firmly anchored to the principle of territoriality, and even following the SEA the guiding criterion of the free movement of labour within the single market is still that of equality of treatment with workers who are nationals of the host member State based on the latter's legislation, as the place where work is actually performed.

The principle of territoriality, albeit in diverse forms and with sometimes major technical differences as regards labour law and social-security law in the strict sense,[330] therefore serves to countersign and defend – even within the Community system – the underlying exclusivity of state jurisdiction in dictating the normative conditions of labour utilization within national borders.

As has been stated, 'territoriality, interpreted as the principle whereby peremptory norms prevail over personal autonomy, is an expression of the most traditional choices inherent in national legal orders as guarantors of the rights of those regarded as the weak contracting parties . . . and, at the same time, jealous guardians of the values fundamental to the particular domestic order concerned'.[331] By applying its own mandatory norms in preference to possibly less protective foreign laws the national order defends itself against forms of social dumping while at the same time admitting migrant workers into its own institutional circuits of citizenship and social integration.

In the context of developments in the Community legal order, the weakening of the territoriality principle and, even more so, its potential at least partial replacement by the contrasting principle of mutual recognition[332]

---

[330] These differences, in some cases significant, obviously cannnot be examined in detail here; for a concise account of them see A. De Matteis and S. Giubboni, 'Rapporti di lavoro con elementi di internazionalità e sicurezza sociale', *Quaderni di Diritto del Lavoro e delle Relazioni Industriali* 1998, no. 20 (issue entitled *I contratti di lavoro internazionali*), pp. 93ff.

[331] A. Lyon-Caen and S. Sciarra, 'La Convenzione di Roma e i principi del diritto del lavoro', *Quaderni di Diritto del Lavoro e delle Relazioni Industriali* 1998, no. 20 (see note 330), pp. 9ff., here p. 12.

[332] A proposal for the total replacement of the territoriality principle (and hence the rule on applying the law of the country of destination) by the principle of mutual recognition or home control has recently been put forward, with respect to the labour market, in ISAE, *Rapporto*, pp. 104ff.

therefore constitute manifestly important aspects of the crisis of Member States' social sovereignty.

A prime factor in eroding the territoriality principle is attributed by some authors[333] to the strengthening – through established case-law of the Court of Justice – of those elements of mutual recognition between different national social-security systems which are indisputably implicit in the logic of Regulation 1408/71.[334] The progressive expansion of the scope of rules on the co-ordination of national social-security systems – rigorously applied by a case-law intent on maximizing their effects in integrating the Community labour market – is said to have 'gradually eroded'[335] some of the most salient derivatives of the principle of territoriality of national laws and, along with them, the very ability of Member States to exert control over important components of their systems of social protection.

Leibfried and Pierson single out, in particular, four main aspects of the weakening of Member States' ability to control the outer limits of their social-security systems. The first is linked to the progressive loss of national control over beneficiaries, owing to the fact that – in deference to the principle of equality of treatment for Community migrants as laid down by Regulations 1612/68 and 1408/71 – Member States are no longer able to confine the benefits they provide solely to their own workers and citizens.

Secondly, Regulation 1408/71 – particularly since the Court of Justice began to include within the ambit of the principle of exportability a new category of special non-contributory benefits – has deprived Member States of 'control over where benefits may be consumed'.[336]

In addition, the obligations imposing co-operation between the administrative and social-security authorities of the several Member States restrict – for mutual cross-border arrangements – autonomy in the assessment and control of the cases which under domestic law confer entitlement to benefits, thereby creating a real commitment to reciprocal recognition of decisions made by the authorities of other member countries.

Lastly – although as we shall see later this aspect extends beyond issues relating to Regulation 1408/71 and interconnects with the effects resulting

---

[333] Leibfried and Pierson, 'Semisovereign Welfare States', pp. 53ff.; but similar comments were made earlier in Streeck, 'La dimension sociale', pp. 56ff.

[334] See M. Cinelli, 'Appunti in tema di incidenza del diritto comunitario sull'ordinamento interno di sicurezza sociale', *Diritto delle Relazioni Industriali* 1996, pp. 95ff.

[335] M. Ferrera, 'Integrazione europea e sovranità sociale dello Stato-nazione: dilemmi e prospettive', *Rivista Italiana di Scienza Politica* 2000, pp. 393ff.

[336] *Ibid.*

from the free movement *of services* in the unified market – there is no longer total exclusivity of national social-security law or control over access to the status of social-services provider within national borders, since a Member State is no longer 'in a position to prevent other social policy regimes from directly competing with the regime it has built on its own territory'.[337]

These are certainly aspects whose overall impact on the autonomy of Member States in deciding the content of their systems of social security and, more generally, social protection cannot be overlooked. Nevertheless, it would be mistaken to overestimate its importance and wrong to see in it – at least in all the cases listed and with the proviso mentioned for the last of them – the symptoms of a weakening of the principle of national-system territoriality that is due to the dynamics of Community integration. In point of fact, the genuine regime-competition effects directly triggered – within national borders – by the insinuation of different (and possibly less generous) rules seem attributable not so much to spillover of the co-ordination principles on which Regulation 1408/71 is constructed as to the comprehensive spread of the provisions on free movement of services (both the freedom to provide services and the freedom to receive services) within the ambit of the single market.

The (partial) loss of national control over eligibility for benefits does not imply any weakening of the territoriality principle; rather, it constitutes an immediate and desired effect of that principle. The absolute and unconditional equality of treatment with workers of the host country which the Treaty of Rome and the large body of secondary legislation adopted in implementation of its ex Articles 48–51 impose on Member States in favour of Community workers who move within the Union requires, in actuality, total observance of the territoriality principle. The fact that it is to be applicable without any possibility of forms of competition from other regulatory systems means, by the same token, that the law of the country of destination is still – subject only to compliance with the basic principle of equality of treatment between national and Community workers – freely decided by Member States, sheltered from conditioning influences deriving from regime competition.

The principle of exportability of benefits, and the upstream principle of aggregation of insurance periods, represent definite derogations from the territoriality of national social-security laws and obvious (albeit partial) acknowledgement of the principle of mutual recognition in this

---

[337] Leibfried and Pierson, 'Semisovereign Welfare States', p. 64.

context. It is, however, significant that the exportability rule applies – in full – only to benefits of a specifically social-security or social-insurance nature, i.e. benefits which, because they are correlated to the payment of contributions, are 'earned' by individuals with work done personally in Community countries of 'immigration'.

Always non-applicable in the case of benefits classed as assistance, which are excluded *tout court* from the material scope of Regulation 1408/71,[338] the exportability rule has more recently been expressly nullified by the Community legislature for practically all of the non-contributory social benefits to which it had been extended during the intervening years by 'praetorian' Court of Justice case-law that had met with heated opposition from Member States.[339]

Regulation 1247/92, which was precipitated by this manifestly unwelcome case-law, was in this sense intended to restore Member States' full territorial control over a range of social citizenship benefits that in many cases have come to represent the barycentre of the basic protection networks offered by national welfare states. The purpose of the 1992 Regulation was mainly to eliminate potential forms of 'social tourism'[340] which, in profiting from the differences in protection offered by those countries with the most generous welfare systems, would in the long run have forced them to lower the level of protection provided for their own citizens and/or residents. It therefore represents an amendment aimed at recovering the original logic of Regulation 1408/71: in relegating non-contributory benefits to an area close to that of social assistance it certainly restores the typically market-oriented rationale that welcomes mobility of the factors of production, including labour mobility, as strictly functional to market requirements[341] but at the same time insulates Member States from external pressures aimed at eroding their capacity to decide their own systems of social protection.

By contrast, the last of the factors singled out by Leibfried and Pierson as corroding the autonomous regulatory capacity of Member States demonstrates more obviously all the weakness of the territoriality principle when it finds itself more openly confronted with forms of regime competition introduced by progressive expansion of the sphere of action of the fundamental principles of free movement of services and of goods.

---

[338] See Giubboni, 'Cittadinanza', especially pp. 100ff.
[339] *Ibid.*, pp. 105ff., also for the necessary case references.
[340] Andreoni, 'Sicurezza sociale', p. 543.   [341] Cinelli, 'Appunti', p. 101.

It is true that, in laying down rules on the cross-border posting of workers, Regulation 1408/71 itself allows limited forms of *intra moenia* competition from regulatory systems other than the national system in cases where the law of the country of origin establishes rules applicable to the fact of being thus posted.[342] This eventuality is, however, construed by Article 14 of the Regulation as a limited and strictly temporary exception to the applicability of *lex loci laboris* on which, in principle, the entire system of co-ordination of national social-security systems hinges. And in so far as practice records persistent instances of evasion of the limits laid down by Article 14 of the Regulation,[343] the Court of Justice continues to oversee with some rigour compliance with the material and temporal preconditions for exemption from the *lex loci laboris* principle in temporary posting situations.[344]

The fact of the matter is, on the contrary, that when associated with exercise of the freedom to provide services within the single market the phenomenon of intra-Community posting symbolizes all the risks of a downward distortion of social competition directly due to the ability to take advantage of regulatory systems offering a weak level of protection within the actual territorial scope of more generous systems. Reference to the notorious Community quarrel that led – as a token of a difficult compromise between Member States – to the adoption of Directive 96/71/EC on the posting of workers in the framework of the provision of services is all too obvious.

The progressive and increasingly rigorous confirmation by Court of Justice case-law of the innovative principle that any kind of obstacle, even if non-discriminatory, to the freedom to provide services is axiomatically precluded by Articles 59 and 60 (now Articles 49 and 50) of the Treaty unless justified by imperative reasons relating to the public interest had effectively paved the way for competing directly on the basis of social costs within the territory of other Member States. The legal concept of temporary posting in the framework of the provision of services, something which was in itself a fairly traditional form of flexible labour utilization, thus came to serve as a cloak for a new attack on the principle of territoriality of national labour-law systems in the name of free competition and

---

[342] See F. Pennings, *Introduction to European Social Security Law*, The Hague-London-Boston 1998, pp. 85ff.

[343] Cf. P. Donders, D. Pieters and P. Schoukens, 'Application of the Provisions of Regulation (EEC) 1408/71 and the Issue of Posting: Facts, Problems and Comments', in P. Schoukens (ed.), *Prospects of Social Security Co-ordination*, Leuven 1997, pp. 49ff.

[344] This has recently been confirmed by ECJ Case C-404/98 *Plum* [2000] ECR I-9379.

economic efficiency within the single market, with an almost complete reversal of the premises on the matter adopted by the Treaty of Rome.

In establishing that ex Articles 59 and 60 of the EC Treaty allowed a company established in Portugal and under contract to perform services in the construction and public-works sector in another Member State to move there temporarily with its own staff without being required to hire labour *in situ* or to obtain a work permit in accordance with the law of the host country, the *Rush Portuguesa* case[345] had, in addition, opened up a possible compromise solution capable of bringing back into play the principle of territoriality of national labour law that had to all appearances been entirely overshadowed and almost engulfed by the principle of freedom to provide services. The Court, citing a precedent which dated from several years earlier but was essentially the opposite in tenor,[346] had stated that Community law did not preclude Member States from extending 'their legislation, or collective labour agreements entered into by both sides of industry, to any person who is employed, even temporarily, within their territory, no matter in which country the employer is established'.[347]

Directive 96/71, based on ex Articles 57(2) and 66 of the Treaty, treads the narrow and difficult path of reconciling the requirements of freedom to provide services with the need to guarantee at least respect for the nucleus of basic principles of the host country's labour law.[348] It thus sets itself obvious objectives of regulating competition within the common market in order to defend the labour laws (and markets) of the Member States (which offer the most generous levels of protection), thereby reasserting an explicit anti-dumping rationale.[349]

---

[345] ECJ Case C-113/89 [1990] ECR I-1417.

[346] ECJ Joined Cases 62/81 and 63/81 *Seco* and *Desquenne* [1982] ECR 223.

[347] Paragraph 18 of the judgment.

[348] Cf. P. Davies, 'Posted Workers: Single Market or Protection of National Labour Systems?', *Common Market Law Review* 1997, vol. 34, pp. 571–602; M. Biagi, 'The Posted Workers EU Directive: From Social Dumping to Social Protectionism?', *Labour Law and Industrial Relations in the European Union – Bulletin of Comparative Labour Relations* 1998, no. 32, The Hague-London-Boston, p. 173; E. Kolehmainen, 'The Directive Concerning the Posting of Workers; Synchronization of the Functions of National Legal Systems', *Comparative Labour Law and Policy Journal* 1998, vol. 20, p. 71; G. Orlandini, 'La disciplina comunitaria del distacco dei lavoratori fra libera prestazione dei servizi e tutela della concorrenza: incoerenze e contraddizioni nella direttiva n. 71 del 1996', *Argomenti di Diritto del Lavoro* 1999, no. 1, p. 465.

[349] In its fifth Recital it is stated that 'any such promotion of the transnational provision of services requires a climate of fair competition and measures guaranteeing respect for the rights of workers.'

Within a range of action broad enough to encompass the main forms of posting connected with cross-border provision of services, the Directive predominantly requires Member States to apply to workers posted to their territory, whatever the law applicable to the employment relationship concerned, a 'hard core' of national terms and conditions of employment as laid down by its laws and collective agreements that are listed in some detail in Article 3(1) of the Directive.[350] However, in a more ambitious attempt to re-extend the territoriality principle beyond this specified nucleus of minimum mandatory protection its Article 3(10) goes farther by authorizing Member States, 'in compliance with the Treaty', both to apply equally to foreign and national undertakings terms and conditions of employment other than those listed in Article 3(1) in the case of 'public policy provisions' and to extend to activities other than those (relating to building and public works) referred to in the Annex to the Directive the scope of collective agreements that have been declared *erga omnes* applicable throughout their national territory.

It is mainly in the practical depth which this latter provision proves to assume that the resistance of the 'territorial sovereignty' of Member States' labour legislation in the face of the cuts and restrictions suffered as a result of the burgeoning exercise of the Community freedom to provide services will be tested.[351] The task of fixing the inevitably fluid line of balance between the two opposing principles has, however, ultimately been left to the Court of Justice. It is for the Court to assess, on a case-by-case basis, whether or not the protectionism expressed by the territoriality principle has transgressed the movable limits set by the need to guarantee respect for the economic freedom of movement, with equal opportunities for competition, within the internal market for services.[352]

Nonetheless, the chances of being able to impose national labour law in more or less its entirety on the strength of Article 3(10) of the Directive seem very remote.

---

[350] The rules in question are those concerning: maximum work periods and minimum rest periods; minimum paid annual holidays; minimum rates of pay, including overtime rates; conditions for the temporary hiring-out of workers; health, safety and hygiene at work; protective measures with regard to pregnant women, women who have recently given birth, children and young people; equality of treatment between men and women and provisions on non-discrimination in general.

[351] Lyon-Caen and Sciarra, 'La Convenzione', p. 25.

[352] Cf. Davies, 'Posted Workers', p. 597.

In *Finalarte*,[353] the Court of Justice had been requested to give a preliminary ruling on the legitimacy, on the basis of ex Articles 59 and 60 of the EC Treaty, of the extension to Portuguese workers temporarily posted to Germany in the context of the provision of services of the system of paid holiday funds provided for by German legislation and collective agreements in order to finance paid holiday entitlements in the construction industry. The Court did not allow the fact that the situation at issue was undoubtedly one covered by the obligation imposed under Article 3(1) of the Directive to deter it from broaching the delicate task of striking a balance – directly on the strength of ex Articles 59 and 60 of the Treaty – between the two potentially conflicting requirements. Although favourable on the whole to recognition of the legitimacy and justification of the German legislators' measure, the reply given to the referring court nonetheless left broad scope for assessment by the national court.

On the main question the Court ruled that ex Articles 59 and 60 of the Treaty do not preclude a Member State from imposing national rules guaranteeing entitlement to paid holidays (such as the scheme under discussion) on a business established in another Member State which provides services in the first (host) Member State. This was, however, said to be on the twofold condition that (1) the posted workers concerned do not enjoy an essentially similar level of protection under the law of the Member State where their employer is established, so that application of the host State's national rules confers a genuine benefit on them which significantly adds to their social protection, and (2) the application of those rules by the host Member State is proportionate to the public-interest objective pursued. The sensitive matter of verification as regards the fulfilment *in casu* of both conditions was left to the national court.[354]

It is not at all impossible that in this context – whether just from the point of view of assessing the actual degree of 'equivalence' of the host Member State's legislation or from the even more elusive aspect of proper observance of the principle of proportionality – what re-emerges in practice is the basic question of the very legitimacy of forms of competition

---

[353] ECJ Joined Cases C-49/98, C-50/98, C-52/98 to C-54/98 and C-68/98 to C-71/98, *Finalarte Sociedade de Construção Civil Lda and Others* [2001] ECR I-7831.

[354] For similar conclusions with reference to a situation involving the potential extension to posted workers of German rules on minimum rates of pay in the construction industry, see also Advocate General Mischo's Opinion in Case C-164/99 *Portugaia Construções Lda* [2002] ECR I-787.

directly based on lower labour costs (cheaper wages and/or labour stan-dards) and, reciprocally, the very legitimacy of measures aimed at restoring the strict territorial sovereignty of national labour law for anti-dumping purposes.

This was the basic problem raised by another German court[355] which essentially asked the Court of Justice whether national rules on minimum rates of pay in the construction industry – the symbolic 'hard core', as it were, that Directive 96/71 seeks to safeguard – did not actually operate precisely contrary to the *social* interests of (Portuguese) posted workers, in making it more difficult to employ them in Germany and aiming, rather, to protect the interests of German insiders (i.e. only the local labour mar-ket of the host country). In *Portugaia Construções* the Court of Justice answered that in assessing whether the application by the host Member State to service providers established in another Member State of domestic legislation laying down a minimum wage is compatible with ex Articles 59 and 60 of the EC Treaty, it is for the national authorities or, as the case may be, the national court to determine whether, considered objectively, that legislation provides for the protection of posted workers. In that regard, although the declared intention of the legislature cannot be conclusive it may nevertheless constitute an indication as to the objective pursued by the legislation. However the Court affirmed that the fact that, in con-sidering a collective agreement specific to one undertaking, a domestic employer can pay wages lower than the minimum wage laid down in a col-lective agreement declared to be generally applicable whilst an employer established in another Member State cannot do so, constitutes an unjus-tified restriction on the freedom to provide services.

In abstract terms, the reply given by the Court in *Finalarte* – as also, to a certain extent, that given in *Portugaia Construções* – was slanted towards the legitimacy of adding measures aimed at hindering social dumping, essentially though the imposition of mandatory forms of protection pro-vided by national law. But despite the Directive the problem of actu-ally comparing and grading these forms of protection in individual cases remains open; and the impression is that the Court tends to restrict them to the real *minimum* core, thereby still leaving considerable scope for *direct regulatory competition in the labour market*. Consequently, although it protects national systems against the worst forms of social dumping the Directive does not eliminate – except for minimum guarantees – the right

---

[355] In the case cited in the preceding note.

of a business to compete on the territory of another Member State while enjoying the greater 'flexibility' margins of its own labour law.[356]

Furthermore the Court has not demonstrated, to date, that it has developed a wholly unambiguous position on the matter. Its *Centros* judgment, delivered in a case relating to the freedom of establishment,[357] offers the example that perhaps carries the most problematic implications of the considerable uncertainties that still exist in this area.[358]

In the complex case referred to the Court the question essentially under discussion was whether or not it was compatible with ex Articles 52, 56 and 58 of the EC Treaty to refuse registration of a branch of a company lawfully formed under the legislation of a Member State in which it had its registered office but in which it conducted no business, when it was clear that the branch was intended to enable that company to carry on its entire business in the Member State in which the branch was to be located, with the main purpose of avoiding having to form a company in the latter State and thereby circumventing its more restrictive rules regarding, in particular, the obligation to pay in minimum company capital. The nub of the question consisted precisely in verifying whether or not conduct deliberately aimed at profiting from the differences in regulatory costs between the two Member States as regards company capital requirements constituted an abuse of the right of establishment conferred by the Treaty.

In its reply, the Court took the view that such conduct is, in principle, fully in accordance with the logic of an integrated market broadly based on competition between different regulatory systems. It cannot, therefore, be deemed abusive or fraudulent conduct in itself since it is legitimately based on a calculation of the economic advantages opened up by the transnational competitive process. Seeking out 'less restrictive' rules – as the Court itself calls them – is a choice inherent in recognition of the right of establishment.

According to the Court, protection of the general interest, which the refusal by the Danish authorities to effect registration was intended to

---

[356] In this sense also see W. Streeck, 'Competitività e sistemi nazionali. L'internazionalizzazione delle relazioni industriali', *Quaderni Rassegna Sindacale* 2000, no. 2, pp. 19ff., especially pp. 47–8.

[357] See ECJ Case C-212/97 *Centros Ltd* [1999] ECR I-1459.

[358] See, in critical terms, K. E. Sørensen, 'Prospects for European Company Law after the Judgment of the European Court of Justice in *Centros Ltd*', *Cambridge Yearbook of European Legal Studies* 1999, vol. 2, pp. 203–30, and S. Deakin, 'Two Types of Regulatory Competition: Competitive Federalism versus Reflexive Harmonisation. A Law and Economics Perspective on *Centros*', *Cambridge Yearbook of European Legal Studies* 1999, vol. 2 pp. 231–60.

serve,[359] could have been achieved with less restrictive measures. This meant that not all four conditions governing the applicability of ex Article 56 of the EC Treaty (any such national measures must be applied in a non-discriminatory manner; they must be justified by imperative requirements in the general interest; they must be suitable for securing the attainment of the objective they pursue; and they must not go beyond what is necessary to attain it) were fulfilled.[360]

It can readily be appreciated that this finding has implications extending far beyond the specific issue in question (minimum capital requirements), with potential consequences for the entire spectrum of issues entailed by intra-Community competition between company-law systems of differing rigidity and restrictiveness, including those connected with the various systems of employee participation or, more generally, 'involvement'. It is difficult to foretell what actual repercussions the judgment will prove to have in practice, particularly on this latter aspect.

Any prospect or perhaps risk of a deregulatory drift of the 'Delaware Syndrome' type possibly seems excessive in the European context.[361] Directive 2001/86 supplementing the Statute for a European company with regard to employee involvement[362] indicates, rather (in this highly sensitive matter), the different prospect of 'reflexive harmonisation'[363] and co-ordinated and regulated competition between the several national regulatory systems.

It nevertheless remains undeniable that in, for example, casting a number of doubts on the total Community legitimacy of the *siège réel* theory as applied in the majority of company-law systems in continental Europe,[364] and in any case reinjecting strong elements into the logic of regulatory competition,[365] *Centros* has helped to increase, at least indirectly, the not

---

[359] As submitted by the Danish Government, the general interest in protecting, first, public creditors against the risk of debts owing to them becoming irrecoverable, and second, all creditors – whether public or private – against the risk of fraudulent bankruptcy.

[360] See paragraph 34 of the judgment.

[361] A view shared by Sørensen, 'Prospects', pp. 222ff.

[362] Adopted contextually with Regulation 2157/2001.

[363] As it is termed by Deakin, 'Two Types', pp. 244ff.

[364] Cf. Sørensen, 'Prospects', especially pp. 220–2.

[365] The Opinion delivered by Advocate General La Pergola is particularly clear in this respect, in stating that 'the fact that a national of a Member State may take advantage of the flexibility of United Kingdom company law . . . must be viewed in that context [that is, in the context of the Community system]. In short, in the absence of harmonisation, competition among rules must be allowed free play in corporate matters' (see point 20 of his Opinion).

inconsiderable cracks in the principle of territoriality in one of the most critical and sensitive areas of national labour law itself.[366]

In reinvigorating the 'liberalist basis of the Community',[367] the judgment is in line with a logic and an economic-constitution model in which national law is directly subject to the dictates of the market, in the sense that the several legal systems are placed in competition with each other and that it is possible to choose whichever is the most favourable (to the enterprise). Comparative competition between legal orders penetrates directly within their borders, fostering law-shopping processes that accentuate what Sabino Cassese has called the tendency towards 'marketization of the State'.[368]

---

[366] See, in this sense, C. Barnard and S. Deakin, 'In Search of Coherence: Social Policy, the Single Market and Fundamental Rights', *Industrial Relations Journal – European Annual Review* 1999/2000, pp. 121–41, especially p. 134.

[367] S. Cassese, *La crisi dello Stato*, Rome-Bari 2002, p. 116.   [368] *Ibid.*

2

Re-embedding liberalism: towards a new balance between negative and positive integration of European welfare states

1. The difficult quest for a new balance between negative integration and positive integration of national welfare states

The weakening of the principle of territoriality of national systems of labour and social-security law as a result of the progressive expansion of the scope of the Community freedom to provide services effectively encapsulates the overall sense of the metamorphoses of the European economic constitution as described in the preceding chapter.

Negative integration came to prevail over positive integration, driven by the institutional and normative asymmetry created, in its favour, as a result of the constitutionalization of the Treaties by the Court of Justice. The latter has opted to give primary consideration to the rules underpinning the construction of a completely unified market around the principles of economic freedom, free enterprise and free competition, principles which have in this way acquired a centrality wholly unknown to the original balances. The direct effect accorded to these economic freedoms, elevated – in contrast to what had formerly been the case in most Member State constitutional traditions – to the status of fundamental rights, immediately achieved the object of removing the obstacles and barriers standing in the way of the construction of the single market, thanks to the supremacy of Community law over the rules of domestic law (including those of constitutional ranking).

The institutional limits of positive integration – as prisoner of the joint-decision trap and the political blocks of the 'intergovernmental method'[1] – prevented it from adequately counterbalancing the varyingly marked

---

[1] To repeat the well-known terminology of F. W. Scharpf, among whose contributions see, for example, 'Negative and Positive Integration in the Political Economy of European Welfare States', *Jean Monnet Chair Papers, Robert Schuman Centre – European University Insititute* No. 95/28 (also in G. Marks *et al., Governance in the European Union,* London 1996, pp. 15–39).

deregulatory effects produced, at the level of national social policies, by the semi-automatic advance of negative integration.

The strengthening of the institutional resources of positive integration under the Single European Act system, primarily through the introduction of qualified-majority voting, essentially related to the internal market and concerned the area of social policies only to a limited extent. In other words, it mainly concerned measures 'of an anti-interventionist stamp'[2] aimed at promoting the regulation and efficient functioning of the internal market.

The institutional gap between negative and positive integration was not filled by the Agreement on Social Policy annexed, together with the relevant Protocol, to the Maastricht Treaty. The opposing factors were: first, the UK's opportunistic self-exclusion, which in confining the Agreement's effects to eleven of the then twelve Member States to some extent further reinforced the contradictions and distortions of a social Europe à la carte that had already emerged on a reduced scale with the proclamation of the 1989 Community Charter of Fundamental Social Rights of Workers; and second, the persistent absence of any recognition of fundamental social rights at Treaty level, a fact which weakened the potentialities of the innovative inclusion of collective bargaining as one of the quasi-legislative sources of Community social policy.

By contrast, the social provisions of the Treaty of Amsterdam – the subject of a renewed (and often sterile) polemic between Euro-pessimists and Euro-optimists[3] – are marked by a feeble but nonetheless significant attempt to correct the fundamental asymmetry between negative and positive integration of national welfare-state systems.

As will be seen in more detail in the subsections below, the innovations on the matter contributed by the Treaty of Amsterdam followed three main lines: reinforcement of the constitutional importance of the social values assumed as fundamental to the European integration process, mainly (but not solely) through repeated reference to the fundamental rights recognized by the Council of Europe's 1961 European Social Charter and the 1989 Community Charter of Fundamental Social Rights of

---

[2] M. Barbera, *Dopo Amsterdam. I nuovi confini del diritto sociale comunitario*, Brescia 2000, p. 49.

[3] Cf., for example, the opposing assessments of R. Blanpain, 'The European Union, Employment, Social Policy and the Law', in Blanpain (ed.), *Institutional Changes and the European Social Policies after the Treaty of Amsterdam*, The Hague London Boston 1998, pp. 1ff., especially pp. 58ff., and F. Carinci and A. Pizzoferrato, '"Costituzione" europea e diritti sociali fondamentali', *Lavoro e Diritto* 2000, pp. 281ff.

Workers;[4] redefinition of a unitary (and formally autonomous) legal basis for Community action in the field of social policy, by incorporating the text of the Agreement on Social Policy into the Treaty; and, last but not least, codification of the strategy for the co-ordination of national employment policies as progressively delineated since the Essen summit of 1994, with the introduction into the Treaty of a new Title on Employment. And the two Intergovernmental Conferences that followed the Amsterdam revision also advanced – to a differing degree – along the same political and institutional contours, in the new context of 'semi-permanent' revision of the Treaties.[5]

Thus, the Treaty of Amsterdam heralded a new phase of Community integration characterized by an attempt to regain a more appropriate and even balance between the necessity of constructing a totally unified market and the need to reaffirm the essential values of the European social model, both with the emergence of guiding principles at the top of the supranational order and with a search for the necessary space for autonomy of national labour-law systems. What in fact emerged clearly at Amsterdam for the first time was an awareness that central aspects of the democratic legitimacy and very sustainability of the entire integration process are linked to such a balance. As the first revision of the Treaties not to make market integration the focus,[6] it was precisely in the identification of new instruments for establishing a different balance between the economic

---

[4] In addition, the new Article 13 of the EC Treaty likewise acquired obvious importance from this point of view as a legal basis for taking 'appropriate action to combat discrimination based on sex, racial or ethnic origin, religion or belief, disability, age or sexual orientation' (see Directive 2000/43 implementing the principle of equal treatment between persons irrespective of racial or ethnic origin and Directive 2000/78 establishing a general framework for equal treatment in employment and occupation); cf. M. Bell, 'Anti-discrimination Law after Amsterdam', in J. Shaw (ed.), *Social Law and Policy in an Evolving European Union*, Oxford-Portland 2000, pp. 157ff.; P. Chieco, 'Le nuove direttive comunitarie sul divieto di discriminazione', *Rivista Italiana di Diritto del Lavoro* 2002, vol. I, pp. 75ff. By contrast, the provision contained in the new Article 7 of the Maastricht Treaty (subsequently amended at Nice) would appear, in confining the political sanctions it envisages to breach of those civil and political rights that form part of the classical liberal tradition of a State governed by the rule of law, to have no impact on the protection of social rights; see B. Hepple, 'Towards a European Social Constitution', in C. Engels and M. Weiss (eds.), *Labour Law and Industrial Relations at the Turn of the Century. Liber Amicorum in Honour of Roger Blanpain*, The Hague-London-Boston 1998, pp. 291–304, especially p. 292.

[5] B. De Witte, 'Il processo semi-permanente di revisione dei Trattati', *Quaderni Costituzionali* 2002, p. 499.

[6] J. Kenner, *EU Employment Law. From Rome to Amsterdam and Beyond*, Oxford-Portland 2002, pp. 375ff., at p. 378.

demands of economic and monetary union and social requirements that the Treaty of Amsterdam sought a concrete response to the growing legitimacy crisis of the construction of the Community.

As we shall see, the gradual strengthening of the European Employment Strategy as a form of 'open method of co-ordination' of national employment policies effectively implemented even before the new Treaty actually entered into force, and the incipient extension of this method to the crucial area of social-inclusion/social-protection policies that had initially been excluded, are paramount aspects of this attempt.

Starting from the Lisbon summit in particular, significant progress has been achieved in attempting to establish a clear connection – and especially a 'two-way' one – between the co-ordination of economic policies and the co-ordination of employment policies. The requirement for delineating the bases of a genuine European economic governance is thus being increasingly perceived as the necessity of exploring the potentialities of effective decision-making circuits capable 'of managing . . . the systematic interdependences between the market and the single currency, employment and social protection'.[7]

The culmination of the Intergovernmental Conference reached at Nice, although hard-won, nonetheless not only consolidated the social *acquis* of the Treaty of Amsterdam but also, with the solemn proclamation of the Charter of Fundamental Rights of the European Union. significantly strengthened and refocused the prospects of the constitutionalization of a weighty catalogue of fundamental social rights at Union level. The Treaty establishing a Constitution for Europe – the subject, in the Intergovernmental Conference that opened at the end of 2003 and ended only recently, of one of the most drawn-out and tortuous compromises in the Community's history – consolidates and enshrines these trends, particularly by incorporating in its Part II the Nice Charter of Fundamental Rights of the European Union. The long march forward of fundamental social rights in the Union legal order therefore exemplifies, it might be said, the slow and laborious process of establishing a new constitutional balance in the construction of the Community. This is the aspect that we shall take as a starting-point in moving on to test the soundness of what is called the new Community 're-embedding liberalism' phase.

---

[7] M. Ferrera, *Le trappole del welfare. Uno stato sociale sostenibile per l'Europa del XXI secolo*, Bologna 1998, p. 98.

2. Social rights and the market in the European constitutional space *in fieri*: developments up to the Treaty of Amsterdam ...

The original absence – in the founding Treaties – of any reference whatever to fundamental rights was not regarded as a lacuna in the Community order.[8]

Before the 'heroic' phase of Court of Justice case-law and the 'quiet revolution'[9] effected by the Court with the constitutionalization of the Treaties starting from its judgments in *Van Gend en Loos*[10] and *Costa*,[11] the need to protect fundamental rights in areas falling under Community law could be said to be fully met by the national constitutions of the founding States, all of which were in any case bound by the European Convention on Human Rights and, later, the European Social Charter itself.[12]

The same could obviously be said in the case of social rights. Affirmed for the first time (albeit with widely differing degrees of emphasis and sensitivity) by the post-war Member State constitutions, these rights were able to count on the secure protection accorded by the several national orders, without any possibility, at least according to the abstract expectations of the founding fathers, of their being suppressed by the Community Treaties. On the contrary, the latter – in guaranteeing the gradual integration of the Member States' economies – were presumed to favour the effective protection of such rights in that they strengthened the dynamics of material development which constitute the essential precondition for the fulfilment, in particular, of social redistribution rights (*Leistungsrechte,* or *diritti sociali di prestazione*).

---

[8] See J. H. H. Weiler, 'Eurocracy and Distrust. Some Questions Concerning the Role of the European Court of Justice in the Protection of Fundamental Human Rights within the Legal Order of the European Communities', *Washington Law Review* 1986, no. 1, pp. 1103ff.

[9] The well-known expressions used by J. H. H. Weiler: see his 'A Quiet Revolution. The European Court of Justice and Its Interlocutors', *Comparative Political Studies* 1994, pp. 510ff., and 'The Transformation of Europe', in Weiler, The *Constitution of Europe. 'Do the New Clothes Have an Emperor?' and Other Essays on European Integration*, Cambridge 1999, pp. 10–101, here pp. 19ff.

[10] ECJ Case 26/62 *Van Gend en Loos* [1963] ECR 1.

[11] ECJ Case 6/64 *Costa* v *ENEL* [1964] ECR 585.

[12] See M. Cartabia, 'Commento all'art. 51', in R. Bifulco, M. Cartabia and A. Celotto (eds.), *L'Europa dei diritti. Commento alla Carta dei diritti fondamentali dell'Unione europea*, Bologna 2001, p. 345.

In such a context, any recognition of fundamental rights in the Treaty of Rome therefore seemed relatively superfluous. In point of fact the omission of any reference to them was, rather, both useful and opportune in that – as pointed out by Weiler[13] – it helped to remove the threat of a surreptitious expansion of the powers conferred on the new Community in the event of a perceived link, as borne out by the historical experience of federalism, between the pronouncement of a Bill of Rights and the extension of 'central' competences to the detriment of the member nation-states.[14]

It was only later that the lacuna emerged, when affirmation of the constitutional doctrines of direct effect, supremacy of Community law and implied powers materialized that threat and introduced the risk, unless it was countered by the development of adequate safeguards at supranational level, of leaving the essential core of Community protection of fundamental rights dangerously exposed.

Although the need to establish adequate forms of protection, and in particular to recognize an express catalogue of social rights effectively guaranteed at supranational level, therefore followed and backed up the analogous need that very quickly presented itself on a more general front, it nevertheless had a logic of its own which took account of the specific nature of the problem of social rights within the Community ambit.

What in fact happened was that the gradual affirmation of a 'praetorian' system of Community fundamental-rights protection – developed and progressively refined by the Court of Justice from the late 1960s onwards in response to strong representations emanating mainly from the German and Italian constitutional courts[15] – to some extent filled the gap that had arisen in the case of the civil and economic rights and freedoms of the liberal tradition, but did not provide adequate answers as regards the specific matter of social rights.

The language of fundamental rights gradually evolved and articulated in Court of Justice case-law in an increasingly frequent dialogue with

---

[13] Reference need only be made to his book *Il sistema comunitario europeo. Struttura giuridica e processo politico*, Bologna 1985, pp. 139ff.

[14] See O. Kahn-Freund, 'L'incidenza delle costituzioni sul diritto del lavoro', *Giornale di Diritto del Lavoro e di Relazioni Industriali* 1979, pp. 77ff., especially p. 79.

[15] Cf. G. F. Mancini, 'La tutela dei diritti dell'uomo: il ruolo della Corte di Giustizia delle Comunità europee', *Rivista Trimestrale di Diritto e Procedura Civile* 1989, pp. 1ff.; G. F. Mancini, 'The Making of a Constitution for Europe', *Common Market Law Review* 1989, vol. 26, pp. 595–614, now also in his *Democracy and Constitutionalism in the European Union. Collected Essays*, Oxford-Portland 2000, pp. 1ff.

national courts touched on social rights only marginally.[16] It essentially concerned first-generation rights:[17] with the important exception of equality of treatment/equal opportunities between men and women at work, the emergence of the Community social dimension as an 'issue' developed, by contrast, outside the language of fundamental rights proper.

At this latter level the case-law in question, paradoxically, actually aggravated the Community protection deficit in exposing the social rights recognized by the Member States' legal systems more directly to the pressures of transnational economic liberalization,[18] amplified by the tendency to accord fundamental rights status solely to economic freedoms, to a degree unknown to many national constitutions.[19]

It is therefore not surprising that – in so far as the asymmetries of protection and hence the risks of conflict between Community economic freedoms and national social rights were becoming correspondingly greater[20] – it was European labour lawyers who, from the late 1980s onwards, were some of the most vociferous advocates of the urgent need for express constitutionalization of fundamental social rights directly within the body of the founding Treaties.[21] Nor, obviously, is it surprising

---

[16] Cf. G. De Búrca, 'The Language of Rights and European Integration', in J. Shaw and G. More (eds.), *New Legal Dynamics of European Union*, Oxford 1995, pp. 29ff.; see, however, for a different account K. Lenaerts and P. Foubert, 'Social Rights in the Case-law of the Court of Justice', *Legal Issues of Economic Integration* 2001, pp. 267ff.

[17] See E. Pagano, 'I diritti fondamentali nella Comunità europea dopo Maastricht', *Diritto dell'Unione Europea* 1996, no. 1, pp. 164ff.

[18] See S. Sciarra, 'Verso una costituzionalizzazione dei diritti sociali fondamentali dell'Unione europea', *EUI Working Papers in Law* No. 96/1, and, more recently, Sciarra, 'Market Freedom and Fundamental Social Rights', *EUI Working Papers in Law* No. 02/3 (also in B. Hepple (ed.), *Social and Labour Rights in a Global Context. International and Comparative Perspectives*, Cambridge 2003, pp. 95ff.).

[19] See A. Cantaro, 'Lavoro e diritti sociali nella "Costituzione europea"', *Democrazia e Diritto* 1999, no. 4, special issue entitled *Lavoro: declino o metamorfosi?*, ed. P. Barcellona, pp. 97ff.

[20] See in more detail in chapter 3 below.

[21] See, for example, W. Däubler, 'Market and Social Justice in the EC. The Rationale and Substance of a European Fundamental Rights Act', in Däubler (ed.), *Market and Social Justice in the EC. The Other Side of the Internal Market*, Gütersloh 1991, pp. 42ff.; A. Lyon-Caen and S. Simitis, 'L'Europe sociale à la recherche de ses références', *Revue du Marché Unique Européen* 1993, p. 109; Lord Wedderburn, 'European Community Law and Workers' Rights after 1992: Fact or Fake?', in Wedderburn, *Labour Law and Freedom. Further Essays in Labour Law*, London 1995, pp. 247ff.; M. A. Moreau, 'Tendences du droit social communautaire: des droits sociaux en quête de reconnaissance', *Droit Social* 1994, p. 612; M. Rodríguez-Piñero and E. Casas, 'In Support of a European Social Constitution', in P. Davies *et al.* (eds.), *European Community Labour Law: Principles and Perspectives. Liber Amicorum Lord Wedderburn*, Oxford 1996, pp. 23–48; Sciarra, 'Verso una

that – accompanying a line of thought presented authoritatively by the Comité des Sages set up by the Commission[22] – this community of labour lawyers put forward its most articulate criticisms and most significant and expert proposals in 1996 during the Intergovernmental Conference that led to the Treaty of Amsterdam,[23] when, with the EMU project launched, the sense of urgency was greater.

Their shared intention was to curb the potential destructuring effects that might be produced as a result of purely negative integration by an uncontrolled expansion of the freedoms of movement and competition, and at the same time to impose the emergence of new substantive principles of Community labour law embodying common fundamental values, protected and recognized as rights of (at least) equal ranking with economic freedoms.

In the background there was also the sensitive issue of the need to re-establish the legitimacy of the Court, which was more and more often being dangerously exposed to the strategic use of Community economic freedoms as a means of dismantling the forms of protection provided by the several national social systems.[24] This meant that the specific nature of the problem inherent in the recognition of social rights could, however, be perceived only in the context of the more general question of the democratic re-legitimation of the Court of Justice's 'constitutional adjudication' activities and of the Community legal order itself. The inclusion of an exhaustive Community catalogue in the Treaties would correct the original defect of a 'praetorian' treatment of fundamental rights developed predominantly as instrumental to the need for effective

costituzionalizzazione'. See also, among the first analyses and proposals at institutional level, the Economic and Social Committee's important Opinion of November 1987: *Opinion of the Economic and Social Committee on the Social Aspects of the Internal Market (European Social Area)*, ESC (1987) 1069.

[22] Commission of the European Communities, *For a Europe of Civic and Social Rights*. Report by the Comité des Sages chaired by Maria de Lourdes Pintasilgo, DG V, Brussels 1996.

[23] This refers to R. Blanpain, B. Hepple, S. Sciarra and M. Weiss, *Fundamental Social Rights: Proposals for the European Union*, Leuven 1996 (who proposed that Article 117 of the Treaty of Rome should be reworded to include the insertion of the binding pronouncement of an extensive catalogue of directly actionable social rights, together with the explicit statement of guiding principles for Community and Member State social-protection policies); and B. Bercusson *et al.*, *A Manifesto for Social Europe*, Brussels 1996, especially pp. 155ff. (who were advocating the incorporation into the EC Treaty of the Community Charter of Fundamental Social Rights of Workers along with the Protocol and Agreement on Social Policy signed at Maastricht as a means of implementing, on a legislative basis, the substantive principles affirmed in the former).

[24] See S. Simitis, 'Dismantling or Strengthening Labour Law: The Case of the European Court of Justice', *European Law Journal* 1996, vol. 2 no. 2, pp. 156–76.

market integration[25] and therefore outside any 'democratic discourse',[26] by circumventing the intrinsic limits of judge-made law and at the same time filling its most obvious gap.

The 1989 Community Charter had obviously not been capable of fulfilling such a complex and ambitious function, nor had it had been conceived with this in mind. Proclaimed without the United Kingdom, the Charter assembled with 'calculated legal imprecision',[27] in a text lacking any binding legal force, a series of rights, principles and simply objectives for social policy. It provided a useful programmatic basis for the social-policy initiatives adopted by the Commission in the first half of the 1990s in a particularly unfavourable climate, using the narrow scope offered first by Article 118a of the EC Treaty and later – but still with the serious limitation of the United Kingdom's self-exclusion – by the Agreement on Social Policy. It is therefore no surprise that the Court of Justice referred to it only with extreme reluctance and infrequency as a possible source of inspiration for the elaboration of Community fundamental social rights and, what is more, that the rare cases in which it did occur almost invariably had negative outcomes.[28]

On the other hand, the Maastricht Treaty – by maintaining unchanged the weak position of social rights and at the same time reinforcing, at least in symbolic terms, the position of first-generation rights – had aggravated the asymmetries and imbalances left unresolved by the 1989 Charter. As one author has put it vividly, it meant that the European Community/Union was, in a way, taken back 'to the first stage in Marshall's

---

[25] In this sense, the well-known analysis by J. Coppel and A. O'Neill, 'The European Court of Justice: Taking Rights Seriously?', *Common Market Law Review* 1992, pp. 669ff.; see, however, in critical vein, J. H. H. Weiler and N. J. S. Lockhart, '"Taking Rights Seriously" Seriously. The European Court and its Fundamental Rights Jurisprudence', *Common Market Law Review* 1995, pp. 62ff.

[26] M. Cartabia, *Principi inviolabili e integrazione europea*, Milan 1995, pp. 54–5, who emphasizes that fundamental rights made their appearance 'at a certain point in the life of the Community to contain potential deviations of the Community institutions without, however, ever assuming the dignity of constituent values of the Community legal order', explains in this way the 'axiological prevalence' accorded to the 'economic objectives that constitute the *raison d'être* of Community integration'.

[27] Rodríguez-Piñero and Casas, 'In Support', p. 35.

[28] Cf. J. Baquero Cruz, 'La protección de los derechos sociales en la Comunidad europea tras el Tratado de Amsterdam', *Revista de Derecho Comunitario Europeo* 1998, pp. 639ff., especially p. 653; L. Betten, 'The EU Charter on Fundamental Rights: a Trojan Horse or a Mouse?', *International Journal of Comparative Labour Law and Industrial Relations* 2001, vol. 17 no. 2, pp. 151–64, especially pp. 157–8, who cites details of the very few examples of the use of the 1989 Charter for this purpose (but with almost always negative outcomes).

evolutionary cycle of rights',[29] contradicting the inspiration of many constitutional traditions of national *welfare* states.

By incorporating a decision on a system favouring market freedom and competition,[30] the Maastricht Treaty increased the hiatus between negative and positive integration precisely inasmuch as it confined itself to codifying, without recognizing autonomous space for social rights, the Court of Justice's settled case-law. Ex Article F(2) – which, moreover, the following Article L (subsequently Article 46 in the consolidated and amended version) excluded from the Court's jurisdiction[31] – mentioned only the 1950 European Convention on Human Rights and the constitutional traditions common to the Member States, in terms which could not but confirm that fundamental social rights were essentially extraneous to the horizon of Community action.[32]

In a context such as this, the provisions introduced by the Treaty of Amsterdam signal, as already mentioned, an obvious and indisputable point of discontinuity with the past. The explicit mention[33] of the fundamental social rights recognized in the 1961 European Social Charter and the 1989 Community Charter that is now contained in the Treaties[34] constitutes a novelty of not only considerable symbolic significance but

---

[29] M. La Torre, 'Citizenship and Social Rights. A European Perspective', *EUI Working Papers – EUF* No. 98/2, p. 12.

[30] '*Gesamtentscheidung*', to use ordoliberal terminology: W. Eucken, *Die Grundlagen der Nationalökonomie*, Berlin-Heidelberg-New York 1989 (first published 1940), p. 52. See, recently, L. Cassetti, *Stabilità economica e diritti fondamentali. L'euro e la disciplina costituzionale dell'economia*, Turin 2002, pp. 118 and 121.

[31] As is well known, of course, the limit imposed in this way on the Court's jurisdiction has been removed as a result of the rewording, in the Treaty of Amsterdam, of the current Article 46 of the EU Treaty.

[32] Cf. S. Sciarra, 'From Strasbourg to Amsterdam: Prospects for the Convergence of European Social Rights Policy', in P. Alston (ed.), *The EU and Human Rights*, Oxford 1999, pp. 473ff., especially pp. 480ff. The author notes that the 1950 European Convention on Human Rights – notoriously lacking any reference to social rights as covered by the Council of Europe's European Social Charter concluded at Turin in 1961 – does not even constitute an adequate basis for the protection of trade union freedom, i.e. the right to organize, although it is mentioned in its Article 11. The Strasbourg Court has in fact interpreted this provision, along with the others, in accordance with the eminently individualistic approach that marks the entire establishment of the Convention.

[33] S. Robin-Olivier, 'La référence aux droits sociaux fondamentaux dans le traité d'Amsterdam', *Droit Social* 1999, p. 609.

[34] See in particular the fourth paragraph of the Preamble to the EU Treaty (where the contracting parties declare that they confirm 'their attachment' to these rights) and Article 136 of the EC Treaty (where the Community and the Member States undertake to 'have in mind' the aforesaid rights in pursuing the social-policy objectives defined by this provision).

also undoubted practical relevance.[35] It has effectively opened up – albeit in the absence of full constitutionalization of these rights – new opportunities for a more even balance to be struck by the Court of Justice between social values and economic values.

In affirming the fundamental nature of social rights and values explicitly for the first time,[36] the Treaties have made the quest for limits to 'the imperialism of negative integration' easier,[37] allowing 'balances to be struck more in favour of the social objectives to which the construction of the Community is becoming more and more closely linked'.[38]

The now famous *Albany International BV* case represents the most emblematic example of the opportunities offered by the Treaty of Amsterdam in this direction.[39] Here it was possible for the social-policy objectives pursued by the Treaty, including through reliance on the 1961 European Social Charter and the 1989 Community Charter mentioned in Article 136, to be treated on an equal footing, in terms of importance and relevance, with those deriving from the common rules on competition, enabling the Court of Justice to carry out a balancing operation between them which would in all probability have been more difficult and perhaps impossible under the pre-existing normative framework.

At the same time, however, the *Albany* case also exemplifies all the limitations of a reference to fundamental social rights that remains tied to the notion of being purely instrumental to the pursuit of social objectives, even those which have been declared essential by the Community and the Member States. Limitations which seem in a sense to be sublimated – as will be argued in more detail in chapter 3 below – by the refusal to see in collective bargaining and its 'products' the exercise of a fundamental social right forming part, as such, of the nucleus of minimum preconditions for an autonomous labour-law system.[40]

With the Treaty of Amsterdam, in fact, social rights – as recognized, although with very unequal degrees of force and effectiveness,[41] by the

---

[35] Cf. Sciarra, 'From Strasbourg', pp. 488ff.

[36] See M. Bonnechère, 'Quelle garantie des droits sociaux fondamentaux en droit européen?', *Europe, Chronique* July 2000, p. 4.

[37] Scharpf, 'Negative and Positive Integration', p. 35.

[38] Robin-Olivier, 'La référence', p. 616.

[39] ECJ Case C-67/96 [1999] ECR I-5751; see, at more length, subsections 6 and 7 of chapter 3 below.

[40] And one which features, not by chance, among the core labour standards more recently envisaged by the ILO Declaration on fundamental principles and rights at work adopted in June 1998.

[41] Cf. T. Treu, 'Diritti sociali europei: dove siamo?', *Lavoro e Diritto* 2000, pp. 429ff., especially p. 437, who states that the two Charters 'give somewhat heterogeneous lists, differing in

two Charters of 1961 and 1989 – were admitted into the *acquis commu-nautaire* essentially 'as guidelines for activities of both the Community and the Member States'.[42] They became part in principle of the Community patrimony of existing law essentially as objective social interests, albeit with fundamental status, and not as directly justiciable subjective positions. 'What the Community (and the Member States) are committed to are social interests presented in the form of objectives (employment, social protection, social dialogue, etc.) and it is these which are protected by the Treaty (which is still the basic law of the Community). Social rights *per se*, however, remain in the background and the opportunity of invoking them is linked to the need to achieve the social objectives stated. In short, they boil down to their status as *Reflexrechte*.'[43]

In this context, there remains an obvious asymmetry in comparison with the fundamental economic freedoms that the EC Treaty guarantees to individuals: the '*Community minority*' status[44] still attaching to social rights.[45]

Thus, even after the Treaty of Amsterdam Community labour law remained enclosed within a dimension that has been described as 'pre-constitutional'[46] inasmuch as, although it rests on the constitutional traditions of Member States, it lacks deep roots in the Treaties.

From this viewpoint, it is perfectly understandable why it has been stated authoritatively that the Treaty of Amsterdam, as the vehicle of the first-ever mention of fundamental social rights in the Treaties, did not lessen but if anything highlighted and increased the urgency of the need for them to be expressly constitutionalized, alongside civil and economic rights, with the maximum level of visibility and effectiveness inherent in

the degree to which they are specific, as regards social rights which are either what may be termed programmatic or those which are directly actionable.'

[42] Commission of the European Communities, *Affirming Fundamental Rights in the European Union. Time to Act*, Report of the Expert Group on Fundamental Rights chaired by Prof. Spiros Simitis, DG V, Brussels February 1999 (referred to hereinafter as the Simitis Report), p. 11.

[43] M. Luciani, 'Diritti sociali e integrazione europea', in Associazione Italiana dei Costituzionalisti, *Annuario 1999. La Costituzione europea*, Atti del XIV Convegno annuale Perugia 7–9 ottobre 1999, Padua 2000, pp. 507ff., here p. 530.

[44] *Ibid.*, p. 529 (the emphasis is in the original).

[45] In this sense see M. V. Ballestrero, 'Brevi osservazioni su Costituzione europea e diritto del lavoro italiano', *Lavoro e Diritto* 2000, pp. 547ff., especially pp. 554–5; B. Veneziani, 'Nel nome di Erasmo da Rotterdam. La faticosa marcia dei diritti sociali fondamentali nell'ordinamento comunitario', *Rivista Giuridica del Lavoro e della Previdenza Sociale* 2000, pp. 779ff.

[46] S. Sciarra, 'Integration Through Courts: Article 177 as a Pre-Federal Device', in Sciarra (ed.), *Labour Law in the Courts. National Judges and the European Court of Justice*, Oxford-Portland 2001, pp. 1–30, here p. 23.

the supranational legal order.[47] And, in particular, this should be done by including an open list in the text of the founding Treaties themselves based on the principle of the indivisibility of civil, political, economic and social rights.

It was in these ideal terms that the Simitis Committee invited the Convention charged with the task of drawing up the Charter of Fundamental Rights of the European Union to re-state the fundamental values of the European social model in the name of the indivisibility and complementarity of first-, second- and third-generation rights. It was felt that the indivisibility resulting from the unitary and equal recognition of the aforesaid rights in a single constitutional text was the only way of translating into practice the idea – underpinning this model – that social rights, in realizing the autonomous goals of social justice and substantive equality specific to them, also contribute to establishing the normative conditions for proper and efficient functioning of the market.

3. ... and the prospects opened up by the Nice Charter

The body, later dubbed a Convention, which was decided on at the Cologne European Council and whose actual composition was specified shortly afterwards at the Tampere summit marks the start of an entirely new method of pursuing the Community process of constitutional reform. Composed for the most part of members of the European Parliament and national parliaments, this 'first' Convention, under its President Roman Herzog, initiated a method that was subsequently extended to the actual revision of the Treaties with the creation of the Convention set up to draft the Treaty establishing a Constitution for Europe: a deliberative method institutionally open to contributions from members of civil society which, with particular reference to this second experience, has rightly been described as 'a fascinating process of quasi-democratization of the traditional method followed by Intergovernmental Conferences in considering amendments to the basic legal order of the European Union on various occasions.'[48] The Convention presided over by Mr Herzog drew up the Charter of Fundamental Rights of the European Union in a constitutional spirit, in full awareness that it might constitute the framework of a future Community Bill of Rights.

---

[47] Simitis Report, p. 13.
[48] As put by N. MacCormick in the Introduction to the 2003 Italian edition of his *Questioning Sovereignty. Law, State, and Nation in the European Commonwealth*, Oxford 1999.

Solemnly proclaimed in December 2000 at the Nice summit by the Parliament, Council and Commission in the presence of the members of the European Council,[49] the EU Charter of Fundamental Rights effectively responds to the wish to bring together with equal ranking, in a single catalogue that is for the first time specific and particular to the entire European Union, the values and rights adopted as being fundamental and underpinning the very legitimacy of the Community order.

In the Treaty establishing a Constitution for Europe finally approved by the Heads of State or Government in the context of the Intergovernmental Conference and signed in Rome on 29 October 2004, the Charter occupies the whole of Part II and is thus fully enshrined as a constitutional source of the Union. However, right from the time of its solemn proclamation at Nice it began to have effect in the European constitutional fabric as a single document bringing together Union fundamental values.

The fact which is most significant for our present purposes, and which will therefore be considered first, consists in the adoption by the 2000 Charter of the principle of indivisibility which represents its most imme-diately perceptible innovative force compared with Community experi-ence in the matter. It is from this aspect which – even beyond what might have been expected, given the cautious wording of the mandate received by the 'first' Convention at Cologne – the most innovative import of the Charter has to be assessed: in the solemn and concrete affirmation of the principle of the indivisibility, interdependence and complementarity of first-, second- and third-generation rights; and in the equal ranking, around the central and unifying value of human dignity,[50] of civil, polit-ical, economic and social rights.

In breaking down the barriers between the various categories of funda-mental rights and endowing social rights with autonomy and equal nor-mative value, the Nice Charter is situated directly on the track of the most advanced European constitutionalism,[51] going beyond the functional

---

[49] On the details and symbolic significance of the particular form of proclamation chosen, see B. De Witte, 'The Legal Status of the Charter: Vital Question or Non-Issue?', *Maastricht Journal of European and Comparative Law* 2001, pp. 81ff.

[50] Cf. S Rodotà, 'La Carta come atto politico e documento giuridico', in A. Manzella *et al.*, *Riscrivere i diritti in Europa. Introduzione alla Carta dei diritti fondamentali dell'Unione europea*, Bologna 2001, pp. 57ff., especially p. 74.

[51] *Ibid.*, p. 73, and also A. Manzella, 'Dal mercato ai diritti', in Manzella *et al.*, *Riscrivere*, pp. 29ff., especially p. 31. For a more critical evaluation see, however, J. Kenner, 'Economic and Social Rights in the EU Legal Order: The Mirage of Indivisibility', in T. Hervey and J. Kenner (eds.), *Economic and Social Rights under the EU Charter of Fundamental Rights. A Legal Perspective*, Oxford-Portland 2003, pp. 1ff.

limits perceptible in this connection in what is stated in the Treaty of Amsterdam.[52] As is emphasized by most commentators,[53] the main input of substantive novelty – as regards the principles and values underlying European Union action – contributed by the Charter therefore resides in its elevation of fundamental social rights to the status of rights ranking equally with economic freedoms.

The fact that the Charter seeks to express the fundamental values of a construction which has for some time transcended the purely market dimension and profoundly affected the political and constitutional dimension also signifies a move beyond the instrumental and ancillary role previously accorded to social rights in the Community perspective. With the symbolic transition from integration through the market to integration through rights,[54] the European social model has regained the centrality which 'seemed to have been nullified by the prevalent logic of the Treaties'.[55]

In a market economy which is 'heterocorrected' and 'heterocompensated' in a solidaristic direction[56] social rights are indivisible from Community economic freedoms, and 'they all share the same nature'.[57]

Solidarity – in its capacity as a meta-criterion underpinning social rights together with substantive equality and human dignity – appears in the Charter as an 'organizing principle of individual and collective rights',[58] alongside the principles of dignity, freedom, equality, citizenship and justice.[59] Its inclusion on an equal footing as one of the classifying

---

[52] And, even more so, going beyond the experience of the 1989 Community Charter, whose function is rightly judged by S. Sciarra, 'Diritti sociali. Riflessioni sulla Carta europea dei diritti fondamentali', *Argomenti di Diritto del Lavoro* 2001, no. 2, pp. 391ff., especially p. 408, to be 'historically ended'.

[53] See, for example, in addition to the authors cited in the preceding notes, E. Paciotti, 'La Carta: i contenuti e gli autori', in Manzella *et al.*, *Riscrivere*, pp. 9ff., especially p. 18; K. Lenaerts and E. E. De Smijter, 'A "Bill of Rights" for the European Union', *Common Market Law Review* 2001, pp. 273ff., especially p. 280; M. Roccella, 'La Carta dei diritti fondamentali: un passo avanti verso l'Unione politica', *Lavoro e Diritto* 2001, pp. 329ff.; R. Del Punta, 'I diritti sociali come diritti fondamentali: riflessioni sulla Carta di Nizza', *Diritto delle Relazioni Industriali* 2001, pp. 335ff.

[54] Cf. Manzella. 'Dal mercato', and, as regards the preceding stages in the process, L. Azzena, *L'integrazione attraverso i diritti. Dal cittadino italiano al cittadino europeo*, Turin 1998.

[55] Rodotà, 'La Carta', p. 79.

[56] To use the terminology of A. Predieri, *Euro. Poliarchie democratiche e mercati monetari*, Turin 1998, pp. 5ff.

[57] G. Arrigo, 'La Carta dei diritti fondamentali dell'Unione europea. Prime osservazioni', *Diritto del Lavoro* 2001, vol. I, pp. 191ff., here pp. 192–3.

[58] Sciarra, 'Diritti sociali', p. 405.

[59] The originality of the technique used in drawing up the Charter, innovatively centred around six fundamental values or principles, is emphasized by R. Bifulco, M. Cartabia and A. Celotto in their 'Introduzione' to their edited volume *L'Europa*, p. 15.

values of EU fundamental rights therefore means that solidarity has been adopted as a fundamental principle of the Community constitutional order.

Although mostly grouped in the chapter headed 'Solidarity', social rights are also given broad and widespread recognition in those headed 'Freedoms', 'Equality' and 'Citizens' Rights'. The indivisibility of civil, political and social rights is also perceptible in the transverse systematic grouping of these latter rights, itself effectively reproduced from the image of the 'reticular nature of European solidarity'.[60]

Despite the limitations and lacunae which are inevitable in a document palpably reflecting the difficulty of compromise and mediation sometimes experienced between different political and constitutional cultures,[61] the catalogue of social rights given express recognition in the EU Charter seems, overall, to be broad and robust. In articulating this catalogue in the various chapters of the Charter, the Convention drew extensively – and with a varying degree of freedom – on the main international sources accepted by the Member States[62] as well as on their constitutional traditions.

The resulting text is in some respects not without originality and in any event potential for innovation and further development even in comparison with those constitutional traditions (such as that of Italy) which are historically the richest and most detailed in terms of their recognition of social rights. One example is the right to protection in the event of unjustified dismissal (Article 30), adopted from Article 24 of the 1996 revised version of the 1961 European Social Charter but non-existent as such in the constitutions of the Member States with the sole exception of Portugal;[63] another is the right to information and consultation within the undertaking 'in good time' conferred on workers or their representatives by Article 27 of the Charter.

There is also – on a different level – the central importance assumed in the Nice Charter by issues related to combating poverty and social

---

[60] Sciarra, 'Diritti sociali', p. 405.

[61] Here, not for the first time, particular influence was wielded by UK hostility towards the notion of the full incorporation of social rights into a text likely to have priority constitutional relevance in the future of the Union: see B. Hepple, 'The EU Charter of Fundamental Rights', *Industrial Law Journal* 2001, vol. 30 no. 2, pp. 225–31.

[62] R. Foglia, 'La Carta dei diritti (sociali) fondamentali dell'Unione europea', *Rivista del Diritto della Sicurezza Sociale* 2001, pp. 6ff., especially p. 8, has spoken in this connection of a 'Communitization of the principles of international labour law'.

[63] Cf. A. Giorgis, 'Commento agli articoli 30 e 31', in Bifulco, Cartabia and Celotto, *L'Europa*, p. 223.

exclusion,[64] all of them re-stated in the language of fundamental rights from a perspective that was at least partly new, particularly for European welfare states of a Bismarckian stamp, and in terms that could prove to have innovative repercussions on the actual social-cohesion functions currently performed by the Community within a solely inter-State or regional dimension.

In this view of things, the right to social and housing assistance so as to ensure a decent existence for all those who lack sufficient resources as laid down in Article 34(3) of the Charter assumes all its importance as a principle in confirming in legally binding terms that ensuring everyone the material conditions of existence constitutes the essential precondition for the enjoyment of any civil or economic freedom that is guaranteed by Community sources.

The Charter has so far existed by virtue of its solemn proclamation by the EU political institutions, remaining formally outside the body of the Treaties in accordance with the programme established at the Cologne European Council in 1999. The question of its incorporation into the Treaties was to be decided by the 2003/2004 Intergovernmental Conference[65] in the context of the more general debate on the constitutional reform of the Union.[66]

As has been mentioned above and will be specified in more detail below, in the Treaty establishing a Constitution for Europe[67] the Nice Charter occupies the whole of Part II, which therefore signifies total acceptance of its content – albeit with certain questionable changes – as a normative text of full EU constitutional relevance. The constitutional Treaty as approved by the Intergovernmental Conference on 18 June 2004 and signed in Rome on 29 October 2004 will have to undergo a lengthy and very hazardous process of ratification over which there hang clouds heavy with profound political uncertainty, and not only because of the serious

---

[64] These are issues which were in fact incorporated into the Community agenda of the 1990s, whose centrality had already been strongly reaffirmed by the Lisbon European Council of 23–4 March 2000 and was subsequently emphasized by the new European Social Policy Agenda endorsed at Nice (particularly in the context of the third main policy area, namely, fighting all forms of exclusion and discrimination).

[65] See the Declaration on the future of the Union annexed to the Treaty of Nice, particularly its point 5, where it was stated that one of the key issues to be addressed by the debate on the constitutional reform of the Union was the status of the Charter of Fundamental Rights of the European Union, in accordance with the Cologne Conclusions. See also point 2 of the Presidency Conclusions of the Nice European Council.

[66] See J. Wouters, 'Institutional and Constitutional Challenges for the European Union. Some Reflections in the Light of the Treaty of Nice', European Law Review 2001, pp. 342ff.

[67] CIG 87/2/04 REV 2, Brussels 29 October 2004.

risks of a 'no' vote in the projected French referendum. Ratification by all of the present twenty-five Member States of the Union is obviously the *sine qua non* for it to be able to enter into force and so exert all its constitutional effectiveness. In the expectation and hope that this happens, the reflections expressed by the open community of European interpreters[68] on the 'paradoxical'[69] legal effectiveness of the Union Charter of Fundamental Rights as solemnly proclaimed at Nice probably remain wholly pertinent. Indeed, although founded solely on a solemn political proclamation, unlike the Community Charter of Fundamental Social Rights of Workers, the Nice Charter – by virtue of the procedure by which it was drafted and the philosophy governing its adoption – found a place at once in the European constitutional fabric as a document of immediate *legal* relevance.

It therefore still seems useful to reconstruct the significance and *legal* relevance of the Union Charter of Fundamental Rights in its form as a *political* document solemnly proclaimed at Nice, since in strictly formal terms that is what its status as yet remains, at least until such time as the constitutional Treaty enters into force through ratification by the twenty-five Member States. It is not improbable – as will also be mentioned later – that its incorporation into Part II of the constitutional Treaty may from now on, even prior to ratification, increase the chances of 'active' use of the Charter by the judges in Luxembourg in particular. Quite apart from this possibility, however, it remains important to stress that *with just its solemn proclamation in 2000* the Nice Charter has already taken on an undoubted *legal* relevance within the Community order.

The fact that the Nice Charter was adopted in the form of a solemn proclamation and hence as an essentially political act does not seem sufficient to justify likening it to precedents which are only apparently (or only superficially) analogous. A comparison with the experience of the 1989 Community Charter of Fundamental Social Rights of Workers based on the presumption that its act of adoption is of the same legally non-binding nature is therefore not feasible.[70]

The aspects which indicate – immediately, and leaving aside for the time being its incorporation into the constitutional Treaty – the different and greater *legal* relevance of the Nice Charter include, in addition to the

---

[68] P. Häberle, 'Die offene Gesellschaft der Verfassungsinterpreten', *Juristenzeitung* 1975, p. 297.

[69] M. Poiares Maduro, 'The Double Constitutional Life of the Charter of Fundamental Rights of the European Union', in Hervey and Kenner *Economic and Social Rights*, p. 269.

[70] As would appear to be suggested by Foglia, 'La Carta', p. 7.

difference in content, the total originality and novelty of the method that presided over its adoption. The 'as if' doctrine that inspired the drafting of the Charter[71] is capable of opening up broad scope for its immediate legal impact on the interpretative development of EU fundamental (social) rights and principles by the Court of Justice and the Court of First Instance.

In delineating its content from the outset 'as if' the Charter were to carry the full legal force of an authentic Community Bill of Rights, the Convention produced – as it has been tellingly put – a text of 'paraconstitutional' relevance,[72] immediately capable of 'becoming self-integrated' into the Treaties through the operation of interpretation.[73] Such an effect – likely to transcend the limits of a soft-law instrument technically imputable to the Charter as a legal document[74] – follows from its import as an act of recognition of the rights and values assumed by the European Union as the indispensable foundation of its democratic legitimacy.

Even by virtue of its solemn proclamation alone, the Nice Charter therefore already represents an inescapable 'document of European Union constitutional reference'.[75] In terms of its legal force in giving specific recognition to the common constitutional traditions of the Member States or to the fundamental rights and values to which they are pledged under the international sources they have accepted (starting with the 1950 Convention on Human Rights), the Charter can be and actually is already the subject of jurisprudential interpretation in the light of Articles 6(2) and 46 of the EU Treaty.[76]

---

[71] See G. De Búrca, 'The Drafting of the European Union Charter of Fundamental Rights', *European Law Journal* 2001, pp. 126ff., especially p. 128.

[72] Bifulco, Cartabia and Celotto, 'Introduzione', p. 31.

[73] Manzella, 'Dal mercato', pp. 38.

[74] See D. Curtin and R. Van Ooik, 'The Sting is Always in the Tail: The Personal Scope of Application of the EU Charter of Fundamental Rights', *Maastricht Journal of European and Comparative Law* 2001, pp. 102ff., especially pp. 110–11.

[75] Manzella, 'Dal mercato', p. 36; in the same sense, Rodotà, 'La Carta', p. 61; J. Dutheil de la Rochère, 'The Charter of Fundamental Rights and Beyond', *Cambridge Yearbook of European Legal Studies* 2001, vol. 4, pp. 133ff.; S. Douglas-Scott, 'The Charter of Fundamental Rights as a Constitutional Document', *European Human Rights Law Review* 2004, pp. 37ff.

[76] See Commission of the European Communities, *Communication from the Commission on the Legal Nature of the Charter of Fundamental Rights of the European Union*, COM(2000) 644 final of 11 October 2000. Among legal scholars there is a convergent view, albeit expressed with differing degrees of emphasis, that the Charter is thereby essentially binding: see, for example, M. Wathelet, 'La Charte des droits fondamentaux: un bon pas dans une course qui reste longue', *Cahiers de Droit Européen* 2000, nos. 5–6, pp. 585ff.; A. Vitorino, 'La Charte des droits fondamentaux de l'Union europénne', *Revue du Droit de l'Union Européenne* 2000, no. 3, pp. 499ff.; Lenaerts and De Smijter, 'A "Bill of Rights"', pp. 298–9

Consequently, it is no surprise that the Charter began 'immediately to develop some binding effect'.[77] In *BECTU* v *Secretary of State for Trade and Industry*,[78] Advocate General Tizzano turned to the Charter (which had only shortly before been proclaimed at Nice) for full confirmation of the fact that entitlement to paid annual leave constitutes a fundamental *social* right. He saw decisive proof of the recognition of such a right by the Community legal order in Article 31(2) of the Charter, on the presumption that the latter represents, in comparison with other declarations of rights, a form of solemn and specific codification of the principles and rights underpinning the supranational order.

In delivering judgment essentially in accordance with the Advocate General's Opinion, and stating in particular that protection of workers' right to health and safety at work should not be subordinated to purely economic considerations, the Court of Justice omitted, for understandable reasons of self-restraint, to make any explicit mention of the Charter. However, this does nothing to detract from the influence that the Nice Charter is capable of exerting in guiding and assisting the Court in the delicate task of extracting, from the general principles of Community law, the fundamental rights to which that law guarantees protection.

Moreover, the Court of First Instance has shown itself less reluctant than the Court of Justice to make explicit reference to the Charter. Particularly in two of its recent judgments it has turned specifically to the Nice Charter for the most authoritative confirmation that the right to good administration and the right to an effective remedy and a fair trial fall within the catalogue of fundamental rights recognized by the constitutional traditions common to the Member States.[79]

Be that as it may, there is particular significance in the fact that it is precisely in the field of fundamental social rights that the Nice Charter has made its appearance on the interpretation scene. This represents a

---

(where the Charter is described as 'a legally enforceable text'); De Witte, 'Legal Status', p. 84; A. J. Menéndez, 'Chartering Europe', *ARENA (Advanced Research on the Europeanisation of the Nation-State) Working Papers* No. 01/13 (who talks of law in force). For an opposing view, however, see U. De Siervo 'L'ambigua redazione della Carta dei diritti fondamentali nel processo di costituzionalizzazione dell'Unione europea', *Diritto Pubblico* 2001, pp. 33ff., especially pp. 45ff.

[77] Bifulco, Cartabia and Celotto, 'Introduzione', p. 24.

[78] ECJ Case C-173/99 [2001] ECR I-4881. See G. Ricci, '*BECTU*: An Unlimited Right to Annual Paid Leave', *Industrial Law Journal* 2001, pp. 401ff.

[79] See Court of First Instance Case T-54/99 *Max.mobil Telekommunikation Service GmbH* v *Commission* [2002] ECR II-313; Court of First Instance Case T-177/01 *Jégo-Quéré et Cie SA* v *Commission* [2002] ECR II-2365.

tangible sign of the potential for a strong 're-balancing' in this direction offered by the Charter.[80]

The fact remains, nonetheless, that this potential can obviously be realized to the full only if the constitutional Treaty, into which the Charter has been formally incorporated, is ratified by all Member States, with all the attendant consequences of the complete constitutionalization of fundamental social rights along with other fundamental rights in the Community legal order. This is an aspect that will be dealt with in more detail at the end of the present chapter, where the 'social' content of the Treaty establishing a Constitution for Europe will be analysed more closely.

4. European social policy after Amsterdam

It was stated earlier that the need to delineate an autonomous basis for Community action in the field of social policy first revealed itself in parallel with the impasse suffered by the model initially adopted by the Treaty of Rome[81] and became more acute as the gap widened in comparison with the progress achieved by the integration of the common market.

This need was made more pressing by the entry into force of the 1986 Single European Act. In introducing the qualified-majority rule in the case only of 'measures for the approximation of the provisions laid down by law, regulation or administrative action in Member States which have as their object the establishment and functioning of the internal market' (ex Article 100a, now Article 95 of the EC Treaty), the Act accentuated the 'minority status' of the social dimension of European integration at the very time when the increased dynamic of the transnational competitive process was for the first time directly lapping at the shores of the formerly protected territories of national labour-law systems.

Read in conjunction with Article 100a(2) of the Treaty,[82] Article 118a quickly revealed, even to scarcely disillusioned eyes, the 'optical illusion' effect[83] produced by the extension of the qualified-majority decision-making procedure to (only) measures aimed at improving the work

---

[80] Cf. Sciarra, 'Market Freedom'.   [81] See subsection 7 of chapter 1 above.

[82] According to which, as is well known, the qualified-majority rule (only formally representing a derogation from Article 100) introduced by the first paragraph of the same provision was *non*-applicable not only to fiscal provisions but also to 'those relating to the rights and interests of employed persons'.

[83] S. Sciarra, 'European Social Policies and Labour Law. Challenges and Perspectives', *Collected Courses of the Academy of European Law* 1995, vol. IV no. 1, pp. 301ff., here p. 317.

environment to protect workers' health and safety. However broadly construed by the Commission with essential endorsement from the Court of Justice,[84] this provision did not permit the surreptitious expansion of the qualified-majority rule to the entire range of (normative) working conditions also advocated by some for the precise purpose of achieving the longed-for goal of an equal extension of the Community bases for action in regard to market and social integration alike.

The Maastricht Treaty, in its turn, deepened the asymmetry between these two dimensions of European integration.

The Agreement on Social Policy (ASP) – which the UK's veto relegated to the status of a normative base binding on only eleven of the then twelve Member States – added a specific and totally new factor of asymmetry, or perhaps rather distortion, in this connection. The differentiation that it institutionalized was in accord with the notion of a Europe *à la carte* in which the legal space of an increasingly deregulated market (or, more accurately, one regulated more lightly at supranational level and less subject to hetero-correction at national level) constituted the sole common element unifying the Member States. By once again sanctioning the legitimacy of the United Kingdom's opt-out, the ASP amplified the intrinsic weakness and contradictory character of the idea of a social Europe *à la carte* already implicitly affirmed by the 1989 Community Charter, leaving 'the future of social policy as uncertain as ever' and that of EC social legislation 'as fragmented and marginalized' as ever.[85] The very idea of not only the possibility but the complete legitimacy of opportunistic self-exclusion of a Member State from the ties of a political and legal area so crucial for the fate of the single market and the Community project constitutes, indeed, the most obvious feature of the crisis of the original model of the Rome Treaty. It meant that social policy lost its role of regulating competition in the common market in line with preservation of the levels of protection guaranteed by the several national social systems: its implementation in accordance with the new basis offered by the ASP risked penalizing the competitive position of the Member States concerned, by rewarding the United Kingdom's free-riding.

Thus, at Maastricht social policy lost the unifying and standardizing role attributed to it by the founding fathers without, however, the new differentiation dynamic being able to rest on a common floor of fundamental

---

[84] See ECJ Case 84/94, *UK* v *Council* [1996] ECR I-5755.
[85] S. Deakin, 'Integration through Law? The Law and Economics of European Social Policy', in J. T. Addison and W. S. Siebert (eds.), *Labour Markets in Europe: Issues of Harmonization and Regulation*, London 1997, pp. 118ff., here p. 127.

rights and principles capable of fixing its insurmountable limits. This element of asymmetry, which in a sense marked a complete reversal of the original assumptions of the Treaty of Rome regarding the role and functions of social policy in the common market,[86] obscures – or at least blurs – the significant aspects of considerable novelty that were contained in the ASP.

In this context, the incorporation – under the Treaty of Amsterdam – of the provisions of the ASP into the text of the new Articles 136 et seq. of the EC Treaty mended the fracture arising from the UK's opt-out and eliminated the risks of 'regime shopping' (and hence of harmonization through the market) it had potentially triggered in that country's favour, by admitting into the Community social *acquis* the innovations already accepted by the other Member States.[87]

Among these innovations, the one that stands out most – apart from the significant increase in the scope of qualified-majority voting – is the quasi-legislative role assumed by the European social partners as a result of the possibility of assimilating into a Decision of the Council, acting on a proposal from the Commission, agreements reached between them in the areas envisaged by Article 137 of the Treaty.

Under the auspices of the ASP, in fact, in the course of the 1990s a new generation of Community social legislation had matured which was a long way away, in its methodological approach and content, from that characteristic of the beginnings of European social policy. The Treaty of Amsterdam made a decisive step in the direction of consolidating and strengthening this new path for Community social policy. And the Treaty of Nice subsequently reinforced such a tendency.

The rewording of Article 137 of the EC Treaty resulting from the amendment introduced at Nice,[88] more than anything else, signals the

---

[86] See Lord Wedderburn, 'European Community Law', especially pp. 258ff.; A. Lo Faro, 'Maastricht ed oltre. Le prospettive sociali dell'Europa comunitaria tra resistenze politiche, limiti giuridici ed incertezze istituzionali', *Diritto delle Relazioni Industriali* 1993, pp. 125ff., especially pp. 137ff.

[87] It is very significant in this connection that the legal base chosen for the extension to the United Kingdom, by Directive, of the social *acquis* developed between the other Member States by virtue of the ASP consisted of Article 100 (now 94) of the EC Treaty. In the Preamble of all the extension Directives it is stated that the United Kingdom's return to the social *acquis* will improve the functioning of the common market inasmuch as it removes a source of distortion of competition linked to the application of different standards: in other words, it removes opportunities for social dumping opened up, in the United Kingdom's favour, by the ASP itself. See Kenner, *EU Employment Law*, p. 383.

[88] The entry into force of the Treaty of Nice on 1 February 2003 following its ratification by the then fifteen Member States means that on the basis of the new Article 137 the Council, acting unanimously on a proposal from the Commission and after consulting the

abandonment of the rigid upward-harmonization model envisaged by the founding fathers in favour of the flexible reflexive-harmonization model[89] whose outlines had already emerged during the 1990s on the basis of the ASP.[90]

In the new text of Article 137 priority even in terms of the order in which they are mentioned is given to forms of intervention designed to give soft encouragement to co-operation between Member States through initiatives aimed at developing exchanges of information and best practices, promoting innovative approaches and benchmarking experiences, to the exclusion of any kind of harmonization of national legislative and regulatory provisions. By generalizing to the whole of social policy what had already been stated in this connection by the Treaty of Amsterdam as regards the integration of persons excluded from the labour market and the fight against social marginalization,[91] the new text of Article 137 thus establishes a kind of ideal bridge with the 'open method of co-ordination' of national employment policies dealt with in the previous Title VIII of the EC Treaty, giving explicit expression to the basic affinity, in terms of their underlying methods and principles, between the two formally autonomous normative blocs.

There is a perceptible intention here to make transparent the relationship of complementarity between the new functions assigned to the common social policy and the strategy of supranational co-ordination of national employment policies[92] which has in a way already been tested in

European Parliament, may decide to extend use of the co-decision procedure in accordance with Article 251 (which would involve qualified-majority voting) to the protection of workers where their employment contract is terminated, the representation and collective defence of workers' interests, and conditions of employment for third-country nationals who are legally resident in Community territory. On the other hand, the ability to extend the qualified-majority rule is still precluded in the area of social security and the social protection of workers, where the unanimity requirement has been controversially preserved by the Nice Treaty even in relation to the provisions on the co-ordination of national schemes as envisaged by Article 42 of the EC Treaty.

[89] See S. Deakin, 'Two Types of Regulatory Competition: Competitive Federalism versus Reflexive Harmonisation. A Law and Economics Perspective on *Centros*', *Cambridge Yearbook of European Legal Studies* 1999, vol. 2, pp. 231–60.

[90] This line of reasoning will be dealt with at more length in chapter 4 below.

[91] See ISAE – Istituto di Studi e Analisi Economica, *Rapporto sullo stato dell'Unione europea*, ed. F. Kostoris Padoa Schioppa, Bologna 2001, pp. 233–4.

[92] Cf. N. Bruun, 'The European Employment Strategy and the "Acquis Communitaire [*sic*]" of Labour Law', *International Journal of Comparative Labour Law and Industrial Relations* 2001, vol. 17 no. 3, pp. 309–24; see, however, in a partly different sense, D. Ashiagbor, 'Soft Harmonisation: Labour Law, Economic Theory and the European Employment Strategy', European University Institute PhD Thesis, Florence 2002, p. 129.

practice and is also emerging in programmatic terms in the 2000 European Social Agenda.

Thus, in the new text of Article 137(2) as amended by the Nice Treaty the possibility of adopting 'by means of Directives, minimum requirements for gradual implementation, having regard to the conditions and technical rules obtaining in each Member State' (subparagraph *b*) is 'postponed' until after the option – envisaged above it in subparagraph *a* – of encouraging voluntary co-operation between Member States. And while it may be true that the fact that the technique of co-operation is mentioned before that of harmonization by minimum-requirement Directives does not necessarily signify any hierarchy in the technical legal sense between the two methods,[93] there is no doubt that at policy level there is an outright preference for the less invasive forms of co-ordination, as indicated clearly by the Social Policy Agenda approved at Nice.[94]

What is more, as well as being excluded, as before, in the case of combating social exclusion hard-law (minimum) harmonization through Directives is also symptomatically excluded as regards the modernization of social-protection systems. The fight against exclusion and the modernization of social-protection systems are the two most recently emerging areas of European social policy and it is not by chance that they have also, even more recently, been brought within the domain (which tends to be exclusive) of open co-ordination. Where the national competences and prerogatives of Member States are most jealously preserved, Community action cannot but follow the logic of the open method of co-ordination.

In any event, the model of normative intervention envisaged in Article 137(2)(6) incorporates the notion, established during the 1990s as a reflection of the subsidiarity principle, that the harmonization of national labour-law systems was now to be regarded 'as a process of differentiation rather than one of imposing uniformity'.[95] 'Reflexive' harmonization

---

[93] In this sense Kenner, *EU Employment Law*, p. 499, who observes that the ambiguous expression 'co-operation' actually encompasses the essential aspects of the open method of co-ordination: 'the reference to "cooperation" rather than "coordination" suggests caution on the part of the Member States who are, perhaps, unwilling to constitutionalise the dynamic and flexible open method of coordination in the Treaty' (p. 500).

[94] Cf. COM(2000) 379 final, especially pp. 7 and 14. The Commission identifies the open method of co-ordination – from a viewpoint of dynamic application of the principle of subsidiarity – as the main means of achieving the Agenda's objectives. At the same time, it emphatically confirms: 'The new Social Policy Agenda does not seek to harmonise social policies.' See, in more detail, subsection 7 below.

[95] M. D'Antona, 'Mercato unico europeo ed aree regionali deboli: le conseguenze giuridiche', *Lavoro e Diritto* 1992, pp. 49ff., here p. 58.

differs radically from the 'constructivist' harmonization prototype originally envisaged precisely because, rather than setting out to make national systems uniform by shaping them to the model that is deemed functionally better, it seeks to open up space for autonomy and differentiation while at the same time avoiding – on the basis of an acceptance of common principles and values – forms of downward regulatory competition.[96]

Although leaving ample space for comparison and hence competition between different national schemes reflexive harmonization, which in this respect operates not unlike the open mechanism of co-ordination of employment and social policies, seeks, in fact, to prevent – thanks to the establishment of common general principles – 'non-co-operative' forms of undesirable downward competition between systems. The idea, therefore, is no longer that harmonization should put 'an end to regulatory competition as such' but rather that it should 'preserve a space for local-level experimentation and adaptation', contrary to 'the "levelling-down" agenda of negative harmonization'[97] guided by the market. This is the leitmotiv which, despite the diversity of the areas of intervention involved and the concrete goals underlying their normative content, unites the new-generation Directives and, in particular, those of them that are the products of the European social dialogue.

A particularly illustrative example is offered by the Directives on part-time work and fixed-term work.[98] As qualified fruits of the European social dialogue, they incorporate framework agreements based on a logic of considerable national-system autonomy while stating basic principles that enrich the patrimony of rights and guarantees offered to 'atypical' workers.[99]

---

[96] See also subsection 4 of chapter 4 below.

[97] C. Barnard and S. Deakin, 'In Search of Coherence: Social Policy, the Single Market and Fundamental Rights', *Industrial Relations Journal – European Annual Review* 1999/2000, pp. 121–41, here p. 134.

[98] These are, respectively, Directive 97/81/EC and Directive 99/70/EC.

[99] Cf. S. Giubboni and S. Sciarra, 'Introduzione', *Giornale di Diritto del Lavoro e di Relazioni Industriali* 2000, no. 4, special issue entitled *La regolamentazione del part-time in Europa*, pp. 547ff.; B. Caruso, 'Alla ricerca della "flessibilità mite": il terzo pilastro delle politiche del lavoro comunitarie', *Diritto delle Relazioni Industriali* 2000, pp. 141ff., especially p. 146; A. Perulli, 'Interessi e tecniche di tutela nella disciplina del lavoro flessibile', in Associazione Italiana di Diritto del Lavoro, *Interessi e tecniche nella disciplina del lavoro flessibile*, Atti delle giornate di studio di Diritto del lavoro Pesaro-Urbino 24–25 May 2002, Milan 2003, pp. 39ff. More generally, see the recent comparative study edited by S. Sciarra, P. Davies and M. Freedland, *Employment Policy and the Regulation of Part-time Work in the European Union. A Comparative Analysis*, Cambridge 2004.

The ability to opt for a wide range of different routes, instruments and forms of implementation, defined in relation to the specific nature of the national contexts, features very frequently, whereas provisions capable of producing the traditional vertical direct effects to which the major Directives of the 1970s had accustomed us are now increasingly absent.

The European Works Council Directive exemplifies a measure aimed at co-ordinating rather than harmonizing national systems,[100] along lines also developed – albeit with different techniques and goals – by other more recent Community normative measures.[101]

Broad scope for choice within the framework of a menu of options mindful of the diversity of national industrial-relations models is now provided for by Directive 2001/86 supplementing the Statute for a European company with regard to the involvement of employees. Likewise, in fixing general criteria the more recent Directive 2002/14, which establishes a general framework for informing and consulting employees in undertakings within the European Community, requires the Member States to define the detailed formalities ensuring exercise of the rights of 'employees' representatives'. In the first of these two Directives in particular, there is an obvious influence of the 'procedural track' of the European Works Council Directive, visible in the priority importance given to the 'negotiation route'.[102]

It is undeniable that this model of flexible and light harmonization, in which the traditional hard-law form is toned down in the preceptive content to leave space for differentiation, is not immune from limitations and risks, and in particular that of exerting too weak an influence on national systems. Directives often come to resemble – in their concrete content, if not in form, which is still binding on the basis of Article 249 of the

---

[100] Directive 94/45/EC, subsequently extended to the UK under Directive 97/74/EC; cf. W. Streeck, 'Il modello sociale europeo: dalla redistribuzione alla solidarietà competitiva', *Stato e Mercato* 2000, pp. 3ff., especially p. 11.

[101] The system of co-ordination of national schemes is adopted by Directive 98/49/EC on safeguarding the supplementary pension rights of employed and self-employed persons moving within the Community, while the Posted Workers Directive (96/71/EC) mentioned earlier adopts a similar logic of 'synchronization' of national systems; see, respectively, S. Giubboni, 'Previdenza complementare e mercato unico. Cenni al quadro normativo comunitario', *Industria e Sindacato* 2000, no. 4, pp. 11ff., and E. Kolehmainen, 'The Directive Concerning the Posting of Workers: Synchronization of the Functions of National Legal Systems', *Comparative Labor Law and Policy Journal* 1998, vol. 20, pp. 71ff.

[102] M. Roccella and T. Treu, *Diritto del lavoro della Comunità europea*, 3rd edn, Padua 2002, p. 390.

EC Treaty – flexible recommendations which articulate general principles and cannot effectively constrain Member States to fulfil obligations that are left too open and unspecified.

This is precisely the reason why it seems increasingly necessary to anchor European social policy to a solid core of fundamental principles endowed with the maximum level of protection by the Community legal order. To quote the lucid warning given by Massimo D'Antona immediately after the Maastricht Treaty was signed, 'no legal order which wants to remain unitary can accommodate processes of decentralization and differentiation without fixing a basic plank of central values or, perhaps rather, fundamental rights and principles that are not, as such, susceptible to differentiation.'[103]

Consequently, a strategy aimed at achieving full constitutionalization of fundamental social rights and principles of the European Union remains the necessary complement of, or indispensable normative precondition for, a Community social policy which, in deference to the requirements imposed by subsidiarity, increasingly follows the strategy of reflexive harmonization and open co-ordination of national systems. Possibly even more in this sphere than in others, only a base strongly rooted in common fundamental principles seems able to guarantee the necessary 'unity in diversity',[104] acting as 'the necessary counterweight to the greater decentralization'[105] and differentiation within social policies demanded by due respect for diverse national identities.

5. The new strategy of supranational 'open' co-ordination of Member States' employment and social policies

The European Employment Strategy, as a first and precocious supranational open method of co-ordination of national employment policies regulated by the new Title VIII of the EC Treaty which, as agreed at the Extraordinary Meeting of the European Council in Luxembourg in November 1997, was put into effect some eighteen months before actual

---

[103] D'Antona, 'Mercato unico', p. 59.

[104] So runs the motto coined to express the sense of the course currently being followed by Europe; see N. Fontaine, *Speech Following the Presentation of the Motto for Europe: 'Europe: Unity in Diversity'* of 4 May 2000 (available at http://europarl.eu.int/president/speeches/en/sp0034.htm).

[105] Hepple, 'Towards a European Constitution', p. 298, in the same sense see Lo Faro, 'Maastricht ed oltre', pp. 133–5.

ratification,[106] perhaps represents the Treaty of Amsterdam's most significant and original institutional innovation. Strongly advocated by the newly elected French delegation in order to re-balance the Stability and Growth Pact negotiated at Dublin, it bears the clear marks of the cultural influence of the Scandinavian experience as well as a certain ideal affinity with the new Labour approach of a Blairite UK.[107] It is precisely in this that the effectiveness of the open method of co-ordination (later extended to other sensitive domains of social policy) lies, i.e. in its intrinsic adaptability and its apparently ambiguous capacity to reflect and at the same time enable the co-existence of ideological and policy stances which, although sharing the intention to restore the issue of employment to the centre of the European political agenda, nevertheless differ greatly from each other.

The Title on Employment is also a response – in the first instance – to the need for the Community's political and symbolic relegitimation that is likewise served by the affirmations, as mentioned earlier, of the 'attachment' of the Member States and supranational institutions to the fundamental social rights of workers introduced by the Treaty of Amsterdam. The specific purpose of elevating the creation of a high level of employment to the ranks of the Community's general and primary objectives (Article 2 of the EC Treaty) was to re-balance the underlying principles of the European economic constitution,[108] albeit without questioning the primacy of the objectives of monetary stability and permanent macroeconomic rigour as confirmed (and indeed corroborated) by the Stability and Growth Pact.

The new system of supranational co-ordination creates the premises for a reduction of the 'institutional gap'[109] between the Community's monetary objectives and employment objectives. However, the latter are still left subordinate to the former, in the belief that there no longer exists, save possibly in the illusory and fleeting contingency of the short term, any trade-off between inflation and unemployment. 'In no way should the shaping of the European employment and social policies be alternative to

---

[106] For a summary account of events see J. Goetschy, 'The European Employment Strategy: Genesis and Development', *European Journal of Industrial Relations* 1999, no. 2, pp. 117ff.

[107] See M. A. Pollack, 'A Blairite Treaty. Neo-Liberalism and Regulated Capitalism in the Treaty of Amsterdam', in K. Neunreither and A. Wiener (eds.), *European Integration after Amsterdam. Institutional Dynamics and Prospects for Democracy*, Oxford 2000, pp. 266ff.

[108] Cf. Barbera, *Dopo Amsterdam*, p. 128.

[109] F. Snyder, 'EMU Revisited: Are We Making a Constitution? What Constitution Are We Making?', *EUI Working Papers in Law* No. 98/6, p. 75.

economic and monetary policies':[110] it must obviously remain 'consistent' (Articles 126(1) and 128(1) of the EC Treaty) with them and combine with them in moulding a framework conducive to growth.

It is nonetheless evident that affirming a high level of employment as an objective – in conjunction with provision for an innovative political and institutional procedure – is aimed at producing the effect of re-establishing an element of *reciprocal* consistencies between the Union's macropolicies. In this sense, it can rightly be said that Article 125 of the Treaty contains 'a rule on transverse or reticular action whereby the objective of a high level of employment is to be taken into account in the definition of Community policies'.[111]

The gradual development – starting from the Cologne Summit in December 1999 – of a macroeconomic dialogue that adopts the creation of more and better jobs as a priority objective, co-ordinated with that of maintaining sound and sustainable public finances, is closely linked to the more general question of strengthening the Union's institutions and sites of economic governance in the face of the competence conferred on the European Central Bank.

Nevertheless, the differences in depth and weight between the powers involved in the different 'poles' are still evident, given that – albeit in a context that is proving increasingly conducive to moderating and 'softening', at least through interpretation, the rigidity of the Stability and Growth Pact[112] – the macroeconomic dimension of employment policies remains weak.[113]

The Presidency Conclusions of the Lisbon Summit of March 2000 have been seen as embodying the re-emergence of a neo-Keynesian language and approach, visible above all 'in the recovery of a positive view of the relationship between economic growth and employment, with full

---

[110] T. Treu, 'The Role of a European Social Policy', in Engels and Weiss, *Labour Law*, pp. 439–59, here p. 456.

[111] Predieri, *Euro*, p. 399.

[112] See M. J. Artis and M. Buti, '"Close-to-Balance or in Surplus". A Policy-Maker's Guide to the Implementation of the Stability and Growth Pact', *Journal of Common Market Studies* 2000, pp. 563ff., especially p. 564. A significant pointer in the direction of interpretative moderation of the rigidity of the Stability and Growth Pact is provided by the recent decision of the Ecofin Council to attribute greater importance, from 2003 onwards, to the structural deficit as compared with the nominal deficit in assessing compliance with the relevant parameters. See G. Della Cananea, 'Dal vecchio al nuovo Patto di stabilità', *Giornale di Diritto Amministrativo* 2004, no. 2, pp. 221ff.

[113] Cf. S. Deakin and H. Reed, 'The Contested Meaning of Labour Market Flexibility. Economic Theory and the Discourse of European Integration', in Shaw, *Social Law*, pp. 71ff., especially p. 99.

employment and the reduction of regional disparities being fixed anew as realistic goals'.[114] The deepening of the link between economic policies and employment policies – with the progressive emergence of quantitative parameters for defining the basic objectives of the latter as well[115] – certainly signals a positive move beyond rigidly monetarist and liberalist approaches in which labour policy tends to boil down to deregulation and the dismantling of forms of protection.[116]

Although essentially inspired by the idea that the primary means of opposing marginalization is inclusion in the labour market through active policies, the more recent extension of the open method of co-ordination to the area of the fight against social exclusion is also intended to focus Community attention on the more traditional question of the redistribution of economic resources in favour of persons who are excluded.[117]

However, in the 'pillars' and 'guidelines' (re)drawn up each year by the Council in the context of the open co-ordination of Member States' employment policies the emphasis is mainly on supply-side measures,[118] even though there is an increasingly evident endeavour to restore the structural modernization of labour markets and associated systems of social protection to a point of balance between flexibility and security, efficiency and solidarity.[119] Following the Lisbon European Council there has been, in particular, a renewed emphasis on the *quality* of work and

---

[114] Barbera, *Dopo Amsterdam*, p. 144, who goes as far as describing the Conclusions as 'a kind of neo-Keynesian manifesto'.

[115] Cf. ISAE, *Rapporto*, p. 214.

[116] The objective of strengthening organic interaction between Union and Member State macropolicies, in particular by convening a special annual session of the European Council dedicated to economic and social problems, is also spelled out in the 2000 European Social Agenda. The Stockholm European Council of 23–4 March 2001 was the occasion of the first annual spring meeting on social and economic issues; for a somewhat critical examination of its Conclusions, see ISAE, *Rapporto*, pp. 251ff.

[117] It is no accident that, in the context of combating exclusion, the current European Social Agenda places the focus on the minimum resources that must be guaranteed by national systems of social protection. In their two-year plans for combating poverty and social exclusion, Member States must also render account of the extent to which they have implemented Recommendation 92/441/EEC concerning sufficient resources and social assistance. This – as well as the provisions of the Charter of Fundamental Rights of the European Union discussed earlier – evidences the rediscovery of a redistributive dimension of the solidaristic functions fulfilled by national systems of social protection.

[118] See, in a critical sense, Deakin and Reed, 'The Contested Meaning', pp. 88 and 90–2, and also D. Ashiagbor, 'EMU and the Shift in the European Labour Agenda: From "Social Policy" to "Employment Policy"', *European Law Journal* 2001, pp. 311ff., especially pp. 322ff.

[119] Cf. S. Giubboni, 'Flessibilità delle forme di lavoro e protezione sociale. Note introduttive', *Rivista del Diritto della Sicurezza Sociale* 2002, no. 2, pp. 419ff.

industrial relations in a context of social cohesion, as a qualifying aspect of the adaptability pillar.[120]

In the context of the procedure of open co-ordination and peer review of implementation of the guidelines, Community-level governance assigns itself a mainly 'driving' and 'enabling' role,[121] one of actively encouraging the reform of national labour markets and their associated social-protection systems but without undertaking direct regulatory functions. The Community puts itself forward as a forum for the discussion and dissemination of the most innovative approaches to promoting employment and fighting unemployment, through the exchange of information on national best practices and the promotion and 'comparative' assessment of the best experiences.

The Commission, assisted together with the Council by the new Employment Committee (Article 130 of the EC Treaty), is thus consolidating its assumption of the institutional role of a catalyst for change[122] towards which it was more and more insistently motivated and directed during the 1990s in the field of social and employment policies.[123]

The guidelines for employment policies drawn up annually by the Council constitute a new, sophisticated and very persuasive form of soft law which at the same time, in observance of the subsidiarity principle (Article 127(1) of the EC Treaty), leaves the Member States' primary regulatory competences intact. Any form of harmonization via hard law is excluded: co-ordination implies co-operation between Member States which is by definition horizontal and non-hierarchical, in accordance with a model that has been persuasively defined as 'co-ordinative governance

---

[120] This is underlined, albeit in the context of a critical overall assessment, by Ashiagbor, 'Soft Harmonisation', p. 182.

[121] J. Kenner, 'The EC Employment Title and the "Third Way": Making Soft Law Work?', *International Journal of Comparative Labour Law and Industrial Relations* 1999, vol. 15 no. 1, pp. 33–60, especially p. 35, talks of the 'enabling role' of the Community institutions.

[122] See, for example, S. Milner, 'Training Policy. Steering Between Divergent National Logics', in D. Hine and H. Kassim (eds.), *Beyond the Market: The EU and National Social Policy*, London-New York 1998, p. 156.

[123] This refers in particular to the Commission's 1993 White Paper on *Growth, Competitiveness, Employment: The Challenges and Ways Forward into the 21st Century* and to its 1993 Green Paper on *European Social Policy: Options for the Union* (COM(93)551) and 1994 White Paper on *European Social Policy: A Way Forward for the Union* (COM(94)333), in which – as significantly observed by the then Commissioner for Social Affairs and Employment Pádraig Flynn – it basically assumed the function of a 'clearing house for information and catalyst for action' (as termed by L. Hantrais, *Social Policy in the European Union*, London 1995, p. 207, from whom the quotation is taken).

by non-hierarchical means'.[124] Although exposed to the risk of a political sanction in the form of a possible individual recommendation as envisaged by Article 128(4) of the EC Treaty, Member States are not under any directly binding obligation to observe the guidelines drawn up by the Council.[125]

However, the iterative nature of the procedure, which is repeated in circular fashion year by year,[126] strengthens the ability of Community guidelines to penetrate national policy practices. The participatory and circular method of drawing up the guidelines progressively reinforces their ability to exert a concrete influence on the Member States' voluntary choices precisely inasmuch as it increasingly highlights the autonomous nature of the option they adopt, albeit within a shared and common framework.[127]

The 'plasma' metaphor suggested by Predieri[128] with respect to those products of Community soft law which, although not binding in strictly formal terms, acquire growing practical political relevance, seems particularly apt in the case of the employment guidelines. There is no doubt that the European Employment Strategy has contributed to pushing forward a number of reforms at national level.[129] As one author has put it, 'the commitment to compare and evaluate national policies with a view to sharing information about "best practices", and to promoting "innovative approaches" . . ., creates conditions that are conducive to the joint

---

[124] G. Thompson, 'Governing the European Economy. A Framework for Analysis', in Thompson (ed.), *Governing the European Economy*, London 2001, pp. 1ff., here p. 14.

[125] Cf. M. Biagi, 'L'applicazione del Trattato di Amsterdam in materia di occupazione: coordinamento o convergenza?', *Diritto delle Relazioni Industriali* 1998, pp. 437ff., who, on the other hand, criticizes the attempts at hegemony demonstrated to some extent in its application practice by the Commission, which do not follow the spirit (and letter) of the provisions in the Treaty of Amsterdam stamped by the construction of 'a peer-pressure system aimed at the co-ordination of Member States' employment policies'.

[126] The simile is suggested by Sciarra, 'Market Freedom', p. 20, who emphasizes that the flexible institutional structure of co-ordination follows a 'circular geometry'.

[127] Cf. D. M. Trubek and J. S. Mosher, 'EU Governance, Employment Policy, and the European Social Model', *Jean Monnet Working Paper, New York University School of Law* No. 15/01; more recently Trubek and Mosher, 'New Governance, Employment Policy, and the European Social Model', in J. Zeitlin and D. M. Trubek (eds.), *Governing Work and Welfare in a New Economy. European and American Experiments*, Oxford 2003, pp. 33ff.

[128] Predieri, *Euro*, pp. 365–6, who explains that in physics 'plasma' means 'a different or fourth state of the aggregation of matter distinct from the traditional states (solid, liquid and gaseous)'.

[129] See Commission of the European Communities, *Taking Stock of Five Years of the European Employment Strategy*, COM (2002) 416 final.

discussion of structures and causes of employment problems, and to the joint exploration of employment policy options at the national level.'[130] It therefore offers 'opportunities for "deliberative" interactions'[131] between all the actors involved, in forms that have rightly been described as dialogue or, more accurately, a multi-language legal discourse,[132] a 'communicative system open enough to include simultaneously the voices of different speakers, and sufficiently understandable for the ears of all those listening'.[133] This is obviously not a dialogue or discourse solely between different 'public' institutions, between the various levels of government (supranational, national, regional and local) of the multitiered system. The involvement of the social partners is constantly sought (even if not always satisfactorily achieved), since their contribution is essential to the feasibility of any concerted strategy for re-regulating labour markets and modernizing European social-protection systems.[134]

At the same time – and this is an equally significant aspect – the multilateral co-ordination and monitoring of national employment policies can now 'for the first time, provide some safeguards against the temptation of all countries to protect domestic jobs through "beggar-my-neighbour" policies, competitive deregulation, and tax cuts.'[135] They represent, in a way, a type of insurance against the most harmful forms of regulatory competition, i.e. potential moves towards the removal of protection and/or distortional social-devaluation practices.[136] From this point of view, the co-ordination of employment and, more recently, social-inclusion policies represents a co-operative response to the risks of a deregulatory spiral arising from forms of regime competition unable to break free of the selfish trap of the prisoner's dilemma.[137]

---

[130] F. W. Scharpf, *Governing in Europe: Effective and Democratic?*, Oxford 1999, pp. 159–60.

[131] *Ibid.*, p. 159.

[132] S. Sciarra, 'The Employment Title in the Amsterdam Treaty: A Multi-Language Legal Discourse', in D. O'Keeffe and P. Twomey (eds.), *Legal Issues of the Amsterdam Treaty*, Oxford 1999, p. 157.

[133] *Ibid.*, p. 160.

[134] See Commission of the European Communities, *A Concerted Strategy for Modernising Social Protection*, COM(1999) 347 final.

[135] Scharpf, *Governing in Europe*, p. 159.

[136] This aspect is also emphasized by Kenner, 'The EC', p. 51.

[137] With the euro now a common currency, the co-ordination of bargaining and pay policies by the European trade-union organizations could symmetrically represent a useful co-operative response to the risks of deflationary spirals inherent in 'beggar-my-neighbour' forms of competition in the euro zone. On the numerous obstacles standing in the way of such a prospect see, however, J. Visser, 'Bargaining in Euros – What Should Unions Do?', in Engels and Weiss, *Labour Law*, pp. 461–88, here pp. 480ff.

However, if the eminently procedural effort to co-ordinate national regulatory policies is to be able to realize all of its potential virtuous effects, a constant dialectic link needs to be maintained with the fundamental social principles and values recently proclaimed by the Charter of Fundamental Rights of the European Union and now re-affirmed by the Treaty establishing a Constitution for Europe.

A connection in this sense is clearly perceptible in the progressive refinement of the content of the 'pillar' on the transverse or, more accurately, 'mainstreaming' horizontal relevance of policies on sex equality and equal opportunities. But the aforesaid dialectic link must be constantly cultivated and deepened in all of the areas affected by the employment guidelines, in order to give substance to the idea of high-quality employment that can effectively reconcile the demands of flexibility with the fundamental values of the security and freedom of workers.[138] The current discussion initiated by the Commission on the rationalization and simplification of the European Employment Strategy seems to be effectively moving in this direction.[139]

6. The Treaty establishing a Constitution for Europe . . .

On 18 June 2004, bringing to an end an Intergovernmental Conference (IGC) launched in the worst of circumstances by the Italian Presidency,[140] the Heads of State or Government of the European Union finally arrived at political agreement on the text of the Treaty establishing a Constitution for Europe, which was eventually signed in Rome on 29 October 2004. The final text of the constitutional Treaty largely mirrors the text drawn up earlier by the European Convention presided over by Valéry Giscard d'Estaing, although not without some major changes[141] found necessary – after the initial breakdown of negotiations – to enable agreement to be reached within the IGC. Following its official signing, the constitutional Treaty faces perhaps its most difficult test: in this case more than ever

---

[138] This point is taken up again in subsection 8 of the present chapter and in subsection 8 of chapter 4 below.

[139] See Commission of the European Communities COM(2002) 487 final.

[140] See S. Giubboni, 'Diritti e politiche sociali nella crisi europea', *Quaderni di Rassegna Sindacale* 2004, no. 1, pp. 23ff. For a broader analysis of the social content of the constitutional Treaty see also Giubboni, 'Lavoro e diritti sociali nella "nuova" Costituzione europea', *URGE (Unità di Ricerca sulla Governance Europea) Working Paper* No. 5/2004, at www.urge.it.

[141] See, for a critical evaluation, G. Amato, 'Dai veleni dell'astensionismo all'agrodolce del nuovo Trattato', *Il Sole 24 Ore*, 20 June 2004.

before, the lengthy process of ratification looks fraught with uncertainties and risks. The threat of rejection, especially in those countries where a national referendum is to be held, is very great nowadays, as demonstrated by, *inter alia*, the widespread feeling of disillusionment and in some cases open disaffection towards the Union manifested by the outcome of the recent European Parliament elections.

Non-ratification of the constitutional Treaty would open up scenarios which are difficult to foresee and for that reason alone are disquieting. No attempt will therefore be made here to essay predictions about a future that is open and unforeseeable as never before; instead, the concluding pages of this chapter will be confined to presenting a critical examination of the 'social' content of the Treaty establishing a Constitution for Europe.

Nor, now that its endorsement within the IGC and its official signing means that the Treaty has acquired a definitive character, will the process of its 'quasi-democratic' drawing-up by the European Convention[142] be analysed in detail. In the matter that is of interest to us here the differences between the text approved by the European Convention and that which has emerged from the IGC are not, in point of fact, particularly significant. It therefore seems right to concentrate all our critical attention on what we are now presented with as the final outcome of this admittedly lengthy, intense, troubled and absolutely fascinating process.

Overall, the Treaty establishing a Constitution for Europe seems stamped by a cautious consolidation of the *acquis* gradually built up in the social field from the Treaty of Amsterdam onwards. The Working Group on Social Europe that was eventually set up more with the intention of remedying an embarrassing formal gap than of opening up a new and substantive stage of debate did not make any genuinely innovative proposals, and the European Constitution has ended up by mirroring, in its wording, the prudent and cautious approach that had been characteristic of the earlier Convention.

This is not to say, naturally, that the body of the constitutional Treaty as a whole does not entail what amount to far-reaching new developments in the field of social rights and policies. The fact that the incorporation of the Nice Charter in Part II of the Constitution for Europe did not ultimately meet with any significant resistance must not allow us to forget that such an

---

[142] For an in-depth examination of the work of the European Convention on the Future of Europe, with special reference to the social dimension, see E. Gabaglio, 'L'Europa sociale nella Convenzione europea', *Quaderni di Rassegna Sindacale* 2004, no. 1, pp. 65ff.

outcome – of absolute importance for the purposes of effective recognition of social rights as fundamental rights in the EU legal order – was far from being a foregone conclusion: it should therefore rightly be seen as 'one of the most spectacular results of the 2003 draft'.[143] Throughout the work of the IGC this extraordinary outcome – difficult to imagine even up to only a few years ago[144] – was not, however, cast in any doubt, a sign that it has come to be regarded as an essential and now inviolable aspect of the constitutionalization of social Europe.[145]

Nonetheless, there is at the same time a danger of the constitutional Treaty also consolidating – and in that sense making it difficult to reverse – a number of the historical weaknesses of this slow and laborious process of the affirmation of social Europe. It is in the most long-standing and classic of its areas – that of social policy in the strict sense, and more particularly harmonization policies – that these weaknesses are most evident. So it is from this aspect that it is appropriate to begin, in the concluding pages of the present chapter, our critical analysis of the Treaty establishing a Constitution for Europe.

7. . . . The constitutional Treaty and social policy . . .

It is now a common observation that in the 'new paradigm for social policy'[146] the space for harmonization of the several national systems – central to the model delineated by the Treaty of Rome – has progressively dwindled, if not totally disappeared. The idea of common models of the protection of working conditions being imposed heteronomously, even if only within the circumscribed limits that had been stipulated in order to equalize the conditions of competition and prevent the associated distortions, very quickly proved incompatible with actual developments in the integration process.

Already in crisis from the early 1980s onwards, the 'upward' harmonization model – possibly always a myth rather than a reality – became largely superseded when the Single European Act was adopted. The 1990s

---

[143] J. Ziller, *La nuova Costituzione europea*, Bologna 2003, p. 17.

[144] Cf. M. Weiss, 'The Politics of the EU Charter of Fundamental Rights', in Hepple, *Social and Labour Rights*, pp. 73ff.

[145] S. Sciarra, 'La constitutionnalisation de l'Europe sociale, entre droits sociaux fonda mentaux et soft law', in O. De Schutter and P. Nihoul (eds.), *Une Constitution pour l'Europe. Réflexions sur les transformations du droit de l'Union européenne*, Brussels 2004, pp. 171ff.

[146] E. Szyszczak, 'The New Paradigm for Social Policy: A Virtuous Circle?', *Common Market Law Review* 2001, vol. 38, pp. 1125–70.

therefore witnessed the progressive prevalence of a social-policy model which tends to eschew harmonization and focuses instead on co-ordination, reflexive self-regulation by the social partners and light regulation that is on principle of a mainly procedural slant.

In the 2000 Social Policy Agenda this lengthy process of transformation of the foundational paradigm of Community social policy would appear to have reached its completion. The European Commission states unreservedly that 'the new Social Policy Agenda does not seek to harmonise social policies. It seeks to work towards common European objectives and increase co-ordination of social policies in the context of the internal market and the single currency.'[147]

In this new context, the main instrument of action in social matters has become – as has already been mentioned and will also be repeated later[148] – the open method of co-ordination, in all its increasingly sophisticated variants. The open method of co-ordination now occupies, in a sense, the central position which in the original model was occupied by the harmonization of social policies (or, more accurately, legislation). 'The Open Method of Co-ordination has now become the instrument of choice for overall policy orientation',[149] the *general* method of social governance in Europe.

The major enlargement of the Union towards the East has now added even more cogent arguments in support of the notion of intervention marked by a light regulatory touch and the greatest possible respect for national differences. There is general consensus among commentators that the differences in economic development and levels of social-protection standards between the old and the new members of the European Union are so marked[150] as to make the idea of pursuing social cohesion in forced stages, by imposing rigid normative obligations, simply unthinkable, let alone impracticable.

The new paradigm has so profoundly shaped the very view of the role and functions of European intervention with regard to social policy that the age-old problem of the limits of Community legislative competence in this field now seems largely resolved. After having dominated both theoretical debate and actual proposals for reform at least throughout the 1980s and much of the 1990s, the question of the limits of legislative

---

[147] COM(2000) 379 final, p. 7, already mentioned at note 94 above.
[148] See chapter 4 below.
[149] N. Bernard, 'A New Governance Approach to Economic, Social and Cultural Rights in the EU', in Hervey and Kenner, *Economic and Social Rights*, pp. 247ff., here p. 263.
[150] Cf. T. Boeri and F. Coricelli, *Europa: più grande o più unita?*, Rome-Bari 2003.

competence and the closely connected issue of the extension of qualified-majority voting appear to have lost their interest and importance. Indeed, the Final Report of the European Convention's Working Group XI on Social Europe[151] regards it as an outdated problem that is now a thing of the past, a question that has been largely settled.

In the Report it is recognized that the range of Community legislative powers in the social field is sufficient and adequate for the purposes of action on the part of the supranational institutions. In so far as Community action is essentially aimed at supporting and complementing that of the Member States, in the eyes of Working Group XI the present legislative powers are therefore sufficient and their exercise should be essentially confined to those fields most directly affecting the functioning of the internal market, for the dual purpose of preventing distortions of competition and assisting transfrontier activities.

This is clearly a particularly narrow view which amounts, *inter alia*, to reinstating the old rationale of European social policy as an anti-dumping instrument of regulation/equalization of the conditions of competition in the single market, and also a step backwards from the idea of social policy as a 'factor of production' which, especially after Lisbon, now marks the new path of events in the Commission's documents.[152]

On the subject of procedures – i.e. the possible extension of qualified-majority voting into numerous sectors still subject to the unanimity rule – the Working Group on Social Europe evinces an undoubtedly more problematic and open approach. The weak prospect of the future generalization of qualified-majority voting is not, however, accompanied by correspondingly innovative proposals. In this case too, the reasonable compromise reached with the Treaty of Nice – not long previously entered into force – features, all things considered, as the point of arrival of essentially satisfactory progress that can be developed only to a very limited extent.

This basic caution on the part of the Working Group on Social Europe is inevitably reflected in the provisions of the draft Treaty establishing a constitution for Europe, as approved first by the European Convention and then by the IGC.[153]

---

[151] *Final Report of the Working Group XI on Social Europe*, CONV 516/1/03 REV 1, WG XI N9, Brussels 4 February 2003.
[152] See J. Hunt, 'Fair and Just Working Conditions', in Hervey and Kenner, *Economic and Social Rights*, pp. 45ff., especially p. 56.
[153] The reference is to CIG 87/2/04 REV 2.

The legal bases of EU action, and hence the actual limits of supra-national legislative competence in the field of social policy, remain unchanged in the Constitution for Europe. First and foremost, therefore, the exclusions currently envisaged by paragraph 6 of the Nice-amended text of Article 137 of the Treaty establishing the European Community are still in place. Article III-210 of the Treaty establishing a Constitution for Europe does not apply – as its paragraph 6 continues to state – 'to pay, the right of association, the right to strike or the right to impose lock-outs'.

The sharp contradiction of excluding issues which are absolutely central to the very fabric of fundamental social rights as recognized in Part II of the constitutional Treaty is thus left unresolved; meaning that it is, as it were, definitively enshrined and constitutionalized as a specific and characteristic identifying feature of European Union labour law. The Union will therefore continue, in the future, to lack powers which are surely indispensable to laying down and affirming minimum standards of protection particularly in areas where supranational normative intervention seems irreplaceable, and any forms of weak co-ordination between Member States would in no way represent an adequate substitute for it.

We need only consider the question of transnational secondary strike action taken as an expression of solidarity to appreciate just how important the potential implications of this 'lacuna'[154] are, not only today but even more so as regards prospects for the future. Whilst the preclusion, as anticipated by some legal scholars,[155] of recourse to alternative legal bases (like Articles 94 and 308 of the EC Treaty, or the corresponding provisions of the constitutional Treaty) is confirmed, all the difficulties of developing satisfactory common standards of protection in this crucial field through interpretation and case-law remain.[156] The several national legal orders exhibit enormous differences in the matter, and comparing the diverse

---

[154] Cf. P. Germanotta and T. Novitz, 'Globalisation and the Right to Strike: The Case for European Protection of Secondary Action', *International Journal of Comparative Labour Law and Industrial Relations* 2002, vol. 18, pp. 67ff.; from a broader perspective, see A. Supiot, 'Revisiter les droits d'action collective', *Droit Social* 2001, pp. 687ff.; Supiot, 'Governing Work and Welfare in a Global Economy', in Zeitlin and Trubek, *Governing Work and Welfare*, pp. 376ff., especially pp. 396ff.

[155] See B. Ryan, 'The Charter and Collective Labour Law', in Hervey and Kenner, *Economic and Social Rights*, pp. 67ff., especially p. 85.

[156] See G. Orlandini, *Sciopero e servizi pubblici essenziali nel processo d'integrazione europea. Uno studio di diritto comparato e comunitario*, Turin 2003, pp. 367ff.; S. Giubboni and G. Orlandini, 'Il conflitto collettivo nell'ordinamento comunitario', *Democrazia e Diritto* 2004, no. 3, p. 119.

standards respectively developed on the basis of the European Convention on Human Rights and ILO sources is no less arduous.[157]

The search for legal instruments capable of establishing a 'countervailing workers' power'[158] in an attempt to counterbalance the extraordinary pressure arising from de-territorialized global capital is thus in danger of coming up against an obstacle in the European constitutional order which will be very difficult to overcome in the future.

Second, the constitutional Treaty perpetuates all the weaknesses deriving from the heavy limitations which still restrict the use of qualified-majority voting within the Council.

In this case the cautious and only virtual progress achieved by the Treaty of Nice is essentially maintained. Paragraph 3 of Article III-210 of the Constitution for Europe also provides that in the fields referred to in its paragraph 1 under (d) (protection of workers where their employment contract is terminated), (f) (representation and collective defence of the interests of workers and employers) and (g) (conditions of employment for third-country nationals legally residing in Union territory), which as things stand remain subject to unanimity, the Council of Ministers may, on a proposal from the Commission, adopt a European decision making the ordinary legislative procedure supported by qualified-majority voting applicable. On the other hand, the field of social security and social protection of workers, mentioned in paragraph 1(c) of Article III-210, is still excluded from this *passerelle* or escalator clause within the Section on Social Policy.

First, therefore – contrary to what is introduced for other important spheres of Union action – there is no direct extension of the new general qualified-majority rule; and second, the issue of policies on social security and social protection of workers is to remain locked within the confines of unanimity.

The only aspect in which in the Treaty establishing a Constitution for Europe the subject of social security is in principle subject to the qualified-majority rule and the ordinary legislative procedure is that of the co-ordination of national legal systems, within the meaning of Article III-136 of the Constitution. Supranational normative intervention is in this case functional to bringing about – through the co-ordination of

---

[157] See P. O'Higgins, 'The Interaction of the ILO, the Council of Europe and the European Union Labour Standards', in Hepple, *Social and Labour Rights*, pp. 55ff., especially p. 63.

[158] Lord Wedderburn, 'Common Law, Labour Law, Global Law', in Hepple, *Social and Labour Rights*, pp. 19ff.

the several Member States' social-security systems – freedom of movement for employed and self-employed workers within the internal market.

Although it represents an important and long-awaited novelty, the extension of the qualified-majority rule and the ordinary legislative procedure to social security for migrant workers is therefore by way of being a natural development of the rules on freedom of movement. However, even in this case Article III-136 introduces major and significant reservations in the form of the proviso 'that a member of the Council considers that a draft European law or a framework law referred to in paragraph 1 would affect the financial balance of that system'. These reservations could, in reality, frustrate the extension of the qualified-majority rule and make it purely apparent, with the risk of a *de facto* return to the unanimity requirement in this field.

In short, when we read the text of the Constitution for Europe we find the clear tendency towards a re-dimensioning of social policy via hard law which represents one of the distinctive connotations of the 'new paradigm'.[159] The Section on Social Policy seems not to introduce anything essentially new and, along with the progress of the past decade, also perpetuates the weaknesses and contradictions inherited from the successive amendments of the Treaties that took place during the 1990s.

8. . . . The constitutional Treaty and the open method of co-ordination . . .

Since the Lisbon European Council, the open method of co-ordination (OMC) has firmly occupied centre stage as regards Union action in social matters. What is more, continuous spillover into increasingly new areas more or less distant from the sphere of Community legislative competence would nowadays indicate that the term should be used in the plural, since it is actually a question of methods, or at least diverse forms of the same method.[160]

The depth and incidence assumed over the years by the European Employment Strategy – the original and still as yet most important area for the OMC in the social field – are not, or at least not so far, matched in other areas. The sector which perhaps is or shows signs of becoming the closest (albeit with notable differences) to the sector of choice, i.e.

---

[159] See also C. Barnard and S. Deakin, 'Corporate Governance, European Governance and Social Rights', in Hepple, *Social and Labour Rights*, pp. 122ff.

[160] Cf., e.g., C. De la Porte and P. Pochet (eds.), *Building Social Europe through the Open Method of Co-ordination*, Brussels 2002.

employment policies, is that of policies on social inclusion;[161] in the field of immigration policy, and even more so in that of policies on pensions, health and social protection, the distances seem — for a number of reasons — even greater, and the use of the plural is therefore still more justified.[162]

But above and beyond the differences in its uses and forms – which in our present context can be ignored – what undoubtedly emerges is the seemingly irresistible ascendancy of a method of social governance of more and more clearly universal applicability. The Commission regards it as a valuable opportunity for exercising its own influence and political initiative in policy areas that are often of great importance but in some cases far removed from the sphere of Community legislative competence or at any rate not accessible to hard law; national governments have no reason to oppose its developments, which by definition are non-binding and allow for national and regional differences; and the social partners see in it another possible locus of interaction and 'concertation'.

So the OMC seems capable of giving rise to what is a positive-sum procedural game for the principle actors involved in it, since it offers all of them some advantage and hence some incentive to participate. Given the widespread consensus that exists with respect to it among the Union's government institutions, it would have been entirely reasonable to expect the OMC to receive special attention. However, when we read through the Constitution this expectation turns out to be rather surprisingly frustrated.

Despite the hopes and express recommendations put forward by various parties,[163] in the constitutional Treaty the OMC is still not given an adequate and definite base of constitutional foundation.

Article I-15 of the constitutional Treaty, entitled 'The coordination of economic and employment policies', contains only a vague reference, little more than 'an allusion'[164] to the OMC. Sandwiched between the provision

---

[161] M. Ferrera, M. Matsaganis and S. Sacchi, 'Open Coordination Against Poverty: The New EU Social Inclusion Process', *Journal of European Social Policy* 2002, pp. 227ff.; S. Giubboni, 'L'incerta europeizzazione. Diritto della sicurezza sociale e lotta all'esclusione in Italia', *Giornale di Diritto del Lavoro e di Relazioni Industriali* 2003, pp. 563ff.

[162] See F. Vandenbroucke, 'The EU and Social Protection: What Should the European Convention Propose?', *Max Planck Institut für Gesellschaftsforschung Working Paper* No. 02/6, http://www.mpi-fg-koeln.mpg.de/pu/workpap/wp02/6/wp02-6.html.

[163] See G. De Búrca and J. Zeitlin, 'Constitutionalising the Open Method of Co-ordination. What Should the Convention Propose?', *Centre for European Policy Studies Brief* No. 31/2003, http://www.cesps.be.

[164] Ziller, *La nuova Costituzione europea*, p. 162.

establishing the (non-exhaustive) list of areas of shared competence and the rule laying down the general bases of common foreign and security policy, Article I-15 does have the unquestionable merit of according the same level of co-ordination to both the economic policies of the Member States (through 'broad guidelines') and their employment policies (in particular in the form of 'guidelines'). Apart from this it contains, first, a reference to the fact that specific provisions are applicable to those Member States which have adopted the euro and, second, empowers the Union to adopt initiatives to ensure co-ordination of Member States' social policies (paragraph 3).

Thus, the European Constitution does not contain even a hint of a general rule on principle regarding the OMC specifically aimed at anchoring this method of governance – as had been suggested[165] – to the Union's institutional architecture. Furthermore, despite the welcome mention on an equal footing of the co-ordination of both economic and employment policies, the links between the two forms of co-ordination are not specified in detail. In particular, it is not ensured that the two (virtually complementary and interdependent) policy co-ordination exercises are in practice on equal terms as regards the instruments available.[166]

Even in the case of the OMC and new models of economic and social governance, therefore, the constitutional Treaty does not seem to indicate any course other than that of timid consolidation of the *acquis* as formerly pursued. Nor does the debate that went on within the Convention seem to have added anything very much as regards some of the critical profiles which are coming increasingly to the fore in this respect.

The worry – not a new one – is that, from being a potential setting for the advancement of open, pluralist and effectively 'shared' forms of deliberative supranationalism, the OMC is in reality turning out to be reduced to an esoteric locus of discussion 'between elites for elites',[167] a new epiphenomenon of what Colin Crouch calls 'post-democracy'.[168]

In particular, the question of the relation between the OMC and fundamental social rights remains largely avoided. One aspect of this question relates to social rights in their procedural dimension of rights to

---

[165] See Vandenbroucke, 'EU and Social Protection', pp. 21ff.

[166] In actuality, as is maintained with strongly critical overtones by J.-P. Fitoussi, *La règle et le choix. De la souveraineté économique en Europe*, Paris 2002, there was no real political discussion within the European Convention on the crucial and very delicate subject of economic governance.

[167] Barnard and Deakin, 'Corporate Governance', p. 147.

[168] C. Crouch, *Postdemocrazia*, Rome-Bari 2003. This point will be taken up again and discussed later, in subsection 8 of chapter 4 below.

full participation in the definition and implementation of the increasingly pervasive steering of social and employment policy which passes through the melting-pot of the OMC.[169] Article I-48 of the constitutional Treaty, reflecting a suggestion put to the European Convention by the Working Group on Economic Governance, enshrines a general principle which is of undeniable importance from this point of view, although it has to find adequate forms of effective translation. The rule in question – which not by chance comes immediately after the innovative provision on 'The principle of participatory democracy' (Article I-47) – has the indisputable merit of affirming that recognition and promotion of the role of the social partners, specifically in the form of facilitating 'dialogue between the social partners', respecting their autonomy, are central aspects of the Union's democratic life. There is no doubt that a strengthening of the role of the social partners and civil-society organizations within the ambit of the OMC entails a guarantee of adequate procedural fundamental social rights; such a guarantee necessarily depends, however, on a prior definition of the channels of representation and criteria of representativeness.[170]

A second aspect concerns the need to guarantee respect for fundamental social rights – including in the substantive sense – in the new soft-law procedures, and particularly in the sphere of employment policies and policies on social inclusion.

Some authors, perhaps with excessive optimism about the maieutic virtues of soft law, see directly in the OMC itself the locus that is at least potentially the best suited to developing the 'fundamental-rights policy', simultaneously respecting diverse national traditions, which the European Union has long been reproached for lacking.[171] In this view of things the OMC could be a particularly effective means of implementing the Charter of Fundamental Rights of the European Union. As has been suggested, 'an OMC process for the purpose of implementing the Charter,

---

[169] For some interesting ideas in this connection, from the theoretical perspective of the 'capability approach', see S. Deakin and J. Browne, 'Social Rights and Market Order: Adapting the Capability Approach', in Hervey and Kenner, *Economic and Social Rights,* pp. 27ff.

[170] B. Caruso, 'The Future of Labour Law: Traditional Models of Social Protection and a New Constitution of Social Rights', *Massimo D'Antona Research Centre for the Study of European Labour Law (Università degli Studi di Catania) Working Paper* No. 10/2002, www.lex.unict.it/eurolabor/ricerca/presentazione, p. 14.

[171] See P. Alston and J. H. H. Weiler, 'Vers une politique des droits de l'homme authentique et cohérente pour l'Union européenne', in P. Alston (ed.), *L'Union européenne et les droits de l'homme,* Brussels 2001, pp. 3ff., and more recently O. De Schutter, 'Des limites à l'action des institutions à une politique des droits fondamentaux', in De Schutter and Nihoul, *Une Constitution pour l'Europe,* pp. 81ff.

offering the prospect of a public debate on National Action Plans for Fundamental Rights followed by exchange of views in the Council would seem a more promising way to introduce into the EU decision-making process a fundamental rights discourse which is at present virtually absent'.[172]

Without going as far as that and perhaps overdoing spillover of the OMC with the risk of dissolving the *entire* fundamental-rights discourse in the European Union in the lukewarm waters of soft law, it would instead be important to start at least ensuring greater consistency between the open co-ordination procedures currently in operation – especially on the subject of employment policies and policies on social inclusion – and fundamental rights as recognized in the Nice Charter. This would mean that it could more realistically and profitably be imagined that 'in the context of the open method of co-ordination – at present chiefly in regard to employment and social inclusion – the drawing-up of national plans for scrutiny by the European institutions devotes room not just to indicating what has been achieved with a view to the co-ordination of policies but also to verifying respect for fundamental rights', with 'a direct link between soft-law procedures and monitoring of the degree to which fundamental rights are complemented in the several national legal orders.'[173]

From the perspective just indicated, it would be particularly useful to establish appropriate benchmarks on respect for European fundamental social rights in translating the guidelines regularly issued by the Council. There is no doubt that the appropriate introduction of a 'human rights mainstreaming clause'[174] into the constitutional Treaty would make this task easier. However, a clause of this kind, although very useful, does not seem strictly necessary as such and has in any case been omitted – in the terms suggested – from the text of the Treaty establishing a Constitution for Europe. The objective in question could, in point of fact, be achieved by making full use of the multiple effects potentially deriving from the constitutionalization of fundamental social rights through the incorporation of the Nice Charter into Part II of the constitutional Treaty.[175] It is not impossible that such an objective could be more easily achieved by 'proper use' of the transverse social clause innovatively introduced by the IGC into the final text of the constitutional Treaty, at Article III-117. This

---

[172] Bernard, 'A New Governance Approach', p. 267.

[173] Sciarra, 'La constitutionnalisation de l'Europe sociale', p. 191.

[174] G. De Búrca, 'Fundamental Rights and Citizenship', in B. De Witte (ed.), *Ten Reflections on the Constitutional Treaty for Europe*, Florence 2003, pp. 11ff., here p. 26.

[175] See Kenner, 'Economic and Social Rights', p. 15.

provision – whose effective significance has yet to be explored at all – prescribes that 'In defining and implementing the policies and actions referred to in this Part [III], the Union shall take into account require- ments linked to the promotion of a high level of employment, the guar- antee of adequate social protection, the fight against social exclusion, and a high level of education, training and protection of human health.' This horizontal social clause completes and enriches the important transverse provisions contained at the start of Part III of the constitutional Treaty (at Articles III-116 et seq.), and is certainly capable of prompting closer atten- tion on the part of the Union institutions to the impact on national social rights and policies of all the policies and actions envisaged in Part III.

9. . . . The constitutional Treaty and the advance of fundamental social rights . . .

As has already been pointed out, the unanimous agreement reached on inserting the Nice Charter into the constitutional Treaty represents one of the most positive and in some ways also most surprising outcomes of the European Convention's work.

It was emphasized above that full constitutionalization of fundamental social rights within the Community legal order remains an inescapable necessity and that it is only with incorporation into the constitutional Treaty that the Charter can develop the whole of its potential as regards the full affirmation of a discourse on fundamental social rights in the European Union.

As is well known, the European Court of Justice (unlike the Court of First Instance) has up till now avoided making any direct use of the Charter, disregarding – in an understandable attitude of self-restraint – the suggestions in this direction frequently put to it by the Advocates General. It is not entirely impossible that, in view of the consensus recorded within the European Convention and the IGC, the Court may now change this attitude and make more active and direct use of the Charter even before the constitutional Treaty comes to be ratified by the Member States. What perhaps seems more likely is that, given the major political uncertainties surrounding the process of ratification of the Treaty in the now twenty- five Member States, the Court will continue to maintain the caution it has displayed so far. And it is for this reason that the thoughts expressed in subsection 3 above on the legal significance of the Nice Charter following its proclamation remain pertinent even now that the constitutional Treaty has been signed.

Incorporation of the Charter into the European Constitution is still the route of choice for full emancipation of the discourse on social rights at Union level.[176] And this notwithstanding the unquestionable weaknesses and ambiguities of its text, weaknesses and ambiguities which the partial rewriting of the Charter's so-called horizontal clauses adopted in the constitutional Treaty might well increase.

In this connection, as is well known, the provision that has particularly attracted worried and rightly strong criticism is the reworded version of Article 52 of the Charter (Article II-112 of the Constitution for Europe), which gives a very debatable definition of the scope and interpretation of 'rights' and 'principles'. There is no doubt that – at least in the intention of its most whole-hearted supporters (i.e. the British Government representatives within the Convention) – the distinction between the two, certainly in the inappropriate and somewhat crude terms in which it has been formulated, will essentially serve to weaken the significance of the recognition of fundamental social rights, banishing them to the empyrean of mere programmatic principles and so separating them off from civil and political rights. In accordance with the new Article II-112, whereas (social) rights are as such directly actionable, principles are observed only when they are put into practical effect through legislative or executive acts of the Union's institutions, with this legislative materialization constituting the necessary medium to make them justiciable.[177]

The pronouncement that the provisions of this Charter which contain principles may be implemented by legislative and executive acts taken by institutions and bodies of the Union and by acts of the Member States when they are implementing Union law, in the exercise of their respective powers, should be enough – in the logic in which it is put forward – to convince anyone of the purely programmatic nature of almost all of the Charter's social rules. And the pronouncement that these provisions

---

[176] It is, for example, reasonable to assume that insertion *pleno jure* into the body of the European Constitution could make variations of the kind already recorded in the 'use' of the social rights contained in the Nice Charter more difficult. See, for instance, the difference in attitude exhibited by Advocate General Tizzano (and indirectly by the Court of Justice) on the subject of the fundamental social right to paid annual leave in, respectively, *BECTU* (see note 78 above) and *Bowden* (Case C-133/00 [2001] ECR I-7031); cf. Kenner, 'Economic and Social Rights', pp. 21–3.

[177] Article II-112(5) of the Treaty establishing a Constitution for Europe reads as follows: 'The provisions of this Charter which contain principles may be implemented by legislative and executive acts taken by institutions, bodies, offices and agencies of the Union, and by acts of Member States when they are implementing Union law, in the exercise of their respective powers. They shall be judicially cognisable only in the interpretation of such acts and in the ruling on their legality.'

can be invoked before a court only for the purposes of interpreting such acts and ruling on their legality is expected to provide a further convincing indication that they cannot per se be relied on before the courts and become invocable only in the event of their discretionary legislative implementation.

The distinction is rightly criticized[178] for the way in which it is formulated and for the manifest and unacceptable contradiction to which it could give rise if taken literally. Indeed, as some authors have pertinently commented, 'a statement that the values on which the Union is founded are indivisible, as well as universal, is not compatible with a statement that some of the rights deriving from these values correspond to principles which are freely disposable by the legislators.'[179] That is to say, it is incompatible with the very nature of fundamental principles of the European Union that they *may* – to use the wording of above-mentioned Article II-112(5) – be freely implemented by the legislators and therefore need to be observed by the courts *only* where the former have chosen to intervene. In reality, fundamental social 'principles' too, once constitutionally enshrined, cannot but be *always and in whatever circumstances* respected and observed – through interpretation – by any court before which they are invoked.[180] To give just one example of their *direct* interpretative relevance, it may be noted that the *effet d'obstacle* (impeding effect) – as a 'means of legal resistance to opportunist movements of deregulation' – pointed out by Antoine Lyon-Caen[181] is directly deducible from these fundamental social *principles* as well.

Nonetheless, although it merits criticism the distinction between rights and principles as set out in Article II-112 of the constitutional Treaty should not, however much it has formerly been emphasized, be overestimated: where correctly understood and, as it were, 'moderated', its effects are likely to be more modest than was hoped by those who championed it. In point of fact, the distinction made by the provision in

---

[178] See, for example, De Búrca, 'Fundamental Rights', pp. 22ff.; Sciarra, 'La constitutionnalisation de l'Europe sociale', p. 192; De Schutter, 'Des limites', pp. 110ff.

[179] C. Pinelli and F. Barazzoni, 'La Carta dei diritti, la cittadinanza e la vita democratica dell'Unione', in F. Bassanini and G. Tiberi (eds.), *Una Costituzione per l'Europa. Dalla Convenzione europea alla Conferenza Intergovernativia*, Bologna 2003, pp. 37ff., here p. 39.

[180] Cf. O. De Schutter, 'La garanzia dei diritti e dei princìpi sociali nella Carta dei diritti fondamentali', in G. Zagrebelsky (ed.), *Diritti e Costituzione nell'Unione europea*, Turin 2003, pp. 192ff.

[181] A. Lyon-Caen, 'The Legal Efficacy and Significance of Fundamental Social Rights: Lessons from the European Experience', in Hepple, *Social and Labour Rights*, pp. 182ff., here p. 188.

question is ultimately nothing other than a merely inappropriate reformulation or explanation of one which is familiar in theoretical debate on the subject of social rights and also very much a feature in the constitutional jurisprudence of those national legal orders which, directly or indirectly, recognize such rights. It must therefore be viewed in relative, or perhaps contextual, terms, storing up the benefit of this rich constitutional experience and remembering that the distinction between rights and principles is nothing really new even within the theoretical and political proposals being put forward at Community level (leaving aside the fact that it is nowadays already implicitly deducible from Article 51 of the Nice Charter).[182] In order to pinpoint the constitutional significance of this distinction within the Union legal order it is consequently absolutely essential properly to recognize the import of the Charter's individual social provisions, apart from everything else in order to dispel the prejudice and misunderstanding which tend to relegate the provisions in question entirely (and erroneously) to the level of mere programmatic principles and the harmless realm of aspirational rights. In the terms in which it was remodelled by the Nice Charter itself, European social law is in fact also rich – in addition to principles – in directly actionable fundamental rights.

The attempts at classifying the fundamental social rights recognized by the Nice Charter and, in future, the Union's constitutional Treaty so far variously essayed by legal scholars[183] are therefore united, above and beyond their differences, by an awareness that an interpretative operation of this kind is absolutely essential in order to gain the true benefit of one of the most innovative and significant features of the present phase of open and 'multilevel' constitutionalism of the European Union.[184]

The typological classification which divides social rights into 'social freedoms', 'unconditional rights' and 'conditional rights'[185] also seems

---

[182] See Kenner, 'Economic and Social Rights', pp. 16ff.

[183] Cf. D. Grimm, 'Diritti sociali fondamentali per l'Europa', in Fondazione Lelio e Lisli Basso, *Sfera pubblica e Costituzione europea*, Rome 2002, pp. 7ff., especially pp. 17ff.; A. J. Menéndez, 'The Rights' Foundations of Solidarity: Social and Economic Rights in the Charter of Fundamental Rights of the European Union', *ARENA (Advanced Research on the Europeanisation of the Nation-State) Working Papers*, WP 03/1, at http://www.arena.uio.no/publications/wp03_1.pdf; S. Giubboni, 'I diritti sociali fondamentali nell'ordinamento comunitario. Una rilettura alle luce della Carta di Nizza', *Diritto dell'Unione Europea* 2003, pp. 325ff., especially pp. 349ff.

[184] The reference is, manifestly, to the well-known theoretical reconstruction by I. Pernice, for whom see his more recent 'Multilevel Constitutionalism in the European Union', *European Law Review* 2002, pp. 51ff.

[185] A. Baldassare, *Diritti della persona e valori costituzionali*, Turin 1997, pp. 208ff. The distinction between 'rights to commutative equality', 'rights to regulatory intervention by the

particularly appropriate in the context that interests us here. Suitably adapted to the peculiarities of the Community experience, it allows an accurate grasp of the actual potentialities of implementing the social rights and principles guaranteed by the Charter.

Social freedoms (or, if preferred, social rights to freedom or autonomy) share with civil and economic freedoms the fundamental structural characteristic of attributing to the respective beneficiaries a sphere of *agere licere*, such that their 'exercise, once they have been effectively guaranteed, depends primarily on the holder's actions or conduct'.[186] It is from this structural connotation that trade union freedom and the right to strike likewise derive their self-applicability in the Community legal order, once – as is the case in Article 28 of the Charter (Article II-88 of the constitutional Treaty) – they have been constitutionally guaranteed. As a consequence, they are also judicially actionable horizontally in the sphere of legal relationships falling beneath the umbrella of Community law and must at all events be respected, at least as regards their 'essential content', in all regulatory action taken by the supranational institutions or by Member States in implementing EU law.

This second profile of relevance in particular, in which the rights in question operate as, to use a well-known terminology, a 'shield' or 'guarantee' (of autonomy) rather than a 'sword', is totally independent of whether or not the Union possesses its own legislative powers in the matter. Thus, even in the presence of the highly debatable exclusions laid down in Article 137(6) of the EC Treaty (and Article III-210(6) of the constitutional Treaty),[187] the EU legal order would nonetheless have to ensure full respect of these fundamental social rights where it interfered with their exercise, as occurs emblematically in the frequent cases of conflict between Community competition law and national systems of labour law. And this in accordance with standards which, in the absence of supranational regulation, would inevitably be inferred, *inter alia*, from the constitutional

---

legislature' and 'rights to distributive equality' proposed, again with reference to the Italian Constitution, by A. Giorgis, *La costituzionalizzazione dei diritti all'uguaglianza sostanziale*, Naples 1999, leads to not dissimilar conclusions. The classic distinction between social rights 'of autonomy', 'to public provision' and 'of participation' used by E. Picard, 'Citizenship, Fundamental Rights, and Public Services', in M. Freedland and S. Sciarra (eds.), *Public Services and Citizenship in European Law. Public and Labour Law Perspectives*, Oxford 1998, pp. 83–98, especially p. 90, also seems inspired by similar classifying and taxonomic criteria, this time with express reference to the Community legal order.

[186] Baldassare, *Diritti della persona*, pp. 212.

[187] The most severe criticism of the real contradiction at the heart of social Europe created by these exclusions of competence is still that of Lord Wedderburn, 'European Community Law', pp. 247ff.

traditions of the Member States. A hermeneutic exercise which – although certainly a difficult one, given the extreme diversity of these traditions[188] – the interpreter is nevertheless required to carry out in conformity with Articles 52 and 53 of the Charter (Articles II-112 and II-113 of the Treaty establishing a Constitution for Europe).

Unconditional social rights are characterized by being inherent in legal relationships 'which are established spontaneously, i.e. on the free initiative of the parties, leaving it to them to qualify the type or quantity of certain performances'.[189] Although they concern a positive performance, or action on the part of a subject other than the holder of the right, they automatically refer to the relationship as provided for and/or regulated by the Community legal order and are therefore directly actionable before the courts. A necessary condition of their exercise is that the employment relationship to which they refer (and which is envisaged by Community rules) has been established, and that at the same time the possibly generic definition of the content of the performances to which they confer entitlement does not prevent the court from arriving at a determination of those performances on the basis of ordinary assessment and interpretative discretion.

The right to paid annual leave – the subject of the *BECTU* judgment already mentioned[190] – is a typical example of this category of fundamental social rights. But probably the most important example, especially in the context of the Community legal order, is offered by the principle of, and consequent right to, equality and equal opportunities/treatment of men and women in working life. A right which the Community legal order – starting from Article 119 (now Article 141) of the Treaty of Rome (Article III-214 of the constitutional Treaty) has made the subject of a fundamental corpus of legislation and case-law, the source of profound repercussions on the Member States' actual constitutional arrangements. Although it may appear more open to question, the right to 'fair and just'[191] working conditions as provided for by Article 31 of the Nice Charter (Article II-91 of the constitutional Treaty)[192] should also be seen as falling into the category of unconditional social rights. This is so even where – as seems more correct – the fundamental social right to equal

[188] See G. Orlandini, 'Il diritto di sciopero nella Carta dei diritti fondamentali dell'Unione europea', *Giornale di Diritto del Lavoro e di Relazioni Industriali* 2001, pp. 649ff.
[189] Baldassare, *Diritti della persona*, p. 214.   [190] See notes 78 and 176 above.
[191] Or to working conditions which respect 'health, safety and dignity', as the text of the provision in question goes on to specify.
[192] Much the same can be said of the right to protection against unjustified dismissal which, as already mentioned, is conferred on workers by Article 30 of the Charter (and now by Article II-90 of the constitutional Treaty).

pay is included in it, or where a legal situation with respect to which the Community lacks, and will continue to lack, concurrent legislative competence is regarded as covered by Article 31 of the Charter. Even in the absence of a definition of the content of these rights by Community legislation, the Court of Justice could and should, in all cases where they come into prominence in the sphere of incidence of supranational law, take its cue from the constitutional traditions of the Member States or from the relevant ILO Conventions and the European Social Charter in order to arrive at a useful determination of the relative content and standards of protection.

By contrast, provisions such as those contained in paragraphs 1 and 3 of Article 34 of the Nice Charter[193] or again in its Article 36 (Articles II-94 and II-96 of the constitutional Treaty) enshrine within the Union legal order what are fundamental principles, and not directly actionable rights. In other words, the fundamental social rights envisaged by these provisions are typical conditional rights to redistribution or public provision:[194] their translation into practice requires – obviously within the limits of the respective powers and responsibilities, which are still essentially national – legislative acts of the Union and of Member States, as explained by the above-mentioned revised text of Article II-112(5) of the constitutional Treaty. The essential principles established by such provisions *must*, in any event, guide and direct the Union's social policies in all the many and varied versions of the latter's conformation and instrumentation: they must therefore also be preserved as a feature within those policies, increasingly characteristic of the role of the supranational institutions, which are pursued in the context of open co-ordination procedures. They can, however, also perform a more direct 'defensive' role in representing some guarantee of the specificity of the diverse national welfare-state approaches and constellations, especially in the face of the excessively invasive tendencies of supranational competition and market law.

Ultimately, it will be for the Court of Justice and the national judges as Community judges to establish where directly actionable social rights end and social principles begin, and what it is that actually differentiates them. And it may be predicted that the imprecise language used by Article II-112

---

[193] As I have attempted to show elsewhere (S. Giubboni, 'Solidarietà e sicurezza sociale nella Carta dei diritti fondamentali dell'Unione europea', *Giornale di Diritto del Lavoro e di Relazioni Industriali* 2001, pp. 617ff., especially pp. 629–30), paragraph 2 of Article 34 of the Charter confers directly actionable rights.

[194] In German constitutional language, *Leistungsrechte*: see Cassetti, *Stabilità economica e diritti fondamentali*, p. 10.

is very unlikely to restrict the Court of Justice 'in drawing on the range of values and norms expressed in the Charter in its adjudicative role'.[195] Just as it is very likely that the 'bizarre reference to the explanations given by the Praesidium of the previous Convention',[196] now contained in the newly worded Preamble to the Charter as well as in Article II-112(7) of the constitutional Treaty,[197] will be even less effective in limiting the interpretative and creative power of the courts of the Union and of the Member States. The least that can be said in this latter connection is that 'any claim to dictate to the courts criteria for the interpretation of legislative texts is the expression of a frightened and culturally primitive legislature and, into the bargain, has sooner or later been contradicted by experience.'[198]

10. . . . A summary assessment of the social content of the constitutional Treaty

It has recently been written that 'the DNA of the social issue . . . has already been inoculated' into the European Union, 'as it is part of the core business of its policies.'[199] Although attended by persistent weaknesses and ambiguities, the Treaty establishing a Constitution for Europe represents an important step which is probably a decisive one in the slowly advancing affirmation of a priority social dimension of the Union. The mixed picture of it that has been sketched in the preceding pages does not prevent the constitutional Treaty from being seen as a unique occasion of consolidation of the constitutional roots of European labour law and re-balancing of social values as compared with those of the integrated market. Despite attempts to reduce its significance directed more narrowly at its horizontal clauses, the insertion of the Nice Charter into Part II of the Treaty establishing a Constitution for Europe is nonetheless destined to represent a

---

[195] De Búrca, 'Fundamental Rights', p. 25.

[196] Ziller, *La nuova Costituzione europea*, p. 69.

[197] The Preamble of the Charter as amended reads as follows: 'In this context the Charter will be interpreted by the courts of the Union and the Member States with due regard to the explanations prepared under the authority of the Praesidium of the Convention which drafted the Charter and updated under the responsibility of the Praesidium of the European Convention'. Article II-112(7) of the constitutional Treaty is aimed at strengthening this odd provision by stating 'The explanations drawn up as a way of providing guidance in the interpretation of the Charter of Fundamental Rights shall be given due regard by the courts of the Union and of the Member States.'

[198] Pinelli and Barazzoni, 'La Carta dei diritti', p. 40.

[199] Caruso, 'Future of Labour Law', p. 13.

turning-point in the long journey towards the full constitutionalization of fundamental social rights in the European Union. Furthermore, the opening provisions themselves of the constitutional Treaty reinforce and expand, from the more general perspective of establishing a new balance that was initiated at Amsterdam, the role and significance of the cardinal values of the 'European social model'.

Article I-2 solemnly declares that the Union 'is founded on the values of human dignity, liberty, democracy, equality, the rule of law and respect for human rights, including the rights of persons belonging to minorities', and confirms that these 'values are common to the Member States in a society in which pluralism, non-discrimination, tolerance, justice, solidarity and equality between men and women prevail'. In going on to restate the Union's objectives, Article I-3 seems very clear in placing those concerned with guaranteeing the full economic integration of the Member States on an equal footing with those which commit the Union to combating social exclusion and discrimination and promoting 'social justice and protection, equality between women and men, solidarity between generations and protection of the rights of the child'. The search for a balance is particularly evident in its provision whereby 'The Union shall work for the sustainable development of Europe based on balanced economic growth and price stability, a highly competitive social market economy, aiming at full employment and social progress, and a high level of protection and improvement of the quality of the environment.'

It is difficult to deny that there has been 'an adjustment in the Union's aims: the reader and the interpreter can no longer infer that its primary goals are of an economic nature'.[200] There is probably also to be seen in this an endeavour to equip the Union with the 'frame of reference in terms of principles, in the context of which the foundational values of rights find expression and which act as a guide for the legislators and the courts in arriving at a balance of interests',[201] which – according to some authors[202] – was until now missing even within the Charter. It could

---

[200] G. Bronzini, 'Il modello sociale europeo', in E. Paciotti (ed.), *La Costituzione europea. Luci e ombre*, Rome 2003, pp. 90ff., here p. 96.

[201] G. F. Ferrari, 'I diritti tra costituzionalismi statali e discipline transnazionali', in Ferrari (ed.), *I diritti fondamentali dopo la Carta di Nizza. Il costituzionalismo dei diritti*, Milan 2001, pp. 1ff., here p. 50.

[202] See, by way of example, P. Ridola, 'La Carta dei diritti fondamentali dell'Unione europea e lo sviluppo storico del costituzionalismo europeo', in P. Costanzo (ed.), *La carta europea dei diritti*, Genoa 2002, pp. 6ff., especially pp. 10–11 and 13, according to whom the strong opening-up of the Nice Charter to the pluralism of values, with the decision to group rights around 'six axiological checklists', also carries 'risks of a non-hierarchized balance between the various rights, which leaves too much room for interpretation by the courts'.

therefore be easier to trace a reference framework of principles which guides the courts of Europe in carrying out a balance of interests and enables them more readily to give a 'face'[203] to European fundamental social rights. It is equally undeniable that achieving such an objective would require a strengthening of the bases for action of the Union's social policy, a strengthening which is almost totally absent in the constitutional Treaty.

It will in any case be possible to explore these prospects – albeit with all the difficulties and uncertainties they hold – only if the Treaty establishing a Constitution for Europe is actually ratified by the twenty-five Member States. The Member States will be called on to make a political choice of vital importance for the future of a united Europe. The threat that rejection of the constitutional Treaty by the more sceptical national parliaments or electorates may ultimately put the great 'adventure'[204] of the Union's unitary journey in a dramatically critical position is a very great one. We can only conclude with the hope that this unitary journey can be continued and that Europe can therefore keep on along the *Sonderweg*[205] that was initiated more than half a century ago.

---

[203] C. Salazar, 'I diritti sociali nella Carta dei diritti fondamentali dell'Unione europea: un viaggio al termine della notte?', in Ferrari, *I diritti fondamentali*, pp. 239ff., here p. 250.

[204] V. Castronovo, *L'avventura dell'unità europea. Una sfida con la storia e il futuro*, Turin 2004.

[205] J. H. H. Weiler, 'Federalism and Constitutionalism: Europe's Sonderweg', *Jean Monnet Working Paper – Harvard University*, 2000.

PART II

The market, competition and social rights in the European constitutional space

3

Infiltration of Community competition law into national systems of labour law, and its antidotes

1. Introduction

The word 'infiltration',[1] like (and perhaps even more so than) all the others such as 'intrusion',[2] 'penetration',[3] 'corrosion' and 'erosion'[4] that have also become part of the common phraseology used by labour lawyers over the past decade or so to describe the troubled relationship between Community competition and market law and national labour-law systems,[5] immediately evokes the idea of a threat, an insidious danger which originates from outside but is capable of penetrating more or less secretly or subtly to the deepest roots of a system to the point of shaking its very foundations and putting its most solid and 'internal'[6] categories in crisis. Consequently, it does not introduce a 'neutral' description of the phenomenon but carries within itself a specific and obviously negative evaluation. And although the sheer familiarity of this usage – felicitously initiated by Gérard Lyon-Caen and now become, in its several 'variants', almost commonplace – may have to some extent blunted the original

---

[1] G. Lyon-Caen, 'L'infiltration du Droit du travail par le Droit de la concurrence', *Droit Ouvrier* 1992, p. 313.

[2] P. Laigre, 'L'intrusion du droit communautaire de la concurrence dans le champ de la protection sociale. À propos de l'arrêt *Coreva*, CJCE 16 novembre 1995', *Droit Social* 1996, p. 82.

[3] K. Michelet, 'Protection sociale et contraintes économiques et monétaires européennes', *Droit Social* 2001, p. 292.

[4] A. Lyon-Caen, 'Droit social et droit de la concurrence. Observations sur une rencontre', in *Les orientations sociales du droit contemporain. Écrits en l'honneur du Professeur Jean Savatier*, Paris 1992, pp. 331ff.

[5] Cf. P. Davies, 'Market Integration and Social Policy in the Court of Justice', *Industrial Law Journal* 1995, vol. 24 no. 1, pp. 49–77; M. Roccella, 'Tutela della concorrenza e diritti fondamentali nella giurisprudenza sociale della Corte di Giustizia', *Giornale di Diritto del Lavoro e di Relazioni Industriali* 1993, pp. 1ff. (now also in Roccella, *La Corte di Giustizia e il diritto del lavoro*, Turin 1997, pp. 25ff.).

[6] See Lord Wedderburn, 'Freedom and Frontiers of Labour Law', in Wedderburn, *Labour Law and Freedom. Further Essays in Labour Law*, London 1995, pp. 350ff., especially pp. 370ff.

negative connotation, it has not altogether lost its intrinsic evaluative, rather than merely descriptive, meaning and so still inevitably contains an unequivocal (dis)value-judgement.

When assessed in terms of the potential for radical and comprehensive effects that is inherent in its asserted function of making social rules conform to market requirements, the infiltration of competition law – as the extreme and purest, and as it were quasi-sublimated, expression of the 'forced' deregulation of employment relationships[7] – would appear, in point of fact, to call directly into question the 'very legitimacy of labour and social-security law'.[8] As Alain Supiot has put it vividly: 'A competition law that recognizes no point of view other than that of the person operating in the market rings the knell of all the legal constructs underpinning social security or occupational solidarity.'[9]

All this means that the intrinsic negative (deregulatory, or simply destructive) potential of the infiltration of labour law by competition law cannot but be remarked upon *in limine*, and in its more general and profound guise, even in a context such as our present one in which it assumes relevance only from the circumscribed viewpoint of observing the changes undergone by the Community economic constitution and their impact on national systems of labour and social-security law. And this is so in more than the mere interests of terminological clarification, of proper explanation (and justification) of the meaning of the words that are used.

However, an overall view of the phenomenon from the specific, but at the same time privileged, point of view of the Community legal order – which is what the present chapter proposes to offer – will enable us to tone down the terms of the value-judgement that is implicit (and now openly

---

[7] Cf. U. Mückenberger and S. Deakin, 'From Deregulation to a European Floor of Rights: Labour Law, Flexibilisation and the European Single Market', *Zeitschrift für ausländisches und internationales Arbeits- und Sozialrecht* 1989, no. 3, pp. 153ff., especially p. 171 for a prompt in this direction; more generally, see S. Deakin and F. Wilkinson, 'Il diritto del lavoro e la teoria economica: una rivisitazione', *Giornale di Diritto del Lavoro e di Relazioni Industriali* 1999, pp. 587ff. Indeed, if taken to its extreme logical consequences, the notion of the subordination of labour law to the specific functionality of the rules on free competition – especially in its classical paradigm and still more in its Hayekian variants (on which see I. Musu, 'Il valore della concorrenza nella teoria economica', in I. Musu and N. Lipari (eds.), *La concorrenza tra economia e diritto*, Milan-Rome-Bari 2000, pp. 5ff.) – possibly represents the most radical form of negation of the legitimacy of labour law, as being an obstacle to efficient allocation of the factors of production and to their free flow and dispersion within the market.

[8] A. Supiot, *Critique du droit du travail*, Paris 1994, p. 189.   [9] *Ibid.*, p. 228.

declared) in the choice of the chapter's title and arrive at a less sweeping assessment.

It will, in fact, be suggested that – especially as regards the construction of an emphatically pluralist constitutional space like the European one[10] – the key issue consists in building a system for the coexistence and adaptation, in mutual respect, of potentially contrasting values.[11] This is in line with a proposal that the protection of labour within the European constitutional system *in fieri* 'can also be realized by bringing the two families concerned, i.e. that of labour law and that of competition law, face-to-face with each other',[12] without involving unjustifiable forms of any 'tyranny' of the values expressed by the latter over those guaranteed by the former in the terms implied by a direct and one-way 'infiltration' of competition law.

According to this approach, the two 'families are not merged but compared with each other in, as it were, mutual respect, each with its own history and particular foundational values'.[13] A not inconsiderable part of the necessary material legitimacy of the emerging original 'common constitutional space'[14] represented by closer and closer inter-penetration between the Community's legal order and those of the Member States depends on such a re-balancing exercise between these several interests and values underlying the European Union.

2. Community competition and market law and national systems of labour law in the original model

The infiltration of Community competition and market law into practically every sphere of the 'social sovereignty' originally reserved to the

---

[10] Cf. N. Walker, 'The Idea of Constitutional Pluralism', *Modern Law Review* 2002, pp. 317ff.

[11] Cf. L. Idot, 'Droit social et droit de la concurrence: confrontation ou cohabitation? (À propos de quelques developpements récents)', *Europe, Chronique* November 1999, pp. 4ff.; S. Giubboni, 'Solidarietà e concorrenza: "conflitto" o "concorso"?', *Mercato Concorrenza Regole* No. 1/2004, pp. 75ff.

[12] S. Sciarra, 'Diritto del lavoro e regole della concorrenza in alcuni casi esemplari della Corte di Giustizia europea', *Diritto del Mercato del Lavoro* 2000, no. 3, pp. 586ff., here p. 590.

[13] *Ibid.*

[14] C. Tomuschat, 'Europe. A Common Constitutional Space', in *The Common Law of Europe and the Future of Legal Education*, The Hague 1992, pp. 133ff.; P. Häberle, 'Per una dottrina della costituzione europea', *Quaderni Costituzionali* 1999, pp. 3ff., especially p. 12, uses the image of the European common constitutional space in an extended sense, also including Council of Europe sources in the supranational level. Among labour lawyers, see M. Rodríguez-Piñero, 'Il dialogo tra Corte di giustizia e giurisprudenza costituzionale', *Lavoro e Diritto* 1998, pp. 445ff., especially pp. 455.

several Member States,[15] including what has possibly been their most exclusive 'preserve',[16] i.e. the organization of social security and social protection, is a relatively recent phenomenon which in practice only began to acquire real depth and to be perceived as a new and threatening front of 'corrosion' of national labour-law systems from the late 1980s onwards.

The determining factors and main aspects of this phenomenon, which although relatively homogeneous in the outcomes and problems it leads to is a particularly complex and multifaceted one, will be examined in the later subsections of this chapter. What we need to do first is to emphasize, in more detail than was done in chapter 1, the substantively novel, and indeed destructive or – to use the highly coloured terminology suggested elsewhere in a wider context[17] – 'subversive' nature of the 'infiltration' phenomenon in regard to the balances originally intended by the founding fathers of the EEC. This will be done by once again running through the essential features of the model which they devised and which effectively governed relations between Community competition law and national labour-law systems largely up to the first half of the 1980s.

In outline, and anticipating the gist of what will be argued more specifically below, it may be said that the Treaty of Rome in the first place incorporated the relationship of essential *non-interference* between Community competition law and national rules on labour and social protection or, more pertinently, of complete autonomy of the latter with respect to the former, which certainly emerges from the overall political and institutional design that had been mapped out, with a view to the general unification of the Member States' markets, in the Spaak Report. And that at the same time, in line with the traditional and dominant conception of the functions of transnational labour law as revisited by the Ohlin Report and the Spaak Report, it further espoused the principle that the EEC's (limited and exceptional) social competences should help to corroborate this *autonomy* of Member State labour laws by protecting and rendering them immune from the risks of unfair forms of competition based on social-dumping practices.

---

[15] See M. Ferrera, 'Integrazione europea e sovranità sociale dello Stato-nazione: dilemmi e prospettive', *Rivista Italiana di Scienza Politica* 2000, pp. 393ff.; Ferrera, 'European Integration and National Social Citizenship: Changing Boundaries, New Structuring?', *Comparative Political Studies* 2003, pp. 611ff.

[16] E. Vogel-Polsky, 'Les compétences sociales de l'Union européenne: protection sociale et sécurité sociale', *Revue Belge de Sécurité Sociale* 1994, pp. 1135ff., here p. 1145.

[17] See M. Rhodes, '"Subversive Liberalism": Market Integration, Globalisation and the European Welfare State', *EUI Working Papers, Robert Schuman Centre – European University Institute* No. 95/10 (also in *Journal of European Public Policy* 1995, pp. 384ff.).

In this sense, it may be said that the specifically and essentially regulatory function of transnational competition inherent in the original social provisions of the Treaty of Rome could not but recognize and codify – at transnational level – the close relationship of complementarity that labour law, by its very nature, maintains with the principles governing the organization of fair conditions of competition between undertakings.[18]

The fundamental assumption of the drafters of the EEC Treaty was that the construction of the common market, a decisive step towards the integration of the European economies in line with the political stabilization of the Old Continent, would be firmly based on safeguarding in full all of the market-correction and wealth-redistribution functions intrinsically performed by national welfare states.

In particular, with the important exception of the common agricultural policy – imbued as it was with a priority welfare function – the EEC was not to appropriate for itself any of the national competences belonging, in this decisive field, to the Member States. The underlying presumption here was that guaranteeing them full political and regulatory autonomy in this respect was the only way of fulfilling the preconditions for their effective participation in the construction of the common market.

The Community's few social competences – as laid down by the scant provisions of the original Title on Social Policy of the founding Treaty – were simply intended to accompany the construction of the common market in an ancillary and instrumental capacity, without detracting from the essential presumption of full autonomy of public and/or collective governance of the redistribution processes and social-protection and social-cohesion functions carried on within national welfare states. At most, the provisions in question were intended to help strengthen – in line with the natural intensification of the economic integration process – the ability of the Member States to steer welfare regimes, from the perspective of the upward harmonization of systems which at the time were already beginning to savour the first signs of their most successful and extraordinary growth stage.

In these circumstances, the fact that the supranational provisions on the free movement of goods and services and on competition were not such as to interfere with national systems of labour and social-security law was quite obvious and therefore did not need to be spelled out. Although such specific pronouncements were certainly made, what is more important is

---

[18] See, in particular, G. Lyon-Caen, 'L'infiltration', *passim*, and also G. Lyon-Caen, *Le droit du travail. Une technique réversible*, Paris 1995, pp. 90ff.

that – above and beyond the formal and express guarantees contained in its text – the entire slant prefigured by the Treaty of Rome presupposed, and so took for granted, this relationship of absolute non-interference between the two normative areas.

Admittedly, the provisions relating to economic freedoms and competition were from the outset formulated as basic general principles characterizing the entire construction of the Community and, as such, having an innate propensity to acquire a status per se superior to the Community's sectoral policies proper including, obviously, social policy.[19] So their potential across-the-board range of action – failing, beyond all else, any express exemptions such as those established for agricultural policy (Article 42, now Article 36 of the EC Treaty) – probably made the inherent possibility of their extension to national social policies immediately apparent. Furthermore, rules certainly intended to (greatly) restrict the freedom of Member States to grant forms of aid to undertakings, such as those contained in Articles 92–94 (now Articles 87–89), made this possibility still more evident, and an undoubtedly less remote one.

Nonetheless, these considerations – which today, with the benefit of hindsight, may seem perfectly obvious – do not account for the attitude of effective non-interference that subsisted for many years, in the construction of the Community, between supranational competition and market law and Member State rules in the social field.

In reality, over a lengthy span of the by no means linear history of the construction of the common market it was never seriously taken into consideration, or even supposed, that Articles 85–94 (now Articles 81–89) of the Treaty could influence the regulatory choices freely made by Member States as regards, to cite just two examples that will be examined in more detail in subsection 6 below, the organization of their public job-placement services or their social-security schemes.[20] And the same can

---

[19] On this categorization, with particular reference to competition, which it would be wrong even for Community rules to class as a 'policy' since, just like the fundamental freedoms of movement of the factors of production, it has the more basic function of shaping and 'structuring the market', see S. Cassese, *La nuova costituzione economica*, Rome-Bari 1995, pp. 40–1.

[20] To appreciate the enormous distance separating the attitude of the time from the interpretative framework that has become common today, it is still very instructive to read what was written about these 'key provisions' of the Treaty in one of the most authoritative of the first European commentaries on it; cf., in particular, the essays by U. Draetta, U. Leanza and A. Pappalardo (with commentaries on Articles 85-94) in *Trattato istitutivo della Comunità economica europea. Commentario*, eds. R. Quadri, R. Monaco and A. Trabucchi, Milan 1965, vol. II.

naturally be said of the provisions on the free movement of goods and services, the other pillar of the 'establishment of the common market'.[21]

Nor must it be forgotten, 'to convey even a brief idea of the complex situation that existed at the time when the Community was being born and hence of the difficulties encountered in first fixing these rules and then, even more so, in fine-tuning and applying them, that there was very little empathy in Europe with the demands of fair competition between undertakings and that the Member States' own legislation bore witness to the lack of degree to which the subject had been developed.'[22]

During the first decades of the Community's history – as it has been authoritatively noted elsewhere – a 'competition culture' even vaguely comparable to the one we have today was simply non-existent. 'French planning concepts were opposed to Germany's "soziale Marktwirtschaft". The presence and interference of the Member States in their respective economies was increasing, instead of decreasing. The promoters of an active industrial policy were more influential in most Member States than the advocates of a rigorous competition policy.'[23]

But even more than the relative underdevelopment of a competition-law culture, which at the time exhibited some degree of advance only in Germany (whose model of course greatly influenced the original Community choices),[24] the decisive factor in shaping practices of peaceful and undisturbed non-interference between the two normative areas was a kind of immediate and common pre-acceptance – initially fully subscribed to by the same supranational institutional actors who were later to be among the most active in overturning it – of the compromise-based stance postulated in this respect by the Treaty and also revealed by it in a number of key provisions such as those laid down in its Article 222 and also Article 90(2).

Only the extraordinary 'constitutional activism' of the Court of Justice, encouraged and backed by the Commission in a show of mutual institutional support, made Articles 30 and 85 (now Articles 28 and 81) – albeit

---

[21] M. Cartabia and J. H. H. Weiler, *L'Italia in Europa. Profili istituzionali e costituzionali*, Bologna 2000, p. 241.

[22] A. Tizzano, 'Le dimensioni internazionali della concorrenza e la pluralità degli ordinamenti giuridici in un contesto di globalizzazione', in Musu and Lipari, *La concorrenza*, pp. 89ff., here p. 93.

[23] C. D. Ehlermann, 'The Modernization of EC Antitrust Policy: A Legal and Cultural Revolution', *Common Market Law Review* 2000, vol. 37, pp. 537–90, here p. 540.

[24] Cf., in addition to Tizzano, 'Le dimensioni', pp. 92ff., D. J. Gerber, 'The Transformation of European Community Competition Law', *Harvard International Law Journal* 1994, pp. 97ff.

later, and in terms very different from those envisaged by the drafters of the Treaty – the formidable instruments of stringent control of Member States' intervention in their respective economies and, ultimately, of the actual level of public regulation of the market (including, to a certain extent, the labour market) established by them, that we know today.[25]

An attempt will be made to explain this extraordinary broadening of the scope of the provisions in question and, in some ways, the real reversal of the relations between supranational market law and national labour law that it caused, in the later subsections of this chapter. All that need be done here is to emphasize once again how different the original balance devised by the founding fathers was from the one that has been brought about today.

This can in any case also easily be gathered from the other aspect of the original model which is in fact entirely consequent upon (and consistent with) the one just highlighted and which was likewise mentioned at the beginning. As we saw there, the creation of a common market conceived in line with and as the outcome of the affirmation of 'strong national economic interests',[26] and intended as such to favour completion of the task of post-war reconstruction of the nation-state, implied acceptance of the corollary that the social provisions of the Treaty of Rome, few and weak as they were, should on the whole merely accompany and support the process of spontaneous levelling-up that was expected from the proper functioning of that market, in accordance with a mechanism whereby 'assimilation of national legal systems should be the last resort and the Commission should only be given the power either to grant subsidies to correct distortions or to promote collaboration among Member States in the social field, as stated in Article 118'.

The creation of the common market, so the thinking went, would trigger a process of spontaneous upward harmonization of living and working conditions in the Member States which would axiomatically be beneficial to their respective systems of labour law and social protection, without any need for heteronomous corrective intervention. The Member States would therefore be able to pursue the objectives assigned to their several domestic social policies entirely freely, according to their particular economic needs and ideological preferences: the differences in the levels of protection thereby offered would not, as a rule, cause distortions of

---

[25] See A. Lyon-Caen, 'Droit social', p. 337.

[26] S. Sciarra, 'From Strasbourg to Amsterdam: Prospects for the Convergence of European Social Rights Policy', *EUI (European University Institute) Working Papers in Law* No. 98/9, p. 5, from which the following quotation in the text is also taken.

competition within the common market to the detriment of the most generous systems providing the most guarantees.

However, in the exceptional cases – identified by the Treaty itself (in ex Article 119 and 120) in line with the indications of the Spaak Report or at any rate subsequently identifiable on the basis of practical experience – in which the above-mentioned differences in the degree of development and cost of their respective systems of social and labour protection proved liable to falsify or distort competition between Member States (or, more accurately, between the undertakings operating within them), *Community labour law* recovered all its coercive force in order to restore conditions of *fair and just competition* through a form of *levelling-up*. In other words, the intention was that in those cases (albeit few and exceptional) where the competitive process triggered by the opening-up of the common market might be distorted by forms of social dumping caused by the differing degree of 'rigour' of national rules in the social field, supranational regulation would guarantee the re-establishment of conditions of fair competition through the upward harmonization of domestic legal systems to the highest standard existing.

In this sense, (Community) labour law reappropriated – (also) at supranational level – what has been described as its primary function, its particular 'essential purpose'.[27] Which consists in avoiding and, ultimately, eliminating social dumping by ensuring 'equalization' of the conditions of competition for undertakings that operate in the same economic sector by establishing a level playing-field in terms of labour costs. This function and purpose belong to both collective agreements and to direct state legislative intervention and make labour law – which is able to exist inasmuch as it is per se outside the scope of the rules on competition – at the same time a system of norms 'born as law directed towards organizing fair competition between enterprises and hence as law which is complementary to competition law and therefore no different from it in spirit'.[28]

---

[27] G. Lyon-Caen, 'L'infiltration', p. 313.

[28] *Ibid.* There is clearly no contradiction between the two aspects. On the one hand labour law is by its very nature a system of norms aimed at restricting or removing competition in the labour market, with a view to safeguarding – by fixing mandatory standards of protection – the liberty and dignity of the worker as a 'human being' (cf. Deakin and Wilkinson, 'Il diritto del lavoro', p. 590). In so doing it expresses a *raison d'être* opposed to that of competition law and needs to be kept outside its scope. The most limpid recognition of this principle is perhaps still to be found in section 6 of the Clayton Act: 'the labor of a human being is not a commodity or article of commerce'. On the other hand, the very fact that it 'equalizes' the conditions of competition between enterprises as regards one of the factors of production and proscribes dumping practices with respect to that

Although expressed in a form that was technically somewhat different, the same conception emerged – as we also saw in detail in chapter 1 above – from the ECSC Treaty. The close contiguity between the provisions on competition and those in the social field, which even followed each other immediately in the text, manifested in a more transparent manner the same relationship of complementarity between Community competition and market law and national systems of labour law as already envisaged in 1951 by the drafters of the Treaty of Paris. In its Article 68, the main Community instrument of (albeit indirect) intervention with regard to wages and welfare benefits was in reality directly functional to guaranteeing fair conditions of competition in the common market for coal and steel. And here too, the explicit anti-dumping rationale of the provisions was linked to the principle of guaranteeing high labour-protection standards within the Member States and, upstream, their actual regulatory autonomy in the social field.

Consequently, in this case again the fairness of conditions of competition was closely linked with, or indeed presupposed, the full guarantee – within each Member State and on the basis of autonomous choices made by the latter – of high levels of social protection for workers.

The Treaty of Paris therefore anticipated, albeit using different techniques and without envisaging forms of normative harmonization, the same virtuous relationship of instrumentality/interdependence/complementarity between competition law and labour law that was later to be found again in the Treaty of Rome. The only thing was that in the Treaty of Paris this link was so strong that much of supranational labour law (already scant as it was) coincided *tout court* with competition law: i.e. it was nothing other than a form of regulation of transnational competition, in its turn functional to the protection of national labour-law systems from 'undue' pressures of the common market.

factor means that labour law is also complementary to competition law. It is, in particular, 'this market-standardization function' – fulfilled *in primis* by collective bargaining but in general by labour-protection legislation – 'that must be seen as the main reason for extending the applicability, in terms of the employees and employers covered, of collective agreements' (G. Giugni, 'Diritto del lavoro (voce per un'enciclopedia)', *Giornale di Diritto del Lavoro e di Relazioni Industriali* 1979, pp. 11ff., and now also in Giugni, *Lavoro legge contratti*, Bologna 1989, pp. 245ff., especially p. 272). Labour law therefore maintains, with competition law, a relationship that is somewhat ambivalent but not contradictory. A relationship that suggested to G. Lyon-Caen, *Le droit du travail*, p. 6, the image of labour law as a collection of 'two-way and entirely reversible' rules and institutions 'which can coincide with the interests of either employers or employees depending on which side they are presented from'.

When we turn to the Treaty of Rome, on the other hand, Community labour law unquestionably featured as serving, and subsidiary to, the political economy of the common market[29] and as such instrumental to its efficient functioning. Equally obviously, however, it is also featured as an instrument of protection (of the most advanced versions) of the Member States' national labour-law systems.

Wherever, in fact, there were perceived to be real risks of social dumping, there was provision for heteronomous intervention at Community level to guarantee compliance with the highest standard, with harmonization of the Member States' systems following the example of the most advanced model and so averting the danger of the freeing-up of common-market forces becoming the source of a ruinous 'race to the bottom' in terms of the protection provided.

In this respect there is clearly no significant difference in the abstract normative model originally adopted by the Treaty of Rome as compared with the logic of action of law originating from the ILO. The contrary opinion upheld by Pietro Ichino[30] that the inspiration (and subsequently the actual normative content) of the European regional legal order signalled a substantial departure from the ILO's intervention logic would therefore appear to be wide of the mark, at least as regards the initial phase of establishing the theoretical bases of Community labour law. According to this opinion, ILO intervention has always targeted situations of 'structural monopsony', typical of the early stages of capitalist development, in which 'distortion is caused by the fact that there is only a single employer in the local labour market who buys labour, in the face of an over-abundant supply';[31] it has therefore consistently been directed towards reacting to these situations by means of traditional intervention protective of the worker as the weaker party to the relationship, achieved by imposing mandatory minimum labour standards aimed at generalizing the highest levels of protection. Community labour law – produced during (and starting from) a more advanced and mature stage of industrial development – has, by contrast, been aimed from the outset at reacting to diverse and less serious distortions that arise in situations of 'dynamic monopsony' mainly caused by problems of asymmetry characterized by disbenefit to

---

[29] See Lord Wedderburn, 'Freedom', p. 387.

[30] Cf. P. Ichino, 'Diversità di ispirazione e contenuti normativi fra l'organizzazione internazionale del lavoro e l'ordinamento comunitario europeo', *Diritto delle Relazioni Industriali* 1999, pp. 295ff.; Ichino, 'Contrattazione collettiva e antitrust: un problema aperto', *Mercato Concorrenza Regole* 2000, pp. 635ff.

[31] Ichino, 'Diversità di ispirazione', p. 295.

the worker. For this reason, it has from the start focused its intervention not on the traditional protective arsenal of labour law (i.e. mandatory minimum standards of protection) but on corrective measures consisting in 'the activation of information services, vocational training and support for mobility within the market, capable of increasing workers' opportunity to choose (which in recent years has come to be referred to as "employability") and hence their negotiating strength'.[32] It has, however, eschewed, essentially *ab ovo*, any objective of outright upward harmonization.

I cannot subscribe to Pietro Ichino's viewpoint. It does not seem convincingly sustainable to argue that the inspiration underlying Community labour law – which deliberately owed much to the indications originating from the ILO group of experts chaired by Bertil Ohlin – was really any different, at least at the outset, from that adopted as its own and advocated, in a global context, by the ILO.[33] The anti-dumping rationale of the standards of protection that the EEC imposed (albeit exceptionally) on Member States, with the upward approximation of their respective labour-law systems, is not really any different from that which primarily (although admittedly not exhaustively)[34] inspired those fixed by the ILO. Nor, above all, were the techniques and objectives of intervention different.[35]

The basic idea was to establish mandatory standards of protection through the upward harmonization of national social rules. It is true that harmonization was in the first place expected to be spontaneously promoted and fostered by the free operation of the common-market forces themselves, and intended in any case to be confined to exceptional cases. But these cases nevertheless entailed strong heteronomous intervention by the EEC. If anything, owing to the greater initial homogeneity of the levels of development of its participants the 'functionalist' harmonization[36] achieved by the EEC certainly bore witness to average standards

---

[32] *Ibid.*, p. 296.

[33] Cf. Lord Wedderburn, 'Freedom', pp. 387ff.; B. Hepple, 'New Approaches to International Labour Regulation', *Industrial Law Journal* 1997, pp. 353ff.

[34] Cf. N. Valticos and G. Von Potobsky, *International Labour Law*, Deventer-Boston 1995, pp. 20ff.

[35] They were the techniques of protective labour law based on a mandatory norm (*sub specie*, here, of harmonization up to the highest standard of protection), which was obviously the dominant model – in all of the Member States – during the EEC's formative years.

[36] As it is described by M. D'Antona, 'Sistema giuridico comunitario', in A. Baylos Grau *et al.* (eds), *Dizionario di Diritto del Lavoro Comunitario*, Bologna 1996, pp. 3ff., especially p. 22.

of protection which were higher than those feasible for the ILO on a worldwide scale and in any case endowed with the superior mandatory and coercive force conferred on them by their supranational source.

It therefore seems right to end by concluding that the Treaty of Rome, like the Treaty of Paris before it, had placed Community competition law and labour law in a relationship of peaceful 'co-existence and complementarity'.[37] On the one hand, there existed between Community competition law[38] and national labour-law systems a clear and generally accepted relationship of mutual 'non-interference' or 'indifference', in the sense that the latter were amicably excluded from the scope of the former. On the other hand, and without in any way contradicting this first presumption since they were both functionally aimed at preserving the autonomy of the several national systems of labour and social-security law, Community labour law was essentially conceived as an instrument for organizing a level playing-field and fair conditions of competition within the common market.

3. Crisis of the original model . . .

The infiltration of competition law into national systems of labour law therefore represents an obvious factor that has disrupted the complex (and certainly unstable) balance devised in this respect by the founding Treaty.

Although what mainly interests us here is to investigate the reasons for the crisis of the first presumption underpinning this original compromise-based approach, it is clear that it has also been superseded – in the context of the profound changes in the Community political economy that have taken place in particular from the mid-1980s onwards – in the second of its supporting elements.

As two eminent authors have remarked: 'There is no doubt that the Single European Act of 1986 marked a departure from the presumption of complementarity between competition and Community social policy.'[39]

---

[37] G. Lyon-Caen, *Le droit du travail*, p. 91.

[38] Once again meant in the broad sense, i.e. here including in the term law aimed at establishing a free market between the Member States (see Lord Wedderburn, 'Freedom', p. 377).

[39] S. Simitis and A. Lyon-Caen, 'Community Labour Law: A Critical Introduction to Its History', in P. Davies *et al.* (eds.), *European Community Labour Law: Principles and Perspectives. Liber Amicorum Lord Wedderburn*, Oxford 1996, pp. 1–22, here p. 9.

In largely abandoning – as has already been pointed out and will be repeated later[40] – the principle of strong upward harmonization of national social systems, the 1986 Act broke the close relationship of complementarity between Community labour law and the organization of fair conditions of competition within the common market that constituted the other characteristic feature of the original model. And whereas this helped to some extent to release Community social policy from the original economic-integration logic of being purely instrumental to the requirements for the proper construction of the common market[41] and in fact justified the establishment (starting with the old Article 118a) of an autonomous normative base for it, albeit initially a partial and restricted one, it at the same time embodied, at least in principle, a rejection of the use of supranational regulation to protect national labour-law systems from the pressures of the competitive dynamic.

It has been said that in 'abandoning the initial conception . . . of the levelling-up of working conditions' the Single European Act actually incorporated the idea of intra-Community competition directly 'based on the reduction of labour costs', thereby overturning the approach of the founding Treaty and injecting into the single market's functioning dynamic a logic of 'tolerated, and encouraged, social dumping'.[42]

Even if we eschew such a radical reading of the Act's intrinsic purport,[43] it is nonetheless certain that severing this initial link of complementarity also helped to make the immunity of national social law from Community competition and market law more fragile, in leaving it more exposed to the pressure emanating from the increased competitive dynamic ignited by the completion of the market 'without internal frontiers'. Viewed from the perspective that became dominant following the Single European Act, national systems of labour and social-security law were more liable to appear to represent, and to be effectively conceptualized and pictured as, concrete obstacles to a free and undistorted movement of goods and

---

[40] See subsection 7 of chapter 1 above and subsections 3 and 4 of chapter 4 below.

[41] Or 'its subservience to the process of market integration', as it was put by P. Davies, 'The Emergence of European Labour Law', in W. E. J. McCarthy (ed.), *Legal Intervention in Industrial Relations: Gains and Losses*, Oxford 1992, pp. 313ff., here p. 346, and also quoted by B. Hepple, 'Social Values and European Law', *Current Legal Problems* 1995, vol. 48 Part 2, pp. 39–61, especially p. 45.

[42] G. Lyon-Caen, 'L'infiltration', p. 319.

[43] See B. Bercusson, 'European Labour Law in Context: A Review of the Literature', *European Law Journal* 1999, pp. 87ff., especially p. 95.

services in the unified market, or an unjustified distortion of competition within it.

From being a presumption or precondition for the evolution of a sound competitive dynamic, labour law thus became 'a brake on economic development'[44] and on the expansion of the internal market.

However, even before the 1986 Act a more direct contribution to this outcome – which, obviously, immediately cast doubt on the primary postulate of reciprocal 'non-interference' between the two normative areas – was made by the extraordinary expansive *vis* assumed in the meantime, in terms which have been emphasized several times and which will now be examined more closely, by the provisions constituting the architrave of the legal construction of a unified European market based on the principles of free competition. Starting, as we shall see next, from that progressively connoted by the provision which has rightly been described as the cornerstone of the Community's economic constitution[45] and which in fact revealed its liberalizing potential earlier: Article 30 (now Article 28 of the EC Treaty).

4. ... particularly in the changing interpretation of Article 30 of the Treaty of Rome (now Article 28 TEC) ...

It has been pointed out – in an essay in which the various historical phases of the complex and stratified changing interpretation of Article 30 were keen-sightedly revisited[46] – that the beginnings of Court of Justice jurisprudence in the matter actually gave no hint at all of the impetuous developments to which we subsequently became accustomed through the increasingly extensive and (at least until recent times) almost uncontrolled application, in all kinds of situations involving public regulation of the market on the part of Member States, of the famous '*Dassonville* formula'.

In the judgment that inaugurated what Joseph Weiler has called the 'foundational period' of this jurisprudence, the Court of Justice, in fact,

---

[44] G. and A. Lyon-Caen, *Droit social international et européen*, 8th edn, Paris 1993, p. 183.

[45] Cf. M. Poiares Maduro, *We, The Court. The European Court of Justice and the European Economic Constitution*, Oxford 1998.

[46] Cf. J. H. H. Weiler, 'The Constitution of the Common Market Place: Text and Context in the Evolution of the Free Movement of Goods', in P. Craig and G. De Búrca (eds.), *The Evolution of EU Law*, Oxford 1999, pp. 349ff. The old numbering of the Treaty is used preferentially here and on the following pages because of the more directly evocative and symbolic force it carries, especially from a retrospective viewpoint.

adopted a relatively narrow and somewhat 'conservative'[47] interpretation of the concept of a 'measure having equivalent effect' (in the case in point, an effect equivalent to customs duties on imports and exports, ex Article 12, now Article 25 of the EC Treaty).

In *Statistical Levy*,[48] the Court had been asked to rule on the legitimacy of a charge levied equally on imported and exported goods in order to finance the collection of statistical data on foreign trade in Italy. The Commission had taken the view that the charge levied – which by its nature, as maintained by the Italian Government, was neither discriminatory nor protectionist – in any event incorporated the essential elements of a charge having an effect equivalent to customs duties.

The Court upheld the Commission's application and ruled that 'any pecuniary charge, however small and whatever its designation and mode of application, which is imposed unilaterally on domestic or foreign goods by reason of the fact that they cross a frontier, and which is not a customs duty in the strict sense, constitutes a charge having equivalent effect within the meaning of Articles 9, 12, 13 and 16 of the Treaty, even if it is not imposed for the benefit of the State, is not discriminatory or protective in effect and if the product on which the charge is imposed is not in competition with any domestic product'.

Although it may seem to all appearances to be inspired by the same rigour, 'the same logic and a similar rhetoric',[49] *Statistical Levy* is in reality very far from anticipating the approach followed in *Dassonville*.[50] The latter, in enshrining the celebrated maxim: 'All trading rules enacted by Member States which are capable of hindering, directly or indirectly, actually or potentially, intra-Community trade are to be considered as measures having an effect equivalent to quantitative restrictions', does not in fact represent 'the natural, seamless extension of *Statistical Levy*, but represents instead an important departure'.[51] It thus carries out a hermeneutic operation that is in a way the opposite of that carried out in *Statistical Levy*.

Statistical Levy falls within a traditional interpretative context and relies on categories conventionally used in the application of agreements on the liberalization of inter-State trade. In ruling against what in reality was held to be a typical charge having an equivalent effect to duties on imports and exports, the judgment is also at pains to make it clear that the concept in question 'does not include taxation which is imposed in the same way

---

[47]   *Ibid.*, p. 354.   [48]   ECJ Case 24/68 *Commission* v *Italy* [1969] ECR 193.
[49]   Weiler, 'Constitution of the Common Market', p. 358.
[50]   ECJ Case 8/74 *Procureur du Roi* v *Dassonville* [1974] ECR 837.
[51]   Weiler, 'Constitution of the Common Market', p. 358.

within a State on similar or comparable domestic products, or at least falls, in the absence of such products, within the framework of general internal taxation, or which is intended to compensate for such internal taxation within the limits laid down by the Treaty'.[52] In so doing the Court makes a clear distinction 'between rules governing market access and rules governing market regulation and considers that the former should, indeed, be obstacle-based and the latter be discrimination-based'.[53] And although this distinction is not always an easy one to make in practice, there is no doubt that it was inspired by a logic essentially shared by the EEC with other international trade regimes such as GATT.[54] And one which therefore reflected, as has again been emphasized by Weiler, 'a conventional and conservative view of a liberal trade regime',[55] in which the firm prohibition on protectionist and discriminatory practices, and hence an undoubted restriction on Member State powers vis-à-vis imported products, was matched by the grant to Member States of substantial freedom as regards 'social and economic regulatory choice'[56] operating at a purely domestic level and, as such, free from discriminatory aspects.

Dassonville, by contrast, signals an interpretative operation that does the complete opposite. The judgment departed from the 'GATT-type' approach and from the model of a balance between free international trade and broad State autonomy in national regulatory options which is inherent in it (and very probably intended by the founding fathers themselves) and imparted to Article 30 of the Treaty a potential meaning endowed with an extraordinary and virtually unlimited capacity to pervade Member States' *domestic choices*. 'Instead of affirming the GATT-oriented distinction between regulation which bars market access and regulation within the market which, however, allows market access to imported products, *Dassonville* conflates the two and then applies to both the same prohibition on unjustified obstacles whether or not discriminatory and/or protectionist.'[57]

This marked a major turning-point in the construction of the common market and the outlines of the Community economic constitution itself. One that was taken up and then sanctioned and further developed by other famous judgments of the next generation which gave full rein to the potential effects of the '*Dassonville* formula'.

---

[52] Paragraph 11 of the judgment.
[53] Weiler, 'Constitution of the Common Market', p. 354.
[54] Cf. M. Egan, *Constructing a European Market*, Oxford 2001, p. 89.
[55] Weiler, 'Constitution of the Common Market', p. 354.
[56] *Ibid.*, p. 357.   [57] *Ibid.*, pp. 358–9.

The very famous *Cassis de Dijon* judgment,[58] which has (perhaps wrongly) passed into history for having first affirmed the principle of mutual recognition that the Commission shortly afterwards made part of the very basis of the entire internal-market project,[59] actually follows in the path of this precedent and is in fact aimed at providing an answer to a number of questions opened up by the latter, at any rate confirming its fundamental *acquis*.

For the purposes of what interests us here, the most relevant consequence of the *Dassonville* jurisprudence is that it 'expands dramatically the number and type of cases in which a Member State is required to justify its social choices in regulating the market place and its public sphere.'[60]

When the criterion governing the application of Article 30 departed from the discrimination test (including indirectly discriminatory effects), this lowered the barriers to spillover of the rules on freedom of movement into practically every area of public regulation of the market, including, obviously, those institutionally reserved to national systems of labour and social-security law.

Article 30 then became – particularly in the hands of those operating economically on a Community scale and thus the most 'naturally' interested in maximizing its liberalizing effects – an instrument that could usefully be invoked, as part of knowingly devised judicial strategies, not only to guarantee access for their goods to the markets of the other Member States (and therefore to further the integration of the latter into the common market) but, more and more frequently, to secure access to the market *tout court* in order to attain greater economic freedom.[61]

It has been argued convincingly that in this the Court was not actually prompted by any specific liberalizing and neoliberal ideology but was, rather, institutionally inclined, in the name of the European polity, towards endowing the provision rightly regarded as the architrave of the entire construction of the common market with maximum effectiveness (*effet utile*).[62] It is, however, undeniable that – at least in the perception

---

[58] ECJ Case 120/78 *Rewe-Zentrale AG* v *Bundesmonopolverwaltung für Branntwein* [1979] ECR 649.

[59] Cf. K. J. Alter and S. Meunier-Aitsahalia, 'Judicial Politics in the European Community. European Integration and the Pathbreaking *Cassis de Dijon* Decision', *Comparative Political Studies* 1994, vol. 26, pp. 535ff.

[60] Weiler, 'Constitution of the Common Market', p. 363.

[61] M. Poiares Maduro, 'Never on a Sunday – What has (EU) Law Got to Do with It?', in S. Sciarra (ed.), *Labour Law in the Courts. National Judges and the European Court of Justice*, Oxford-Portland 2001, pp. 273–90, here p. 273.

[62] This, as already mentioned in subsection 8 of chapter 1 above, is the soundly argued reading put forward by Poiares Maduro, *We, The Court*, especially pp. 61ff.

prevalent in economic circles concerned to exploit it 'strategically' and 'actively' – Article 30 lent itself to becoming a useful instrument for directly challenging an increasingly broader range of national regulatory measures, even in cases where any concrete link with the freedom of intra-Community trade was more tenuous or simply non-existent. That is to say, it is undeniable that certainly in symbolic terms the enormous expansion of the scope of Article 30 (and the consequent need to construe the associated derogations narrowly) 'meant, of course, an inbuilt conservative bias, or at least presumption, in favour of free trade, creating an ethos that any obstacle to free trade is in some ways improper and has to be justified'.[63]

Through Article 30 the Court thus came to be called upon to decide at one and the same time what is the level of governance competent to regulate the market, Community or national, and what is the actual appropriate level of public regulation of the market.[64] And it is clear that the interpretation adopted inevitably tended to predispose the Court's view towards both expanding Community competences to the detriment of national ones and strengthening decision-making/allocation mechanisms directly determined by the market to the detriment of those guided by the political process, in accordance with a logic different from that of maximizing the allocative efficiency of productive resources.

The *Dassonville/Cassis de Dijon* jurisprudence can therefore rightly be seen as having essentially transformed Article 30 – far beyond what appeared to be the (albeit ambiguous) intention crystallized in the rule drafted by the founding fathers – 'into a formidable instrument of the redistribution of power from the Member States to the Community institutions and from political decision-making processes to the market', inasmuch as it meant that 'the task of defining the limits of state regulation is ultimately shifted onto the Court and . . ., through the promotion of regulatory competition, the choice of the optimum level of regulation is entrusted to the market and not to national or Community political decision-makers'.[65]

The considerable broadening of Community (regulatory) competences did not reside solely in the decisive role of arbitrator in the matter assumed by the Court of Justice (and indirectly, in the shade of the latter, by

[63] Weiler, 'Constitution of the Common Market', p. 363.

[64] Cf. Poiares Maduro, *We, The Court*, pp. 35ff., and also Poiares Maduro, 'Reforming the Market or the State? Article 30 and the European Constitution: Economic Freedom and Political Rights', *European Law Journal* 1997, pp. 55ff.

[65] M. Barbera, *Dopo Amsterdam. I nuovi confini del diritto sociale comunitario*, Brescia 2000, p. 54.

the Commission) but in the expansion of the scope of ex Article 100 and, therefore, ex Article 100a of the Treaty, which became immediately enforceable where the national legislative measure in question, although *prima facie* constituting an obstacle according to the *Dassonville* formula, is nevertheless justifiable (if discriminatory) in the light of the express derogations provided for by Article 36 or (if applicable indiscriminately) of the 'mandatory requirements' that can be invoked by virtue of *Cassis de Dijon*.

It is, however, plain, at least from the viewpoint of relevance here and especially given the merely residual or subordinate nature of the broadening of legislative competences within the meaning of ex Articles 100 and 100a, that the decisive element was in fact the extraordinary expansion of the role of the Court of Justice as constitutional adjudicator. Institutionally, the Court thus placed itself at the centre of 'substantive policy dilemmas', becoming 'the arbiter of delicate social choices, reconciling trade with competing [national] social policies'.[66] This is not a case solely (or so much) of regulatory dilemmas that are per se inappropriate and excessive for the Court, which in fact has found itself continually constrained to explore all of its legitimation resources and put them to the test.[67]

Regulatory dilemmas of the kind are actually recurrent in (and in some ways typical of) any curb on the legitimacy of the acts of legislators: that is, they are inherent in the very logic of checks on constitutionality and constitutional adjudication. From this point of view, they are experienced by the Court of Justice insofar as it performs such a function,[68] in exactly the same way as they are encountered by a national constitutional court.

The crucial point, in reality, is that in undertaking these delicate balancing operations between conflicting interests and values the Court of

---

[66] Weiler, 'Constitution of the Common Market', p. 363.

[67] Cf. S. Simitis, 'Dismantling or Strengthening Labour Law: The Case of the European Court of Justice', *European Law Journal* 1996, vol. 2 no. 2, pp. 156–76.

[68] It is now common among legal scholars to draw an analogy between the functions that the Court of Justice has progressively taken upon itself by virtue of Article 177 (now Article 234) in its vigorous activity in constitutionalizing the founding Treaty and the functions specific to a federal constitutional court. In this sense see, recently, R. Dehousse, *The European Court of Justice. The Politics of Judicial Integration*, London-New York 1998, pp. 21ff., and – among labour lawyers – R. Foglia, 'Il ruolo della Corte di Giustizia e il rapporto tra giudice comunitario e i giudici nazionali nel quadro dell'art. 177 del Trattato (con particolare riferimento alle politiche sociali)', *Diritto del Lavoro* 1999, vol. I, pp. 138ff. For an earlier suggestion in this direction see P. Pescatore, 'La Cour en tant que juridiction fédérale et constitutionnelle', in *Dix ans de jurisprudence de la Cour de Justice des Communautés européennes*, Cologne, 1965.

Justice takes its cue from criteria that tend to preassign a natural prevalence to the requirements of the market. From, therefore, interpretative (or, more accurately, assessment) principles which do not always coincide with those that govern the balancing operations allowed by national constitutional systems in which economic freedoms are not elevated to the 'fundamental' status accorded them by Community law and so have to give way on various fronts relating to the protection of the individual in all the complexity and profundity of his *social* relations.[69]

By its very logic, the fundamental principle of free movement of goods[70] lends a bias, in the sense just mentioned, to the criteria that are effectively available to the Court in assessing and weighing up the interests at issue.

It is undoubtedly true that assessment of the 'imperative reasons in the general interest' allowed by the *Cassis de Dijon* jurisprudence accommodates interests other than those directly protected by Article 30 of the Treaty. Nevertheless, it is equally clear that the rigour with which the Court grants access to possible justifications under this heading for regulatory choices made by a Member State – in terms such as to hinder, actually or potentially, free trade within the common market – is inclined to relegate these requirements to an uncertain and increasingly recessive position. It is undeniable, in this sense, that the fundamental principle underpinning the application of Article 30 is 'potentially highly destructive of national regulatory regimes'.[71]

The judicial control exercised by the Court of Justice directly involves the merit of the choice made by national legislators; the balance test is calibrated according to a rigorous (and largely discretionary) analysis of the (economic) costs and the (social) benefits of the measure being

---

[69] The subject will be taken up again at more length below, mainly with reference to the potential clashes in values and associated conflicting assessments that can arise in relation to the Italian Constitution. For the time being, however, cf. M. Cartabia, *Principi inviolabili e integrazione comunitaria*, Milan 1995, pp. 37ff.

[70] But similar considerations can be repeated with respect to the principle of free movement of services, which more and more frequently tends to be combined with the former in concrete developments in the Court's jurisprudence. Take, for example, the events (to which we shall return in more detail later) that led, on 28 April 1998, to the judgments in *Decker* (Case C-120/95 [1998] ECR I-1831) and *Kohll* (Case C-158/96 [1998] ECR I-1931), one relating to Article 30 and the other to Article 59 of the Treaty but both entirely in tune with each other as regards the line of reasoning followed and the judicial outcome. Among legal scholars see, for instance, S. O'Leary, 'Free Movement of Persons and Services', in Craig and De Búrca, *Evolution*, pp. 377ff.; V. Hatzopoulos, 'Recent Developments of the Case Law of the ECJ in the Field of Services', *Common Market Law Review* 2000, pp. 43ff

[71] P. Davies, 'Posted Workers: Single Market or Protection of National Labour Systems?', *Common Market Law Review* 1997, vol. 34, pp. 571–602, here p. 587.

challenged.[72] The latter, provided they meet mandatory requirements in the general interest, are not only to be assessed in relation to the resultant cost in terms of loss of economic efficiency and reduction of the scope for free trade but are also subject to comparison, in deference to the principle of proportionality, with all of the possible alternative measures which, in being less restrictive, are capable of producing a higher net benefit.[73] As one author has defined it precisely, the 'strict scrutiny standard' used in this way by the Court 'means that the justification demanded for national legislators' actions is extremely rigorous, since: (*a*) the social goal to be achieved must fulfil a criterion not just of political appropriateness but *necessity*; and (*b*) the circumstances must be such that it is not possible to apply alternative measures that are less of a hindrance to trade'.[74]

Given these premises, it is not surprising that in the cases in which – for the most part from the second half of the 1980s onwards – national legislative measures on more or less traditional and significant aspects of the regulation of employment relationships or social-security systems have had to face the test imposed by Article 30,[75] the balancing exercise carried out by the Court of Justice has seemed imperfect or elusive, if not concealed or even denied.[76]

The superior status of a fundamental individual right that is accorded by the Court of Justice to the principle of free movement of goods[77] means that legal situations or objective values protected by national law which operate contrary to that principle or are at any rate brought face to face with it are rendered uncertain and precarious.

Indeed, the increasingly interwoven dialogue conducted by the Court of Justice with national legal communities that have been far from passive

---

[72] See Poiares Maduro, *We, The Court*, p. 49ff.

[73] *Ibid.*, p. 58.   [74] Barbera, *Dopo Amsterdam*, p. 54.

[75] But this is an observation that can also be directly extended, as stated above, to other aspects of the infiltration of competition law into national labour-law systems. We need only think – to give an example that cannot be examined in more detail in the present study – of the increasingly difficult relationship between traditional forms of financial employment assistance and Community rules on state aids, in the terms in which, essentially from the early 1990s, these rules have started to be rigorously applied by the Commission with the endorsement of the Court of Justice. See M. Tiraboschi, *Incentivi all'occupazione, aiuti di Stato, diritto comunitario della concorrenza*, Turin 2002.

[76] Davies, 'Market', pp. 51 and 66ff.; M. Poiares Maduro, 'Striking the Elusive Balance between Economic Freedom and Social Rights', in P. Alston (ed.), *The EU and Human Rights*, Oxford 1999, pp. 449ff.

[77] See, for example, ECJ Case 240/83 *Procureur de la République* v *ADBHU* [1985] ECR 531; J. Baquero Cruz, *Between Competition and Free Movement. The Economic Constitutional Law of the European Communities*, Oxford-Portland, 2002, especially chapter 5.

in accepting the promptings and pointers issuing from Luxembourg[78] reveals fairly clearly an imbalance in the meaning and concrete normative content of the 'messages' conveyed through Article 30 of the founding Treaty. There have been numerous cases of the strategic use of preliminary references shrewdly piloted by a limited and strongly identified and motivated 'community of interests and actors'.[79] Thus, we find a significantly high percentage of strategic court actions focused on expanding the *effet utile* of Article 30 to the maximum degree possible and co-ordinated – even between lawyers and litigants in different Member States – by the same economic actors with the backing of expert legal assistance for the main purpose of overcoming unwelcome limits or obstacles interposed by national legislation (the famous Sunday Trading Saga is one of the most interesting examples of the activism demonstrated in this direction by one of the most seasoned 'repeat players' to appear on the scene).[80]

The risks of 'advancing instrumentalization of the European Court of Justice for the resolution of national disputes'[81] are only too evident. It is in the light of this context that we need to view the efforts made by the Court to curb such attempts and so stem the growing unease caused to it – mainly in terms of the substantive legitimation of its activity – by the increasing politicization of its role.[82]

The signs of what, after *Keck and Mithouard*,[83] came to be seen as a marked reversal of its tendency on the part of the Court are in fact already clearly visible in the final stages of the Sunday Trading Saga. What is more, from its very outset Advocate General Van Gerven had given the Court a clear warning of the considerable risk it could incur by concerning itself

---

[78] See Poiares Maduro, 'Never on a Sunday', pp. 283ff.

[79] Poiares Maduro, *We, The Court*, p. 30.

[80] R. Rawlings, 'The Eurolaw Game: Some Deductions from a Saga', *Journal of Law and Society* 1993, vol. 20 no. 3, p. 309, from whom the expression used in the text has been taken; also C. Barnard, 'Sunday Trading: A Drama in Five Acts', *Modern Law Review* 1994, vol. 57, pp. 449ff., here p. 450, again on the subject of (British) cases regarding the prohibition on shops opening on Sundays (and hence on working on Sundays), talks of 'an orchestrated campaign' on the part of several large retail concerns. See also A. Arnull, 'What Shall We Do on Sunday?', *European Law Review* 1991, pp. 112ff.

[81] Simitis, 'Dismantling', p. 173.

[82] The politicization of the Court's role – due to the shifting of regulatory issues from the national political and democratic process to that which takes place in the lists of the supranational judiciary – is the other side of the coin of the judicialization of 'domestic' policy disputes by actors with an interest in overcoming or, more accurately, bypassing, blocks or impasses inherent in the national political process. Cf. Dehousse, *The European Court*, pp. 97ff.

[83] ECJ Joined Cases C-267/91 and C-268/91 [1993] ECR I-6097.

with 'areas of policy for which Community law provides no, or at any rate few, criteria of assessment' and therefore suggested that 'such a difficult inquiry relating to national measures such as those at issue here should be avoided as far as possible by interpreting Article 30 in accordance with the intendment of the Treaty'.[84] It is well known that the Court forbore at the time to follow the Advocate General's prudent advice and that it was only later, after the appearance of the first negative consequences of this new episode of the provision's spillover[85] and in response to the clear call made to it by the House of Lords to 'assume responsibility',[86] that it went into 'full retreat' from the tricky entanglement of issues involved in assessing the legitimacy of a Community ban on Sunday opening for (and hence Sunday work in) retail outlets, 'insisting that no Article 30 point arose for consideration in such cases'.[87]

This 'retreat' presaged, in a way, the 'turnabout' that the Court was to make with its judgment in *Keck and Mithouard*. Here again, it had been confronted with the basic question arising from the uncontrolled expansion of the scope of the principle of free movement of goods: 'Is Article 30 of the Treaty a provision intended to liberalize intra-Community trade or is it intended more generally to encourage the unhindered pursuit of commerce in individual Member States?'[88]

That the Court felt an urgent need to free itself from its growing unease at the proliferation of 'instrumental' use of Article 30 and to signal its clear intention to change course seems beyond dispute. 'In view of the increasing tendency of traders to invoke Article 30 of the Treaty as a means of challenging any rules whose effect is to limit their commercial freedom even where such rules are not aimed at products from other Member States, the Court' – it is stated peremptorily in paragraph 14

---

[84] See point 33 of the Advocate General's Opinion in Case C-145/88 *Torfaen Borough Council v B&Q plc* [1989] ECR 3851, here p. 3883.

[85] As recorded by Poiares Maduro, 'Never on a Sunday', p. 274, 'the temporary deregulation of Sunday trading was effective in causing a reassessment of national policy on Sunday trading by the political process, leading to the adoption of new British rules which favoured those wishing to trade on Sundays.'

[86] Cf. ECJ Case C-169/91 *Stoke-on-Trent* [1992] ECR I-6635, in which, answering the specific questions referred to it by the House of Lords, the Court in fact expressly ruled that the challenged national rules were legitimate within the meaning of Article 30. Thereafter it held fast to the same principle in successive judgments delivered in answer to similar questions also referred to it in the meantime by other national jurisdictions; see Roccella, *La Corte di Giustizia*, pp. 85ff.

[87] Davies, 'Market', p. 52.

[88] This is the question with which Advocate General Tesauro significantly opened his Opinion, delivered on 27 October 1993, in Case C-292/92 *Hünermund* [1993] ECR I-6787.

of the judgment – 'considers it necessary to re-examine and clarify its case-law on this matter'.

In its judgment the difficult task of restoring much-needed balance in the application of Article 30 is entrusted by the Court to the introduction of the notion of 'selling arrangements' as a case broadly lying outside the scope of the provision. On the one hand, obstacles which, in the absence of harmonization of national legislation, are the consequence of applying to goods coming from other Member States where they are lawfully manufactured and marketed rules that lay down *requirements* to be met by such goods are still regarded as constituting measures of equivalent effect prohibited by Article 30, even if those rules apply without distinction to all products and are not necessarily justified by a public-interest objective taking precedence over the free movement of goods. On the other hand, the application to products from other Member States of national provisions restricting or prohibiting certain *selling arrangements* is not, by contrast, deemed to hinder trade between Member States within the meaning of the *Dassonville* formula, so long as those provisions apply to all relevant traders operating within the national territory and affect in the same manner, in law and in fact, the marketing of domestic products and those from other Member States.

The *Dassonville* and *Cassis de Dijon* jurisprudence has therefore not been totally abandoned, or directly reversed or refracted. Rather, *Keck* 'restricted *Cassis de Dijon* to measures relating to product requirements and reinterpreted *Dassonville* but only with reference to measures restricting or prohibiting "selling arrangements"'.[89] The former were still to be subject, as before, to the balance test,[90] while the latter were made subject to a test that undoubtedly 'brought the concept of discrimination back to the heart of Article 30'.[91]

The subsequent evolution of Community case-law on Article 30[92] has in a way borne out the prediction of those who had taken the view that the 'reform' brought about by *Keck* – although enough to curb to some extent exploitation of the rule as a means of challenging any national rule aimed at restricting freedom of trade – would not, in itself, increase the

---

[89] Poiares Maduro, *We, The Court*, p. 79, who consistently with this sees *Keck* as 'more of a reform than a revolution'.

[90] See G. Tesauro, *Diritto comunitario*, Padua 1995, p. 287.

[91] Poiares Maduro, *We, The Court*, p. 78; similarly, S. Weatherill, 'After *Keck*: Some Thoughts on How to Clarify the Clarification', *Common Market Law Review* 1996, vol. 33, pp. 885ff.

[92] On which see L. González Vaqué, 'La jurisprudence relative à l'article 28 CE (ex article 30) après l'arrêt *Keck et Mithouard*', *Revue du Droit de l'Union Européenne* 2000, no. 2, pp. 395ff.

degree of legal certainty in this crucial area nor, therefore, greatly reduce the Court's workload.[93]

And it is no accident that it is still social litigation based on Article 30 that reveals, with particular clarity, the persistent expansive dynamic of the fundamental freedom it guarantees and the still unresolved difficulty encountered by the Court in finding an adequate basis for striking a balance with interests opposed to those to which it still gives preferential protection.

Mention has already been made above of the situation that was the subject of *Commission* v *France*[94] and also of that ruled on in the *Decker* judgment.

In the former case, the Commission of the European Communities had brought an action claiming that France was in infringement of Article 30 because it had failed to fulfil its obligation to take all necessary measures in order to prevent the free movement of goods from being obstructed by campaigns including acts of vandalism, threats or bans carried out within its territory for more than a decade by groupings of French farmers against agricultural products from other Member States (particularly Spain).

As is well known, in upholding the Commission's claim the Court pronounced the innovative principle whereby 'As an indispensable instrument for the realization of a market without internal frontiers, Article 30 does not merely prohibit measures emanating from the State which, in themselves, create restrictions on trade between Member States, but may also apply where a State abstains from adopting the measures required in order to deal with obstacles to the free movement of goods which are not caused by the State', meaning that in such circumstances an act of omission can represent an obstacle just as much as an act of commission. Article 30 therefore requires the Member States 'not merely themselves to abstain from adopting measures or engaging in conduct liable to constitute an obstacle to trade but also, when read with Article 5 of the Treaty, to take all necessary and appropriate measures to ensure that the free movement of goods, a fundamental freedom, is complied with on their territory'.

This pronouncement is notable not merely, and not so much, for the strong reaffirmation of the *Dassonville* doctrine[95] as for the significant

---

[93] Cf. M. Poiares Maduro, '*Keck*: The End? The Beginning of the End? Or Just the End of the Beginning?', *Irish Journal of European Law* 1994, vol. 1, pp. 30ff.

[94] ECJ Case C-265/95 [1997] ECR I-6959.

[95] See González Vaqué, 'La jurisprudence', p. 401.

and entirely new extension of the scope *ratione personae* of Article 30, owing to its being read in conjunction with Article 5 (now Article 10 of the EC Treaty) to also include actions (creating obstacles) carried out by private individuals.[96] And from the viewpoint that most interests us here, it is notable in particular for the force *ratione materiae* it appears to inject afresh into 'freedom of trade *tout court*'[97] as a fundamental principle of the Community legal order which as such prevails over opposing interests involving the freedom to take collective action in situations that are safeguarded by national legal systems.

As signalled by the doctrine thus put forward, the wording used by the Court in denouncing on the basis of Article 30 any kind of conduct such as to create a climate of insecurity or uncertainty which has 'a deterrent effect on trade flows as a whole'[98] is so broad that it can be 'applied to situations that go far beyond pure and simple acts of vandalism visited upon goods'[99] and potentially also extended to forms of industrial action that are totally legitimate under the national legal system concerned and possibly recognized by it as a fundamental right or freedom for workers. In the obvious tension between economic freedoms and collective action, the former tend *naturaliter* to take precedence over the latter. Any balancing with legal positions such as those relating to strike action, which particularly in 'Mediterranean constitutional traditions'[100] are elevated to the status of fundamental social rights, takes place in a hidden manner or, rather, is 'cut off at the roots' owing to the tendency to accord absolute pre-eminence – based on a scale of values that is exactly the reverse of that accepted by the above-mentioned constitutional traditions – to the freedom of intra-Community trade.

Any possibility of striking a balance is preserved solely thanks to a piece of compensatory Community legislation which – although endorsing the marked broadening of the material and personal scope of Article 30 – avoids or at least reduces the most dangerous corrosive effects of an unconditional affirmation of the freedom of trade as a Community limit on industrial action by expressly stipulating that the new 'praetorian' rules may not be interpreted 'as affecting in any way the exercise of

---

[96] Cf. G. Orlandini, 'Libertà di circolazione delle merci: un limite "comunitario" al conflitto sindacale', *Giornale di Diritto del Lavoro e di Relazioni Industriali* 1999, pp. 623ff., especially pp. 628.

[97] *Ibid.*, p. 629.   [98] Paragraph 53 of the judgment.

[99] Orlandini, 'Libertà', p. 632.   [100] *Ibid.*, p. 647.

fundamental rights as recognised in Member States, including the right or freedom to strike'.[101]

Although in terms of the conceptual development it represented it was probably not as innovative as that explored by *Commission* v *France*, the case-law that culminated in the *Decker* judgment[102] would appear no less significant in revealing the potential for expansion, *in casu* to the detriment of the consolidated balances of national social-security systems, left intact for the freedom of trade as envisaged by Article 30.

It is true that strategic use of this provision as a means of overcoming regulatory limits and restrictions imposed by Member States mainly to control public expenditure in the health sector is nothing really new. What is, however, new is the effectiveness demonstrated more recently by the use of Article 30 (and Article 59) of the Treaty – as opposed to what was still evident, for example, in the *Duphar* judgment of 1984[103] – in circumventing one of the firmest principles (one might almost say institutional assumptions) in the matter: the almost absolute reservation

---

[101] As provided for by Article 2 of Council Regulation No. 2679/98 [1998] OJ L337/8, on which see A. Mattera, 'Un instrument d'intervention rapide pour sauvegarder l'unicité du Marché intérieur: le règlement 2679/98', *Revue du Marché Unique Européen* 1999, no. 2, pp. 99ff. More recently, the Court of Justice found itself having to strike a balance of interests between the principle of free movement of goods on the basis of Article 28 of the EC Treaty and exercise of the fundamental freedoms of assembly and expression as guaranteed, in the case in point, by Austria's Constitution and by Articles 10 and 11 of the European Convention on Human Rights (see Case C-112/00, *Eugen Schmidberger, Internationale Transporte und Planzüge* v *Austria* [2003] ECR I-5659). The Court held that the Austrian Government's decision to authorize (or not to ban) a demonstration by environmental protesters which impeded the freedom of movement guaranteed by Article 28 of the Treaty was based on legitimate protection of the fundamental rights recognized by Articles 10 and 11 of the ECHR and was proportionate to the pursuit of that legitimate aim. For a comment on the judgment see A. Biondi, 'Free Trade, a Mountain Road and the Right to Protest: European Economic Freedoms and Fundamental Individual Rights', *European Human Rights Law Review* 2004, no. 1, pp. 73ff.

[102] For the relevant references, see note 70 above. For a wide-ranging analysis of this and the judgment delivered on the same date in *Kohll*, see: P. Mavridis, 'Une libéralisation des soins de santé? Un premier diagnostic après les arrêts *Kohll* et *Decker*', *Droit Social* 1999, pp. 172ff.; Mavridis, 'Libéralisation des soins de santé en Europe: un premier diagnostic', *Revue du Marché Unique Européen* 1998, no. 3, pp. 145ff.; A. P. Van der Mei, 'Cross-Border Access to Medical Care within the European Union – Some Reflections on the Judgments in *Decker* and *Kohll*', *Maastricht Journal of European and Comparative Law* 1998, pp. 277ff.; L. González Vaqué, 'Aplicación del principio fundamental de la libre circulación al ámbito de la seguridad social: la sentencia *Decker*', *Revista de Derecho Comunitario Europeo* 1999, pp. 129ff.; A. Bosco, 'Are National Social Protection Systems Under Threat? Observations on the Recent Case Law of the Court of Justice', *Groupement d'Etudes et de Recherches Notre Europe – European Issues* 2000, no. 7.

[103] ECJ Case 238/82 *Duphar BV* v *Netherlands* [1984] ECR 523.

to individual Member States of competence in the financial organization of their respective social-security and public healthcare systems.

In *Decker* the question that had been referred concerned the legitimacy, within the meaning of Article 30, of a requirement for prior authorization from the competent national social-insurance institution – in this case the Luxembourg Caisse de Maladie des Employés Privés – in order to qualify for reimbursement of the medical expenses incurred in another Member State for the purchase of a pair of spectacles with corrective lenses as duly prescribed by an ophthalmologist.[104] The national rules at issue, which were being alleged to constitute an unjustified barrier to the free movement of goods as envisaged by Article 30, in fact followed the principle laid down in Article 22 of Regulation No. 1408/71 without any significant variations, and so were seen as being consistent with it.

In pronouncing the incompatibility of the Luxembourg rules with Articles 30 and 36 of the Treaty as constituting a barrier to the free movement of goods within the internal market, the Court states quite definitely that, despite what was maintained by the Member State governments which submitted observations, these rules are not justified 'by the risk of seriously undermining the financial balance of the social security system . . ., nor are they justified on grounds of public health in order to ensure the quality of medical products supplied to insured persons in other Member States'.[105] Consequently, the mandatory requirements which were mentioned earlier and which in abstract terms are certainly such as to justify the rules being challenged, could not in practice be invoked in the case in point. And the Court is equally clear in pointing out, with regard to the first and more significant category of justification, that a serious risk of undermining the financial balance of the system could justify obstacles to the free movement of goods (or services) only on the basis of the customary canons of (strict) scrutiny applied in the matter and with the burden of proof obviously resting on the Member State concerned.

Furthermore, it states trenchantly that 'the fact that the national rules at issue in the main proceedings fall within the sphere of social security cannot exclude the application of Article 30 of the Treaty'.[106]

---

[104] In *Kohll* the challenge concerned in wholly analogous terms the legitimacy, this time on the basis of Article 59 of the Treaty, of a refusal to grant the authorization requested by a Luxembourg insured person in the name and on behalf of his youngest daughter to obtain from the insurance institution to which he belonged the cost of dental treatment to be carried out in another Member State.

[105] As put in the official summary of the judgment. Entirely corresponding conclusions are reached in *Kohll* with reference to Article 59.

[106] Paragraph 25 of the judgment.

The premiss – confirmed with little conviction on the basis of *Duphar*[107] and borrowed case-law on Regulation No. 1408/71 – whereby 'Community law does not detract from the powers of the Member States to organize their social security systems' and that 'In the absence of harmonization at Community level, it is therefore for the legislation of each Member State to determine, first, the conditions concerning the right or duty to be insured with a social security scheme . . . and, second, the conditions for entitlement to benefits',[108] is emptied of any real content by the Court's pronouncement and given what is now the flavour of purely ritual acknowledgement.

In reality, these powers are directly detracted from and limited by the law of the transnational market. The sphere of full sovereignty that was guaranteed to the Member States in the original approach adopted by the Treaties is now directly 'encapsulated'[109] by Article 30, with effects 'that can have somewhat "destructuring" consequences as regards the institutional and organizational status quo',[110] especially in view of the uncertainty (and opaque nature) of the non-articulated balancing operations carried out to date by the Court of Justice in such delicate and politically sensitive matters.

On the other hand, the Court is more cautious when it comes to including hospital treatment in the scope of the freedom of movement guaranteed by the Treaty. In the face of the more likely risks of undermining the financial balance of national health and social-security systems that are implied by such an eventuality, it did not rule against the legitimacy, within the meaning of Article 59, of a requirement for prior authorization from the competent institution in order to benefit from hospital treatment provided in another Member State for which the costs are reimbursed by the national insurance body.[111] It has, however, rigorously restricted the margins for discretion in deciding the conditions governing such authorization[112] and even here 'encapsulated' the powers thus reserved to the Member States within the limits imposed by the principle of proportionality.

---

[107] And also of the similar ruling delivered in Case C-70/95 *Sodemare* v *Regione Lombardia* [1997] ECR I-3395.
[108] Paragraphs 21 and 22 of the judgment.   [109] Ferrera, 'Integrazione europea', p. 408.
[110] *Ibid.*, p. 411.   [111] See ECJ Case C-157/99 *Geraets-Smits* [2001] ECR I-5473.
[112] See also ECJ Case C-368/98 *Vanbraekel and Others* [2001] ECR I-5363; ECJ Case C-385/99 *Müller-Fauré and van Riet* [2003] ECR I-4509 (and, for a comment, M. Fuchs, 'Il diritto di cura all'estero nella giurisprudenza della Corte di giustizia europea: la prospettiva tedesca', *Rivista del Diritto della Sicurezza Sociale* 2004, no. 2, pp. 621ff.).

The total absorption of social security into the scope of the free movement of goods and services, despite the autonomy and discretionary powers formally accorded to the Member States in this field, inevitably carries a 'destructuring' potential that in all probability outweighs the actual efforts, albeit commendable, made by the Court of Justice to balance and reconcile the different interests at stake.[113]

5. . . . and of Articles 85, 86 and 90 of the Treaty of Rome (now Articles 81, 82 and 86 TEC)

Even a superficial glance reveals that the changing interpretation of the rules underpinning Community competition law *sensu stricto* has followed a course very similar to that which has marked the progressive expansion of the scope of Article 30.

Here too, we find a convergent thrust towards extending beyond the boundaries indicated by what was agreed in the founding Treaty; a thrust which tends to make competition, initially relegated to the role of an 'economic-law category of relations between producers . . ., [the] model governing every relationship that has economic relevance'.[114] In this case, it is the primary Community sources themselves that express the sense of the radical change of approach as compared with the early days: it has rightly been said that 'by inserting at Article 3(g) as one of the Union's objectives that of achieving "a system ensuring that competition in the internal market is not distorted", the Maastricht Treaty endowed freedom of competition with a status different from that attributed to the other freedoms'.[115]

Commentators are at one in taking the view – albeit with differing degrees of emphasis and assessments – that the focus of Community policy on competition has progressively shifted from an objective of integrating national markets into the common market to an objective of promoting efficiency of the market as such, by distilling the latter into the principle of 'undistorted' competition.[116] In these circumstances, it seems fair to say that starting from the second half of the 1980s what has evocatively been called the 'public turn'[117] of Community intervention on competition has to some extent marked, albeit without totally abandoning the first

---

[113] Cf. M. Fuchs, 'Free Movement of Services and Social Security – Quo Vadis?', *European Law Journal* 2002, pp. 536ff.

[114] L. Di Via, 'Considerazioni sulle "mobili frontiere" del diritto della concorrenza', *Contratto e Impresa/Europa* 2000, no. 1, pp. 1ff., here p. 2.

[115] *Ibid.*, p. 1.   [116] Cf. Gerber, 'The Transformation', pp. 98ff.   [117] *Ibid.*, p. 137.

objective but rather absorbing it in or lumping it together with the second, the point of passage from the one to the other.

With the Single European Act signalling achievement of the objective of creating a virtually unified internal market, the fight against distortions of competition caused by the persistent presence – in all of the major Member States except for Thatcherite Britain – of large public monopolies or, at any rate, penetrating forms of state intervention in key sectors of the several national economies, became the instrument for both giving practical effect to the process of market unification and promoting, within its context, a system of undistorted competition.

As one author put it admirably: 'Since the middle of the 1980s the attention of the Commission has increasingly turned to the issue of the impact of the public sector on the creation of a single market, for national public-sector or state-supported monopolies now constitute the most obvious embodiment of the old pattern of nationally segmented markets which it is the object of the Community to destroy. Although the Commission has never said that public ownership as such is inconsistent with the Treaty, it has pursued a rigorous policy of liberalization in the name of market integration.'[118]

This drastic shift of focus in Community intervention – formerly concentrated almost exclusively on the conduct of private individuals and now mainly directed towards national government interference in the competitive process – has also brought about a profound change in the original balances between supranational competition law and national systems of labour law.

For the purposes of the present study, it will be sufficient to examine the significance of the radical change of course adopted – with the active support of the Court of Justice – in the interpretation and application of Articles 85, 86 and 90 (now Articles 81, 82 and 86 of the EC Treaty). However, entirely similar considerations could be repeated in the case of the extraordinary emphasis placed by the Commission (and by the Court), from as far back as the early 1990s, on the Community rules relating to state aids, which after a lengthy phase of maintaining an almost totally 'frozen' profile suddenly became one of the most acute and pressing obstacles to the development of the traditional economic (anti-competition) intervention of the old Keynesian state.

The subject will be taken up again in subsection 6 below, where two developments that are in a way paradigmatic of this change in the

[118] Davies, 'Market', p. 69.

Community's attitude towards public monopolies (of a social nature) will be analysed more closely. However, it is timely at this point to draw attention to what may be called the main determining factors of this process, which can as a whole be usefully depicted with the perhaps slightly conventional but effective image of the expansion, both *ratione materiae* and *ratione personae*, of the highly moveable boundaries of the scope of Articles 85 et seq. of the Treaty.[119]

Expansion of the limits *ratione materiae* of competition law has essentially taken place through the large-scale reversal of the terms of application of Article 90, or through what an alert commentator has figuratively dubbed 'the velvet revolution'[120] in its interpretation effected by the Court of Justice in the early 1990s.

Awoken from the 'deep sleep'[121] and state of inoffensive non-application[122] or, to put it more kindly, marginality[123] in which it had long languished, Article 90 – bursting the banks of its application as originally envisaged by the founding fathers – became the keystone of the strategy for the liberalization of services of general economic interest adopted by the Commission, with the full backing of the Court of Justice, from the end of the 1980s onwards.[124]

Although it did so with the inevitable lexical ambiguity of compromise rules, Article 90 expressed clearly enough the sense of the contradictory mix of liberalism and interventionism, of a free (transnational) market and strong public intervention in the (national) economy, that gave substance to the original Community balance of 'embedded liberalism'. In the oxymoron-like form of what Advocate General Tesauro was later to refer to as its 'manifest obscurity',[125] Article 90 confirmed, with respect to

---

[119] Cf. Di Via, 'Considerazioni', pp. 5ff.

[120] A. Gardner, 'The Velvet Revolution: Article 90 and the Triumph of the Market in Europe's Regulated Sector', *European Competition Law Review* 1995, no. 2, pp. 78–86.

[121] A. Pappalardo, 'State Measures and Public Undertakings: Article 90 of the EEC Treaty Revisited', *European Competition Law Review* 1991, no. 1, pp. 29ff., here p. 30.

[122] C.-D. Ehlermann, 'The Contribution of EC Competition Policy to the Single Market', *Common Market Law Review* 1992, vol. 29, pp. 257–82, especially p. 264, where it is stated that the Article's provisions began to be effectively applied as part of the more general strategy for the implementation (and liberalization) of the single market only after the entry into force of the Single European Act in 1986.

[123] P. Fattori, 'Monopoli pubblici e articolo 90 del Trattato CE nella giurisprudenza comunitaria', *Mercato Concorrenza Regole* 1999, pp. 127ff., especially p. 129.

[124] Cf. also L. Hancher, 'Community, State and Market', in Craig and De Búrca, *Evolution*, pp. 721ff.; J.-F. Auby, *Les services publics en Europe*, Paris 1998, pp. 76ff.

[125] The wording used in point 1 of his Opinion delivered in ECJ Case C-202/88 *France v Commission* [1991] ECR I-1223, better known as *Telecommunications Terminals*.

public monopolies and exclusive rights, what was established more generally but less ambiguously by Article 122 in relation to systems of property
ownership that were acceptable in the context of the common market.
Monopolies, as also public ownership of undertakings and the means of
production, were in themselves perfectly legitimate; and the construction
of the common market was not to interfere with them in any way, with
the principle to be followed being one of absolute neutrality save for a
proper safeguard for the Community – which although established from
the outset by Article 90(1) was never applied until relatively recently –
against any more overtly abusive measures on the part of the Member
States.

As stated by a leading authority,[126] Article 90 was therefore based on
the assumption that Member States were in reality entirely free to grant
exclusive rights, the sole restriction being a prohibition on their enacting
and applying any measure that allowed undertakings possessing those
exclusive rights to act in a discriminatory manner.

The overall tenor of a compromise between the free-trade volition
underlying the creation of a common market firmly founded on the (gradual) application of the four freedoms of movement and the maintenance of
institutional arrangements capable of securing maximum public control
over the several national economies also emerged clearly from Article 37
of the Treaty of Rome (now Article 31). In imposing on Member States the
obligation to 'progressively adjust any State monopolies of a commercial
character so as to ensure that when the transitional period has ended no
discrimination regarding the conditions under which goods are procured
and marketed exists' between their nationals, it in fact in no way curbed
the freedom to make national political choices creating public monopolies in the *production* of goods and services deemed to be of general
interest.[127]

On the very rare occasions throughout the 1960s and 1970s on which
it had been called upon to consider questions falling within the triangle
traced by Articles 37, 90 and 222 of the Treaty, the Court had always
been very clear in reaffirming the principle of neutrality and essential
Community non-interference established in the matter by the founding

---

[126] See G. Amato, 'Citizenship and Public Services – Some General Reflections', in M. Freedland and S. Sciarra (eds.), *Public Services and Citizenship in European Law. Public and
Labour Law Perspectives*, Oxford 1998, pp. 145–56, here p. 153.

[127] Cf. Gardner, 'Velvet', p. 78; Pappalardo, 'State', p. 32; J. J. Montero Pascual, 'I monopoli
nazionali pubblici in un mercato unico concorrenziale. Evoluzione e riforma dell'art. 90
del Trattato', *Rivista Italiana di Diritto Pubblico Comunitario* 1997, pp. 663ff.

fathers in the shape of these provisions. In perfect harmony with the position adopted by the Commission itself, the Community judges had decisively pointed to the principle whereby 'Member States were free to confer exclusive rights on undertakings for considerations of public interest of a non-economic nature' and according to which, consequently, 'the grant of such rights could not of itself violate Article 90(1)'.[128]

In the judgment it delivered on 30 April 1974 in *Sacchi*[129] (an obligatory point of reference that is universally mentioned by specialist scholars for an understanding of the original interpretive stance adopted by the Commission and the Court of Justice) the Court, finding itself confronted for the first time with the meaning of the relationship between Articles 90 and 86, established, with the full support of the Commission, a strong presumption of legitimacy in favour of a public monopoly as such. In ruling that it was not incompatible with the competition rules for the Italian Republic to grant exclusive rights to carry out television transmissions to a limited company like RAI (Radiotelevisione Italiana), it held that Article 90 does not prohibit – of itself – the grant of such rights to particular undertakings, declaring that: 'Nothing in the Treaty prevents Member States, for considerations of public interest, of a non-economic nature, from removing radio and television transmissions, including cable transmissions, from the field of competition by conferring on one or more establishments an exclusive right to conduct them'[130] and possibly extending the content of that right when deemed appropriate.

On this first important occasion, the interpretation of Articles 86 and 90 taken together therefore led the Court 'to the conclusion that the fact that an undertaking to which a Member State grants exclusive rights has a monopoly is not as such incompatible with Article 86'.[131] The applicability of the rules on competition to public monopolies was therefore given a very restrictive interpretation and in principle excluded.

Admittedly, undertakings in a legal monopoly situation were still required to comply with Article 86 and were prohibited from engaging in behaviour of a discriminatory nature, at least – by reason of Article 90(2) – 'so long as it is not shown that the said prohibitions are incompatible with the performance of their tasks'.[132] Nevertheless, the decisive way in which the presumption of the legitimacy of granting exclusive rights

---

[128] Gardner, 'Velvet', p. 78.
[129] ECJ Case 155/73 [1974] ECR 409.   [130] Paragraph 14 of the judgment.
[131] *Ibid.* For a confirmation *a contrario*, as it were, of the principle, see ECJ Case 59/75 *Manghera* [1976] ECR 91.
[132] As worded in particular in paragraph 15 of the *Sacchi* judgment.

was underlined obviously led to a natural exemption of the subject from the rules on freedom of competition. 'The simple reason is that the very notion of monopoly is not really in line with that of competition';[133] and once the presumption has been established that a monopoly is legitimate save where the relevant national court identifies particular instances of abuse, it is obvious that the dilemma has already been resolved in principle in the sense of the natural exclusion of the rules on competition. Control by the Community institutions thus remains both external and also potential and remote, concentrated solely on the hypothetical abuse of exclusive rights and never on the mere fact of the existence of the public monopoly.

In consequence, the creation of national public monopolies in the provision of services was *de facto* not subject to Community law, in the precise sense that – in deference to the balance of interests that characterized the first phase of European integration – they 'were not actually made subject to the rules on competition and freedom of movement'.[134]

It is easy, at this point, to grasp the significance of the genuine overturning of the original politico-institutional and interpretative balances that was brought about, starting from the mid-1980s and with growing intensity in the early 1990s, by the 'discovery'[135] or *renouveau*[136] of Article 90 by the Commission and the Court of Justice.[137]

The change lies in what amounted to a reversal of the original direction of the presumption of the legitimacy of monopoly status operated by the Court, with the invention of the concept of 'inevitable' or 'automatic' abuse by a monopolist undertaking of its dominant position.[138]

---

[133]   G. Tesauro, 'Intervento pubblico nell'economia e art. 90, n. 2, del Tratto CE', *Diritto dell'Unione Europea* 1996, no. 3, pp. 719ff., here p. 725.

[134]   Montero Pascual, 'I monopoli', p. 665.   [135]   Tesauro, 'Intervento', p. 724.

[136]   R. Kovar, 'La peau de chagrin ou comment la droit communautaire opère la réduction des monopoles publics', *Europe, Chronique* July 1992, p. 1; in the same vein see also A. Wachsmann and F. Berrod, 'Les critères de justification des monopoles: un premier bilan après l'affaire *Corbeau*', *Revue Trimestrielle de Droit Européen* 1994, pp. 39ff.

[137]   Cf. also L. Pascal, 'Les apports de la Commission européenne et de la Cour de Justice des Communautés européennes à l'identification des activités de service public', in R. Kovar and D. Simon (eds.), *Service public et Communauté européenne: entre l'intérêt général et le marché*, Actes du colloque de Strasbourg 17–19 octobre 1996, vol. I, *Introductions et approche sectorielle*, vol. II, *Approche transversale et conclusions*, Paris 1998, vol. II, pp. 103ff.

[138]   See C.-D. Ehlermann, 'Managing Monopolies: The Role of the State in Controlling Market Dominance in the European Community', *European Competition Law Review* 1993, pp. 61ff.

A clear forewarning of the change is given by the important judgment in *Telecommunications Terminals*,[139] in which the Court – asked to rule on the legitimacy of Commission Directive 88/301/EEC within the meaning of Article 90(3) – had already significantly declared that, even though it had to be admitted that the rule in question presupposes the existence of undertakings which have certain special or exclusive rights, implying the presumed legitimacy of monopoly status conferred in this way by the state, 'it does not follow that all the special or exclusive rights are necessarily compatible with the Treaty',[140] which depends in each particular case on verifying their compatibility with different rules to which Article 90(1) refers. Thus, whereas on the one hand the presumption of the legitimacy of public monopolies or the grant of special rights was *formally* confirmed, this affirmation was on the other hand given a largely new dimension since it was made clear that the appearance of conformity with the Treaty was only relative and that it was for the Court in Luxembourg to subject it, in the light of the characteristics involved on a case-by-case basis, to close and meticulous scrutiny. Thus, as has been stated, 'albeit on the particular legal basis associated with supervision of the legitimate exercise by the Commission of the "quasi-legislative" power conferred on it by Article 90(3), the question was also raised which was to become central in subsequent pronouncements, namely, that of the link which must necessarily exist between a state measure and abusive conduct by undertakings for the purposes of applying Article 90, in terms of *inducing or determining* abuse'.[141] Hence, a question was raised which already carried within it the seeds of the doctrine of inevitable abuse regarding the actual manner in which the special or exclusive rights of public or monopolist undertakings are configured or structured by national legislators.

The about-turn, of which *Telecommunications Terminals* had been merely a forewarning, was to be completed shortly afterwards with a historic quartet of judgments all delivered in response to preliminary references at short intervals from each other.[142] It is with these judgments – and especially that delivered in *Höfner and Elser v Macrotron Gmbh*, which

---

[139] Already referred to in note 125 above.   [140] See paragraph 22 of the judgment.

[141] Fattori, 'Monopoli', p. 133 (the italics are in the original).

[142] These are the judgments delivered by the Court of Justice on 23 April 1991 in Case C-41/90 *Höfner and Elser v Macrotron Gmbh* [1991] ECR I-1979; on 18 June 1991 in Case C-260/89 *ERT (Elleniki Radiophonia Tileorasi) v Dimotiki* [1991] ECR I-2925; on 10 December 1991 in Case C-179/90 *Merci Convenzionali Porto di Genova v Siderurgica Gabrielli* [1991] ECR I-5889; and on 13 December 1991 in Case C 18/88 *Régie des Télégraphes v GB – Inno* [1991] ECR I-5941.

marks what is perhaps one of the most pointed instances of the infiltration of competition law into the body of national labour-law systems that the Court of Justice laid down the outlines of the new concept of inevitable or automatic abuse of a dominant position by a public monopoly or undertaking granted special rights.

The essence of the new doctrine can be summarized as follows: given that on the basis of Article 5 (now Article 10 of the EC Treaty) Member States are under an obligation neither to enact nor to maintain in force any measures that may prejudice the *effet utile* of the rules on competition, Articles 86 and 90(1) taken together are infringed when an undertaking that has been granted an exclusive right is led, through the mere fact of exercising that right, to make use in an abusive manner of the dominant position thereby conferred upon it, or when the grant of the right in question is capable of creating a situation in which the undertaking granted it is necessarily led to commit such an abuse.

Obviously, deference to the principle that 'merely creating a dominant position by granting exclusive rights within the meaning of Article 90(1) of the Treaty is not in itself incompatible with Article 86'[143] continues to feature in subsequent Court case-law.[144] But it is plain that in the new jurisprudential course being followed the principle has completely lost the central and diriment relevance effectively attributed to it in *Sacchi* and become no more than the pivot 'of a line of reasoning focused on the concrete details of the organization and exercise of a monopoly on the basis of which the very existence of an exclusive right conferred through Member State provisions can, in the presence of such conditions, prove to be contrary to the Treaty rules on competition'.[145]

The original logic, 'which saw a monopoly as per se legitimate, unless it is found that the concrete details of its exercise are contrary to market and competition rules, has therefore undergone a not inconsiderable correction'.[146] The approach adopted in *Sacchi* has clearly been abandoned by the new reading of the rules in question. To quote once again the words of one of the most accomplished advocates of the new line of reasoning, that approach 'is no longer to be found in the interpretation given to

---

[143] ECJ Case C-163/96 *Silvano Raso* [1998] ECR I-533, paragraph 27 of the judgment.

[144] See, for example, ECJ Case C-266/96 *Corsica Ferries France* [1998] ECR I-3949, at paragraph 40.

[145] Fattori, 'Monopoli', p. 135.

[146] Tesauro, 'Intervento', p. 725; in the same vein see, by way of example, Pappalardo, 'State', p. 38; D. Simon, 'Les mutations des services publics du fait des contraintes du droit communautaire', in Kovar and Simon, *Service public*, vol. I, pp. 65ff.

Article 90 by the Court in its case-law of the early 1990s, which exhibits the emergence of the very concept that a law granting exclusive rights is capable of inevitably leading the undertakings granted those rights to abuse the dominant position thereby conferred on them and therefore to infringe the rules on competition. *The presumption deduced from the original reading of Article 90 has therefore been completely overturned.*'[147]

The 'silent revolution'[148] effected by the Court is summed up in this: in the fact that the direction of the original presumption has been reversed and that – under certain conditions that are still not that clearly defined – recognition of a monopoly *ex lege*, or the grant of a special right, is presumed to infringe Articles 86 and 90(1) taken together unless it can be proven that exclusive rights and powers have been exercised properly or, rather, that their grant is essential to the performance, in law or in fact, of the particular function of general interest entrusted to the undertaking concerned.

It is this radical change of outlook operated by the judges in Luxembourg which explains the emphasis placed by the Court's more recent case-law[149] on the clause contained in Article 90(2) of the Treaty, on which the decision as to the legitimacy of any monopoly or special right being challenged[150] is increasingly focused.

If, aside from any detailed aspects of its exercise, the mere creation of a monopoly, or the forms in which national legislation structures its very existence, can be viewed as (inevitably or automatically) infringing the Treaty rules, independently of the actual behaviour of the subject enjoying that position, it is in fact perfectly understandable that attention should have shifted to the exception envisaged by the second paragraph of Article 90, as the only route left whereby the choices made by a Member State in the name of the public (non-economic) interest could potentially once more be justified.

It would therefore be totally misleading to impute to the decisions delivered in *Corbeau* and *Municipality of Almelo* – which in comparison with the heavy one imposed at the time in *Sacchi* represent an apparent lightening of the burden of proof resting on Member States on the basis of

---

[147] Tesauro, 'Intervento', p. 725. The emphasis has been added.

[148] Gardner, 'Velvet', p. 80.

[149] Starting from its well-known judgments in Case C-320/91 *Corbeau* [1993] ECR I-2533 and Case C-393/92 *Municipality of Almelo* [1994] ECR I-1477.

[150] Cf. D. Waelbroeck, 'Les conditions d'applicabilité de l'article 90 paragraph 2 du Traité CE', in Kovar and Simon, *Service public*, vol II, pp. 447ff.; D. Triantafyllou, 'Les règles de la concurrence et l'activité étatique y compris les marchés publics', *Revue Trimestrielle de Droit Européen* 1996, pp. 57ff.

Article 90(2) – a kind of restoration, albeit subject to different conditions, of the original approach to the rule's application.

In reality, in moderating the conditions governing the exception, now deemed admissible even when what is at risk is simply the financial equilibrium (and not the very survival) of the monopolist undertaking entrusted with the task of providing a service of general economic interest, *Corbeau* and *Municipality of Almelo* presupposed, and indeed kept a firm hold on, the 'bold' interpretation of Article 90(1) adopted a few years earlier by the Court's case-law, overturning the set of presumptions upheld in *Sacchi*.[151] And at the same time, they sought, by restating the 'minimum' conditions for a balance between the opposing requirements involved, to give a plausible answer to the fierce controversies aroused by the new approach, which was accused, particularly in France,[152] of unleashing the dismantling and forced deregulation of one of the cornerstones of the 'European social model': that consisting in the tradition of solid public-service systems.

The 'softening' of the interpretation of Article 90 unquestionably effected by the Court through the (relative) broadening of the scope for invoking the *exception* envisaged in its second paragraph was in fact inevitable and, on careful reflection, almost obligatory, since – in the new balance adopted in applying the provision – the latter ultimately represents the only way of taking into account those interests 'other' than protection of the 'competition' public good which in *Sacchi* were, by contrast, given their maximum recognition 'upstream' owing to the full presumption of the legitimacy of legal-monopoly positions.[153]

As will be demonstrated below, however, the significance of this 'softening'[154] – although not negligible – should not be exaggerated. That contained in Article 90(2) is still an exception, and one that is a matter of narrow interpretation.[155]

---

[151] Amato, 'Citizenship', p. 153, who talks in this connection of 'bold interpretation' of the provision by both the Commission and the Court of Justice 'on the grounds of the overriding principle of competition in the integrated market'.

[152] See R. Kovar, 'Droit communautaire et service public: esprit d'orthodoxie ou pensée laïciste', *Revue Trimestrielle de Droit Européen* 1996, respectively pp. 215ff. (part 1) and pp. 493ff. (part 2).

[153] This is recognized, with his customary lucidity, by Tesauro, 'Intervento', pp. 773–4, where he explains that it was the 'about-turn' in the reading of Article 90(1), 'and therefore abandonment of the presumption of the legitimacy of monopolies', that 'led to a reassessment of Article 90(2).'

[154] To repeat once again the expression used by G. Caire, 'Services publics et construction européenne', *Droit Social* 1999, pp. 176ff., here p. 180.

[155] Cf. Kovar, 'Droit', pp. 502–3; Simon, 'Les mutations', pp. 80ff.; Pascal, 'Les apports', p. 115.

A monopoly, in certain circumstances, still has to be justified by the Member State concerned within what remain the narrow limits of the exception. An assessment of whether the grant of special or exclusive rights is really essential in order to enable the general-interest function in question to be performed in conditions of financial equilibrium or on an economically viable basis delimits, at any rate in restrictive terms – leaving a broad margin for appraisal by the Court of Justice – the space within which exemption from the rule on competition can be successfully invoked. The implicit presumption remains that the general interest is best served by the regulatory mechanisms of a competitive market and that exemption from them should therefore be permitted only in the exceptional cases in which 'the free play of competition can compromise the performance of the general-interest function entrusted to the undertaking concerned'.[156]

Robert Kovar has spoken tellingly in this connection of 'regulated deregulation'.[157] In point of fact, *Corbeau* and *Municipality of Almelo* contain *in nuce* the essential outlines of the doctrine of 'universal service' developed shortly afterwards by the Commission in its well-known 1996 Communication on Services of General Interest in Europe. They reveal clearly the idea that, precisely because they represent exceptions to the application of competition principles, monopoly or exclusive-right situations should be confined within the narrowest possible space.

In deference to the principle of proportionality, Article 90(2) imposes the definition of a minimum core of exclusive rights that are essential to the achievement, on an economically viable basis, of the function entrusted to the entity in question.

Hence, the sphere of action of a public service which as such is exempt from the rules on competition tends to coincide with that of the basic or minimum level of essential services provided to all members of the general public, in conditions ensuring equality of access at prices they can afford, of the 'adequate' extent and quality characterizing the concept of a universal service in the terms used by the EC Commission itself in its Communication.[158]

Without discounting the admittedly significant readjustment of the balancing criteria brought about by *Corbeau* and *Municipality of Almelo*, it therefore seems right to conclude that, whereas the Court previously

---

[156] Kovar, 'Droit', p. 230.
[157] R. Kovar, 'La Cour de Justice et les entreprises chargées d'un service d'intérêt économique général, un pas dans le bon sens vers une dérégulation réglée', *Europe, Chronique* July and August/September 1994, p. 6.
[158] COM(96) 443 final of 11 September 1996.

'sought to define the maximum sphere of exclusive rights which these undertakings [entrusted with a public-interest function] may enjoy without infringing the competition rules, it now seeks to define the minimum sphere of exclusive rights compatible with these undertakings' financial viability', using an approach which at any rate 'encourages a far more restrictive policy towards public monopolies and privileged undertakings'.[159]

Furthermore, the same approach underlies the other front of expansion of the Community rules on competition, i.e. what was singled out at the start of this subsection as the *ratione personae* aspect of the extension of the coverage of Articles 85 et seq. of the EC Treaty. This is, of course, an aspect of considerable and indeed priority importance, since the widening of the circle of natural and legal persons deemed to fall within the scope of the competition rules is to some extent a precondition for the strengthening of their content *ratione materiae*.

The expansion of the concept of an undertaking within the meaning of Articles 85 et seq. effected by the Court's case-law is certainly in line with a purpose that is in a way inherent in the more general dictates of Community hermeneutics.[160] Centred as it is on the material substrate of the rules and on their economic objective rather than on the traditional structural elements of the legal form, purposive and functional interpretation of the fundamental concepts of the construction of the Community unquestionably corresponds to primary necessities for the supranational order. It is in conformity with, in the first place, the priority economic function and relevance of the Community order; and secondly with the need – clearly vital in order to ensure the unified construction of a common market without any risks of fragmentation – to separate from the several Member State legal orders, stamped as they are by very different traditions, the definition of the notions and rules underpinning the very identity of the supranational order as an autonomous system.

Interpretation of the notion of an undertaking for the purposes of applying competition law follows this logic and takes it to extreme consequences. The omnivorous force inherent in the concept of an undertaking as adopted in *Höfner* v *Macrotron* exceeds the standard requirements for a functional interpretation of Community economic rules in general and is perhaps better explained as a specific political option for the right to

---

[159] Gardner, 'Velvet', p. 82.
[160] See J. Joussen, 'L'interpretazione (teleologica) del diritto comunitario', *Rivista Critica di Diritto Privato* 2001, pp. 491ff.

attribute to the provisions on competition the maximum sphere of coverage in terms of the natural and legal persons affected.

It should, however, be mentioned that in its early pronouncements in the matter on the basis of the ECSC Treaty provisions,[161] the Court of Justice had still been essentially adhering to a traditional interpretative logic, i.e. focused on the form and structure of the 'undertaking' as a legal concept.

In *Klöckner-Werke AG and Hoesch AG*,[162] in fact, the Court had stated that 'an undertaking is constituted by a single organization of personal, tangible and intangible elements, attached to an autonomous legal entity and pursuing a given long-term economic aim'. Consequently, although it is perhaps excessive to regard this definition as 'exclusively the fruit of formal legal assessments'[163] it would nevertheless seem to resemble a conceptual system not unlike that adopted by the Italian Civil Code itself. That is to say, an at least partly familiar set of concepts with defining categories in which key elements connected with the structure of the case in point (organization, professionalism, economic operation) which, by contrast, the subsequent total functionalization of the notion of an undertaking, even if not completely expunging them from the arsenal employed by the Court, was certainly to make entirely subordinate to assessment of the functional profiles.

Be that as it may, it was not until *Höfner* that the Court really explored to the full the potential of a functional interpretation of the notion of an undertaking, affirming a move towards its all-inclusive coverage of any activity of an economic nature that is directed at the production or exchange of goods or services.[164] Using a formula that was to be constantly cited in its subsequent case-law, the Court declared that 'in the context of competition law, . . . the concept of an undertaking encompasses every entity engaged in an economic activity, regardless of the legal status of the entity and the way in which it is financed'.[165]

---

[161] But its first pronouncements relating to the EEC Treaty provisions on competition also followed the same approach focused on legal form: see Joined Cases 56 and 58/64 *Consten and Grundig* [1966] ECR 299.

[162] Joined Cases 17 and 20/61 [1962] ECR 325.

[163] Di Via, 'L'impresa', in N. Lipari (ed.), *Diritto privato europeo*, Padua 1997, vol. I, pp. 252ff., here p. 265.

[164] See T. Scudiero, 'La nozione di impresa nella giurisprudenza della Corte di Giustizia', *Il Foro Italiano* 1994, vol. IV, col. 113.

[165] So reads paragraph 21 of the judgment, which – as is well known – continues with the apodictic statement that 'employment procurement is an economic activity'.

What has thus come to assume decisive importance is the circumstance that the entity in question is engaged in an activity for which there is an actual or potential market. Consequently, irrespective of the legal nature of the subject in question in accordance with the relevant domestic legal order, whenever that subject is engaged in an activity that is, or could be, carried on by private operators for profit-making purposes an undertaking is deemed to exist within the meaning of Community competition law. To put it differently, the basic test – as pointed out by Advocate General Jacobs in referring to this case-law[166] – 'is therefore whether the entity in question is engaged in an activity which could, at least in principle, be carried on by a private undertaking in order to make profits'. The only activities that can be excluded as a matter of principle are therefore those which are '*necessarily carried out by public entities or their agents*'.[167]

It can easily be seen that such a 'liberal' notion[168] is in danger of losing – at least if applied rigorously in all its logical consequences – any really selective value as regards entities potentially falling within the scope of the rules on competition.

Even discounting its extreme implications, which have indeed been rejected by the Court of Justice itself, this notion is likely to extend its range of action well beyond the circle of 'customary' entities covered by competition law and encompass a whole range of 'entities that are traditionally unconnected with entrepreneurial logic'.[169] And proof of this lies in the extraordinary rash of preliminary references regarding the most disparate entities engaged in activities that were *sensu lato* economic although devoid of any of the traditional and qualifying connotations of entrepreneurship (starting with the absence of any profit-making purpose, or the pursuit of purely social objectives) which were submitted to the Court throughout the 1990s in the wake of the broad interpretation established in *Höfner*.

This extension of the scope *ratione personae* of the rules on competition has accompanied and completed the parallel broadening of their scope *ratione materiae*. The two trends strengthen and support each other or, perhaps more accurately, are the two sides of the same coin.

With the general principle of neutrality symbolized by Article 222 of the Treaty discarded for good, starting from the mid-1980s onwards and in the name of the efficiency of allocative processes within the unified market

---

[166] In his Opinion delivered in Case C-67/96 *Albany International BV* [1999] ECR I-5751, at point 311.
[167] *Ibid.*, at point 330 (the italics are in the original).
[168] Wachsmann and Berrod, 'Les critères', p. 47.   [169] Di Via, 'L'impresa', p. 275.

Community competition law has become a penetrating instrument of the control (and, not infrequently, effective liberalization) of some of the most traditional forms of state intervention in the economy.[170]

6. Two illustrative examples: public job-placement monopolies and national social-security monopolies

During the 1990s public monopolies in the areas of placement in employment and (basic and complementary) social security constituted perhaps the most significant test bed of the problems of coexistence and unresolved tensions between Community competition law and national systems of labour law. The dense body of case-law that successfully built up over more than a decade up to and including the *INAIL* case[171] reflects the entire gamut of problems and contradictions that can arise as a result of the unrestrained infiltration of Community competition law, and also bears witness to the tortured development of the Court of Justice's attitudes in this delicate area.

It has already been mentioned above that the judgment in *Höfner* ushered in the 1990s by giving the most tangible sign of the potential clash likely to be aroused by the infiltration of Community competition law.

In accepting unconditionally that Germany's Federal Employment Office constituted an undertaking that was abusing its dominant position on the market, this judgment marks the moment of maximum expansion of the scope, both *ratione personae* and *ratione materiae*, of Community competition rules. The Court laid down the conditions of the new concept of 'necessary' or 'inevitable' abuse in terms that a few years later, *mutatis mutandis*, were also to confirm the illegality of the monopoly granted to

---

[170] The parallelism with the changing interpretation of Article 30 is now entirely obvious. Both Article 30 and Article 90 have become, mainly from the end of the 1980s, formidable instruments of the control of Member State public regulatory choices in all kinds of different areas of economic and social life. The crucial question which unites the profound change in the balance on which application of the two provisions was based is increasingly becoming that of the material legitimation of the Court of Justice's 'constitutional adjudication' activity. In both cases, in fact, it is plain that the ethos guiding application of the two provisions is that of the free market, and just how precarious the protection of competing values very often is as a result. See Baquero Cruz, *Between Competition and Free Movement*, pp. 85ff.

[171] I have analysed this case-law in detail elsewhere: see S. Giubboni, 'Social Insurance Monopolies in Community Competition Law and the Italian Constitution. Practical Convergences and Theoretical Conflicts', *European Law Journal* 2001, pp. 69ff., Giubboni, 'Fondi pensione e "competition rules" comunitarie', in M. Bessone and F. Carinci (eds.), *La previdenza complementare*, Turin 2004, pp. 110ff.

public employment offices under Italian legislation.[172] This line of reasoning holds that the state is in breach of the prohibitions imposed by Articles 86 and 90(1) of the Treaty where an undertaking that has been granted an exclusive right cannot avoid, through the mere exercise of that right, using its dominant position in an abusive manner, which in the case in point was mainly demonstrated first by the fact that the public employment service was manifestly incapable of satisfying the demand prevailing in the market and, second, by the maintenance in force of statutory prohibitions which made it impossible for other persons to operate lawfully in the same market.

The conceptual system upheld by the Court in *Höfner* and *Job Centre II* leaves no room for the possibility of assessing the conditions for the potential applicability of an exception on the basis of Article 90(2). In the 'circularity'[173] of the Court's line of reasoning the exception envisaged by this provision is precluded from the start by the concept of inevitable abuse.

The Court adopted an 'efficiency-slanted'[174] approach which meant that from the point of view of applying Article 90(2) 'the social arguments for the monopoly conferred in the Federal Employment Office'[175] were completely ignored. The categories used in the two cases by the Court remained entirely within the 'market' or 'consumer' paradigm of citizenship,[176] and took almost no account of the solidaristic redistributive dimension of the traditional functions performed by public employment offices which is, by contrast, assessable from the different viewpoint

---

[172] See ECJ Case C-55/96 *Job Centre Coop.* [1997] ECR I-7119 (known as *Job Centre II*) and comment on the case by M. Roccella, 'Il caso *Job Centre II*: sentenza sbagliata, risultato (quasi) giusto', *Rivista Giuridica del Lavoro e della Previdenza Sociale* 1998, vol. II, p. 29; also the earlier Case C-111/94 [1995] ECR I-3361 (known as *Job Centre I*) and comment on the case by G. Meliadò, 'Il monopolio pubblico del collocamento e il lavoro interinale in Italia dinanzi ai giudici di Lussemburgo: mancate risposte e problemi aperti', *Il Foro Italiano* 1996, vol. IV, col. 77.

[173] N. Reich, 'Competition Between Legal Orders: A New Paradigm of EC Law?', *Common Market Law Review* 1992, pp. 861ff., here p. 887.

[174] Hancher, 'Community', p. 742; also E. Ales, '"*Macrotron II*", ovvero la Corte di Giustizia "abroga" il monopolio pubblico del collocamento?', *Diritto del Lavoro* 1998, vol. II, pp. 93ff., especially p. 105.

[175] Davies, 'Market', p. 64.

[176] M. Freedland, 'Law, Public Services, and Citizenship – New Domains, New Regimes?', in Freedland and Sciarra, *Public Services*, pp. 1ff., especially p. 10; M. Everson, 'The Legacy of Market Citizenship', in J. Shaw and G. More (eds.), *New Legal Dynamics of European Union*, Oxford 1995, pp. 77ff.

of 'constitutional citizenship'.[177] It was left to the national legislature – obviously in ways compatible with the principles of free competition – to restore such a dimension, possibly in favour of the weakest labour-market categories.[178]

In a series of social-security cases,[179] on the other hand, although these represent something of a mixed bag the Court of Justice has shown itself more inclined, overall, to assess the legitimacy of measures adopted by the state, at least from the viewpoint of Article 90(2), one of the reasons possibly being the greater political and economic importance of the issues raised.

In the first of its judgments in this string of cases the Court appeared to give the notion of social solidarity a range and force somewhat comparable to that given to the opposing notion of an undertaking within the meaning of Article 85.

Taking its cue from the Opinion delivered by Advocate General Tesauro, in *Poucet and Pistre* the Court ruled that the French organizations charged with the management of compulsory social-security schemes that were under scrutiny were not to be classed as undertakings for the purposes of competition law. A reaffirmation of the broad notion of an undertaking (as any entity engaged in an economic activity, regardless of the legal status of the entity and the way in which it is financed) was matched here by an equally broad notion of 'national solidarity', based on all three of the indices or criteria specified by the Advocate General: 'distributive solidarity', in the form of the redistribution of income between those who are better off and those who are worse off; 'intergenerational solidarity', with active workers' contributions serving to

---

[177] See again M. Freedland, 'The Marketization of Public Services', in C. Crouch, K. Eder and D. Tambini (eds.), *Citizenship, Markets, and the State*, Oxford 2001, pp. 90ff.

[178] See R. Foglia, 'La Corte di Giustizia e il collocamento pubblico: opportuno un nuovo intervento del giudice comunitario e del legislatore nazionale?', *Argomenti di Diritto del Lavoro* 1998, no. 2, pp. 539ff.; S. Sciarra, 'Job Centre: An Illustrative Example of Strategic Litigation', in Sciarra, *Labour Law*, pp. 241ff.

[179] See ECJ Joined Cases C-159/91 and C-160/91 *Poucet and Pistre* [1993] ECR I-637; Joined Cases C-430 and C-431/93 *Van Schijndel* [1995] ECR I-4705; Case C-244/94 *Fédération Française des Sociétés d'Assurance and Others* [1995] ECR I-4013 (also known as *Coreva*); Case C-238/94 *García* [1996] ECR I-1673; Case C-67/96 *Albany International BV* [1999] ECR I-5751; Joined Cases C-115, C-116 and C-117/97 *Brentjens' Handelsonderneming BV* [1999] ECR I-6025; Case C-219/97 *BV Maatschappij Drijveden Bokken* [1999] ECR I-6121; Case C-222/98 *van der Woude* [2000] ECR I-7111; Joined Cases C-180/98 and C-184/98 *Pavlov and Others* [2001] ECR I-6451; Case C-218/00 *INAIL* [2002] ECR I-691; Joined Cases C-264/01, C-306/01 and C-355/01, *AOK Bundesverband And Others* (judgment 16 March 2004, not yet reported).

finance the pensions of retired workers; and 'financial solidarity', with the social-security schemes in surplus contributing to the financing of those in deficit.[180]

The subsequent judgment in *Coreva*, concerning a situation in which the special rights conferred on the body in question related to a purely optional form of supplementary insurance, led to an opposite outcome on the basis of a line of reasoning which, although apparently analogous to that pursued in *Poucet and Pistre*, was essentially largely different.[181] The Court held that the body in question was to be classed as an undertaking,[182] primarily on the grounds that it operated in accordance with the principle of capitalization rather than on a 'pay as you go' basis, i.e. in accordance with the redistribution principle of 'intergenerational' solidarity.

Thus, among the 'set of indices'[183] used by the Court the tendency became for 'intergenerational' solidarity to prevail: the focus of scrutiny shifted decisively to the technical profile of systems of financial management, with the fact of whether a body is operated in accordance with the principle of redistribution or with the principle of capitalization acquiring diriment relevance. This logic means that the indices of distributive solidarity and financial solidarity play a secondary part, in the sense that they are of relevance 'downstream' for the purposes of potentially justifying exclusive rights within the meaning of Article 90(2) of the Treaty, but no longer for the purposes of the preliminary assessment of whether or not an entity managing a social-security scheme is engaged in an economic activity that classes it as an undertaking.

This marked a very significant change of direction on both a practical and a theoretical level. The Court's subsequent pronouncements – from that delivered in the famous *Albany International BV* case up to and

---

[180] See J.-M. Binon, 'Solidarité et assurance: marriage de cœur ou de raison? Réflexion sur la ligne de partage entre l'assurance publique et l'assurance privée à la lumière des arrêts *Poucet/Pistre, Coreva, García* de la Cour de Justice des Communautés Européennes', *Revue du Marché Unique Européen* 1997, no. 4, pp. 87ff.

[181] Cf. F. Kessler, 'Droit de la concurrence et régimes de protection sociale: un bilan provisoire', in Kovar and Simon, *Service public*, vol. I, pp. 421ff.; M. Fuchs, 'Die Vereinbarkeit von Sozialversicherungsmonopolen mit dem EG-Recht', *Zeitschrift für ausländisches und internationales Arbeits- und Sozialrecht* 1996, pp. 338ff.

[182] The French Conseil d'Etat then gave immediate recognition to the conditions of (automatic) abuse of a dominant position on the market by the managing body of the pension-insurance scheme in question: see Binon, 'Solidarité', p. 110.

[183] D. Gadbin, 'Les fonds de pension obligatoire face au droit communautaire de la concurrence: des positions dominantes à préserver dans le future marché intérieur des services financiers', *Droit Social* 2000, pp. 178ff., here p. 180.

including that delivered in the *INAIL* case – confirmed this interpretative 'adjustment'.

In consequence, only operation according to the 'pay as you go' (redistribution) method axiomatically precludes the activity engaged in by an entity managing forms of basic or supplementary social security from being regarded as an economic activity carried on by an undertaking. As explained by Advocate General Jacobs in his Opinion delivered in *Albany*, it is only in a case of this kind (a pension scheme based on the redistribution principle) that there is no possibility, even in theory, that private undertakings could offer such a scheme on the markets without state intervention. The reason being that 'nobody would be prepared to pay for the pensions of others without a guarantee that the next generation would do the same', which is 'precisely why it was historically necessary to introduce such systems, managed or at least protected by the state'.[184] It was in the light of this criterion that in *Albany* the Court recognized the economic nature of the activity carried on by the Netherlands compulsory supplementary pension funds set up by collective agreement, whereas in *INAIL* it recognized the opposing social-solidarity nature of the Italian public entity.

In so doing, however, the Court ultimately adopted a narrow notion of solidarity, predefined and tailored to the canons of rationality inherent in competition law.[185] Only the specific form of solidarity that finds expression in the redistribution method was to be capable of excluding upstream the applicability of the rules on competition and placing social-security activities outside the domain of the omnivorous notion of an undertaking. The other indices of solidarity could be of relevance only for the purposes of applying the exception envisaged by Article 90(2) of the Treaty.

This is because in *Albany* the Court, accepting the argument of what was referred to as a 'negative spiral',[186] justified compulsory affiliation to the supplementary schemes managed by these funds as well as the other special rights granted to them by the Netherlands legislature, in view of the distributive solidarity they effected within the body of

---

[184] Point 338 of the Advocate General's opinion.

[185] In a similar vein, see Kessler, 'Droit', p. 446.

[186] That is, the argument that, in the absence of compulsory affiliation and hence of an exclusive right, the (public or collective) fund in question would be left only with the 'bad risks', while the 'good risks' would look for more advantageous arrangements with private insurers.

insured persons concerned. The 'essential social function'[187] performed by the Netherlands supplementary funds was therefore recognized and safeguarded, but within the very narrow margins permitted by the *exception* envisaged by Article 90(2).[188]

Generally speaking, the sphere of exclusive rights justifiable by virtue of this provision coincides with that which causes the least possible restriction on competition, in accordance with the principle of proportionality.[189] There is therefore an obvious propensity on the part of the 'Community judges to regard the solidarity effected by social-security organizations as an exception, narrowly construed, to the principles of free competition'.[190]

Critical considerations of a similar tenor can be repeated with respect to another fundamental issue, although one that features less in the series of social-security cases: that of the limits of the antitrust immunity of collective agreements.[191]

Both in *Albany* and in *van der Woude* the Court of Justice recognized that the social-security activities entrusted to pension funds set up by collective agreement or freely selected on the insurance market fall within the domain of core issues of collective bargaining and that in this sphere the products of collective autonomy must therefore be held as immune from the rules on competition. According to some observers, in so doing the Court adopted a notion of an area immune from competition law that has not been adequately defined and delimited, and is certainly broader than that which can be justified on the basis of criteria of strict allocative efficiency.[192] In actual fact the Court, albeit without repeating in detail

---

[187] Paragraph 105 of the judgment.

[188] See also, in critical vein, G. Leone, 'La nozione di impresa e le sue ricadute sui diritti sociali nella giurisprudenza della Corte di giustizia', *Rivista Giuridica del Lavoro e della Previdenza Sociale* 2000, pp. 993ff.

[189] See L. Gyselen, 'L'applicabilité des règles de concurrence communautaires à des régimes de protection sociale', in *Mélanges en hommage à Michel Waelbroeck*, Brussels 1999, vol. II, pp. 1071ff.

[190] A. Supiot, *L'évolution du droit du travail et les tâches de la doctrine en l'an 2000*, Hugo Sinzheimer Institut, Amsterdam 2000, p. 51.

[191] See, at length, N. Bruun and J. Hellsten (eds.), *Collective Agreements and Competition Law in the EU*, Uppsala 2001.

[192] This is the opinion of R. J. Van den Bergh and P. D. Camesasca, 'Irreconcilable Principles? The Court of Justice Exempts Collective Labour Agreements from the Wrath of Antitrust', *European Law Review* 2000, pp. 492ff.; for a similar view, see also P. Ichino, 'Collective Bargaining and Antitrust Law: An Open Issue', *International Journal of Comparative Labour Law and Industrial Relations* 2001, pp. 185ff.

the conditions specified by Advocate General Jacobs in the Opinion he delivered in *Albany*,[193] essentially adopted the conception of the limitations of the antitrust immunity for collective agreements that he had upheld.[194]

In *Albany* the Court ruled that the agreement at issue did not fall within the scope of Article 85(1) of the Treaty simply because, 'by reason of its nature and purpose',[195] it performed functions that are typical and 'normal' for collective bargaining. This was inferred from the fact that first, it 'was concluded in the form of a collective agreement' and was 'the outcome of collective negotiations between organizations representing employers and workers'; and second, that it established, 'in a given sector, a supplementary pension scheme managed by a pension fund to which affiliation may be made compulsory' and therefore with respect to all workers in that sector contributed 'directly to improving one of their working conditions, namely their remuneration'.[196]

Subsequently, the Court was also to follow an entirely similar line of reasoning in *Pavlov and Others*[197] and *van der Woude*, in partly different contexts.[198]

Apart from this, the Court also showed itself to be fully in harmony with the restrictive approach adopted by Advocate General Jacobs in *Albany* from another important aspect, in likewise excluding the existence in the Community legal order of a fundamental right to bargain collectively.

---

[193] At points 191–3 of his Opinion he had proposed three conditions for the *ipso facto* immunity of collective agreements: they must be 'made within the formal framework of collective bargaining between both sides of industry'; they should be concluded 'in good faith' and not as a way of circumventing antitrust prohibitions; and they must deal with 'core subjects of collective bargaining such as wages and working conditions' and not 'directly affect third parties or markets'.

[194] Cf. S. Vousden, '*Albany*, Market Law and Social Exclusion', *Industrial Law Journal* 2000, pp. 181ff.; M. Pallini, 'Il rapporto problematico tra diritto della concorrenza e autonomia collettiva nell'ordinamento comunitario e nazionale', *Rivista Italiana di Diritto del Lavoro* 2000, vol. II, pp. 225ff.

[195] Paragraph 64 of the judgment.   [196] Paragraphs 62 and 63 of the judgment.

[197] In this judgment (see note 179 above) the Court, consistently with its application of the analytical grid previously proposed by Advocate General Jacobs in *Albany*, ruled that an agreement establishing a sectoral pension fund reached between the members of a liberal profession could not be classed as a collective agreement since it did not fulfil the condition of having been concluded within the 'formal' framework of collective bargaining and in the context of negotiations between management and labour.

[198] See J.-P. Lhernould, 'Nouvelles dérives libérales de la CJCE en matière de retraite complémentaire', *Droit Social* 2000, pp. 1114ff.

As will shortly be explained in more detail, it is the absence of the 'language of fundamental rights'[199] that casts a shadow of worrying uncertainty over the nature and extent of the 'immune' area of collective autonomy. The severing of any link with the language of fundamental rights, dominant as it is in many Member State constitutional traditions and rooted in international sources of labour law, brought back – in *Albany* as also in *van der Woude* – the image of a rigidly 'functionalized' collective bargaining.[200]

As a result collective autonomy is in actuality only free to operate, without having to contend with the prohibition imposed by Article 85(1) of the Treaty, within the sphere of what are regarded as its 'normal' functions of regulating terms and conditions of employment. The social partners remain free and autonomous only if they pursue in good faith the objectives specific to them within the formal framework of collective bargaining and confine themselves 'narrowly'[201] to regulating terms and conditions of employment without directly affecting the market in products and services.

Given this perspective, there is an obvious risk of considerable suppression of what in some national Constitutions is unreservedly deemed an original power of self-determination and autonomy for the social partners, guaranteed at the topmost level of the legal order as the expression of a fundamental right. To give one concrete example, it is highly likely that regulatory measures adopted by the social partners in order to limit and control forms of segmentation of the productive apparatus or outsourcing, or in order to reconcile working and family life or combat exclusion from the labour market, are thereby excluded, at least as regards their associated strong effects *ultra partes*, from the immune sphere *ratione materiae* of collective agreements.

Just as in the case of the definition of solidarity as no more than an 'exception' – subject to careful justification and assessment – to the principles of free competition, here too the impression is therefore one of a persistent imbalance of the categories used by the Court of Justice, biased in favour of the requirements of market integration. An imbalance which

---

[199] M. Roccella, 'La Carta dei diritti fondamentali: un passo avanti verso l'Unione politica', *Lavoro e Diritto* 2001, pp. 329ff., here p. 340.

[200] Pallini, 'Il rapporto', p. 242, who underlines the clear contrast of this conception with that of collective autonomy as the social partners' power of self-determination which is enshrined in the Italian Constitution.

[201] As stated by Advocate General Fennelly at point 28 of his Opinion delivered in *van der Woude*.

plainly leaves unresolved, at least on a theoretical level, the dilemmas posed by the incursion of Community competition law into national systems of labour law.

These are dilemmas which directly involve the central issue of the substantive legitimacy of Community law and policies, inasmuch as they reveal one of the most insidious sources of its potential crisis.[202] Consequently, identifying the most effective 'antidotes' to an infiltration which continues to bear the hallmarks of a purely negative integration of national systems of labour law is not unconnected with the search for a sounder base for the legitimacy of the Community legal order that Joseph Weiler has singled out as one of the main tasks of 'European neo-constitutionalism'.[203] In the following pages this search will be conducted along three interrelated lines of analysis and reflection.

7. Antidotes to the infiltration of competition law: (a) Economic freedoms and social rights in the aftermath of the Nice Charter and the constitutional Treaty . . .

It has already been mentioned that – with growing intensity over the course of the 1990s – the community of European labour lawyers was among the most active and consistent advocates urging in scientific and political debate, with a variety of proposals and solutions, the need to include in the founding Treaty, i.e. in what the Court of Justice has tended to regard as the 'constitutional charter' of the European Community,[204] a catalogue of fundamental rights that also contained extensive and full recognition of the Community social rights of citizens and workers.[205] It is equally well known that the urgency of some form of express constitutionalization of fundamental social rights at the topmost level of importance and visibility offered by the supranational order was also the focus – with some difference in the more technical and operative content

---

[202] Cf. F. W. Scharpf, *Governing in Europe: Effective and Democratic?*, Oxford 1999, pp. 50ff.; Simitis, 'Dismantling', pp. 156ff.

[203] See J. H. H. Weiler, 'European Neo-constitutionalism: In Search of Foundations for the European Constitutional Order', *Political Studies* 1996, p. 517, also Weiler, 'Epilogue: The European Courts of Justice: Beyond "Beyond Doctrine" or the Legitimacy Crisis of European Constitutionalism', in A.-M. Slaughter, A. Stone Sweet and J. H. H. Weiler (eds.), *The European Court and National Courts: Doctrine and Jurisprudence. Legal Change in its Social Context*, Oxford 1998, pp. 365ff.

[204] See ECJ Case 294/83 *Les Verts – Parti Écologiste* [1986] ECR 1339, and Opinion 1/91 on the Draft Agreement on the European Economic Area [1991] ECR I-6079.

[205] See subsection 2 of chapter 2 above.

of the proposals – of the authoritative indications emanating from the Comité des Sages chaired by Maria de Lourdes Pintasilgo[206] and from the Expert Group set up more recently for the same purposes by the European Commission under the chairmanship of Spiros Simitis.[207]

In the name of the principle of the indivisibility and complementarity of (first-, second- and third-generation) fundamental rights, the recognition of social rights forms part of the general objective of a necessary deepening of the value-system dimension of the construction of the Community[208] – whose political aspect has now irreversibly exceeded the functional limits of market integration – and of the resultant affirmation of a clear foundation of democratic legitimacy for European public power.[209]

In addition to this, two more specific functions are commonly attributed to it.

First, and within the limits in which it is pursued by the Community, there is the function of anchoring the positive integration of national social systems to a firm base of common principles and values. This specific 'cohesive' function[210] of fundamental social rights becomes all the more necessary in so far as the positive integration of national labour-law systems departs from the more centralizing and 'constructivist' forms of harmonization that have been known in the past and changes into those of co-ordination via soft law or reflexive harmonization.[211] So the supranational rooting of (individual and collective) fundamental social

[206] For a Europe of Civic and Social Rights, Report by the Comité des Sages chaired by Maria de Lourdes Pintasilgo, Commission of the European Communities DG V, Brussels 1996.

[207] Affirming Fundamental Rights in the European Union. Time to Act, Report of the Expert Group on Fundamental Rights chaired by Prof. Spiros Simitis, Commission of the European Communities DG V, Brussels 1999 (referred to hereinafter as the Simitis Report).

[208] See Cartabia, Principi inviolabili, p. 137. Fundamental rights are first and foremost 'value structures' (A. Baldassarre, 'Costituzione e teoria dei valori', Politica del Diritto 1991, pp. 639ff.) and are therefore of direct constitutive relevance to the entire constitutional value system on which a legal order is based (P. Häberle, Die Wesensgehaltgarantie des Art. 19 Abs. 2 Grundgesetz, Heidelberg 1983). Consequently, the proposition – in which Häberle refers to the German constitutional order – that fundamental rights have a dual valency, first in representing 'supreme values' and second in enabling individuals and groups to identify values and update them, guaranteeing them the status of a freedom, can appropriately be generalized on the theoretical level.

[209] See Y. Mény, Tra utopia e realtà. Una costituzione per l'Europa (Conversazione con Renzo Cassignoli), Florence 2000, pp. 103 and 143ff.

[210] To repeat, with some readaptation, the well-known expression used by D'Antona, 'Sistema giuridico comunitario'.

[211] S. Deakin, 'Two Types of Regulatory Competition: Competitive Federalism versus Reflexive Harmonisation. A Law and Economics Perspective on Centros', Cambridge Yearbook of European Legal Studies 1999, vol. 2, pp. 231–60.

rights performs the associated function of a limit to or defence against the temptations of competitive deregulation on the part of Member States.[212] Potential forms of social devaluation or intra-Community regime shopping induced to some extent by the 'rigours' of the macroeconomic environment resulting from monetary unification, especially in view of the recent enlargement of the Union's borders towards the East, may find a significant limit in an adequate articulation of supranational social rights.[213]

Second – and this, obviously, is the profile that interests us more here – the constitutionalization of Community social rights has the recognized ability to establish a more rigorous limit to the negative integration which takes place in the direct and frontal form represented by the (deregulatory) incursion of Community competition and market law into national systems of labour and social-security law.[214] From this second and concurrent perspective, the importance of affirming a strong constitutional core of Community social rights is seen essentially in terms of preservation of the autonomy and, to some degree, the actual specific identity of the several national labour-law systems.[215]

To date, in Court of Justice case-law consideration of the requirements which, at least in some Member State labour-law systems, are given maximum protection in the form of constitutional recognition of fundamental social rights has been confined within rather restricted areas. These requirements have found some citizenship – in the expanding 'empire'

---

[212] See, albeit in a highly sceptical vein as regards the solutions in this direction that can be extrapolated from the Nice Charter, O. De Schutter, 'La contribution de la Charte des droits fondamentaux de l'Union européenne à la garantie des droits sociaux dans l'ordre juridique communautaire', *Revue Universelle des Droits de l'Homme* 2000, nos. 1–2, pp. 33ff., especially pp. 35–6.

[213] See, for example, A. Lo Faro, 'Maastricht e oltre. Le prospettive dell'Europa comunitaria tra resistenze politiche, limiti giuridici ed incertezze istituzionali', *Diritto delle Relazioni Industriali* 1993, pp. 125ff., especially pp. 131–2.

[214] A. Lyon-Caen, 'The Legal Efficacy and Significance of Fundamental Social Rights: Lessons from the European Experience', in B. Hepple (ed.), *Social and Labour Rights in a Global Context. International and Comparative Perspectives*, Cambridge 2002, pp. 182ff., especially p. 188, spoke tellingly in this connection of an '*effet d'obstacle*' of Community fundamental social rights.

[215] The complementarity of the two perspectives under discussion is obvious in this regard. The factor linking them together is the defence – both in a positive (or active) and a negative (or passive) sense – of a relative autonomy of social policies and labour law itself as against macroeconomic policies and integrated-market regulatory processes at both Community and national level. See, for a number of indications from this viewpoint, Sciarra, 'From Strasbourg', p. 23, and also, in a wider context, Sciarra, 'Parole vecchie e nuove: diritto del lavoro e occupazione', *Argomenti di Diritto del Lavoro* 1999, no. 2, pp. 369ff., especially pp. 380ff.

of competition and integrated-market law – first within the areas made available by the 'mandatory requirements' accepted as admissible (subject to the limits fixed by an assessment of necessity and proportionality) by the *Cassis de Dijon* jurisprudence with respect to Article 30, and second within the shifting areas marked out by analogous consideration of the public interests that are protected to a varying degree by Articles 55, 56 and 90 of the Treaty.

The remarkable expansion of the rules on the free movement of goods and services, and particularly the increasingly rigorous application of Article 30 even to non-discriminatory restrictions on the freedom of trade, has inevitably also led the Court to give correspondingly more extensive recognition to reasons in the general interest not directly explained or standardized by the Treaty, thus making way for the protection of interests which in national legal orders are normally 'associated with social rights'.[216]

Nonetheless, it has also been noted that in balancing them with the basic economic freedoms with which they clashed, the resistance of these objective interests has proved to be notably weakened by the standard of strict scrutiny usually applied by the Court, albeit with widely differing degrees of intensity and rigour depending on the *de facto* and *de jure* contexts under examination on particular occasions. In any event, they have almost never featured as rights accorded a ranking at least equal to that of the economic freedoms with which they were being compared, even when this was the status reserved to them within the legal order of the Member State concerned.

From this point of view, as already mentioned in chapter 2 above, not even the Treaty of Amsterdam – despite the increased importance accorded to social objectives in the context of European integration – essentially changed the situation. Although it certainly strengthened the position of social values and objectives within the overall supranational design, and in this sense conferred greater autonomy on these objectives vis-à-vis that of the construction on a continental scale of an open market based on free competition, the Treaty of Amsterdam did not bring about outright constitutionalization of Community fundamental social rights.[217]

---

[216] Poiares Maduro, 'Striking', p. 452.

[217] A. Cantaro, 'Lavoro e diritti sociali nella "costituzione europea"', *Democrazia e Diritto* 1999, no. 4, special issue entitled *Lavoro: declino o metamorfosi?* ed. P. Barcellona, pp. 97ff., has spoken incisively of 'a *vague constitutionalization* that is mainly decorative' or, still

The references to the Council of Europe's 1961 European Social Charter and the 1989 Community Charter of the Fundamental Social Rights of Workers made first in the new Preamble to the Maastricht Treaty and then, in particular, in Article 136 of the EC Treaty using wording of a clearly programmatic nature did not, in fact, serve to incorporate in the Community legal order a catalogue of social rights that are directly justiciable or at any rate protected as such.[218]

Although the reference to the fundamental status of social rights, and no longer solely of economic freedoms, represented 'a political choice of strong symbolic impact'[219] and one certainly not without important repercussions at interpretive level, the fact remains that, even after the entry into force of the Treaty of Amsterdam, 'action on the part of the Community and the Member States remains directed towards a number of objective social interests: employment, proper social protection, social dialogue, etc. Not, that is, the protection of social rights as individual subjective legal situations.'[220]

Albany International BV exemplifies this limbo-like position of social rights in the Community legal order and confirms the status of purely '*Reflexrechte*' (to quote once again the effective characterization used by Massimo Luciani[221]) assigned to them by the Treaty of Amsterdam.

The relative immunity of the products of collective autonomy from the antitrust rules responds to the need to prevent the 'social policy objectives pursued by such agreements'[222] from being seriously undermined. A need that in its turn derives from a consistent and appropriate interpretation of all the Treaty provisions, which assign an undoubted importance to those very objectives.[223]

---

more eloquently, of '*a kind of constitutionalization without rights*', in which 'the "correction in a social direction" took place without any real rethinking on or rearrangement of the Community's set of values, without the Treaties calling into question the pre-eminent status of competition and market law' (p. 115) and, in particular, without according an adequate 'level of legal protection' to an absolutely mandatory catalogue of social rights (p. 116).

[218] Cf. G. Maestro Buelga, 'Constitución económica y derechos sociales en la Unión europea', *Revista de Derecho Comunitario Europeo* 2000, pp. 123ff., especially pp. 148–9; M. V. Ballestrero, 'Brevi osservazioni su costituzione europea e diritto del lavoro italiano', *Lavoro e Diritto* 2000, pp. 547ff., especially p. 561.

[219] M. Luciani, 'Diritti sociali e integrazione europea', in Associazione Italiana dei Costituzionalisti, *Annuario 1999. La Costituzione europea*, Atti del XIV Convegno annuale Perugia 7–9 ottobre 1999, Padua 2000, pp. 507ff., here p. 511.

[220] *Ibid.*, p. 517.   [221] *Ibid.*, p. 530.

[222] Paragraph 59 of the judgment.   [223] See paragraph 57 of the judgment.

On the other hand, there is no recognition of a fundamental social right to bargain collectively. Furthermore, the language of fundamental rights is likewise absent when the Court turns to an evaluation – albeit expressly invoking Directive 98/49/EC – of 'the importance of the social function attributed to supplementary pensions',[224] especially within a system such as the Netherlands one in which the latter represent an almost indispensable supplementation of the basic state pension.

Although at least the exclusion of a fundamental right to bargain collectively may seem questionable in the light of a fuller recognition of Member State constitutional traditions[225] and a less formalistic reading of the relevant international sources than that offered by Advocate General Jacobs, it is nevertheless undeniably consistent with the overall design of the Treaties and with the eminently 'aspirational' dimension within which, even following the amendments introduced at Amsterdam, they enclose social rights.[226]

It might, on the other hand, be said that – inasmuch as the Court was in a position anyhow to exempt collective bargaining on the Netherlands supplementary pension funds, and indeed the subsequent extension *erga omnes* of its effects by the public authorities, from the rules on competition – the recognition of a fundamental right serves no purpose, since the protection *ratione materiae* thus accorded to the legitimate aims pursued by the social partners is enough in itself.

---

[224] Paragraph 106 of the judgment.

[225] Largely different results are in fact arrived at by the perspicacious review of B. Bercusson, 'Trade Union Rights in EU Law', in F. Snyder (ed.), *The Europeanisation of Law: The Legal Effects of European Integration*, Oxford-Portland 2000. On their side, N. Bruun and B. Veneziani ('The Right of Freedom to Transnational Industrial Action', in *A Legal Framework for European Industrial Relations*, European Trade Union Institute, Brussels 1999, p. 84) point out that the 'artificial split between the right to collective bargaining and the freedom to take industrial action' upheld by Advocate General Jacobs 'is clearly not in accordance with the constitutional traditions of the Member States nor the guidelines given by the relevant international treaties'. Nor, moreover, does it seem without significance in this context that the fundamental right to bargain collectively is one of the core labour standards recently reaffirmed by the 1998 ILO Declaration on fundamental principles and rights at work. In this sense, it would not appear inappropriate to attribute to the right to bargain collectively the character of a fundamental right that is, in a way, a preliminary to and governing condition for the individual social rights that operate within the employment relationship: a character which, to put it somewhat boldly, is 'super-fundamental' compared with the latter.

[226] Cf. the Simitis Report, where it is explained that Article 136 of the EC Treaty qualifies the fundamental social rights as determined by the two Charters of 1961 and 1989 simply 'as guidelines for activities of both the Community and the Member States', 'only seen as a basis of Community policies'.

This was, in essence, the line of reasoning expressly argued and suggested to the Court by Advocate General Jacobs, when he had stated in the Opinion he delivered in *Albany* that the recognition of such a right would not have made any difference to the terms of the question referred and the judgment to be delivered in this controversial case. 'The mere recognition of a fundamental right to bargain collectively', he had explained,[227] 'would... not suffice to shelter collective bargaining from the applicability of the competition rules'.

But this is a laboured argument[228] which is in fact subtly contradicted and belied by the painstaking interpretative effort made by the Advocate General himself to refute – by denying the positive existence of such a right in the Community legal order – the opposing thesis put forward both by the Commission and by a number of Member States in the course of the proceedings.

This effort appears, in point of fact, to be driven by an awareness that the admittance of a fundamental right to bargain collectively into the interpretative scheme would actually have changed the nature of things very considerably.[229] It would have significantly influenced not so much the *an* of antitrust immunity, which can be regarded as essentially settled as soon as the perspectives of extreme liberalism are discarded, but rather its *quomodo* and *quantum*, that is, the two aspects that are the most important in *practical terms*. It may indeed be said that the recognition of such a right would have been (and would be) capable of overturning, and reversing, the methodological perspective expounded by Advocate General Jacobs and ultimately adopted by the Court.

If we assume the existence of a fundamental right for the social partners to bargain collectively, it must by definition be accepted that the rules on competition are in reality totally inapplicable. Consequently, it will not be a question of fixing the (varying) limits within which a collective agreement is, by reason of its nature or its purpose, to be deemed

---

[227] At point 163 of the Opinon.

[228] It is, for example, difficult to imagine the extraordinary success story of Article 30 of the Treaty *without* the economic freedom it protects being construed as a *fundamental right*. The powerful penetrative force of this freedom – especially within national legal orders (such as that of Italy) in which economic freedoms are given far less consideration and decidedly weaker constitutional protection – is, in reality, largely due to its affirmation as a fundamental right and claim of the individual that has been guaranteed with maximum effectiveness by Court of Justice case-law (cf. P. Ridola, 'Diritti di libertà e mercato nella "Costituzione europea"', in Associazione Italiana dei Costituzionalisti, *Annuario*, pp. 323ff., especially pp. 347–8).

[229] What is more, it was the Advocate General himself who acknowledged, very significantly, that it 'is a seminal question since if there is such a right, any impairment of the substance of the right, even in the public interest, might be unlawful' (point 133 of the Opinion).

immune; the reverse will be true, and it will be a question of defining the very narrow margins within which – without ever being able to erode its substance, its inviolable nucleus – competition law may, purely by way of exception, require the original sphere of freedom of collective autonomy to be curtailed in the general interest.

In this view of things, the alleged all-pervasive force of Community competition law finds a constitutive limit in the autonomy of the social partners. An original limit which is untouchable other than on a purely exceptional basis and to a degree rigorously circumscribed by the need to guarantee the fundamental right in question the maximum possible effectiveness. A limit, therefore, which itself acts as an autonomous and fundamental organizing principle of the dynamics of the Community legal order and is more than a mere exemption from the (usually predominant) principles of competition law.

The recognition of any fundamental right necessitates identifying carefully those other legally protected interests which are of equal or higher ranking in comparison with the fundamental right in question[230] and with which it has to be correlated in accordance with proper procedures for a balancing operation arriving at equilibrium and co-ordination.[231]

That being so, comparison with the economic freedoms and the principles of free competition in the single market will have to start at least from the presumption that the values protected through recognition of the fundamental right to bargain collectively and other associated manifestations of the social partners' autonomy enjoy equal ranking with those economic freedoms and principles.[232] The weighting of the potentially conflicting legally protected interests will mean, in any case, that only strictly essential limitations of the fundamental right are admissible,[233] without any possibility of incursion into its sphere that is accorded absolute protection.[234]

Turning to one of the most problematic fronts opened up by *Albany*, in the context being assumed here it would be difficult to accommodate the 'intimacy' criterion proposed in the literature (modelled on the Opinion delivered by Advocate General Jacobs) as a means of identifying

---

[230] Häberle, *Die Wesensgehaltgarantie*.   [231] *Ibid.*

[232] Similar ideas are to be found in J. Baquero Cruz, 'La protección de los derechos sociales en la Comunidad europea tras el Tratado de Amsterdam', *Revista de Derecho Comunitario Europeo* 1998, pp. 639ff., especially p. 656.

[233] See again Häberle, *Die Wesensgehaltgarantie*.

[234] *Ibid.* If we adopt the wording used in the Nice Charter, we can call it the 'essence' of the fundamental right in question.

with certainty the demarcation line beyond which a collective agreement will be regarded as going outside the specific regulation of employment relationships and so loses its immunity.[235]

Nor, even more so, would it be lawful to claim – which the Court of Justice itself rejected – that the functions performed by collective bargaining[236] are subject to a systematic comparison with the rules of competition law.[237] This is because in both cases, albeit with differing degrees of emphasis, the approach adopted would still be that of an 'unequal balancing operation in favour of the common-market freedoms',[238] which the affirmation at Community level (as well) of an enshrined fundamental right to bargain collectively would axiomatically preclude.

Consequently, the express recognition of a fundamental right to bargain collectively (and this of course also applies to other social rights potentially in a similar situation of confrontation/conflict with the rules on competition)[239] is undoubtedly such as to alter the overall significance of the normative context in which it takes place, inasmuch as 'the terms of its balancing with other constitutional rights or interests will inevitably change'.[240]

The Charter of Fundamental Rights of the European Union that was proclaimed at Nice contains such an express recognition: its Article 28 prescribes 'Workers and employers, or their respective organizations, have, in accordance with Community law and national laws and practices, the right to negotiate and conclude collective agreements at the appropriate levels and, in cases of conflicts of interest, to take collective action to defend their interests, including strike action.'

This is not the place to offer a detailed analysis of the provision and to weigh up *minutatim* its weaknesses and strong points compared with other international or constitutional pronouncements on rights to negotiate and to take collective action. Here, it suffices (and is necessary) to confine ourselves – referring the reader to what was said in general in chapter 2 above regarding the significance and legal force of the Charter – to take specific note of the express grant, at European level, of a fundamental right to bargain collectively.

---

[235] See L. Di Via, 'Sindacati, contratti collettivi e antitrust', *Mercato Concorrenza Regole* 2000, no. 2, p. 294.

[236] But more generally by the mandatory rules of labour law.

[237] Ichino, 'Contrattazione collettiva', pp. 642ff.   [238] Cartabia, *Principi inviolabili*, p. 43.

[239] In particular, the right to strike; see G. Orlandini, *Sciopero e servizi pubblici essenziali nel processo di integrazione europea. Uno studio di diritto comparato e comunitario*, Turin 2003; T. Novitz, *International and European Protection of the Right to Strike*, Oxford 2003.

[240] Luciani, 'Diritti sociali', p. 543.

The acquired existence at European level of the fundamental character of a justiciable right to bargain collectively[241] is capable on its own, whatever may have been said to date, of shifting and re-balancing the logic and method of comparison with the (potentially opposing) Community constitutional values of competition and unity of the internal market.[242]

In restoring to the Union legal order the full range of fundamental values of the modern-day constitutionalism of rights it certainly seems capable, like the analogous 'acquisitions' effected by the Nice Charter in social matters, of breaking, at the structural level, the 'supremacy rule' regarding market and competition values that has so far prevailed in the jurisprudence of the Court of Justice, and imposing in its place a 'compatibility rule'[243] that respects the autonomy of the values protected by fundamental social rights.

Recognition of the fundamental social rights of individuals and groups also (and perhaps particularly) means that the Union *Gemeinwohl* is enriched expressly in harmony with the effective expansion of its political dimension and comes to incorporate, in all their fullness and autonomous relevance, values and legally protected interests other than the long-dominant construction of the common market, thereby re-balancing the dynamic of the integration process.

At the same time, the Nice Charter establishes new bases for a more profitable constitutional dialogue on the founding values of the European polity. This is because, particularly considering its incorporation into Part II of the Treaty establishing a Constitution for Europe, the Nice Charter conveys more than ever the sense of a dynamic of reciprocal constitutional enrichment founded on the values which the more authentic *ubi consistam* of the Union as an 'osmotic constitutional community'[244] will represent. The Charter in fact expressly prefigures a dynamic relationship, with respect to the several national Constitutions, of reciprocal or two-way

---

[241] As strongly emphasized by A. J. Menéndez, 'Chartering Europe', *ARENA (Advanced Research on the Europeanisation of the Nation-State) Working Papers* No. 01/13, p. 15, once prescribed explicitly and in positive terms in the Nice Charter a right becomes obvious and per se irrebuttable by the Court of Justice itself. This is, manifestly, even more so the case following the incorporation of the Charter into the constitutional Treaty.

[242] For similar assessments, also with respect to the other rights of collective and industrial-relations relevance spelled out by the Nice Charter, see M. Roccella, 'La Carta', especially p. 336.

[243] S. Rodotà, 'Diritto, diritti, globalizzazione', *Rivista Giuridica del Lavoro e della Previdenza Sociale* 2000, pp. 765ff., here p. 777.

[244] P. Häberle, 'Dallo Stato nazionale all'Unione europea: evoluzioni dello Stato costituzionale', *Diritto Pubblico Comparato ed Europeo* 2002, vol. II, pp. 455ff., here p. 456.

subsidiarity, extending to a maximum 'interconstitutional' guarantee of the values now *also* protected by fundamental social rights.[245]

For this reason too, therefore, it seems capable of helping to overcome what has rightly been deemed the anomalous '*proprium* of the Community legal order'[246] as against many national constitutional systems: namely, the fact that in its scale of values the Court of Justice has, to date, placed 'the Community's *economic* objectives on the same level as (if not a higher level than) fundamental rights'.[247] A *proprium* which in recent years has more and more insistently featured as a potential source of dangerous clashes between Community constitutional principles and national constitutional principles, particularly (even if not solely) in the area of social rights.

8. . . . (b) Constitutional dialogues . . .

The emergence of the problem of risks of 'constitutional collision'[248] between the Community legal order and the several national legal orders against the background of the disputed issue of jurisdictional *Kompetenz-Kompetenz* is a relatively recent development, albeit one anchored to theoretical presuppositions which are hardly new.[249]

The famous *Maastricht-Urteil* of the German Federal Constitutional Court in Karlsruhe signals what is symbolically and institutionally perhaps the most acute moment of a legitimacy crisis of the European constitutional discourse which coincided, at the beginning of the 1990s, with the difficult process of negotiating and ratifying the Maastricht Treaty.[250] After Maastricht, what has retrospectively been regarded as a *modus vivendi* marked by a relatively peaceful acceptance of the progressive affirmation by the Court of Justice of the founding constitutional doctrines of the

---

[245] A. Ruggeri, 'Sovranità dello Stato e sovranità sovranazionale, attraverso i diritti umani, e prospettive di un diritto europeo "intercostituzionale"', *Diritto Pubblico Comparato ed Europeo* 2001, vol. II, pp. 544ff., especially p. 561.

[246] Cartabia, *Principi inviolabili*, p. 42.

[247] *Ibid.* (the emphasis is in the original).

[248] N. MacCormick, 'Risking Constitutional Collision in Europe?', *Oxford Journal of Legal Studies* 1998, pp. 517ff.

[249] See by way of example, C. U. Schmid, 'From Pont d'Avignon to Ponte Vecchio. The Resolution of Constitutional Conflicts Between the European Union and the Member States through Principles of Public International Law', *EUI (European University Institute) Working Papers in Law* No. 98/7.

[250] See Weiler, 'Epilogue', especially pp. 366–7, who gives an indicative list of 'some of the signs of the new, more hostile, constitutional landscape' inaugurated by the post-Maastricht context.

European Community[251] gave way to a 'new discussion which goes to the fundamental myths of the Community or Union calling into question the very foundations of European constitutionalism'.[252]

The conjunction of sovereignty and fundamental rights[253] underlies the rediscovery and assertion of *Kompetenz-Kompetenz* by the German Federal Constitutional Court and – in a more indirect but no less 'insidious'[254] form – is also the source of the reaffirmation by the Italian Constitutional Court of its exclusive competence to establish 'counter-limits' to Community integration.[255]

Concern for an adequate (strong) protection of fundamental rights at Community level as well as at national level – albeit somewhat overshadowed, particularly in the *Maastricht-Urteil*,[256] by an attempt to mount a tardy and rather backward-looking defence of the irretrievably out-of-date conception of State sovereignty as a *suprema potestas* of the *Herren der Verträge*[257] – does appear to occupy a central position. Even though not entirely free from the risk of instrumentalization,[258] its genuineness would

---

[251] B. De Witte, 'Sovereignty and European Integration: The Weight of Legal Tradition', in Slaughter, Stone Sweet and Weiler, *European Court*, pp. 277–304, especially pp. 281–93, comments that, in retrospect, the two-year period 1989–90 can be seen as the high-water mark of (relative) 'peaceful coexistence' between the Court of Justice and national supreme and constitutional courts, with the historic acceptance of the doctrine of supremacy of Community law by the French Conseil d'Etat (with its *Nicolo* decision) and by the British House of Lords (with its *Factortame* judgment).

[252] Weiler, 'Epilogue', p. 377.

[253] G. Silvestri, 'La diretta applicabilità delle norme comunitarie: implicazioni teoriche', in Associazione Italiana dei Costituzionalisti, *Annuario*, pp. 149ff., especially p. 186, talks of 'sovereignty-power and sovereignty-values'.

[254] J. H. H. Weiler, 'L'Unione e gli Stati membri: competenze e sovranità', *Quaderni Costituzionali* 2000, pp. 5ff., especially p. 12.

[255] See, by way of example, M. Cartabia, 'The Italian Constitutional Court and the Relationship Between the Italian Legal System and the European Union', in Slaughter, Stone Sweet and Weiler, *European Court*, pp. 133–46.

[256] See J. Kokott, 'Report on Germany', in Slaughter, Stone Sweet and Weiler, *European Court*, pp. 77–131, especially p. 107.

[257] Cf., in particular, the stern criticism of J. H. H. Weiler, 'The State "über alles". Demos, Telos and the German Maastricht Decision', *EUI Working Papers, Robert Schuman Centre – European University Institute* No. 95/19, and the no less searching criticism of N. MacCormick, 'The Maastrict-Urteil: Sovereignty Now', *European Law Journal* 1995, vol. 1 no. 3, pp. 259–66.

[258] See N. Reich, 'Judge-made "Europe à la carte": Some Remarks on Recent Conflicts between European and German Constitutional Law Provoked by the Banana Litigation', *European Journal of International Law* 1996, pp. 103ff., especially p. 110, who sees a materialization of the risk of instrumentalization of the defence of fundamental rights and state sovereignty under the *Kompetenz-Kompetenz* umbrella in the famous German controversy over bananas.

seem undeniable, as witness (to mention just one aspect) the lengthy history of its non-suspect 'usage'.[259]

It is no accident that, mainly in Italy (but also, with the difference in sensitivity reflected by its different constitutional tradition, to a certain extent in Germany),[260] this concern has consistently involved social rights.[261] Especially after Maastricht, concerns for the overall guardianship of the strong system of social rights protected by the Italian Constitution multiplied[262] along with increasingly frequent warnings of possible risks of 'constitutional collision' in this crucial area.[263] This is because, comparatively speaking, the Italian Constitution is characterized by the exceptional extent of the catalogue of social rights which it protects and elevates in positive terms to the rank of fundamental rights.[264]

The 'guiding rule laid down by the second paragraph of Article 3 of the Constitution, the true characterizing token'[265] of the Italian Constitutional Charter, casts its light over the entire plexus of organic connections

---

[259] This dates back to at least the early 1970s (we need mention only the *Solange I* decision of the German Federal Constitutional Court). What is more, conventional wisdom holds that the actual construction of the protection of fundamental rights as general principles of Community law by the Court of Justice was largely a shrewd response by the judges in Luxembourg to pressure in this direction exerted mainly by the German and Italian Constitutional Courts (see, by way of example, G. F. Mancini: 'The Making of a Constitution for Europe', *Common Market Law Review* 1989, vol. 26, pp. 595–614, now also in his *Democracy and Constitutionalism in the European Union. Collected Essays*, Oxford-Portland 2000, pp. 1ff.).

[260] See, for example, W. Däubler, 'Instruments of Community Labour Law', in Davies *et al.*, *European Community Labour Law*, pp. 151–67, especially pp. 157 and 167. Likewise, Häberle, 'Per una dottrina', pp. 26–7, stresses that the lack of protection of social rights at Union level as against the strong guarantee of economic rights can represent a threat for the 'constitutional welfare state', whose primary constitutional objective is precisely the achievement of 'distributive justice'.

[261] The same observation can, however, be extended to other national constitutional contexts. With respect to Spain, see M. R. Alarcón Caracuel, 'La necessità di un capitolo sociale nella futura Costituzione europea', *Lavoro e Diritto* 2000, pp. 607ff.

[262] Cf. M. Luciani, 'La costituzione italiana e gli ostacoli all'integrazione europea', *Politica del Diritto* 1992, pp. 557ff., especially pp. 578–81; Cartabia, 'Italian Constitutional Court', p. 144.

[263] Cf. M. V. Ballestrero, 'Corte costituzionale e Corte di Giustizia. Supponiamo che . . .', *Lavoro e Diritto* 1998, pp. 485ff. (regarding substantive equality between men and women); Pallini, 'Il rapporto', p. 232 (regarding the protection of collective autonomy as enshrined in Article 39 of the Italian Constitution); Giubboni, 'Social Insurance', p. 105 (regarding Article 38 of the Italian Constitution).

[264] According to Ballestrero, 'Brevi osservazioni', p. 548, in terms of social rights the Italian Constitution represents an absolute '*unicum* in the European landscape'.

[265] M. Luciani, 'Economia nel diritto costituzionale', *Digesto delle Discipline Pubblicistiche* vol. V, Turin 1990, pp. 373ff., here p. 378. (Article 3 of the Italian Constitution reads as follows: '1. All citizens are vested with equal social status and are equal before the law,

between the values and rights protected by it and directs the interpreter towards the '*unequal balance between considerations of an economic nature and those (connected but sometimes conflicting) relating to social development*'[266] which is in a way the reverse of that adopted so far by Court of Justice jurisprudence.

Although perhaps not in terms as clear as those that connote the Italian case, this considerable shortfall in the protection of social rights by the Community legal order also exists in comparison with other national constitutional experiences: the latent risks of conflict in this area are, in fact, fairly widespread.[267]

The spectre of 'collision' and more generally of a constitutional 'legitimacy crisis' – with the dangerous disintegrative effects that its actual 'explosion' could bring – has prompted leading Community scholars to launch an intense and impassioned process of re-examining the very foundations of European constitutionalism.[268]

This is obviously not the place to enter into the merits of a debate which in its breadth and complexity goes far beyond the particular theme of the present book. Suffice it to note that, over and above the diversity of the theoretical approaches followed, the common denominator of the proposals put forward for avoiding an impasse and the *practical* intractability of a potential explosion of the conflict of principle hidden behind the *Kompetenz-Kompetenz* issue[269] consists in the pragmatic suggestion of dialogue and co-operation, in an open and pluralist context, between all of the constitutional actors involved.

---

without distinction as to sex, race, language, religion, political opinions and personal or social condition. 2. It is the responsibility of the Republic to remove all obstacles of an economic and social nature which, by limiting the freedom and equality of citizens, prevent the full development of the individual and the participation of all workers in the political, economic and social organization of the country.')

[266] *Ibid.* (the emphasis is in the original).

[267] See also B. De Witte, 'Community Law and National Constitutional Values', *Legal Issues of European Integration* 1991, no. 2, pp. 1–22.

[268] See, among the most highly regarded contributions, N. MacCormick, *Questioning Sovereignty. Law, State, and Nation in the European Commonwealth*, Oxford 1999 (paperback 2002); J. H. H. Weiler, *The Constitution of Europe. 'Do the New Clothes Have an Emperor?' and Other Essays on European Integration*, Cambridge 1999; T. C. Hartley, *Constitutional Problems of the European Union*, Oxford-Portland 1999.

[269] A. Stone Sweet, 'Constitutional Dialogues in the European Community', in Slaughter, Stone Sweet and Weiler, *European Court*, pp. 305–30, especially p. 319, comments that – if the presuppositions on which the Court of Justice and, for example, the German Federal Constitutional Court respectively operate are taken to their consistent logical conclusions – the potential situations of constitutional conflict over competence are 'in fact irresoluble'.

Thus, the route of 'constitutional dialogue' on the foundational values of the Community polity has come to be ever more insistently invoked as a means of avoiding, in mutual respect, risks of conflict that are prejudicial to the entire system in being likely to damage the dynamic and open equilibrium that characterizes European multilevel constitutionalism.[270]

This route would mean more discussion and consultation between the Court of Justice and national constitutional and/or supreme courts, on a totally equal footing of 'conversational rights',[271] in a dialogue capable of deepening the value dimension of European integration and accommodating – albeit still within a *common* framework – respect for different national constitutional sensitivities. For example, the competence reserved to itself by the Italian Constitutional Court in regard to 'counter-limits' could become 'the locus in which the voice of the [national] constitutional order is expressed'[272] in the process of Community integration and constitute the starting-point of a positive strategy of co-operation with the Court of Justice. In drawing attention to the values that are specific to its national constitutional order the Italian Constitutional Court can, in fact, 'actively participate in the identification of the common constitutional traditions from which the Court of Justice, in its turn, derives European fundamental principles and thereby contribute to the process of material integration on values that is indispensable to the Community'.[273]

Viewed from this angle, preliminary references submitted by the Constitutional Court could become a valuable instrument of direct dialogue with the Court of Justice which this national court that pronounces on the constitutionality of legislation could utilize to express with authoritativeness the voice of the Italian constitutional order on Community matters that involve its fundamental principles, while at the same time excluding destructive exit strategies.[274] In order to do so the Italian Constitutional Court would, obviously, need to move beyond its own restrictive jurisprudence[275] and regard itself as legitimized (and obliged),

---

[270] I. Pernice, 'Multilevel Constitutionalism and the Treaty of Amsterdam: European Constitution-Making Revisited?', *Common Market Law Review* 1999, pp. 704ff.

[271] A. Lo Faro, 'La Corte di giustizia e i suoi interlocutori giudiziari nell'ordinamento giuslavoristico italiano', *Lavoro e Diritto* 1998, no. 3, pp. 621ff., here p. 622.

[272] Cartabia, *Principi inviolabili*, p. 243.   [273] *Ibid.*, p. 215.

[274] To use the well-known terminology of A. O. Hirschman, *Exit, Voice, and Loyalty. Responses to Decline in Firms, Organizations and States*, Cambridge, Mass. 1970.

[275] See, for example, Constitutional Court Order No. 536 of 1995, in *Giurisprudenza Costituzionale* 1995, pp. 4459ff.

as a court of final instance, to submit references for a preliminary ruling to the Court of Justice within the meaning of Article 234 of the EC Treaty.

In particular, as suggested by Marta Cartabia[276] the Constitutional Court could, in submitting a reference for a preliminary ruling, indicate directly to the Court of Justice the interpretation of the Community rule concerned (in the case in point, rules on competition) which could be regarded as conforming to the inviolable (social) principles of the national constitutional order, and in this sense warn the judges in Luxembourg of the unacceptability of other possible interpretations likely to call the constitutional legitimacy of the 'Community' rule[277] into question by infringing the counter-limits.

A strategy for the 'co-operative management'[278] of possible conflicts has likewise been devised with respect to the German experience.[279] Actual adherence to the principle of 'co-operation' and 'co-ordination' between the Court of Justice and the German Federal Constitutional Court[280] – albeit without entirely eliminating the possibility of a collision – would, nevertheless, have the effect in practice of defusing the *Kompetenz-Kompetenz* issue by favouring, for example, essential agreement between

---

[276] Again in *Principi inviolabili*, pp. 248ff. For similar suggestions with regard to other national experiences as well, see J. Wouters, 'National Constitutions and the European Union', *Legal Issues of Economic Integration* 2000, no. 1, pp. 25ff., especially pp. 83 and 90.

[277] The Community rule itself would not, obviously, be the direct point of emphasis since the review of constitutionality would, technically speaking, take place with reference to the national Act implementing the Treaty in so far as it introduces a Community rule essentially in conflict with inalienable human rights or the fundamental principles of the Italian constitutional order and thereby infringes the 'counter-limits' to supranational integration. See, for example, Italian Constitutional Court Decision No. 232 of 21 April 1989 (*Fragd* decision) in *Giurisprudenza Costituzionale* 1989, p. 1001, with a note by M. Cartabia, 'Nuovi sviluppi delle "competenze comunitarie" della Corte costituzionale', and, in the literature, F. Sorrentino, *Profili costituzionali dell'integrazione comunitaria*, Turin 1996, pp. 10ff.

[278] E. Cannizzaro, 'Democrazia e sovranità nei rapporti fra Stati membri e Unione europea', *Diritto dell'Unione Europea* 2000, pp. 241ff., here p. 261.

[279] See Schmid, 'From Pont d'Avignon', pp. 22–3.

[280] This line of reasoning has been significantly adopted by one of the selfsame judges of the Federal Constitutional Court who, as the rapporteur in the case, influenced the *Maastricht* judgment: see J. Kirchhof, 'Die Gewaltenbalance zwischen staatlichen und europäischen Organen', *Juristenzeitung* 1998, p. 965. See also M. Kumm, 'Who is the Final Arbiter of Constitutionality in Europe? Three Conceptions of the Relationship between the German Federal Constitutional Court and the European Court of Justice', *Common Market Law Review* 1999, vol. 36, pp. 351–86.

the respective courts on the standard of protection of the fundamental right and/or value under discussion.[281]

The virtues of indirect dialogue between the Court in Luxembourg and national constitutional courts are usually emphasized by all those who root in the general duty of reciprocal collaboration arising from Article 10 of the EC Treaty a specific obligation on the latter systematically to take account of their respective jurisprudential stances whenever questions arise that cut across, with risks of substantial divergences, constitutional essentials of the legal orders involved.

In this view of things, the Court of Justice could never arrive at its own conclusions without giving due regard to 'their potential impact on national constitutions',[282] and for their part the several Member State constitutional courts would always have to bear in mind the notion of being fully part of a polity broader than the national one.[283]

The Nice Charter, while the fact that it established for the first time a specifically EU-level catalogue of fundamental rights means that it makes explicit and transparent the *minimum* of constitutional homogeneity shared in this respect by the Member States,[284] nowadays facilitates comparison between the different national constitutional traditions in the search for a more adequate and satisfactory standard.

As stated earlier, the establishment of an EU catalogue of fundamental rights which is inspired by the principle of their indivisibility and for the first time encompasses social rights on an equal footing helps to make good the deficit of supranational protection of social values which is seen as causing some of the risks most relevant to the material legitimacy of the integration process, as well as – more specifically – the risk of 'constitutional collision'.

---

[281] Faint and very indirect confirmation could be found in the latest developments of the 'banana litigation': in declaring the inadmissibility of the question addressed to it (see Interim Order of 7 June 2000, *Human Rights Law Journal* 2000, vol. 21, p. 251), the German Federal Constitutional Court was in fact able to 'count on' at least partial acceptance by the Court of Justice of its submissions of fact regarding the level of protection of the fundamental right being challenged (the right to property of German banana importers). See also the critical assessments of C. U. Schmid, 'All Bark and No Bite: Notes on the Federal Constitutional Court's "Banana Decision"', *European Law Journal* 2001, pp. 95ff.

[282] MacCormick, *Questioning Sovereignty*, p. 120.

[283] See also Häberle, 'Per una dottrina', p. 15, who maintains the urgency 'of a theory of fundamental rights at Community level' that is sufficiently 'flexible in accommodating the differences between national dogmatics' and recalls that 'the open society of European constitutional interpreters' is necessarily 'multinational'.

[284] For some ideas in this direction, see Pernice, 'Multilevel', p. 726.

The Nice Charter is not intended, in any event, to replace the other forms of fundamental-rights protection that exist within the European constitutional space. In providing the Union with a catalogue of its own, it is intended to represent 'an added value to the protection of fundamental rights in Europe, without prejudice to the forms of protection that exist at various levels',[285] while at the same time filling the objective lacunae in the Community system. As one author has put it, the Union Charter thus forms part 'of the multilevel protection of fundamental rights . . . as one of the many planets in the overall galaxy of European fundamental rights'.[286]

The wording of its Article 53 seems, at any rate, quite enough to give a reassuring answer to all those who rightly point out that the introduction of a Community catalogue does not, in itself, necessarily eliminate the problem of divergence, and hence potential conflict, between standards of fundamental-rights protection in the composite and pluralist European space.[287]

What Article 53 of the Charter does, in fact, is to provide a means of defusing potential conflicts arising from the non-harmonized superimposition of different standards of protection. In such circumstances, it stipulates that the rights protected by the Union Charter must be interpreted in a manner that does not prejudice or reduce the protection ensuing from the international legal order or from national Constitutions. In prescribing that the provisions of the Charter may not be seen as restricting or adversely affecting the rights and freedoms recognized not only by Union and international agreements to which the Union or all the Member States are party[288] but also by the national constitutions, Article 53 appears to give explicit expression in positive terms to the criterion of the prevalence of the highest standard of protection, thereby observing the special nature of the solutions provided at this level in providing the 'greatest guarantee' for the value being protected.[289]

---

[285] M. Cartabia, 'Commento all'articolo 53', in R. Bifulco, M. Cartabia and A. Celotto (eds.), *L'Europa dei diritti. Commento alla Carta dei diritti fondamentali dell'Unione europea*, Bologna 2001, p. 360.

[286] *Ibid.*, p. 363.

[287] L. F. M. Besselink, 'Entrapped by the Maximum Standard: On Fundamental Rights, Pluralism and Subsidiarity in the European Union', *Common Market Law Review* 1998, pp. 629ff., especially p. 630.

[288] Including, in particular, the European Convention for the Protection of Human Rights and Fundamental Freedoms (ECHR) that was signed in Rome in 1950.

[289] See, in this vein, L. F. M. Besselink, 'The Member States, the National Constitutions and the Scope of the Charter', *Maastricht Journal of European and Comparative Law* 2001, pp. 68ff., especially p. 80.

This criterion is very different from the one which, although without ever really spelling out its choice, the Court of Justice mostly followed in the past in extracting from the 'constitutional traditions common to the Member States' the *an* and the *quantum* of Community protection of fundamental rights. In applying the praetorian principle subsequently codified by the present Article 6(2) of the Maastricht Treaty, the Court had in fact hitherto particularly (and mainly) adopted the criterion of the lowest common denominator both for the purposes of verifying the existence of a right and for the purposes of determining the relative standard and *quantum* of protection.[290]

Such an approach was unsatisfactory for two reasons. First, it entailed a trend towards the sacrifice or relinquishment of 'unique'[291] fundamental values and/or rights, i.e. those recognized on a specifically national and idiosyncratic basis only by the Constitution of a single Member State (or by those of a minority of Member States).[292] Second, it entailed a trend towards a process of levelling-down to a common minimum standard of protection accorded to a given right, blunting the effect of national provisions providing a higher level of protection. It thus tended to generalize over the entire Community system the *common minimum standard* that could be found by comparing the (main) solutions offered by the Member State national Constitutions.[293]

By contrast, in incorporating in the shape of its Article 53 what has been vividly described as a 'criterion of constitutional subsidiarity "on the up" (*al rialzo*)'[294] the Nice Charter appears to opt for the solution – more respectful of national constitutional identities – of safeguarding, in the event of discrepancy, the local maximum standard.[295]

As thus prescribed, in cases where, in the light of the provisions of the Charter itself and of Community law in general, the level of protection accorded to a given fundamental right (for example, a fundamental *social* right such as the right to bargain collectively or the right to strike) is lower than that deducible from the Constitution of the Member State

---

[290] See De Witte, 'Community', p. 11, who notes that this is the approach developed in *Hoechst* v *Commission* (ECJ Joined Cases 46/87 and 227/88 [1989] ECR 2859, especially paragraphs 17–18 of the judgment) and subsequently mostly used by the Court.

[291] Besselink, 'Entrapped', p. 636.

[292] De Witte, 'Community', p. 7, states that 'Constitutions are not mere copies of a universalist ideal, they also reflect the idiosyncratic choices and preferences of the constituents and are the highest legal expression of the country's value system.'

[293] That is, the opposite of the solution wished for by Besselink, 'Entrapped', pp. 670ff., in the form of a universalized maximum standard.

[294] Ballestrero, 'Brevi osservazioni', p. 568.

[295] See Besselink, 'Entrapped', pp. 674ff.

concerned, it is the latter which – in the event of any dispute – must take precedence, irrespective of the extent to which (if at all) it is shared by the other national constitutional traditions.[296] Conversely, the level of protection provided by the Community legal order is ensured precedence only where and in so far as it guarantees a standard of protection higher than the relevant national (or international) standard.

Consequently, while it elevates social rights to the rank of fundamental rights of the Community legal order itself, the Nice Charter at the same time facilitates the co-operative search for an agreement on the substantive standard of protection and directs it towards the goal of the maximum protection available in any particular case.[297] In this way it increases the possibilities of dialogue between courts and the opportunities for communication processes aimed at strengthening the fundamental rights of individuals and groups.

In fully reconciling social values with the specific language of fundamental rights at supranational level as well, the Charter thus establishes solid bases whereby the plurality of sources – which is and will continue to be specific to the multilevel constitutionalism typical of the European Union – actually increases the opportunities for affirming and giving effect to social rights and opens up new channels for the social emancipation of the individual.[298] There is no doubt that it favours the prospective development of new and more effective antidotes to an infiltration of Community competition and market law that may prove excessively invasive of the constitutional traditions in which national systems of labour law are rooted.

9. . . . (c) Negative integration and social jurisdiction of the Member States

The third and last aspect on which to reflect – obviously connected with the previous one and also central to the more general problem of establishing

---

[296] For some ideas along this line, see De Witte, 'Community', pp. 21–2.

[297] Cf. S. Rodotà, 'La Carta come atto politico e come documento giuridico', in A. Manzella et al. (eds.), *Riscrevere i diritti in Europa. Introduzione alla Carta dei diritti fondamentali dell'Unione europea*, Bologna 2001, pp. 57ff., here p. 85, according to whom 'the system is structured in accordance with the criterion of the maximum protection possible, since subjects enjoy either the greater guarantees provided by the other sources mentioned in Article 53 or those introduced by the Charter.' Similarly, A. Manzella, 'Dal mercato ai diritti', in Manzella et al., *Riscrevere*, pp. 43 and 45.

[298] S. Sciarra, 'Diritti sociali. Riflessioni sulla Carta europea dei diritti fondamentali', *Argomenti di Diritto del Lavoro* 2001, no. 2, pp. 391ff., especially pp. 399ff.

a new balance between negative and positive integration – concerns the issue of a more precise delimitation of the sphere of competence already guaranteed and reserved to the Member States by the founding Treaty in the matter of employment policy and labour law and, in particular, social protection.

The entire phenomenon of the infiltration of competition law continually poses an obvious question of competence in this respect.[299] In all cases where this arises the same applies as was stated, for example, with regard to *Job Centre*: the basic question consists in verifying whether, in the absence of Community measures directed towards positive integration, national legislators still enjoy an essential sphere of autonomy and freedom in organizing their own welfare system, or whether the choices relating to the actual *quomodo* of the system of social protection as a whole must now in any case be regarded as determined by 'obligations deriving from participation in the process of European integration'[300] in the *specific* form of the market-compatibility requirements[301] imposed by supranational competition and market law.

The question is particularly pressing in regard to those matters of social policy which, although in principle falling within the sphere of shared Community competence as envisaged by Articles 136 and 137 of the EC Treaty (and now Articles III-209 and III-210 of the constitutional Treaty), are nevertheless more jealously protected by the Member States and are in fact still reserved to unanimous decision within the Council and only marginally touched upon by Community regulatory measures of a binding nature. Among these matters, that of social security and protection – an absolute top priority in the effective structuring of national welfare states – occupies an obviously central position.

In abstract terms, the response of the Court of Justice would indeed appear to be clear enough, at least as regards such core issues of Member State social sovereignty. Once again in *Poucet and Pistre*, reiterating what had previously been pronounced in *Duphar*, it peremptorily confirmed that 'Community law does not detract from the powers of the Member States to organize their social security systems.'[302]

---

[299] See A. Lyon-Caen, 'Droit social', p. 335.

[300] Roccella, 'Il caso', p. 37; see also Roccella, 'Tutela del lavoro e ragioni del mercato nella giurisprudenza recente della Corte di giustizia', *Giornale di Diritto del Lavoro e di Relazioni Industriali* 1999, pp. 33ff., especially pp. 60ff.

[301] S. Leibfried and P. Pierson, 'Semisovereign Welfare States: Social Policy in a Multitiered Europe', in Leibfried and Pierson (eds.), *European Social Policy between Fragmentation and Integration*, Washington DC 1995, p. 45.

[302] Paragraph 6 of the judgment.

Except in relation to very marginal aspects and always, of course, subject to observance of the fundamental general principle of non-discrimination between national citizens (workers) and those of other Member States, Community law does not in fact impose any direct and positive constraints with respect to the content and the *quomodo* of national systems of social protection. The Community has intervened in the matter solely in order to ensure – within the framework of guaranteeing the free movement of workers – the co-ordination of national social-security schemes (Article 51, now Article 42 of the EC Treaty and Regulation 1408/71). The notion of their harmonization, much-discussed at the start and to some extent suggested by the Spaak Report itself, was essentially excluded by the Treaty of Rome and, strictly speaking, remains so today, despite the fact that Article 137(3) of the EC Treaty now offers, in theory, an independent legal basis, certainly broader than in the past, for supranational regulatory interventions including those of a binding nature.[303]

Today, in this as also in other areas of social policy, Community action is directed instead towards 'light' (but not for that reason weak) co-ordination of *diverse* national policies, in accordance with active encouragement of the 'concerted modernization'[304] of Member States' social-protection systems. Attention is systematically drawn to the complete autonomy of the choices that individual countries – although within a framework of general guiding principles – are voluntarily invited to make in this direction and to the necessary differentiation, along the diverse political and institutional contours of national welfare-state families, of paths of reform.

The problem posed by the infiltration of Community competition law is that, in the face of a framework so 'positively' mindful of respect for the Member States' prerogatives in organizing their social-protection systems, the strongest and mandatory constraints derive, in the form of purely negative integration, precisely from the spillover of supranational market law into increasingly extensive and 'sensitive' areas of social law. A spillover which takes place far away from the political process – Community and/or national – in the rarefied tranquillity of the Luxembourg chambers of the Court of Justice, and is for the most part driven by a limited and combative 'community of interests' particularly active in entering the litigation lists and very quick to exploit the space opened up by the judicial-dialogue channel provided by Article 177 (now Article 234) of the EC Treaty.

---

[303] See also subsection 6 of chapter 4 below.

[304] Commission of the European Communities, *A Concerted Strategy for Modernising Social Protection*, COM(1999) 347 final.

The apparent schizophrenia of the situation is palpable in the difference in the language used by the different Community institutional authorities involved in the two areas. Whereas in the minutes and documents of various kinds that constitute, in a very broad sense, the precipitate of the Community political process the emphasis is increasingly placed on the autonomy of the Member States, the Court of Justice in, for example, its *Albany* judgment, introducing a by no means fortuitous or non-influential change of language register compared with *Duphar*, merely notes in passing the existence of a residual 'margin of appreciation' for the Member States 'in organising their social security systems'.[305]

This change in linguistic tone, although seemingly minor and perhaps easily overlooked, actually reflects a situation very different from that still to be found in 1984 in *Duphar*.[306] What it reflects is a situation where the Member States are encountering a drastic reduction of their freedom of manoeuvre as regards the organization of their respective social-security systems, potentially even in the crucial respect of the choice (which in 1984 was still not affected, and in particular could not be affected, by Community competition law) of the financing mechanisms considered most appropriate for them.

Nowadays, the possible option of the capitalization method – more and more frequently indicated (and to some extent also practised) as an almost obligatory way of overcoming the crisis of public redistribution systems – directly determines a move into the area governed in principle by Community competition law. This is capable of producing important consequences for the structuring and institutional design of national welfare-state systems, in which the redistribution pay-as-you-go pillar, albeit in forms and to degrees that differ widely from one country to another, is more and more closely interrelated – on the functional level – with a pre-funded supplementary pillar.

A similar out-of-step situation, again in both 'words' and 'reality', is, however, discernible in other contexts as well. In the context (also at the centre of 'common' interests) of the reform of labour-market systems, reference is increasingly made to the hiatus between the extensive autonomy accorded to the Member States for the purposes of the 'modernization', also involving the subnational level, of the respective systems and, at the same time, the rigidity of the constraints nevertheless deriving from, for example, the Community rules on state aids, constraints that can preclude

---

[305] Paragraph 122 of the judgment.
[306] See D. Pieters and J. A. Nickless, *Pathways for Social Protection in Europe*, Helsinki 1998, pp. 73ff.

the use of quite a range of measures theoretically available to national (or regional) legislators.[307]

The need to reduce this hiatus, reverting in a way to *Duphar* and giving more credence to the freedom which the Treaty – including in the light of the principle of subsidiarity – accords to the Member States as regards organizing their national systems of social protection, is very often mentioned by all those who are anxious to establish a new balance between positive and negative integration at Community level. In their view, when applying the rules on competition the Court of Justice should pay more attention to the other side of the coin and take care not to disrupt the delicate and changeable balance that presides over the distribution of powers between the European Union and the Member States in the matter of social policies.[308]

The Treaty of Amsterdam contained more than an invitation in this direction, and not just through the emphasis newly placed on the principle of subsidiarity also in the field of social policies and through the greater attention to respect for the inevitable 'specificity' of national choices which – albeit within a framework inspired by shared interests and objectives – characterizes the strategy for the co-ordination of Member State employment policies in the light of Title VIII of the EC Treaty.

In the domain of competition law itself, Article 16 of the EC Treaty – as introduced by the Treaty of Amsterdam – has the actual function of signalling 'politically' to the Commission and, from there, to the Court of Justice the essential role of services of general economic interest in promoting social and territorial cohesion of the countries that make up the Union. Here too, although subject to the proviso of its being without prejudice to Articles 73, 86 and 87, the subject of respect for the Member States' 'respective powers' and hence, indirectly, for diverse national sensitivities and traditions, is restored as a focus of attention for all the institutional actors involved.

First, Article 16 helps to build up an authentic notion of Community services of general interest based on the counterbalancing values of

---

[307] See Roccella, 'Tutela del lavoro', p. 61; Vousden, '*Albany*', p. 190.

[308] In annulling Directive 98/43/EC on the prohibition of tobacco advertising as infringing the limits of the powers conferred by Article 95 of the EC Treaty, the Court of Justice (Case C-376/98, *Germany* v *European Parliament and Council*) has already demonstrated that it can take a robust line in defending certain Member State prerogatives in regard to regulation of the internal market. Cf. the comments of P. Hecker, *Revue du Droit de l'Union Européenne* 2000, no. 4, pp. 942ff., and of P. Syrpis, 'Smoke without Fire: The Social Policy Agenda and the Internal Market', *Industrial Law Journal* 2001, vol. 30 no. 3, pp. 271–88.

competition and efficiency and those of infra- and inter-State social justice.[309] Second, in expressly elevating services of general economic interest
to the status of 'common values of the Union'[310] it at the same time reinforces the importance of subsidiarity as a principle that actively defends
the specificity of the different national public-service constellations.

Similar lines of reasoning re-emerged from the Lisbon European Council that were faithfully echoed in the Commission's new Communication
on *Services of General Interest in Europe*.[311] They were subsequently reinforced by the Declaration on services of general economic interest annexed
to the Presidency Conclusions of the Nice European Council[312] and by
that adopted at Barcelona on 15/16 May 2002.[313]

The actual revision of the text of the Treaties that was approved at Nice,
and also the Charter of Fundamental Rights of the European Union,
contain new and even more significant indications in the same direction.

In its wording that has been in force since the Treaty of Nice was ratified, Article 137(4) of the EC Treaty is symptomatically clear in strongly
reaffirming the principle that the preceding provisions cannot compromise 'the right of Member States to define the fundamental principles of
their social security systems and must not significantly affect the financial
equilibrium thereof'. So strong a statement of principle – even though
expressly referred to the provisions that delineate the regulatory bases of
'positive integration' of the European welfare states – cannot but mean
that a similar limit applies, at least indirectly, on the negative-integration
side as well. It must, that is, also constrain the effects, equally if not more
damaging to the sphere of competence reserved to the Member States in

---

[309] In this sense see M. Ross, 'Article 16 E. C. and Services of General Interest: From Derogation to Obligation?', *European Law Review* 2000, pp. 22ff., who stresses that in so doing
Article 16 ventures beyond the logic of the single market and embraces the richer logic
of European citizenship. G. Napolitano, 'Il servizio universale e i diritti dei cittadini
utenti', *Mercato Concorrenza Regole* 2000, no. 2, pp. 429ff., also links Article 16 to the
construction of Community citizenship. See, additionally, C. Scott, 'Services of General
Interest in E. C. Law: Matching Values to Regulatory Technique in the Public and Privatised
Sectors', *European Law Journal* 2000, pp. 310ff.; A. Héritier, 'Market Integration and Social
Cohesion: The Politics of Public Services in European Regulation', *Journal of European
Public Policy* 2001, pp. 825ff.

[310] Pernice, 'Multilevel', p. 735.

[311] COM(2000) 580 final; see also, more recently, the Green and White Papers on Services of
General Interest COM(2003) 270 final and COM(2004) 374 final.

[312] Cf. F. Chaltiel, 'La déclaration de Nice sur les services d'intérêt économique général', *Revue
du Marché Commun et de l'Union Européenne* 2001, pp. 89ff.

[313] Cf. S. Rodrigues, 'Réforme des entreprises de réseau et services publics de qualité:
le mandat de Barcelone', *Revue du Marché Commun et de l'Union Européenne* 2002,
pp. 291ff.

this area, that result from the progressive expansion of the freedom of movement of goods and services and from Community principles of free competition themselves.

In the case of the Charter, the point of relevance here is not only (and not so much) its Article 36, which – significantly included in its Chapter IV entitled 'Solidarity' – reaffirms the value of services of general economic interest in order to promote the social and territorial cohesion of the Union, in that it commits the latter to recognize and respect access to such services as provided for in national laws and practices, albeit in accordance with the provisions of the EC Treaty. The main point to be mentioned is Article 34(1) of the Charter, which establishes that the Union recognizes and respects entitlement to social-security benefits and social services in accordance with the *procedures* established by Community law and national laws and practices.[314]

In the crucial area of social security and protection this provision not only confirms the primary competence of the Member States but seems expressly to link the influence of Community action to the specific delineation of positive intervention *procedures*, irreducible as such to the logic of purely negative integration.

From this aspect too, therefore, the Nice Charter seems capable of restoring the prospect of full citizenship, at the level of the Community legal order itself, to the fundamental social values rooted in the Member States' systems of labour and social-security law, helping 'in circular fashion' to strengthen them at domestic level. Its formal incorporation into the constitutional Treaty would lay solid foundations for a more balanced pluralist comparison between values that necessarily have to be adapted to each other, without claims to hegemony or forms of 'tyranny' on one or the other side.

Competition – as 'a value instrumental to the affirmation of other fundamental values'[315] such as the encouragement of innovation and responsibility in the exercise of economic freedom – will continue to occupy a central place in the construction of the Community. It must, however, always be carefully matched with the values of solidarity and equal liberty of the *homme situé*,[316] which form the common substrate of fundamental

---

[314] Similar principles are confirmed by paragraph 3 of the same Article as regards measures to combat social exclusion and poverty and, in largely similar terms, by the following Article 35 with regard to health protection.

[315] Musu, 'Il valore della concorrenza', p. 26.

[316] To repeat the felicitous expression used by G. Burdeau, 'La démocratie gouvernante, son assise sociale et sa philosophie politique', in *Traité de sciences politique*, Paris 1973,

social rights. The formula of 'a highly competitive social market economy' innovatively used by the constitutional Treaty in defining the fundamental objectives of the Union (Article I-3(3)) now forcefully pinpoints this crucial need for a balancing of values.

The entire slant of the constitutional Treaty that was signed in Rome is marked by the conjunction of these regulatory principles. In addition to the above-mentioned 'summarizing' formula set out under Article I-3 and, before it, the detailed enumeration of the Union's foundational values as now contained in Article I-2 consistently with the incorporation of the Nice Charter into Part II of the Treaty, mention must be made in this connection of the horizontal clauses introduced at the start of its Part III.

The innovative provision laid down under Article III-117 is certainly of considerable interest, in committing the Union to take into account, in all policies and actions brought into being by virtue of Part III of the constitutional Treaty, requirements linked to, *inter alia*, an adequate level of social protection, the fight against exclusion, a high level of education and training and health protection. This rule – read together with the other mainstreaming social clauses at the start of Part III of the constitutional Treaty, particularly the following Article III-118 – is capable of giving fresh impetus to the requirements of a 'virtuous' conjunction between solidarity and competition in the spirit of what is confirmed by Article III-122 based on the 'old' text of Article 16 of the EC Treaty.

From the point of view of a correct balance between equally important constitutional values labour law can better demonstrate its special innermost function by presenting itself not simply as 'a system for protecting workers from the market but also, in its own right, as an instrument that can contribute to the efficiency of undertakings'.[317]

The 'reformist'[318] spirit of labour law manifests itself precisely in the capacity to balance – in contexts that today are profoundly different from those that marked the historical beginnings – 'the opposing interests and values of labour and business' and to 'promote both of them in a perspective of sustainable economic development'.[319]

vol. VII, pp. 39ff. As regards the concept of 'equal liberty', it is also obviously essential to refer to J. Rawls, *A Theory of Justice*, Cambridge, Mass. 1971, especially chapter 4.

[317] P. Davies, 'Lavoro subordinato e lavoro autonomo', *Diritto delle Relazioni Industriali* 2000, pp. 207ff., here p. 208.

[318] S. Sciarra, 'Market Freedom and Fundamental Social Rights', *EUI (European University Institute) Working Papers in Law* No. 02/3, p. 1.

[319] T. Treu, 'Diritto del lavoro: realtà e possibilità', *Argomenti di Diritto del Lavoro* 2000, no. 3, pp. 467ff., here p. 522.

4

Forms of regulation of social Europe and models of the European economic constitution

1. Introduction

The purpose of this final chapter is twofold.

Its first aim is to 'systematize', and at any rate analyse organically, a theme that has in a way been a strand running through the entire book: the far-reaching evolution (or considerable transformation) which has taken place, from the entry into force of the founding Treaties to the present day, in the forms of positive integration of national social systems.

The centrality of this theme within the more general discourse on the metamorphoses of the Community economic constitution, and on the different role gradually assumed in such a context by the forms in which European 'social policy' has been conceived and given practical implementation, is quite obvious. The transition from forms of social policy centred on the model of 'hard' upward harmonization to increasingly light and flexible methods of regulatory intervention somewhat removed from the traditional protective logic, and even more so the use of instruments of co-ordination of the 'post-regulatory' type, constitute essential elements of these metamorphoses and therefore need to be focused more carefully.

The second aim of the chapter consists in correlating these changes with the ideal economic-constitution models that they entail. An analytical comparison of the various ideal models of a European economic constitution as viewed in the abstract will serve to highlight the (differing) problems of effectiveness and legitimacy (inevitably) inherent in any given form of supranational intervention in social matters. It will consequently attempt to offer summary and abstract criteria for a normative evaluation of the significance and implications of the actual transformations undergone by the Community economic constitution, which have so far been analysed on a mainly dynamic and diachronic level.

2. Rise and decline of the 'upward' harmonization model

In the Treaty of Rome harmonization was conceived as the typical remedy for distortions of competition potentially arising from differences in national regulatory regimes: it was 'the key to the creation and development of the European common market'.[1]

Mention has already been made on several occasions of the subtle contradiction underlying the model originally adopted by the Treaty of Rome with respect to social harmonization.[2]

On the one hand, the preventive harmonization of national social systems was in principle regarded as irrelevant, if not counterproductive, from an economic point of view. In accordance with the philosophy of the Spaak Report harmonization 'while the improvement is being maintained', i.e. upward harmonization, of these systems was not the condition (and premiss) but at most the natural consequence of the construction of the common market. Convergence towards higher social standards was seen as axiomatically resulting from the progressive levelling-up of productivity that would be spontaneously induced by the creation of the common market.

Profession of this 'ethic of (economic and social) thriving'[3] through the common market was fed by views on the theory of comparative advantage and convergence that were the foundations of the doctrine of international trade (of that era) and was at the same time an expression of the wish to safeguard national 'social sovereignty' as far as possible from the inevitable restrictions resulting from adherence to a pervasive plan of normative harmonization. Only in exceptional cases of *specific* distortion of the conditions of competition would it be 'productive' to have recourse to the typical remedy of upward harmonization of the standards of social protection causing disruption of the competitive process: otherwise, given that a country in a situation of competitive disadvantage could correct its exchange rate accordingly, the proper functioning of the common market would ensure a spontaneous 'race to the top'.[4]

---

[1] M. Egan, *Constructing a European Market*, Oxford 2001, p. 62.

[2] See above, in particular, subsection 7 of chapter 1 and subsections 4 and 5 of chapter 2.

[3] As it is dubbed by A. Cantaro, 'Lavoro e diritti sociali nella "costituzione europea"', *Democrazia e Diritto* 1999, no. 4, special issue entitled *Lavoro: declino o metamorfosi?* edited by P. Barcellona, pp. 97ff., here p. 103.

[4] See S. Deakin, 'Integration Through Law? The Law and Economics of European Social Policy', in J. T. Addison and W. S. Siebert (eds.), *Labour Markets in Europe: Issues of Harmonization and Regulation*, London 1997, pp. 117ff., especially p. 121.

On the other hand, in cases where (total or partial) harmonization proved necessary or useful, the intervention model was conceived in the ambitious terms of a rigorous functional levelling up to the most protective standard among those available.[5] The idea was that Community intervention would complement developments in national social policy and labour law,[6] strengthening and extending them to the supranational context.

The implicit labour-law model that was to inspire Community social policy during the period of its 'maximum expansion',[7] between 1974 and 1980, was a rigidly protective one based on mandatory rules of labour protection.[8] Although this was certainly a very ambitious objective, 'confidence in the possibility of achieving such a Community harmonization of labour law was nurtured by the fact that during those years in many national legal orders of continental Europe labour law had reached the peak of its expansion and its mandatory effectiveness, and by the widespread conviction, not just among lawyers, that the fundamental protection it provided could prevail above and beyond national borders and specific characteristics'.[9]

However, it was not long before this ambition, and the confidence supporting it, began to develop cracks and become weakened. A decisive influence in this was exerted by the sudden changes in the socio-economic scenario, which also gave rise to the three important Directives of the second half of the 1970s on the restructuring and insolvency of enterprises. But a part was also played – in so far as what most interests us here – by the contradictions intrinsic to the model of rigid upward social harmonization.

The latter suffered, in fact, from a congenital incongruity between its presuppositions, means and ends. The normative base of Community social policy – rigidly anchored to the economic rationale assumed by ex Article 100 of the EEC Treaty[10] – was weak: it was to be activated with (relative) success only during times of widespread political consensus, and was subsequently relegated to frustrating inoperability in the face

---

[5] Cf. J. Holloway, *Social Policy Harmonisation in the European Community*, Farnborough 1981, pp. 17 and 49.

[6] Cf. E. Szyszczak, 'The New Paradigm for Social Policy: A Virtuous Circle?', *Common Market Law Review* 2001, vol. 38, pp. 1125–70, especially p. 1126.

[7] G. and A. Lyon-Caen, *Droit social international et européen*, 8th edn, Paris 1993, p. 181.

[8] See T. Treu, *Politiche del lavoro. Insegnamenti di un decennio*, Bologna 2001, p. 81.

[9] *Ibid.*, p. 79.   [10] See, for example, Holloway, *Social Policy*, p. 18.

of the veto systematically wielded against it by the British Conservative Government from the start of the 1980s onwards.[11]

But there were even earlier warning signs of the model's basic ambiguity: the symptoms of its decline began to show themselves during the very years of its greatest ascendancy. It is particularly significant in this connection that as early as 1977, at a stage which was witnessing the relatively painless implementation of the first Social Action Programme of 1974, Michael Shanks, former Director-General for Social Affairs in the European Commission, drew attention to all the 'weakness of the legal base provided by the Treaty of Rome'.[12] In the face of growing unemployment and inflation, 'the more one looks at the complexity of social systems in the EEC', wrote Shanks, 'the clearer it becomes that the overall harmonisation or equalisation of social systems is simply not a feasible objective'.[13] So the proper task of the Community in this field, he urged, was not to level-up national social systems but 'to establish *minimum standards*, below which nobody should be allowed to fall, but on the basis of which those [Member States] who can afford to do so should build their own more ambitious systems.'[14] Careful note should be taken of what was already effected by the 'functionalist' Directives of the 1970s,[15] providing for forms of only partial harmonization of national systems centred on the adoption of minimum standards of protection that could be departed from *in melius* by the Member States.[16]

3. The regulatory impasse of the 1980s and its remedies

The crisis of the harmonization model is actually a general one extending beyond the social field itself, in which its influence in overall terms had in

---

[11] Cf. J. Kenner, *EU Employment Law. From Rome to Amsterdam and Beyond*, Oxford-Portland 2002, pp. 186ff.

[12] M. Shanks, 'Introductory Article: The Social Policy of the European Communities', *Common Market Law Review* 1977, vol. 14, pp. 375–83.

[13] *Ibid.*, p. 376.

[14] *Ibid.*, p. 380 (the emphasis is in the original); and see earlier the Guidelines for the Social Action Programme published in 1973, on which J. H. Petersen, 'Harmonization of Social Security in the EC Revisited', *Journal of Common Market Studies* 1991, pp. 505ff., especially p. 508.

[15] As is well known, the description – quoted on several occasions – is that of M. D'Antona, 'Sistema giuridico comunitario', in A. Baylos Grau *et al.* (eds.), *Dizionario di Diritto del Lavoro Comunitario*, Bologna 1996, pp. 3ff., especially p. 22. A somewhat different discourse applies in the case of the Directives (on equal treatment for men and women and health and safety at work) which are referred to what D'Antona calls 'cohesive' harmonization. See also Treu, *Politiche del lavoro*, p. 81.

[16] Cf. Deakin, 'Integration', p. 138.

any case been marginal, albeit significant. The 'normative imbalance'[17] of harmonization in social matters merely mirrors the more general 'perfectionist'[18] and 'dirigiste'[19] style of the first method of achieving the common market. It is the same lack of balance as that which afflicts an approach generally directed towards the rigid and detailed definition of the Member States' obligations, overly complicated in the increasingly difficult search for unanimous agreement and inefficient because it is inevitably left wanting by accelerated changes in the reality being regulated, in accordance with the well-known diagnosis of 'regulatory mismatch'.[20]

At the end of the transitional period the common market was still, in actuality, nationally fragmented by 'a multitude of non-tariff barriers'[21] which a return to the protectionist practices aimed at coping with the crisis initiated in the mid-1970s would have increased farther, in both quantity and quality.

In terms of the techniques for constructing the common market the turnabout is due to the jurisprudence of the Court of Justice and the promptness displayed by the Commission in seizing on the window of opportunity opened up by the *Cassis de Dijon* doctrine.

The new approach that was codified, in the wake of this jurisprudence, by the White Paper of 1985 on *Completing the Internal Market* and then (partially) endorsed by the Single European Act overturned the previous one. It was aimed at accelerating the Community's regulatory capacity for the purposes of creating the internal market on the basis of two cardinal principles: '(1) where possible, there was to be mutual recognition of regulations and standards, as well as the means of conformity with them; and (2) where necessary, the harmonization of technical regulations would be undertaken by reference to European standards.'[22] Directives, which could

---

[17] T. Treu, 'Le politiche sociali europee'. Paper presented at the AISRI (Associazione Italiana di Studio delle Relazioni Industriali) Conference on *Regolazione e Riregolazione del mercato del lavoro: il ruolo delle parti sociali*, Milan, 1 February 2002, p. 1 (of the typescript).

[18] C.-D. Ehlermann, 'Compétition entre systèmes réglementaires', *Revue du Marché Commun et de l'Union Européenne* 1995, pp. 220ff., here p. 225, who describes the original approach to harmonization as 'a combination of the German tendency towards perfectionism and the French one towards centralism'. In the same vein, with specific regard to the 'old approach' in social and labour matters, G. A. Bermann, 'Regulatory Federalism: A Reprise and Introduction', *Columbia Journal of European Law* 1996, pp. 395ff., especially pp. 399–400.

[19] A. McGee and S. Weatherill, 'The Evolution of the Single Market – Harmonisation or Liberalisation', *Modern Law Review* 1990, vol. 53, pp. 578ff., especially p. 582.

[20] S. Breyer, 'Analysing Regulatory Failure: Mismatches, Less Restrictive Alternatives, and Reform', *Harvard Law Review* 1979, vol. 92, pp. 549ff.

[21] Egan, *Constructing*, p. 41.   [22] *Ibid.*, p. 122.

be adopted on a qualified-majority basis as envisaged by ex Article 100a, were henceforth to be confined to fixing essential safety requirements, leaving the detailed specification of their content to standardization bodies.[23]

In this way, 'the focus of harmonisation of laws in the Community has shifted from positive integration to negative integration'.[24] Harmonization now serves essentially to reduce the opportunities for (legitimate) recourse on the part of the Member States to exceptions based on imperative reasons in the public interest, thereby becoming an instrument for 'removing market barriers, rather than formulating common policies'.[25]

In the complex combination of liberalization measures, mutual recognition and standardization, there is a clear tendency for the strong thrust towards negative integration, more openly linked to the neoliberal and profoundly 'market-oriented' inspiration of the system embedded in the Single European Act, to prevail.

On the social-policy front, the framework is appreciably different, and definitely more problematic.

As early as in its 1985 White Paper on *Completing the Internal Market*, the Commission had indicated clearly that the horizon of social policy was to be essentially limited to the objectives most strictly functional to market integration and to boosting freedom of movement and therefore, in essence, to the promotion of common standards in the field of health and safety at work. More extensive use of the base provided by Article 100, of the type made in the past, now seemed to the Commission to be inappropriate.[26]

Abandonment of the old policy – or perhaps more accurately the old category – of social harmonization was, however, to become even more evident after the adoption of the Single European Act. This is because the Act institutionalized the asymmetry of social policy with respect to the sphere of Community regulation functional to the freeing-up of the internal market, in stating expressly that the new rule on qualified-majority voting was not to apply in the case of Directives 'relating to the free

---

[23] Cf. B. Kurcz, 'Harmonisation by Means of Directives – Never-Ending Story?', *European Business Law Review* 2001, pp. 287ff.

[24] W. Sauter and E. Vos, 'Harmonisation under Community Law: The Comitology Issue', in P. Craig and C. Harlow (eds.), *Lawmaking in the European Union*, London-The Hague-Boston 1998, pp. 169ff., here p. 186.

[25] *Ibid.*, p. 172.

[26] See Commission of the European Communities White Paper, *Completing the Internal Market*, COM(85) 310 final, paragraph 65.

movement of persons nor to those relating to the rights and interests of employed persons' (ex Article 100a(2)).

The only chance of breaking away from the total 'intergovernmental immobilism'[27] into which social policy had plunged from the beginning of the 1980s owing (mainly but not solely) to British obstructionism[28] was offered by ex Article 118a, which allowed qualified-majority voting for Directives relating to health and safety and the work environment.[29] Here, abandonment of the old approach took place *in primis* in the form of a re-appraisal of social-harmonization ambitions from the 'flexibliza-tion' perspective that pervaded the programme incorporated by the Single European Act. Article 118a abandoned the concept of 'upward harmo-nization'[30] – with its burden of expectations for a 'levelling-up to the best of the national laws, with which the other countries were to bring themselves into line'[31] – and introduced instead the idea of minimum requirements to be implemented gradually while, however, taking care not to compromise the competitiveness of European undertakings, par-ticularly small and medium-sized ones.

Even though 'minimal' harmonization is not necessarily 'minimalist',[32] it is nevertheless definitely dissociated from the notion of an attempt to level-up to the protective outcomes of the most advanced social system. Practical experience of its application was to show that an approach cen-tred on the idea of minimum standards to be implemented gradually (while avoiding any threat to the competitiveness of, in particular, small and medium-sized undertakings) entails a tendency towards 'a reduc-tionist interpretation of social standards rather than upward harmoniza-tion'.[33]

In providing social policy with an (albeit limited) autonomous legal base, freed as such from a strict economic rationale, Article 118a allowed

---

[27] P. Teague, *Economic Citizenship in the European Union*, London 1999, p. 142.

[28] Cf. S. Fredman, 'Social Law in the European Union: The Impact of the Lawmaking Process', in Craig and Harlow, *Lawmaking*, pp. 386ff., especially p. 390.

[29] These are, however, matters that G. Majone (for example, 'From the Positive to the Regu-latory State: Causes and Consequences of Changes in the Mode of Governance', *Journal of Public Policy* 1997, pp. 139ff.) attributes, significantly, to the sphere that he describes as social *regulation*, not social *policy*.

[30] See T. Treu, 'L'Europa sociale: problemi e prospettive', *Diritto delle Relazioni Industriali* 2001, pp. 307ff., especially 311.

[31] G. and A. Lyon-Caen, *Droit social*, pp. 167–8.

[32] That is to say, it does not necessarily coincide with the 'lowest common denominator', as made clear by the Court of Justice in Case C-84/94, *UK v Council* [1996] ECR I-5755, especially at paragraphs 17 and 56 of the judgment; see also Kurcz, 'Harmonisation', p. 297.

[33] Kenner, *EU Employment Law*, p. 238.

the resumption of a (steady) production of Community normative standards in the field of health and safety and the work environment.[34] Particularly after the proclamation of the 1989 Community Charter of Fundamental Social Rights of Workers (and the associated implementation programme), the base offered by this provision was to be used fairly lavishly by the Commission in a 'treaty base game'[35] that was to see it constantly invoked against the United Kingdom.

It was only later that the tensions created by the narrowness of the basis for action under Article 118a were to be resolved – once the subsequent phase of uncertainty and fragmentation opened up by the Maastricht Treaty was ended – with the definitive incorporation of the Agreement on Social Policy by the Treaty of Amsterdam.

However, the fact of acquiring in the founding Treaty the new 'quasi-general' legal base provided by the Agreement on Social Policy – with the accompanying significant extension of qualified-majority voting (and co-decision procedures) – did not mark the go-ahead for a new stage of 'hard' harmonization.

'The somewhat ironic conclusion must therefore be that, precisely at the moment in time when the mechanisms have finally been put in place to allow a significant body of social legislation to be adopted at Community level, events have conspired to ensure that soft law is not only the most likely but also the most promising way forward for EC social policy'.[36] The Treaty of Amsterdam can thus be read as having institutionalized total abandonment of the original harmonization model and given express recognition to alternative methods of positive integration in social matters.[37]

4. Alternatives to the traditional harmonization model

As mentioned earlier, the emergence of forms of regulation wholly or partly alternative to the old harmonization model is a phenomenon which from the mid-1980s onwards has profoundly informed the entire theoretical and institutional arsenal of Community integration.

---

[34] The fundamental instance was the adoption of the Framework Directive on Health and Safety 89/391: see, by way of example, G. Arrigo, *Il diritto del lavoro dell'Unione europea*, Milan 2001, vol. II, pp. 160ff.

[35] Deakin, 'Integration', p. 123.

[36] E. A. Whiteford, 'W(h)ither Social Policy?', in J. Shaw and G. More (eds.), *New Legal Dynamics of European Union*, Oxford 1995, pp. 111ff., here p. 128.

[37] Cf. Fredman, 'Social Law', p. 395.

The new approach endorsed by the 1985 White Paper, and then by the Single European Act, aims to provide answers to the 'regulatory deficit'[38] caused by the harmonization crisis, emphasizing the role of mutual recognition between systems for the purposes of implementing the internal market, together with increasing recourse to the closely woven 'web of committees' (so-called 'comitology')[39] and the complex network of semi-independent regulatory bodies that make up the organizational fabric of standardization processes.[40] The development of a network of Community agencies,[41] although still far from the stage seen as appropriate by supporters of the European Union as a 'regulatory state',[42] also forms part of this process of reform of the institutional mechanisms of governance of the internal market.[43]

An equally profound change of paradigm in the regulatory techniques used is informing Community social policy. From this aspect too, consensus is being progressively built 'around . . . new techniques of multi-level governance employing horizontal, consensual, co-ordinating subsidiarity'.[44] The development of this polycentric and light approach to Community social policy was consolidated at Amsterdam, once the phase of 'intergovernmental block' and British opting-out was ended.

The main characterizing features of the 'new paradigm'[45] for European social policy have already been described:[46] what we shall do here is to specify its essential aspects from the point of view of an analysis of regulatory techniques and forms of governance. Abandonment of the model (or perhaps merely 'myth')[47] of upward harmonization goes hand in hand first and foremost with a profound change in the basic objectives of Community action in the social field, with a gradual shift

---

[38] R. Dehousse, 'Regolazione attraverso reti nella Comunità Europea: il ruolo delle agenzie europee', *Rivista Italiana di Diritto Pubblico Comunitario* 1997, pp. 629ff., here p. 637.

[39] See C. Joerges and E. Vos (eds.), *EU Committees: Social Regulation, Law and Politics*, Oxford-Portland 1999, and especially the introductory essay by C. Joerges, 'Bureaucratic Nightmare, Technocratic Regime and the Dream of Good Transnational Governance', pp. 33ff.

[40] Cf. Egan, *Constructing*, pp. 133ff.   [41] Cf. Dehousse, 'Regolazione', pp. 641ff.

[42] See Majone, 'From the Positive to the Regulatory State', pp. 152ff.; A. La Spina and G. Majone, *Lo Stato regolatore*, Bologna 2000, pp. 254ff.

[43] See also K. Armstrong and S. Bulmer, *The Governance of the Single European Market*, Manchester-New York 1998.

[44] Szyszczak, 'New Paradigm', p. 1167.   [45] *Ibid.*, p. 1125.

[46] See subsections 4, 5, 7 and 8 of chapter 2 above.

[47] M. Laroque, 'Coordination et convergence des systèmes de Sécurité sociale des États membres de la CE', *Droit Social* 1993, pp. 792ff., here p. 795.

of its axis from *social* policy to *employment* policy.[48] The starting-point of this 'quiet revolution'[49] is usually seen as lying in the publication of the 1993 White Paper on *Growth, Competitiveness, Employment*, with the subsequent identification in 1994 of the 'Essen priorities'.[50] The 'constitutionalization'[51] of the European Employment Strategy by the Treaty of Amsterdam was to consolidate and reinforce this profound change of course by establishing the premiss for a subsequent refinement of the open method of co-ordination as an emergent form of Community social governance.

Two other qualifying elements of the new paradigm are also correlated with this shift in the focus of Community action towards employment policy: the growing use of soft law[52] and the tendency towards a transition from substantive to procedural social law.[53] What we are actually looking at here are two sides of the same coin: together, they make up the framework of what has earlier been called the transition from the model of 'constructivist' harmonization to that of 'reflexive' harmonization. Here, the adjective is the centre of gravity of the definition, since harmonization means something entirely different in each of the two cases: in the former, it evokes the idea of achieving functional (if not also structural) uniformity for the purposes of regulating (*rectius*: correcting) the competitive process in the common market, while in the latter it is conceived more as a process of differentiation, albeit in the context of common general

---

[48]   See D. Ashiagbor, 'Soft Harmonisation: Labour Law, Economic Theory and the European Employment Strategy', European University Institute PhD Thesis, Florence 2002, pp. 85 and 107ff.; and, earlier, M. Freedland, 'Employment Policy', in P. Davies *et al.* (eds.), *European Community Labour Law: Principles and Perspectives. Liber Amicorum Lord Wedderburn*, Oxford 1996, pp. 275–309.

[49]   E. Szyszczak, 'The Evolving European Employment Strategy', in J. Shaw (ed.), *Social Law and Policy in an Evolving European Union*, Oxford-Portland 2000, p. 197.

[50]   See S. Sciarra, 'Integration through Coordination: The Employment Title in the Amsterdam Treaty', *Columbia Journal of European Law* 2000, pp. 209ff., especially p. 212.

[51]   C. Barnard, 'The United Kingdom, the "Social Chapter" and the Amsterdam Treaty', *Industrial Law Journal* 1997, vol. 26, pp. 275ff., here p. 281.

[52]   See, by way of example, Teague, *Economic Citizenship*, pp. 152.

[53]   Cf. M. Weiss, 'The Future Role of the European Union in Social Policy', in C. Engels and M. Weiss (eds.), *Labour Law and Industrial Relations at the Turn of the Century. Liber Amicorum in Honour of Roger Blanpain*, The Hague-London-Boston 1998, pp. 489–506, especially p. 505; U. Mückenberger, 'Un'Europa senza regolazione sociale? Il dialogo sociale e l'importanza crescente della sfera procedurale', in H. Friese, A. Negri and P. Wagner (eds.), *Europa politica. Ragioni di una necessità*, Rome 2002, pp. 209ff., especially pp. 220 and 238.

principles, without any aspiration to impose itself as an instrument of *direct* regulation of competition between national systems.[54]

Despite its problematic implications, a return to theories of reflexive law,[55] now frequent both in the case of 'pre-legislative' collective bargaining on the basis of Articles 138 and 139 of the EC Treaty and in that of the open co-ordination of employment policies, thus seems fully justified. Primary Community law and European hard law in general are tending to confine themselves to providing the 'institutional ribs of social self-regulation processes'[56] or institutionalizing procedures designed to promote voluntary mutual-learning processes centred on the non-coercive spread of national 'best practices' through benchmarking. This should hinder pure and simple (de)regulatory competition, which is undoubtedly encouraged by any deficit of positive integration at supranational level, and at the same time leave the Member States ample space for differentiation and hence also for maintaining (or trying out) autonomous national or subnational paths.[57]

5. Collective bargaining as a 'regulatory resource' of the Community legal order

European collective bargaining is, in point of fact, conceived and designed by the Agreement on Social Policy (and hence by the present Articles 138 and 139 of the EC Treaty) as a regulatory technique alternative to the old approach to harmonization, as a 'resource of the Community legal order' capable of overcoming the 'regulatory deficit' (or, more accurately, the

---

[54] See W. Streeck, 'Competitività e sistemi nazionali. L'internazionalizzazione delle relazioni industriali', *Quaderni Rassegna Sindacale* 2000, no. 2, pp. 19ff., especially p. 29.

[55] Cf. G. Teubner, 'Substantive and Reflexive Elements in Modern Law', *Law and Society Review* 1983, vol. 17 no. 2, pp. 239–85; and, more recently, Teubner, *Diritto policontesturale: prospettive giuiridiche della pluralizzazione dei mondi sociali*, Italian version edited by A. Rufino, Naples 1999. Teubner, 'Substantive' as cited here, p. 242, defines reflexive law as 'a system for the coordination of action within and between semi-autonomous social subsystems'. It 'means to create the structural premises for a decentralized integration of society by supporting integrative mechanisms within autonomous social subsystems' (*ibid.*, p. 255) and is characterized by a predominantly procedural rationality (and legitimation) (*ibid.*, pp. 274–5).

[56] L. Mengoni, 'La questione del "diritto giusto" nella società postliberale', *Relazioni Industriali* 1988, no. 1, pp. 13ff., here p. 25.

[57] Cf. S Deakin, 'Two Types of Regulatory Competition: Competitive Federalism versus Reflexive Harmonisation. A Law and Economics Perspective on *Centros*', *Cambridge Yearbook of European Legal Studies* 1999, vol. 2, pp. 231–60, especially pp. 232 and 245–6.

semi-paralysis) arising from the crisis of the traditional model in social matters.[58]

Freed (again in the Treaty of Amsterdam) from any constitutional tie to recognition of the fundamental rights to organize collectively and to strike, it therefore takes on a '"purpose-serving" dimension . . . with respect to the functionality of the Community law-making system',[59] undergoing a 'kind of functional metamorphosis'[60] as compared with the idea of collective autonomy cultivated in national systems.[61] As an alternative form of law-making, it takes on the qualities of a para-legislative regulatory phenomenon fundamentally different from the traditional notion of a collective agreement,[62] which has always been an object of concern for labour lawyers. Even though it does not give rise to socially typical negotiating processes, given the absence of the material presuppositions for such a development, Community collective bargaining does have the merit of reactivating a process for the production of 'negotiated' social legislation that is entirely homogeneous with the new paradigm of 'reflexive' harmonization.

The Directives whereby the Council has absorbed the content of the framework agreements concluded to date by the European social partners on the basis of Articles 138 and 139 of the EC Treaty constitute perhaps the fullest and most emblematic expression of the new path.[63] The agreements in question, because of their cross-sectoral horizontal effect, tend to assume a content of a general nature that lies halfway between the guidelines or common recommendations of the past and mandatory legal rules: precisely the sort of soft regulation suitable for incorporation in second-generation flexible Directives that the European authorities and national governments were relying on more and more in order to surmount the obstacles to normative harmonization.[64] Consequently, the Directives that incorporate them are close in content – if not

---

[58] In this sense, A. Lo Faro, *Regulating Social Europe. Reality and Myth of Collective Bargaining in the EC Legal Order*, English translation, Oxford 2000, especially pp. 132ff.

[59] *Ibid.*, p. 132; in the same sense, see Teague, *Economic Citizenship*, pp. 158–9.

[60] A. Lo Faro, 'Europei, comunitari e comunitarizzati: i contratti collettivi nell'era della sovranazionalità', *Rivista Giuridica del Lavoro e della Previdenza Sociale* 2000, pp. 860ff., here p. 881.

[61] See also Mückenberger 'Un'Europa', pp. 220 and 228.

[62] In this sense see also Kenner, *EU Employment Law*, pp. 263 and 292.

[63] They represent the quintessence of what I. Pernice, 'The Framework Revisited: Constitutional, Federal and Subsidiarity Issues', *Columbia Journal of European Law* 1996, pp. 403ff., especially p. 416, calls harmonization based on partnership, of an essentially voluntary and non-coercive nature.

[64] Treu, 'L'Europa sociale', p. 315.

in form, which is obviously still binding – to the procedural slant typical of soft law.[65] Furthermore, this flexible and light approach[66] characterizes the whole of the new generation of social Directives, and not just those that are the direct fruit of European social dialogue and collective bargaining.[67]

6. Convergence of national systems of social protection via soft law

It is not by chance that the express and definitive abandonment of any ambition for normative harmonization has taken place in the field in which the results of the old approach had been the most meagre (where not wholly non-existent): the field of social-security and social-protection systems. Nor is it by chance that this is the scene of the first attempts at convergence on basic objectives by means of soft law.[68]

The illusory nature of any effort to impose the normative harmonization of national systems of social protection, given the enormous economic, political and cultural differences that separate them, is given express acknowledgement in what may be regarded as the last large-scale project for bringing Community social policy into being through recourse to the traditional instrument of legislation. The Action Programme for implementing the 1989 Community Charter of Fundamental Social Rights of Workers does not envisage measures of this kind for social security. Instead, Council Recommendations 92/441/EEC and 92/442/EEC inaugurate the new stage of soft-law convergence on general objectives, agreed by the Member States in accordance with the principle of subsidiarity.[69]

---

[65] Cf. Treu, *Politiche*, pp. 90 and 94.

[66] P. Teague, 'Deliberative Governance and EU Social Policy', *European Journal of Industrial Relations* 2001, pp. 7ff., especially p. 13, talks of 'light touch decentralised labour law'.

[67] I am thinking here of the more recent Directive 2001/86 supplementing the Statute for a European company with regard to the involvement of employees and Directive 2002/14 establishing a general framework for informing and consulting employees in undertakings within the European Community. These incorporate the indications given by the Davignon Report and adopt the principle that 'the EU should set out a menu of different employee involvement schemes, so that the member-states can devise an arrangement that best suits their own circumstances' (Teague, *Economic Citizenship*, p. 195).

[68] See S. Giubboni, 'Cittadinanza comunitaria e sicurezza sociale: un profilo critico', *Argomenti di Diritto del Lavoro* 1997, no. 6, pp. 67ff.

[69] Cf. M. Dispersyn, 'La stratégie européenne de convergence des objectifs et politiques de protection sociale (recommandation du Conseil du 27 juillet 1992)', *Revue Belge de Sécurité Sociale* 1994, pp. 1195ff. It seems significant that the final decision to eschew

The convergence strategy is based on a flexible approach characterized by the combined use of soft-law instruments and the exchange of information and social know-how between the Member States: its aim is to trigger processes of voluntary convergence towards shared objectives (*in primis* the fight against social exclusion and the introduction of common criteria concerning sufficient resources and social assistance), leaving the individual countries entire freedom and responsibility as to organization, detailed operational arrangements and, in particular, the forms of financing used.

To some extent, the decisive change of direction towards light convergence in the two 1992 Recommendations paved the way for the similar option made shortly afterwards with more general reference to social policy by the Medium-Term Social Action Programme 1995–7 launched by the Commission in the wake of the Green and White Papers of 1993–4:[70] here again, the proposals for binding legislative measures are toned down, ceding increasingly greater space to *employment* policy.[71] But above all, the strategy of convergence of social objectives served as a prelude to the techniques for promoting, via soft law, mutual learning and exchange of best practices between Member States that were to be one of the fundamental features first of the European Employment Strategy and then, after Lisbon – and on a more general scale – of the open method of co-ordination.[72]

7. The European Employment Strategy: from the 'Luxembourg process' to institutionalization of the open method of co-ordination

The search for a political and institutional alternative to the harmonization method reached a turning-point with the translation into positive

the harmonization route in social-security matters should take place exactly when the Agreement on Social Policy was providing the Community (albeit one 'of eleven') with an explicit legal base in this direction; see S. Piccininno, 'La natura dei fondi pensione alla luce degli orientamenti della Corte di Giustizia europea', *Argomenti di Diritto del Lavoro* 2000, no. 2, pp. 277ff., especially p. 279.

[70] See COM(95) 134 final.

[71] Cf. Whiteford, 'W(h)ither Social Policy?', p. 127.

[72] C. De la Porte, P. Pochet and G. Room, 'Social Benchmarking, Policy Making and New Governance in the EU', *Journal of European Social Policy* 2001, pp. 291ff., especially p. 296, talk in this connection of a 'premature version of OMC'. And see, in similar terms, M. Ferrera, M. Matsaganis and S. Sacchi, 'Open Coordination Against Poverty: the New EU Social Inclusion Process', *Journal of European Social Policy* 2002, pp. 227ff., who talk of the 'open method of coordination in embryonic form'.

terms of the European Employment Strategy and the open co-ordination of national employment policies.

It has been mentioned several times that the Treaty of Amsterdam defines, in regard to employment policy, an innovative form of co-ordination competence[73] borrowed from (but not coinciding with) the model already tried and tested from the point of view of the co-ordination of economic policies in the context of economic and monetary union.[74] The 'Luxembourg process' has followed, along the lines set out by the Treaty a course of progressive evolution which after the Lisbon European Council of 2000 brought it to extend beyond the chosen field of employment policy and the Employment Strategy.[75]

The open method of co-ordination, although it exists in diverse forms in terms of technical details and methods of application,[76] can be regarded as a kind of sublimation or generalization of the form of governance used first for the co-ordination of economic policies and then for the co-ordination of employment policies. It is a form of governance which represents, in a way, an innovative natural development of the proven instruments of sectoral co-ordination that have long been anchored in firm legal bases. Promoted for the first time at Lisbon as a new form of governance of overarching and comprehensive relevance, it is nevertheless still in search of a specific constitutional base in the Treaties, a search which – given the weakness of the solutions envisaged – could still be left without any satisfactory outcome even after the 2003/2004 Intergovernmental Conference and the signing of the constitutional Treaty. Indeed the constitutional Treaty, disregarding a number of proposals that emerged

---

[73] Cf. M Barbera, *Dopo Amsterdam. I nuovi confini del diritto sociale comunitario*, Brescia 2000, pp. 131–2, who talks of a shared competence in the co-ordination and direction of policy; and see Sciarra, 'Integration', p. 218, who spells out how this differs from 'co-operation'. See, now, Article I-15 of the Treaty establishing a Constitution for Europe, entitled 'The coordination of economic and employment policies'.

[74] See S. Cafaro, *Unione monetaria e coordinamento delle politiche economiche. Il difficile equilibrio tra modelli antagonisti di integrazione europea*, Milan 2001, p. 78.

[75] See Ashiagbor, 'Soft Harmonisation', pp. 227ff.

[76] These still differ greatly even within the sphere of social policy in the broad sense. There are, for example, differences of emphasis between the fully developed architecture of the European Employment Strategy – which became more 'stringent' after Lisbon, with a strong role for the Commission in taking the initiative and ensuring co-ordination – and the weaker version of the open method of co-ordination in regard to social inclusion and, even more so, pensions and social protection. In the areas of its more recent extension, where competence is more jealously reserved to the Member States, the open method of co-ordination emphasizes its more distinctly intergovernmental features. Cf. Kenner, *EU Employment Law*, pp. 482ff.

during the work of the European Convention, does not contain a general prescription on principle (even merely procedural) of the open method of co-ordination. Article I-15 of the constitutional Treaty actually goes no farther than mentioning it as a form of 'co-ordinating' competence on the part of the Union, and essentially refers to the partial and sectoral rules which already existed and are now contained in Part III of the European Constitution.

Despite the cautious detachment with which it is treated in the Commission's White Paper of 2001,[77] the open method of co-ordination now features, in the European Union's effective political dynamics, as an emergent and increasingly general form of Community governance whose centrality for the purposes of achieving the 'strategic goal' set at Lisbon[78] is emphasized unreservedly by the Social Policy Agenda of 2000.[79]

Particularly in its various applications to employment policy and social policy, the open method of co-ordination accurately sums up the characterizing features of the Community system as a 'post-modern'[80] polity, as a form of polymorphic governance distributed 'network-wise' over several interdependent and interconnected levels without any predefined hierarchies.

In embracing open co-ordination the Union represents, more than ever before, a 'polycentric legal system' in which Europeanization (of the employment policies and actual labour *law* of the Member States) cannot help but proceed with respect for 'national peculiarities'.[81]

---

[77] COM(2001)428 final, *European Governance. A White Paper*; cf. the critical assessments by C. Joerges, 'The Commission's White Paper on Governance in the EU. A Symptom of Crisis?', *Common Market Law Review* 2002, pp. 441ff., and A. Cygan, 'The White Paper on European Governance. Have Glasnost and Perestroika Finally Arrived to the European Union?', *Modern Law Review* 2002, pp. 229ff.

[78] For the European Union to become, by 2010, 'the most competitive and dynamic knowledge-based economy in the world capable of sustainable economic growth with more and better jobs and greater social cohesion'.

[79] See Commission of the European Communities, *Social Policy Agenda*, COM(2000)379 final, and also *Scoreboard on Implementing the Social Policy Agenda*, COM(2001)104 final, especially p. 4.

[80] J. A. Caporaso, 'The European Union and Forms of State: Westphalian, Regulatory or Post-Modern?', *Journal of Common Market Studies* 1996, pp. 29ff., especially pp. 45ff.

[81] S. Sciarra, 'Global or Re-Nationalised? Past and Future of European Labour Law', in F. Snyder (ed.), *The Europeanisation of Law: The Legal Effects of European Integration*, Oxford-Portland 2000, pp. 269ff., here p. 288; the same author has talked elsewhere of a form of 'legal system which is losing the rigid configuration that was typical of the European positivist tradition and producing a destructured and multiform legal system' (as she says in 'Parole vecchie e nuove: diritto del lavoro e occupazione', *Argomenti di Diritto del Lavoro* 1999, no. 2, pp. 369ff., here p. 380).

Title VIII of the EC Treaty explicitly adopts the 'logic of promotional-reflexive law'[82] and centres Community action on the procedural dimension, 'on the method, rather than on its results',[83] thereby overcoming the 'static' approach that still marks the strategy of convergence of social-protection policies. Although a drive towards the convergence of results is undoubtedly present in the co-ordination exercise carried out annually in accordance with Articles 128–30 of the Treaty, especially through the thrust in this direction provided by the Commission[84] and the progressive refinement of quantitative and qualitative targets and indicators,[85] the qualifying aspect of the process is its actual recurring and circular nature, or in other words its predominant procedural dimension.

The emphasis, increasingly clear after the Lisbon summit, on benchmarking as the epicentre of the open method of co-ordination[86] in no way implies that there is *one best* model at European level towards which it is necessary to converge.[87] The existence of differences in the several Member States' policy and re-regulatory responses consistently with the profound diversity of the national and local contexts involved[88] remains, as a matter of principle, the most authentic keynote of open co-ordination as a form of social governance. Consequently, within the process of open co-ordination both dynamics of convergence towards policy models which tend to become common by virtue of their better performance (and hence, from this aspect, forms of 'voluntary' Europeanization) and dynamics of differentiation (and hence, as it were, re-nationalization) along the contours of the diverse national welfare traditions, are conceivable and, in principle, equally legitimate. As it has been accurately put: 'At one level "benchmarking" leads to "Europeanisation" or policy transfer of employment policies, with the Commission playing a vital coordinating role in seeking to engineer convergence, and yet it can also be seen as a form of "renationalisation" whereby the process is driven by national best practice rather than rules imposed from Brussels.'[89]

Convergence is one of the possible outcomes, and in this sense not even some form of *spontaneous* harmonization, following logics and sequences obviously very far removed from the normative model envisaged by Article 137 of the Treaty, can be excluded *a priori*. But there is no

---

[82] Barbera, *Dopo Amsterdam*, p. 96.   [83] Ashiagbor, 'Soft Harmonisation', p. 254.
[84] *Ibid.*, pp. 161 and 163.   [85] See Treu, *Politiche*, pp. 91–2.
[86] Cf. Szyszczak, 'New Paradigm', p. 1145.
[87] Cf. De la Porte, Pochet and Room, 'Social Benchmarking'.
[88] Cf. Sciarra, 'Parole vecchie', pp. 375–6.   [89] Kenner, *EU Employment Law*, pp. 477–8.

'inexorability'[90] about convergence outcomes, which are purely potential, given that dynamics of re-nationalization or differentiation, including at subnational level, are equally legitimate and possible in the context of the open and pluralist narrative of the open method of co-ordination.

8. Open co-ordination as a new form of Community economic and social governance

Although presented as an essentially 'post-regulatory'[91] intervention technique, as a form of management by objectives chiefly aimed at steering *policies* (first employment and then, more generally, social policies), open co-ordination is nevertheless capable of exerting a significant impact on national *legal orders* themselves.[92] The persuasive and directive force of the Employment Guidelines seems in this sense to go beyond what might be surmised from the objective fragility of the system for imposing any form of sanction for failure to comply,[93] which in formal terms is very weak (especially in comparison with that available in the case of the Stability and Growth Pact and, indirectly, the broad economic guidelines for the conduct of economic policy), being wholly centred on the political effectiveness of an (individual) recommendation issued by the Council as a (potential) source of discredit among public opinion.

This unexpected and unsuspected force of the weak and procedural law of Title VIII of the EC Treaty worries all those who see in it confirmation that the European Employment Strategy is in reality still entirely subordinate to the logic governing economic and monetary union and therefore remains fundamentally aligned with neoliberal orthodoxy, instrumental to affirming the same discourse on the 'flexibilization' (i.e. 'deregulation') of the labour market.[94]

---

[90] As tends, on the contrary, to be the view held by Kenner, *EU Employment Law*, p. 476, at least as regards the area in which application of the open method of co-ordination is the most established and incisive, i.e. employment policies.

[91] De la Porte, Pochet and Room, 'Social Benchmarking'; S. Régent, 'The Open Method of Coordination: A New Supranational Form of Governance?', *European Law Journal* 2003, pp. 190ff.

[92] Cf. Ashiagbor, 'Soft Harmonisation', pp. 240 and 294ff.; N. Bruun, 'The European Employment Strategy and the "Acquis Communitaire [*sic*]" of Labour Law', *International Journal of Comparative Labour Law and Industrial Relations* 2001, vol. 17 no. 3, pp. 309–24, especially p. 310.

[93] See, for example, Treu, *Politiche*, pp. 108 and 110.

[94] Cf. in this sense especially Ashiagbor, 'Soft Harmonisation', pp. 7, 132 and 145ff.

However indubitable the predominance of the supply-side approach[95] may be, including in the case of employment policy, this criticism would nevertheless seem to underestimate the strong re-balancing pressure which the European Employment Strategy has actually brought to bear with respect to the one-sided monetary emphasis of the Maastricht Treaty.

The Lisbon summit reinstated in European political discourse words which by then seemed to belong to a past that had gone forever: even though recalled without a trace of nostalgia for deficit-spending policies, the objective of 'full employment' made its reappearance, with renewed emphasis on the necessary 'quality' of employment relationships and the social context in general in which this was to be attained.[96] And although it did not entirely overcome the difference in level that still separates the various co-ordination processes which go to make up Community economic governance, the Lisbon Council nonetheless introduced greater elements of systematic connection between them, restoring more visibility and importance to the social and employment dimension.[97]

Be that as it may, the limitations (and high risks of blockage or regression) of a strategy for revitalizing the European social dimension that was to be entrusted solely (or mainly) to soft- and procedural-law mechanisms remain obvious: a stronger and more stable *normative* anchorage of the open method of co-ordination therefore seems indispensable.[98] It seems equally necessary for the Community, in order to bridge the persistent 'phase differences between economic and employment policies', to succeed in arranging resources that are effectively 'capable of supporting promotional actions tailored to each national or local system and likely to activate its ability to react positively'.[99]

In particular, the establishment of normative principles and fundamental social rights on which to base the 'reflexive' harmonization of national systems can only take place at the maximum level of *constitutional* force available to the Community legal order. In the final analysis,

---

[95] See Treu, 'Le politiche sociali europee', p. 4 (of the typescript).

[96] See at length Commisssion of the European Communities, *Employment and Social Policies: A Framework for Investing in Quality*, COM(2001)313.

[97] Likewise Ashiagbor, 'Soft Harmonisation', p. 183, recognizes that at Lisbon: 'For the first time since the introduction of the Employment Title, an explicit attempt was made to fully integrate policies on employment, economic reform and social cohesion.' This brought about a reduction of the 'co-ordination deficit' (Teague, *Economic Citizenship*, p. 165) between the Luxembourg, Cardiff and Cologne processes by giving greater weight and visibility to social issues.

[98] See Ashiagbor, 'Soft Harmonisation', pp. 240 and 250; Szyszczak, 'New Paradigm', p. 1169.

[99] Treu, 'Le politiche sociali europee', p. 6 (of the typescript).

the viability of reflexive law and its effective suitability as a tool for governing and directing the dynamics of the market are dependent on the 'hardness'[100] of these fundamental principles, as also on the actual ability of the European public authorities (in all their complexity) to implement and translate them into policies.[101] For example, the establishment of multilevel social standards through hard-law instruments,[102] combined with the constitutional enshrinement of Community fundamental social rights, could provide useful answers in this direction.

The suggestion put forward by Scharpf for using the instruments of strengthened co-operation provided by the EC Treaty[103] to give *binding* definition to different levels of overall social protection, measured by the differing rates of social spending (as a share of GDP) of the several Community countries, as mandatory lower thresholds that Member States must meet at the very least,[104] would not recreate a model of (social) Europe with variable geometry or, worse, *à la carte*. On the contrary, it would have the advantage of siting the processes of open co-ordination and convergence of national employment and social policies within a framework of strong constraints (comparable to those envisaged by the Stability Pact) that would not only 'eliminate the danger (or the promise) of "competitive welfare dismantling"'[105] but trigger phenomena of upward virtuous competition *without* thereby prejudicing the necessary diversity of national policy choices.

9. An analytical comparison of three ideal-type models of a European economic constitution

So far, I have examined the dialectic relationship between construction of the unified market and (national and supranational) social law and policies in its dynamic and diachronic dimension.

---

[100] Cf., for useful indications in this sense (although they are referred to a different area of the effect of Community law and policies), G. G. Howells, '"Soft Law" in EC Consumer Law', in Craig and Harlow, *Lawmaking*, pp. 310ff., especially pp. 317 and 330.

[101] For general ideas in this direction cf., for example, Mengoni, 'La questione', p. 28; J. Black, 'Constitutionalising Self-Regulation', *Modern Law Review* 1996, pp. 24ff., especially pp. 52ff.

[102] Teague, *Economic Citizenship*, p. 186.

[103] See, recently, F. Tuytschaever, *Differentiation in European Union Law*, Oxford-Portland 1999. The mechanisms in question have been the subject of further revision by the Treaty of Nice.

[104] Cf. F. W. Scharpf, *Governing in Europe: Effective and Democratic?*, Oxford 1999, pp. 175ff.

[105] *Ibid.*, p. 179.

The changes undergone by the European economic constitution – both from the point of view of the relationship between Community competition and market law and national social regulatory systems and from that of the evolution of supranational forms of the latter's positive integration – have been reconstructed in a historical perspective, comparing the various normative models underlying their practical (and often confused and contradictory) development.

In the following pages, these models – cleansed, as it were, of the 'contaminations' by which they have inevitably been marked in their historical implementation – will be analysed and compared in their abstract and stylized form, or their 'pure' and 'ideal-type' form.

None of the three models examined has ever, as such, been effectively and fully translated into the idealized form in which they will be compared with each other here using a 'static' approach. Nevertheless, albeit to a differing extent and with a differing degree of intensity, the 'competitive', 'solidaristic' and 'co-operative' federalism models have all been (and are) present in the dynamics of European integration, and have all variously circulated (and are circulating) in the increasingly lively debate on the presuppositions for the legitimacy of the European economic constitution.[106]

The alternative (at least in abstract terms) economic-constitution models under discussion pose widely differing issues of the legitimacy of European law, both from the point of view of the relationship between the various levels of governance in the Community multitiered system and from the closely interrelated point of view of the institutions responsible for (regulatory and/or corrective) intervention in the market by Community and/or national public authorities.[107]

The precise intention here is to sum up, in its abstract outlines, the constitutional dimension of the relations between social rights and the market in Community integration, developing in a more systematic form concepts that have already emerged in the preceding pages in line with the profoundly different presuppositions for the legitimacy of the various

---

[106] Cf. C. Joerges (with the collaboration of A. Furrer and O. Gerstenberg), 'Challenges of European Integration to Private Law', Collected Courses of the Academy of European Law 1997, vol. VII no. 1, pp. 281ff.; M. Poiares Maduro, We, The Court. The European Court of Justice and the European Economic Constitution, Oxford 1998, pp. 103ff.

[107] On the close interconnection between the two dimensions, see Poiares Maduro, We, The Court, pp. 104–8. In the three alternative models of the European economic constitution discussed by him ('centralised model', 'competitive model' and 'decentralised model'), the two dimensions are examined contextually or, rather, regarded as two sides of the same coin.

models of a European economic constitution. The focus will therefore be mainly concentrated on the question of the 'constitutional justification' of the individual models, from an eminently normative point of view.[108]

This explanation of the essential outlines of the models being compared will, consequently, highlight the aspects of their internal consistency, without any attempt to sketch – by venturing into the realms of prediction – future scenarios of varying degrees of probability.[109] Problematic assessments in this latter direction have in any case already been offered in the course of the book and will also feature later in our conclusions.

The alternative models of 'competitive', 'solidaristic' and 'co-operative' federalism that are suggested here should therefore be regarded as heuristic instruments of normative analysis, freely drawn from the theoretical debate on the present and future reality of the European economic constitution and, more generally, of the European polity. Even the very terminology used for this purpose – as also applies to similar examples[110] – merely corresponds to what is conventionally accepted. In particular, the word 'federalism', whose semantic range is very broad, if not vague,[111] is used in a deliberately non-technical sense, without in any way joining in the debate, at least in its usual terms, on the possible (completely) federal or otherwise future of the Euro-polity.[112] Nor are the qualifying adjectives that connote it, even where they coincide with those sometimes used to

---

[108] The problem of the 'substantive legitimacy' of Community social law is broached from a similar point of view, with an express invitation to 'tackle straightforwardly the issue of the bases of [its] legitimacy', by Barbera, *Dopo Amsterdam*, p. 80.

[109] For a partly comparable approach, see also Commissariat Général du Plan, *Emploi, négociations collectives, protection sociale: vers quelle Europe sociale? Rapport du groupe présidé par Joël Maurice*, Paris 1999, pp. 100–1.

[110] See C. Barnard, 'Regulating Competitive Federalism in the European Union? The Case of EC Social Policy', in Shaw, *Social Law*, pp. 49ff., for the contrast between the 'competitive federalism' model and the 'centralised legislation' model; or, further, A. M. Petroni and R. Caporale, *Il federalismo possibile. Un progetto liberale per l'Europa*, Soveria Mannelli 2000, pp. 17ff., for the similar choice between 'competitive' and 'centralizing' federalism.

[111] I. Pernice, 'Harmonization of Legislation in Federal Systems; Constitutional, Federal and Subsidiarity Aspects', in Pernice (ed.), *Harmonization of Legislation in Federal Systems*, Baden-Baden 1996, pp. 9ff., here p. 15, states that, in its more general perception, 'a "federal system" is any legal entity comprised of states for the purpose of pursuing certain common ends and which has been given, to this effect, the power to exercise limited but direct jurisdiction over their citizens, but where for all other fields of public action the individual states maintain their full autonomy. This definition, therefore, includes federal states, but does not necessarily mean that only states can be a federal system.' See also, by way of example, G. Bognetti, *Federalismo*, Turin 2001, pp. 5ff.

[112] Cf., among the most recent and significant examples, G. F. Mancini, 'Europe: The Case for Statehood' and J. H. H. Weiler, 'Europe: The Case Against the Case for Statehood', *European Law Journal* 1998, vol. 4 no. 1, respectively pp. 29–42 and 43–62. As is well

describe the historical forms or phases of certain federal-state experiences (such as those of the United States and Germany, for example) intended to evoke any particular reminiscence of the specific debate relating to these.

10. The neoliberal 'competitive federalism' model

In the neoliberal 'competitive federalism' constitutional model, the tendency is for supranational law to be assigned the sole task of promoting the *negative integration* of national markets.

Community law has as a priority function the legal unification of the common market, conceived as an economic space without internal frontiers, through the abolition of all (normative) obstacles to freedom of movement for the factors of production (capital, labour, goods and services) and to the free operation of competition. In the wake of the German tradition of ordoliberalism – to which this conception of the Community economic constitution is more directly (although certainly not exclusively)[113] linked – supranational law, conceived in the special sense of economic constitutional law,[114] therefore has the exclusive task of constructing and guaranteeing an open and competitive common market.

The open and free market is established by Community law through a system decision which – finding its practical expression in the grant of fundamental rights to economic freedom and in strong regulation of the competitive process directed simultaneously against distortive interference by the state and the concentration and abuse of a private monopoly position – constitutionally guarantees its efficient functioning.[115]

---

known, the debate on the desirability or otherwise of a completely federal future for the European Union was rekindled by the speech delivered on 12 May 2000 by the German Foreign Minister Joschka Fischer (reproduced, with various comments, in C. Joerges, Y. Mény and J. H. H. Weiler (eds.), *What Kind of Constitution for What Kind of Polity? Responses to Joschka Fischer*, Florence 2000).

[113] The 'public choice' school proposes similar solutions (see Petroni and Caporale, *Il federalismo*, pp. 26ff.), while the recipe that can be inferred from Hayekian liberal constitutionalism, although built on largely common ground, is even more radical (see F. A. von Hayek, *Law, Legislation and Liberty*, 3 vols., London 1973, vol. III, p. 105). For a summary outline of the different cultural origins of the model, see A. M. Petroni, 'L'analisi economica del federalismo e la sua applicazione alla struttura costituzionale dell'Unione europea', in Petroni (ed.), *Modelli giuridici ed economici per la Costituzione europea*, Bologna 2001, pp. 193ff.

[114] Joerges, 'Challenges', p. 292.

[115] Cf. D. J. Gerber, 'Constitutionalizing the Economy: German Neoliberalism, Competition Law and the "New" Europe', *American Journal of Comparative Law* 1994, vol. 42, pp. 25ff. For further details, see also subsection 8 of chapter 1 above.

An aspect of considerable difference is discernible here between the ordoliberal conception of the Freiburg School and Hayekian liberal constitutionalism:[116] the latter tends to think of a market as a spontaneous order – upstream of (and not established by) any system decision institutionalized in (Community) law on the economy – and, correspondingly, to regard economic rights as natural and pre-political freedoms that are in a sense independent of their constitutional recognition,[117] while the former entrusts economic constitutional law with a constitutive, i.e. properly foundational, role. In other words, liberal constitutionalism *à la* Hayek attributes to law (and especially, for our present purposes, to the Community legal order) a less significant role, or more specifically here a role that does not extend to founding and establishing the common market. This is a difference which affects the identification of the legitimacy base of Community law as economic constitutional law, since full recognition of this legitimacy presupposes the idea that a market does not exist as a spontaneous order upstream of any public regulatory intervention but represents, rather, an entity which is 'politically instituted and socially regulated'[118] through law.

Hence, the characterizing feature of the model is a clear *separation between the common market and the nation-state*,[119] i.e. the legal construction of a transnational market *without* the development of equally extensive mechanisms of control and political hetero-correction and, therefore, without the formation of a statal organization at supranational (federal) level.[120] In other words, the model is characterized by 'the co-existence of a single European market together with a number of distinct states on

---

[116] Cf. N. Irti, *L'ordine giuridico del mercato*, Rome-Bari 1998.

[117] See, in critical vein, E. O. Eriksen, 'The Question of Deliberative Supranationalism in the EU', *ARENA (Advanced Research on the Europeanisation of the Nation-State) Working Papers* No. 99/4, p. 8.

[118] Egan, *Constructing*, p. 1.

[119] Corrective and redistributive intervention by the state is permitted exclusively within national borders, in such a manner as not to form an obstacle to free movement of the factors of production and freedom of competition within the integrated market. The social dimension of the market economy – to which ordoliberal theory assigns a prominent role for the purpose of pursuing autonomous goals of distributive justice – is therefore sited within the political confines of the nation-state and can be implemented in so far as it does not interfere with the proper functioning of the European market. On the concept of a 'social market economy' cf., recently, R. Miccú, '"Economia e costituzione" : una lettura della cultura giuspubblicIstica tedesca', *Quaderni del Pluralismo* 1996, pp. 243ff., and, with particular reference to the European Community, cf. Cantaro, 'Lavoro', pp. 103–8.

[120] See C. Joerges, 'The Market Without the State? The "Economic Constitution" of the European Community and the Rebirth of Regulatory Policies', *European Integration Online Papers* 1997, vol. I no. 19, http://eiop.or.at/eiop/texte/1997-019a.htm.

the same territory without a degree of political control equivalent to the degree of economic integration.'[121]

The governance mechanism typical of the model is the market,[122] and the main instrument of the realization of its institutional virtues is the generalized application of the principle of *mutual recognition*. This principle lies at the centre of the institutional universe of 'competitive federalism',[123] inasmuch as it ensures regulatory competition between the different national political and normative systems vying with each other in the same integrated economic space.

Full mobility of the factors of production and comprehensive circulation of the information needed to compare the different national political and institutional systems[124] enable economic actors to choose between the latter on the basis of particular advantages and rational preferences. The role of the institutions and supranational law on the economy is precisely that of making regulatory competition possible, first and foremost in guaranteeing complete freedom of movement of the factors of production (capital and labour).

According to the proponents of this model, natural convergence of the preferences of rational actors (employers, workers and consumers) towards the most efficient and advantageous system is such as to produce a process of 'bottom–up' harmonization, guided by the market and directed at the selection and spread, through imitation, of the best regulatory model.[125] The harmonization likely to ensue from this form of 'bottom–up' and *ex post* harmonization[126] is, as they see it, inherently different from and better than 'top–down' harmonization imposed *ex ante* through heteronomous political intervention, since on the one hand it

---

[121] M. Jachtenfuchs, 'Democracy and Governance in the EU', *European Integration Online Papers* 1997, vol. I no. 2, http://eiop.or.at/eiop/texte/1997-002a.htm, p. 10.

[122] On the 'governance by market' model, see G. Thompson, 'Governing the European Economy: A Framework for Analysis', in Thompson (ed.), *Governing the European Economy*, London 2001, pp. 15ff.: a market claims to secure 'economic order and the co-ordination of economic activities without any conscious organizing centre directing it. It is based upon "decentralized" decision-making, involving a competitive process between dispersed economic agents who make their decisions according to the price mechanism.'

[123] Cf., by way of example, Petroni and Caporale, *Il federalismo*, pp. 126ff.; ISAE –Istituto di Studi e Analisi Economica, *Rapporto sullo stato dell'Unione europea*, edited by F. Kostoris Padoa Schioppa, Bologna 2001, pp. 57 and 169ff.

[124] For a more analytical enumeration of the institutional preconditions for regulatory competition, see Barnard, 'Regulating', p. 54.

[125] Cf. (albeit in a critical sense), J.-M. Sun and J. Pelkmans, 'Regulatory Competition in the Single Market', *Journal of Common Market Studies* 1995, pp. 67ff., especially p. 70.

[126] On this point, in critical terms, see Commissariat Général du Plan, *Emploi*, p. 106.

represents the 'spontaneous' and 'natural' outcomes of the competitive process and on the other it guarantees – precisely because it is the fruit of decision-making mechanisms that are by definition decentralized – axiomatic conformity with the principle of subsidiarity.[127]

The Hayekian virtues of competition as a 'process of discovery'[128] would thus be achieved simultaneously in a maximization of the allocative-efficiency function in the integrated market and a limitation of corrective and, above all, redistributive intervention by individual States, thanks in particular to the comprehensive spread of the effects of fiscal competition.[129]

The principle of mutual recognition would therefore have to have a general range of application, certainly extended to the sphere of regulation of the labour market and employment relationships, in the latter case mainly in order to stimulate convergence towards the model that is the most flexible and favourable to growth in employment.[130] This is because regulatory competition on a European or international scale 'in the field of the welfare state serves as a kind of process of discovery to identify which welfare state package – for whatever reason – turns out to be economically viable in practice'.[131]

While it sets national systems of social law and policy in competition with each other, the supranational legal order does not deliberately – *and should not* – carry out corrective or redistributive functions aimed at compensating, at the more general level, the (predetermined) reduction of autonomous powers of intervention arising from regulatory competition.[132]

---

[127] For the idea that mutual recognition fulfils the requirements of subsidiarity, both vertical and horizontal, in the most complete form see, for example, ISAE, *Rapporto*, pp. 18–19 and 63, and also S. Woolcock, 'Competition Among Rules in the Single Market', in W. Bratton *et al.* (eds.), *International Regulatory Competition and Coordination. Perspectives on Regulation in Europe and the United States*, Oxford 1997, p. 290.

[128] F. A. von Hayek, *Conoscenza, competizione e libertà*, edited and with a foreword by D. Antiseri and L. Infantino, Soveria Mannelli 1998.

[129] Petroni and Caporale, *Il federalismo*, pp. 31ff.

[130] In this sense, see ISAE, *Rapporto*, pp. 105ff., and H. Siebert, 'Labor Market Rigidities and Unemployment in Europe', *EUI Working Papers, Robert Schuman Centre – European University Institute* No. 97/28. For a discussion of this aspect in relation to the actual Community normative context, see subsection 11 of chapter 1 above.

[131] K.-H. Paqué, 'Does Europe's Common Market Need a "Social Dimension"? Some Academic Thoughts on a Popular Theme', in Addison and Siebert, *Labour Markets*, pp. 105ff., here p. 100.

[132] This central aspect of the model under discussion is pointed out (in critical vein) by W. Streeck, 'La dimensione sociale del mercato unico europeo: verso un'economia non regolata?', *Stato e Mercato* 1990, pp. 29ff.

In point of fact, from the perspective of the 'competitive federalism' model Community law is *legitimate* to the extent that it confines itself to the negative integration of national markets and to guaranteeing the free operation of competition in the common market. Its purpose, and hence also the basis of its legitimacy, consists solely in the establishment of a European market which is open and competitive.

Consequently, Community law – seen as constitutional law of the European market – could not legitimately address the positive integration of national social systems. The legitimacy of European law comes essentially from the guarantee of individual (civil and economic) rights that it grants 'against [national] public power'.[133] It is a normative and functional legitimacy centred on recognition of the fundamental freedoms of movement and the resultant guarantee of the efficient functioning of the common market.[134]

The legitimacy of Community law therefore rests on the efficiency and freedom ensured for (and in) the European common market, and for this reason does not require or presuppose extension to the sphere of supranational governance of the (representative and majoritarian) forms of democratic legitimacy peculiar (solely) to the national political process.[135]

Since they go beyond the conditions of legitimacy of Community law inasmuch as they are based on value choices that are legitimized only by the national democratic political process, 'Individual social rights should not exist on the European level but remain restricted to the domain of the nation state, together with political rights.'[136]

In this view of things, the European Community/Union does not suffer from a democratic deficit in so far (only) as it confines itself to the paradigm of the formal rationality of economic constitutional law. On the other hand, the problem of a democratic-legitimacy deficit of Community action arises whenever the European Union goes beyond the functional

---

[133] Poiares Maduro, *We, The Court*, p. 128.

[134] *Ibid.*, p. 129, where the author goes on to observe that – from the neoliberal viewpoint of 'competitive federalism' – 'Private law transactions are seen as the real source of the contractual and democratic legitimacy of any society and, thus, of the constitution upon which it is founded.'

[135] See E.-J. Mestmäcker, 'Politische und normativ-funktionale Legitimation der Europäischen Gemeinschaft', in Mestmäcker, *Recht und ökonomisches Gesetz*, Baden-Baden 1978, pp. 82ff.

[136] Jachtenfuchs, 'Democracy', p. 10.

limits inherent in the *paradigm of formal law* of the market[137] and appropriates for itself tasks that can be performed democratically only by the several (social) nation-states. And the tasks of reallocating social power in the area of the relationships of the production and/or redistribution of wealth that are specific to national social rights and policies are among the functions for which the Community would, in point of fact, entirely lack the necessary resources of democratic legitimacy.[138]

11. The neo-social-democratic 'solidaristic federalism' model

In the neoliberal 'competitive federalism' model the social sovereignty of the Member States, although preserved in formal terms, is reduced to a shell deprived of all substance.[139] The negative-integration effects that arise jointly from exercise of the economic freedoms of movement and

---

[137] On which see, in general, J. Habermas, 'Paradigms of Law', in M. Rosenfeld and A. Arato, *Habermas on Law and Democracy. Critical Exchanges*, Berkeley-Los Angeles-London 1998, pp. 13ff., especially pp. 14–15. Cf. also G. Teubner, 'Juridification. Concepts, Aspects, Limits, Solutions', in Teubner (ed.), *Juridification of Social Spheres. A Comparative Analysis of the Areas of Labor, Corporate, Antitrust and Social Welfare Law*, Berlin-New York 1987, pp. 3ff.

[138] From this aspect there is a firm element of affinity between the 'competitive federalism' constitutional model and the theory of the European Community as a 'regulatory state' (this is rightly emphasized by M. Jachtenfuchs, 'The Governance Approach to European Integration', *Journal of Common Market Studies* 2001, pp. 245ff., especially p. 252, and C. Joerges, 'Challenges', pp. 290 and 303). Giandomenico Majone bases the impossibility of welfare redistributive policies at Community level on the same assumption of the absence, in the supranational institutions, of the necessary democratic (majoritarian) legitimation base. This, together with the financial resources essential for such solidaristic policies, is available *only* at national level. By contrast, the Community level of governance is particularly well suited and possesses full legitimacy, especially after the entry into force of the Single European Act, to perform purely common-market re-regulation functions (including social-regulation functions). That is to say, as well as market-building tasks in the strict sense it could also legitimately perform – preferably by making use of independent agencies – tasks which, although essential, are confined to correcting the failures of the common market. Tasks, therefore, which as such have a bearing on the allocation of resources and not on their redistribution on the basis of some political criterion of social justice. See, for example, G. Majone, 'The European Community as a Regulatory State', *Collected Courses of the Academy of European Law* 1996, vol. V no. 1, pp. 321ff.

[139] In this sense see, for example, C. Offe, 'The Democratic Welfare State in an Integrating Europe', in T. Greven and L. W. Pauly (eds.), *Democracy Beyond the State? The European Dilemma and the Emerging Global Order*, Lanham 2000, pp. 63ff., especially p. 71; M. Poiares Maduro, 'Europe's Social Self: "The Sickness Unto Death"', in Shaw, *Social Law*, pp. 324ff., especially p. 331.

regulatory competition *within* the several Member State jurisdictions[140] contain an obvious, and in reality perfectly calculated, potential for destructuring national welfare systems.[141]

Furthermore, it is an explicit assumption of the neoliberal model that regulatory competition within national jurisdictions – in the presence of full mobility of the factors of production – produces a spontaneous convergence towards the system deemed most efficient *by the market*.[142]

Convergence towards the lightest or lowest social standard,[143] as also the containment of public (and especially social) spending to a minimum arising from the 'taming the Leviathan' effect induced by fiscal competition,[144] therefore represent nothing other than the strictly liberal quality of the model.

The 'solidaristic federalism' model starts from concern about the progressive decline of the Member States' social sovereignty, as being an essential presupposition of their democratic legitimacy,[145] and proposes a solution which is radically alternative to the purely negative integration of markets and characterized by the need to reconstruct at supranational level the same powers of political control of the economic sphere that are now lost or at any rate diminished at national level. It therefore sets itself the objective of full *positive integration* of national welfare systems, or the creation of a Europe-wide sphere of social-protection policies and social 'entitlements to a decent livelihood' through the construction of a genuine political and democratic governance of the common market possessing substantial capacity to change the market distribution of life chances[146] at the only level that now seems functionally appropriate, i.e. supranational level.

---

[140] See Poiares Maduro, *We, The Court*, p. 144.

[141] Cf. also Deakin, 'Two Types', especially p. 244.

[142] Cf., in critical vein, H. Tjiong, 'Breaking the Spell of Regulatory Competition: Reframing the Problem of Regulatory Exit', *Rabels Zeitschrift für ausländisches und internationales Privatrecht* 2002, pp. 66ff., especially pp. 85 and 92.

[143] For an up-to-date discussion of the (at least potential) 'race to the bottom' effects regarding national standards of social protection that are inherent in the 'competitive federalism' model, see Barnard, 'Regulating', pp. 57–60.

[144] See S. Sinn, 'Taming the Leviathan: Competition Among Governments', *Constitutional Political Economy* 1992, vol. 3 no. 2, pp. 177ff.

[145] Cf. J. Habermas, *The Postnational Constellation. Political Essays* (translated, edited and with an introduction by M. Pensky), Cambridge 2001, pp. 80ff.

[146] S. Leibfried and P. Pierson, 'The Prospects for Social Europe', in A. De Swaan (ed.), *Social Policy Beyond Borders. The Social Question in Transnational Perspective*, Amsterdam 1994, pp. 15ff., here p. 20.

In this view of things, the European Union should take on all the characteristics of a *federal welfare state*, endowed with a political Constitution capable of synthesizing the diverse traditions which today already come together in an essentially unitary 'European social model'. The single market therefore needs to be accompanied – precisely in order to offset the erosion of the legitimacy bases of the European democratic welfare states, through their regeneration at Europe-wide level – by complete federalization of the foundations of social citizenship.

European law needs to be able to draw its own legitimation from a political Constitution, as an expression of the democratic will of the peoples of Europe and the social solidarity pact signed by them.[147]

In point of fact the economically functional and technocratic reasoning on which the neoliberal model bases the legitimacy of Community law[148] would on the one hand no longer take account of the dimensions that European integration has attained, which now go far beyond the sphere of market integration, and on the other would in no way be able to justify the increasingly important pressures brought about at the expense of national democratic political pressures, particularly with respect to questions of social justice.[149] It is based on 'a normatively diminished conception of the person'[150] which is centred solely on the instrumental rationale of the subject as an economic actor and quite incapable of encompassing the idea of equal respect for the human dignity of every individual on which the recognition of fundamental social rights is founded.

Regaining the necessary political control over the process of Community economic integration therefore requires, according to the neo-social-democratic 'solidaristic federalism' model, a transition to a European welfare state democratically legitimized to perform – at the only level now appropriate – the solidarity and social-cohesion functions that at present are carried out individually, with ever-increasing difficulty and decreasing effectiveness, by the Member States.[151]

The arrival of complete European political union – necessary for governing a market that reached full integration with the entry into force of the single currency – would therefore find its most defining moment in

---

[147] See Poiares Maduro, *We, The Court*, pp. 111–13.
[148] For similar criticism of the legitimacy criterion on which the 'competitive federalism' model is based, see Eriksen, 'Question', pp. 2–3; and Offe, 'Democratic Welfare State', p. 75.
[149] Cf. Scharpf, *Governing in Europe*, pp. 34ff.
[150] Habermas, *The Postnational Constellation*, p. 94.
[151] Cf. B Bercusson *et al.*, *A Manifesto for Social Europe 2000*, Brussels 2000, pp. 17ff.

the construction of supranational welfare-state structures[152] designed to offer European citizens a high level of social protection. The 'solidaristic federalism' model entails, in accordance with a neo-Keynesian logic, the reinstatement of a capacity for the centralized management of overall demand, for which the Union would need to be provided with an adequate budget and appropriate fiscal resources commensurate with the goals to be pursued.

In its most ambitious version,[153] the development on a pan-European scale of a system of industrial relations and collective bargaining ('Euro-corporatism') would need to be accompanied by federalization of the main social-protection programmes (minimum income, unemployment insurance and pension provision)[154] and harmonization towards the highest of the existing national labour standards. The European Constitution – accorded a hierarchical ranking higher than those of the Member States – would need to contain an extensive catalogue of fundamental social rights that are *common* (i.e. uniformly applicable throughout Union territory) and directly justiciable.

A 'Scandinavia of the world' Europe[155] could thus represent the only global player really capable of actively contributing to the political governance of economic globalization, above all else offering Europeans security against its most destabilizing effects with respect to the historical achievements of the democratic welfare state.[156]

Europe would need to become fully aware of, and regain, its solidaristic identity and vocation to civilize the capitalist economy in social terms, i.e. its 'social self,'[157] and make full use of the potential opened up by the present 'foundational moment'[158] to arrive at a post-national democratic

---

[152] See B. Veneziani, 'Nel nome di Erasmo da Rotterdam. La faticosa marcia dei diritti sociali fondamentali nell'ordinamento comunitario', *Rivista Giuridica del Lavoro e della Previdenza Sociale* 2000, pp. 779ff., especially pp. 787–8, where the route of 'European parliamentary democracy' combined with 'a policy for restoring Europe-wide welfare based on common thresholds that cannot be departed from *in peius* by individual Member States' is seen as the only 'lever for recovery of the political role of Community governance'.

[153] On which see, at length, Commissariat Général du Plan, *Emploi*, pp. 116ff.

[154] Cf. also A. Graser, 'Confidence and the Question of Political Levels. Towards a Multilevel System of Social Security in Europe?', in D. Pieters (ed.), *Confidence and Changes. Managing Social Protection in the New Millennium*, EISS Yearbook 2000, The Hague-London-New York 2001, pp. 215ff., especially pp. 232–5.

[155] G. Therborn, 'Il futuro dell'Europa: la Scandinavia del mondo?', *Europa Europe* 1999, no. 5, p. 93.

[156] Cf. also M. Telò, 'L'Europa attore internazionale: potenza civile e nuovo multilateralismo', *Europa Europe* 1999, no. 5, pp. 37ff.

[157] Poiares Maduro, 'Europe's Social Self', p. 324.   [158] *Ibid.*, p. 324.

Constitution based on the principles of freedom, substantive equality and solidarity. 'This constitutive moment of the EU arises out of the exhaustion of the functional model and its incapacity to legitimise the current institutional and political developments of the EU.'[159]

In this view of things, the redistributive and cohesion functions performed to a significant degree for some time by the Community demonstrate that it is already perfectly capable of bringing about the abstract solidarity 'among strangers'[160] that constitutes the basis of a democratic welfare state. Consequently, the presuppositions for transferring welfare functions from the (prevalently) national level to the European level already exist today. They would, furthermore, become strengthened in a virtuous circle fed by the force of legitimation emanating from the effective implementation of solidaristic functions by the European Union institutions.[161]

Transformation of the European Union's political institutions in a fully democratic and majoritarian direction therefore needs to be founded on 'an underlying social contract based on a criterion of distributive justice to guarantee the social legitimacy of the majority decisions'.[162] Discursive construction of the supporting elements of this new social contract, and of the bond of civic solidarity 'among strangers' in which it is rooted, thus needs to be at the centre of a constituent process committed to redefining the outlines of the crucial European 'social identity question'.[163]

12. The mixed 'co-operative federalism' model

Criticisms of the model just discussed, and in particular of its legitimacy presuppositions, do not emanate solely from the ranks of those who maintain that such a development is precluded by the non-existence of a

---

[159] *Ibid.*, p. 347.

[160] To repeat the expression used by Habermas, *Postnational Constellation*, p. 102.

[161] The argument, frequently invoked by advocates of the 'solidaristic federalism' model, is that redistribution presupposes, but at the same time generates and expands, a bond of 'solidarity among strangers'. It may thus be recalled that in Germany, in a reversal of Marshall's evolutionary cycle (see T. H. Marshall, *Citizenship and Class*, London 1950 and 1992), social rights historically preceded rights to political participation, helping to cement nation-state unity and solidarity. On the German example (albeit in the sense of the extreme improbability of its transposition to the Community experience), see S. Leibfried, 'Towards a European Welfare State? On Integrating Poverty Regimes into the European Community', in Z. Ferge and J. E. Kolberg (eds.), *Social Policy in a Changing Europe*, Frankfurt am Main-Boulder 1992, pp. 245ff., especially pp. 247–8.

[162] Poiares Maduro, 'Europe's Social Self', p. 346.   [163] *Ibid.*, p. 349.

European *demos* and the realistic impossibility of one being formed,[164] at least within a time frame which is less than 'geological'.[165] Their specific objection is based on an assumption that it fails to take adequate account of the present-day normative and political reality of the European Union, and in particular of the fact that the latter already undermines the (conservative) idea of a sovereign people as an ethnically, linguistically, culturally and spiritually homogeneous entity that necessarily pre-exists in a statal (democratic) political order.[166]

Actually, the 'solidaristic federalism' model also encounters the objections of those who maintain that a post-national democracy – pluralistically embracing the 'multiple *demoi*'[167] of Europe – is not only possible (and foreseeable) but in a way already 'sighted' by the constitutional developments of European integration.

It has in fact been pointed out that because the elements of *pragmatic* negotiations and multilateral agreements between Member States that are decisive today cannot disappear without a trace even for a European Union under a *political* Constitution, a European Federation will need to take on a *different* legal identity from that of national federations of the classical type and cannot simply copy their modes of legitimation.[168] Although refuting the thesis that only a sense of national belonging understood as membership in a 'pre-political community of fate' can exert the kind of 'binding effect',[169] and produce the sort of solidarity, which underpin

---

[164] Probably the most well-known and succinct statement of the thesis is to be found in the repeatedly cited *Maastricht-Urteil* of Germany's Federal Constitutional Court. It is also set out and shrewdly elaborated in D. Grimm, 'Una costituzione per l'Europa?', in G. Zagrebelsky, P. P. Portinaro and J. Luther (eds.), *Il futuro della costituzione*, Turin 1996, pp. 339ff., especially pp. 350–4 and 362–5 (and also in the reply by J. Habermas, 'Una costituzione per l'Europa? Osservazioni su Dieter Grimm', *ibid.*, pp. 369ff.).

[165] As it is graphically put by Mancini, 'Europe: The Case for Statehood', p. 34, in criticizing the cultural-ethnic 'no European *demos*' thesis.

[166] Cf. in particular – apart from Habermas, 'Una costituzione per l'Europa?', and Habermas, 'Lo stato-nazione europeo. Passato e futuro della sovranità e della cittadinanza', in *L'inclusione dell'altro. Studi di teoria politica*, edited and with an afterword by L. Ceppa, Milan 1998, pp. 119ff. – J. H. H. Weiler, *The Constitution of Europe. 'Do the New Clothes Have an Emperor?' and Other Essays on European Integration*, Cambridge 1999, pp. 221ff.; D. Curtin, *Postnational Democracy: European Union in Search of a Political Philosophy*, The Hague-London-Boston 1997; N. MacCormick, *Questioning Sovereignty. Law, State, and Nation in the European Commonwealth*, Oxford 1999. For a useful summary of the debate see, lastly, E. Scoditti, *Una costituzione senza popolo. Unione europea e nazioni*, with an introductory essay by G. Palombella, Bari 2001.

[167] J. H. H. Weiler, 'European Neo-constitutionalism: In Search of Foundations for the European Constitutional Order', *Political Studies* 1996, p. 517.

[168] Habermas, *Postnational Constellation*, p. 99.   [169] *Ibid.*, p. 101.

the democratic redistributive policies of a nation-state, it is maintained, 'It is neither possible nor desirable to level out the national identities of member nations, nor melt them down into a "Nation of Europe".'[170]

It would, in any event, be difficult or even impossible for the European Union to reproduce the same forms of democratic majoritarian legitimation on which the unity of redistributive policies within the nation-state is based.

From this point of view, the profound diversity of national institutional forms of the welfare state – rooted in extremely heterogeneous historical, political, economic and social contexts – is not only at the bottom of an empirical and functional objection to the thesis of their becoming unified/uniform in common supranational structures,[171] but also gives rise to a specifically normative objection centred on seeing the diverse national identities as having a positive value in their own right that must, as such, be preserved.[172] However implausible, a harmonization process tending towards making national systems of legislation uniform, and even more so the construction of a European system of social law that is common to them all, would have destructive or disintegrating effects on the diverse national welfare-state constellations just as great as those resulting from negative integration.[173] And it is difficult to imagine that such outcomes could ever be legitimized on the basis of decisions taken democratically by a majority on a European scale.[174]

A complete federalization of matters of distributive justice would, therefore, run up against the necessity of preserving the diverse national democratic and social identities.

---

[170] *Ibid.*, p. 99.

[171] On the improbability (if not downright impossibility) of a European system of social law and social policy common to all Member States, owing to the insurmountable obstacles posed by the irreducible diversity of European welfare states, see, purely by way of example, C. Closa, 'EU Citizenship as the Institutional Basis of a New Social Contract: Some Sceptical Remarks', *EUI Working Papers – Robert Schuman Centre, European University Institute* No. 96/48.

[172] See Sciarra, 'Global', pp. 285ff., and also Sciarra, 'Diritti sociali. Riflessioni sulla Carta europea dei diritti fondamentali', *Argomenti di Diritto del Lavoro* 2001, no. 2, pp. 391ff.

[173] In this sense see, for example, S. Simitis, 'Europeizzazione o rinazionalizzazione del diritto del lavoro', *Giornale di Diritto del Lavoro e di Relazioni Industriali* 1994, pp. 639ff.; Offe, 'Democratic Welfare State', p. 71; T. Treu, 'Diritti sociali europei: dove siamo?', *Lavoro e Diritto* 2000, pp. 429ff, especially p. 442.

[174] Cf. also M. Luciani, 'Diritti sociali e integrazione europea', in Associazione Italiana dei Costituzionalisti, *Annuario 1999. La costituzione europea*, Atti del XIV Convegno annuale Perugia 7–9 ottobre 1999, Padua 2000, pp. 507ff., especially pp. 543ff.; Barbera, *Dopo Amsterdam*, p. 38.

The 'co-operative federalism' constitutional model seeks to take on board the need to respect these identities by simultaneously safeguarding the Member States' social autonomy from the destructive effects of a competitive process that is not governed politically at Union level. In this sense it is presented as a 'mixed model', a solution that is in a way intermediate between those offered respectively – as alternatives to each other – by the 'competitive federalism' and 'solidaristic federalism' models.

In the 'co-operative federalism' model, market correction and the redistribution of life chances remain functions that are, on the whole, the prerogative of the individual Member States. Systems of labour and social-security law, and welfare policies in general, therefore retain their predominantly national connotation and specificity, drawing on the resources of 'input-oriented'[175] democratic material legitimacy that as yet, in the absence of a fully developed European public sphere, only the nation-state can guarantee.

The role which the Community level of governance undertakes is essentially one of co-ordination, direction and control aimed, on the one hand, at encouraging processes of mutual learning between Member States and, on the other, at stimulating effective lines of response to common problems leading to the solution that is the best locally, while at the same time preventing destructive forms of regulatory competition of the beggar-my-neighbour type.

The European Union limits direct regulatory activity in social matters and in any event gives preference to forms which are the most flexible and the most likely to encourage differentiation at national and subnational level. Harmonization that tends to produce uniformity or approximation to a common model is replaced by 'reflexive harmonization'.[176] The latter consists in the establishment of general basic principles which find effective translation into practice in the first place through active support in the social partners' self-regulatory processes and at any rate through autonomous processes of adaptation at national or subnational level, in a form intermediate between pure centralization and mere decentralization, between heteronomous positive integration and anomic regulatory competition.

In the 'co-operative federalism' model, the 'construction of Europe is pursued by developing institutional arrangements that make it possible to reconcile the common defence of European values with the heterogeneity

---

[175] Scharpf, *Governing in Europe*, pp. 7ff.   [176] Deakin, 'Two Types', pp. 241–2.

of the national models that constitute its translation into practice.'[177] Thus, preservation of the heterogeneity of the several national systems allows forms of competition between them but anchors them to acceptance of common fundamental principles and – with the establishment of mandatory thresholds and non-regression clauses – spurs them on to a search for the 'best rules'.[178] Variation (even considerable) in standards of social protection from one territorial jurisdiction to another is therefore not left to the logic of the market but controlled and directed by the supranational level of governance. The latter – in defining those fundamental rights and guarantees that have Community-wide ranking – also, in a way, defines 'the elements of justified diversity'[179] between individual national orders.

As in the case of the 'solidaristic federalism' model, therefore, the 'co-operative federalism' model likewise assigns a decisive role to the constitutionalization of a robust catalogue of fundamental social rights directly at Union level. However, the difference between the two, which is appreciable, is that whereas in the former these feature as *common* rights in the strict sense of the word, i.e. aimed at rooting directly at Union level the functions of redistribution and reallocation of social power that are particular to them, in the 'co-operative federalism' model the European 'social' constitution essentially serves as a guarantee of and yardstick for the protection of social rights at *national* level.[180] In other words, it does not aspire to replace national forms of social-rights protection but essentially to safeguard them while at the same time opening them up to the co-operative discovery – in their dialectic comparison with the constitutional traditions of other Member States – of new meanings in the sharing of common fundamental values. The constitutional enshrinement of European fundamental social rights serves to preserve the nucleus of common values in a dynamic and pluralist sense, without any claim to providing a uniform protective layer 'constructed as a mechanical mean between the rules in force in the Member States.'[181]

Consequently, the relationship between Community sources and national sources of fundamental social rights is not structured, as in the

---

[177] Commissariat Général du Plan, *Emploi*, p. 120.
[178] Barnard, 'Regulating', p. 66.
[179] T. Treu, 'Il diritto del lavoro: realtà e possibilità', *Argomenti di Diritto del Lavoro* 2000, no. 3, pp. 467ff., here p. 533.
[180] This difference is rightly emphasized by Poiares Maduro, 'Europe's Social Self', pp. 342–3.
[181] Treu, 'L'Europa sociale', p. 328.

'solidaristic federalism' model, in hierarchical terms but is configured, instead, as 'a dynamic relationship of reciprocal subsidiarity',[182] axiologically extended towards the maximum possible realization – under the conditions specifically prevailing on any given occasion – of the social value protected by the rule in question.

The basic idea is, therefore, one of a 'system in which there co-exist many decision-making levels involving numerous institutions, each of them with its own regulatory mission, which are united with each other by a common social model and common constitutional traditions'.[183]

Here, the prevalent European governance mechanism is that of the network:[184] the linkage between the different levels of governance of the system is not entrusted either to the market (as in the case of 'competitive federalism') or to the hierarchical relationship between legal orders and public authorities (as in the case of 'solidaristic federalism'). Instead, it is entrusted to open and widespread mechanisms of 'decentralized co-ordination'[185] and is 'polycentric', with 'mutual and reflexive interdependence' between the different decision-making levels and the various actors (public, quasi-public, social and private) involved.[186]

Supranational intervention, although based on a foundation of common values, is predominantly procedural and therefore essentially relies on the legitimacy that derives from the deliberative, open and participatory nature of the 'polyarchic'[187] co-ordination processes activated by it. The debate on the conditions of 'deliberative supranationalism'[188] is likely to represent, in this sense, the most fertile theoretical ground for grasping the implications of the model's discursive and process-oriented

---

[182] A. Ruggeri, 'Sovranità dello Stato e sovranità sovranazionale, attraverso i diritti umani, e prospettive di un diritto europeo "intercostituzionale"', *Diritto Pubblico Comparato ed Europeo* 2001, vol. II, pp. 544ff., here p. 561.

[183] As put by Barbera, *Dopo Amsterdam*, p. 24.

[184] Cf. Thompson, 'Governing', p. 29ff.; see also K.-H. Ladeur, 'Towards a Legal Theory of Supranationality – The Viability of the Network Concept', *European Law Journal* 1997, vol. 3 no. 1, pp. 33–54.

[185] M. Jachtenfuchs, 'Theoretical Perspectives on European Governance', *European Law Journal* 1995, vol. 1 no. 2, pp. 115–33, here p. 125.

[186] I.-J. Sand, 'Understanding the New Forms of Governance: Mutually Interdependent, Reflexive, Destabilised and Competing Institutions', *European Law Journal* 1998, vol. 4 no. 3, pp. 271–93.

[187] J. Cohen and C. Sabel, 'Directly-Deliberative Polyarchy', *European Law Journal* 1997, pp. 313ff.

[188] See, by way of example, C. Joerges, '"Deliberative Supranationalism": Two Defences', *European Law Journal* 2002, pp. 133ff.

legitimation. The idea of the EU as a 'deliberative polyarchy' adds insight into a similar conceptualization of the legitimacy foundations of this model. 'In deliberative polyarchy, problem-solving depends not on harmony and spontaneous co-ordination, but on permanent disequilibrium of incentives and interests imperfectly aligned, and on the disciplined, collaborative exploration of the resulting differences.'[189] Thus, in this perspective, reflexive harmonization and the open method of co-ordination are seen as 'a highly promising mechanism for promoting crossnational deliberation and experimental learning across the European Union'.[190]

13. A preliminary summing up

It was stated earlier (see subsection 9 above) that none of the models – viewed in stylized and ideal-type form – outlined here makes any claim to hegemonically moulding the actual course of European integration. They have, nevertheless, influenced the theoretical debate in various ways and also affected the actual shaping of the Community institutions.

Echoes of the ordoliberal conception are, for example, clearly discernible in the configuration of Community competition law as the driving centre of the legal unity of the unified market. The actual reading of Article 30 of the Treaty of Rome (now Article 28) as an economic due process clause, largely accepted by the Court at least in recent years, has obviously been greatly influenced by it.[191] It is clearly from this model that the infiltration of European competition and market law into national systems of social law obtains its strongest legitimacy base.

The 'solidaristic federalism' model has never enjoyed particular success, probably not even in the years when 'social democratic consensus'[192] was at its peak. It has, however, shaped a vision of Europe which – although always a minority one politically – retains an undoubted attraction of its

---

[189] J. Cohen and C. F. Sabel, 'Sovereignty and Solidarity: EU and US', in J. Zeitlin and D. M. Trubek (eds.), *Governing Work and Welfare in a New Economy. American and European Experiments*, Oxford 2003, p. 366.

[190] J. Zeitlin, 'Introduction: Governing Work and Welfare in a New Economy: European and American Experiments', in Zeitlin and Trubek, *Governing Work*, p. 5.

[191] See Poiares Maduro, *We, The Court*, pp. 49ff.

[192] This is rightly pointed out by D. M. Trubek and J. S. Mosher, 'EU Governance, Employment Policy, and the European Social Model', *Jean Monnet Working Paper, New York University School of Law* No. 15/01, p. 4.

own,[193] and is certainly not absent from the debate on the constitutionalization of fundamental social rights in the Union legal order.[194]

Because of the intermediate features it offers, the 'co-operative federalism' model opens up what are perhaps the most meaningful prospects
as regards the tendencies that nowadays seem mainly to stamp the (far
from defined and linear) path of European integration. But its very *medi-
etas* also makes it the model that is the least clearly defined and the most
beset by uncertainties, especially when it is superimposed on the concrete
dynamics of European integration.

It has been suggested that the decentralized and non-hierarchical mechanisms of the open method of co-ordination, focused as they are on the
legitimate defence of national particularities, conceal 'not so much the
intention to preserve the specific features of each of the welfare systems as
the opposite aim of the Member States to utilize sovereignty in the social
field as a competitiveness-adjusting mechanism that is an alternative to
their lost sovereignty over currency and exchange rates'.[195]

The eminently procedural slant of the model runs the risk of interpos-
ing less than symbolic barriers to the force of the 'self-regulatory' mechanisms of the integrated market[196] and in fact ending up by strengthening
their legitimacy in offering them the purifying filter of 'supranational
deliberation'. Whereas – with monetary unification achieved under the
sway of the anti-inflationary principles of economic stability – the force
of market integration is nowadays able to exert its most potent effects,
the mechanisms of deliberative governance have not reached their full
maturity[197] and are in danger of being simply called on to take note of
(and re-legitimize *ex post*) choices that have already been dictated by the
market.

---

[193] Cf. B. Stråth (ed.), *After Full Employment. European Discourses on Work and Flexibility*,
Brussels 2000, and especially the concluding chapter by the editor and P. Wagner, 'After
Full Employment. Theoretical and Political Implications', pp. 261ff.

[194] See, for example, L. Betten and D. MacDevitt (eds.), *The Protection of Fundamental Rights
in the European Union*, The Hague-London-Boston 1996.

[195] Cantaro, 'Lavoro', p. 101.

[196] This is a concern shared by, for example, S. Deakin and H. Reed, 'The Contested Meaning
of Labour Market Flexibility. Economic Theory and the Discourse of European Integration', in Shaw, *Social Law*, pp. 71ff., here p. 97: 'As long [as] there is no institutional means
by which the harmonisation of social rights can be built into the employment strategy,
there is a danger that the kind of convergence to which the Employment Title will give
rise is one based on the kinds of "structural adjustment" which are envisaged by EMU –
or, in other words, deregulation.'

[197] Teague, 'Deliberative Governance', p. 24.

In reality, the risks of a destructuring of national labour and social-security law traditions inherent in an approach that is oriented in a markedly post-regulatory and merely procedural direction can be off-set only through the decisive reaffirmation at EU Constitution level of the binding force of the foundational and common values of the European social model. As emphasized earlier,[198] a purely procedural approach is not enough: 'States, and at its own level the European Union, cannot con-fine themselves to organizing procedural rules that allow individuals and intermediate groups to participate in the definition and implementation of the general interests assigned to their care. It is also their duty to fix the basic principles that are to govern this definition and to guarantee fundamental social rights to individuals and groups.'[199]

The full affirmation of fundamental social rights as part of the Com-munity legal order therefore represents 'a necessary step in this critical phase of European integration.'[200]

As stated, the constitutionalization of these rights within the Commu-nity order (also) constitutes the supporting plank of the 'co-operative fed-eralism' model. In the absence of the common *substantive value base* that the affirmation of Community fundamental social principles and rights provides,[201] it is difficult to see how the pluralism of national welfare-state traditions can be preserved and adapted to the new socio-economic requirements without simply giving way to the levelling pressure of mar-ket integration.

The Nice Charter launched, in this sense, a process which has yet to find its culmination and crowning moment in the direct modification of the founding Treaties. It laid down the necessary premises of a path of constitutional reform to which the ratification of the European consti-tutional Treaty is expected to bring the necessary completion by giving substance to a specific political choice underlying the significance of Euro-pean social identity. The illusion that such an outcome can come about 'automatically, through a functional integration manufactured from eco-nomic interdependences', nowadays extraordinarily increased by the entry

---

[198] See subsection 8 above, and also subsections 4 and 5 of chapter 2.

[199] A. Supiot (ed.), *Au-delà de l'emploi. Transformations du travail et devenir du droit du travail en Europe. Rapport pour la Commission européenne*, Paris 1999, p. 235.

[200] S. Sciarra, 'Market Freedom and Fundamental Social Rights', *EUI (European University Institute) Working Papers in Law* No. 02/3, p. 11.

[201] The difference in approach in this respect as compared with the 'solidaristic federalism' model is emphasized in subsection 12 above.

into force of EMU, has in fact now lost even the features of its presumed ingenuity.[202]

The thrust towards Community constitutionalization of fundamental social rights does not come solely from the need to safeguard essential principles of social justice and solidarity from (and *against*) the logic of the market.[203] It also comes from considerations of economic efficiency.

Fundamental social rights are, in point of fact, a decisive component of the long-term dynamic efficiency and competitiveness of open and complex market economies: 'far from being adverse to market relationships, they should be regarded as central in a European labour market that is becoming increasingly flexible and individualized.'[204]

An awareness of this essential economic, as well as 'cohesive' and 'emancipatory', function of social rights was not entirely without a part in the post-war 'embedded liberalism' compromise on which the founding fathers based the construction of the Community. Today it should, even more so, guide the indispensable redefinition of the outlines of the 'European social model'.

The values of freedom and solidarity embodied – albeit with differing sensitivities – by the several national labour-law traditions constitute a fundamental heritage of the European democracies. Restated and necessarily updated, they must remain at the centre of the construction of the Community.

Today, more than ever, a strengthening of the constitutional roots of European social law and a reinforcement of the institutional powers of the social partners – who have always been principal actors in the dynamism of labour law and its extraordinary adaptability to the changing needs of the market – constitute unavoidable presuppositions for the democratic

---

[202] See in this sense Habermas, *Postnational Constellation*, p. 102, from whom the words quoted in the text are taken and who rightly criticizes the stance of those who still maintain that it will sooner or later be the functional requirement created by the single currency that determines – by spillover – the development of a strong European economic and social governance capable of matching up 'on equal terms' to the federalization of monetary policy.

[203] The fact that social rights fulfil a primary function of 'de-commodification' of the person (G. Esping-Andersen, *The Three Worlds of Welfare Capitalism*, Cambridge 1990, pp. 35ff.), and therefore have a logic of their own which is antagonistic to that of the market and as such aimed at remedying the forms of social deprivation produced by the latter, is an aspect that is constantly underlined in the literature. However, the relationship of complementarity vis-à-vis market mechanisms (as a means of guaranteeing the dynamic efficiency of the market) that is mentioned here has received less attention.

[204] S. Deakin and F. Wilkinson, '"Capabilities", ordine spontaneo del mercato e diritti sociali', *Diritto del Mercato del Lavoro* 2000, no. 2, pp. 317ff., here p. 344.

legitimacy of any way forward in the process of European integration. The Treaty establishing a Constitution for Europe could bring about a significant redefinition of the fundamental values and objectives inspiring the EU's mission in a globalized world. The insertion of the European Charter of Fundamental Rights into Part II of the constitutional Treaty could imply a full constitutionalization of social rights within the EU legal order on a par with economic freedoms, in accordance with the principle of indivisibility of fundamental values and rights. The constitutional Treaty, notwithstanding its limitations and shortcomings, therefore represents a fundamental step in the process of building solid constitutional roots for the European social model.[205] Its ratification by the Member States would be a decisive move in pursuing what Joseph Weiler has called 'Europe's Sonderweg'.[206]

---

[205] See S. Giubboni, 'Lavoro e diritti sociali nella nuova Costituzione europea. Spunti comparatistici', *Diritti Lavori Mercati* 2004, no. 3, p. 557.

[206] J. H. H. Weiler, 'Federalism and Constitutionalism: Europe's Sonderweg', *Jean Monnet Working Paper – Harvard University*, 2000.

CONCLUSIONS

'The main characteristics of what will be the social model of a united Europe', wrote Wolfgang Streeck recently, 'are less clear today than they were ten or twenty years ago.'[1]

The welfare states of the Old Continent crossed the threshold of the twenty-first century in a state of profound uncertainty.[2] Despite gloomy predictions of their irreversible crisis and inevitable collapse, they are by no means in their death throes and still enjoy widespread and deep-seated political consensus,[3] as foundational elements of the specific identity of European societies and of the European model of 'civilizing' a capitalist economy. Nevertheless, the political-economy presuppositions on which they had been re-established as supporting planks of the social contracts underpinning the post-war reconstruction of the nation-states of Western Europe have altered drastically and definitively.

The state of uncertainty concerns the actual meaning and direction of the processes of restructuring or readaptation, experimentally launched as early as the 1990s,[4] that were imposed by the radical changes brought about by the new political economy, both domestic and international.

More and more commentators are rightly remarking that – although very significant, especially in terms of the future outlook – the challenges

---

[1] W. Streeck, 'Il modello sociale europeo: dalla redistribuzione alla solidarietà competitiva', *Stato e Mercato* 2000, p. 3 (in its original English version the article was published, under the title 'Competitive Solidarity: Rethinking the "European Social Model"', in K. Hinrichs *et al.* (eds.), *Kontingenz und Krise: Institutionenpolitik in kapitalistischen und postsozialistischen Gesellschaften*, Frankfurt am Main 2000, pp. 245–61).

[2] See M. Ferrera, A. Hemerijck and M. Rhodes, *The Future of Social Europe: Recasting Work and Welfare in the New Economy. Report for the Portuguese Presidency of the European Union*, Lisbon 2000, p. 70 (here, and below, of the typescript).

[3] See P. Pierson, 'Coping with Permanent Austerity. Welfare State Restructuring in Affluent Democracies', in Pierson (ed.), *The New Politics of Welfare State*, Oxford 2001, pp. 410ff.; T. Boeri, A. Börsch-Supan and G. Tabellini, 'Would You Like to Shrink the Welfare State? A Survey of European Citizens', *Economic Policy* 2001, no. 32, pp. 9ff.

[4] See the comparative research carried out by F. W. Scharpf and V. A. Schmidt, *Welfare and Work in the Open Economy* (2 vols.), Oxford 2000.

arising from the globalization of capital and financial markets and from increasingly fierce international commercial competition are not the only ones that European welfare states find themselves having to confront today, and probably not even the most important and impelling.[5] The influences at work also include, perhaps even more deeply, the demands for the reform or, to use today's Eurojargon, 'modernization'[6] of the welfare state that are simultaneously dictated by the epochal 'endogenous' changes in progress in European economic and social systems. The rapid transition to a post-industrial economy – based on methods of production of goods and services that are increasingly more information- and knowledge-intensive and less energy-intensive[7] – is radically altering the material framework of reference of national systems of labour and social-security law and means that the forms of solidarity crystallized in them in the phase of their maximum (Fordist and Keynesian) expansion during the hectic thirty-year period of economic recovery in the aftermath of the Second World War known as the *Trente Glorieuses*[8] are becoming increasingly inadequate, in terms of both going too far and not going far enough.

The EMU constitution has in a sense internalized the fundamental principles of the new international political economy. Today, macroeconomic rigour and monetary stability are directly ensured by the rules of the EC Treaty and the Stability and Growth Pact and, in particular, guaranteed by the complete autonomy and independence of the European Central Bank, specifically 'purpose'-designed along the lines typical of the so-called 'conservative institutions'.

It has also increased the competitive dynamic within the Community. 'Up till now the European integration process has in fact accentuated rather than attenuated competition, and so increased the responsibilities of national policy precisely while transferring some of them to a

---

[5] Cf. Ferrera, Hemerijck and Rhodes, *Future*; N. Acocella (ed.), *Globalizzazione e Stato sociale*, Bologna 1999.

[6] See, for example, Commission of the European Communities, *Modernising and Improving Social Protection in the European Union*, COM(97)102 final.

[7] C. Freeman and L. Soete, *Work for All or Mass Unemployment? Computerised Technical Change into the Twenty-first Century*, London-New York 1994.

[8] See, just by way of example, A. Supiot (ed.), *Au-delà de l'emploi. Transformations du travail et devenir du droit du travail en Europe. Rapport pour la Commission européenne*, Paris 1999; M. D'Antona, 'Diritto del lavoro di fine secolo: una crisi d'identità?', *Rivista Giuridica del Lavoro e della Previdenza Sociale* 1998, vol. I, pp. 311ff. (now also in D'Antona, *Contrattazione, rappresentatività, conflitto. Scritti sul diritto sindacale*, edited and with an introductory essay by G. Ghezzi and a foreword by S. Cofferati, Rome 2000, p. 273); U. Romagnoli, 'Per un diritto del lavoro post-industriale e sovranazionale', *Lavoro e Diritto* 1999, pp. 209ff.

supranational level.'[9] The intrinsic pervasiveness of the competitive process is being reinforced and driven on by the law of the economy of the European Union.

On the other hand, it is now quite clear that – even after monetary unification – there is not to be a single European welfare state, i.e. a centralized welfare system organized and operating directly at supranational level. What Norbert Reich called the *Versozialstaatlichung*[10] of the European Community in no way preludes a completed 'federalization' of matters relating to distributive justice, or a transfer en masse to the Union of the fiscal powers necessary for fulfilling at the single higher level the extensive social-protection functions currently performed by the Member States in forms that are still highly diverse.[11] Responsibility, both political and fiscal, for the basic institutions of welfare and social citizenship is – and in all probability will remain – essentially national, i.e. specific to each Member State of the Union.

As a corollary, main responsibility for the necessary processes of readaptation and/or modernization of their welfare systems still lies with the individual Member States. Although governments can no longer rely on the protective mechanisms set up during the post-war years to achieve the objectives of full employment and social protection and equality, the nation-state remains the principle locus of political change.[12]

In tune with the call for 'regulatory moderation'[13] that is in a sense inherent in its affirmation of the principle of subsidiarity, the role that

---

[9] Streeck, 'Il modello', p. 3.

[10] N. Reich, *Schutzpolitik in der Europäischen Gemeinschaft im Spannungsfeld von Rechtsschutznormen und institutioneller Integration*, Hanover 1988, p. 7.

[11] The answer to the everlasting question whether the re-regulation of national labour markets and social-protection systems under way in Europe and also being boosted by the Community itself is tending to accentuate convergences or, on the contrary, to widen divergences remains irreducibly dependent on the analytical outlook chosen, and therefore intrinsically relative and very variable. Answers that are soundly reasoned and persuasive in both directions are to be found in the legal literature. For a prognosis of the tendency towards hybridization of European welfare-capitalism models, see M. Rhodes and B. Van Apeldoorn, 'The Transformation of West European Capitalism?', *EUI Working Papers, Robert Schuman Centre – European University Institute* No. 97/60, p. 12.

[12] Ferrera, Hemerijck and Rhodes, *Future*, p. 5.

[13] S. Simitis, 'Europeizzazione o rinazionalizzazione del diritto del lavoro?', *Giornale di Diritto del Lavoro e di Relazioni Industriali* 1994, pp. 639ff., here p. 648. The same author has also talked elsewhere in this connection, in even more critical terms, of 'a withdrawal to regulatory minimalism' (see 'Il diritto del lavoro ha ancora un futuro?', *Giornale di Diritto del Lavoro e di Relazioni Industriali* 1997, pp. 609ff., here p. 637). These are critical thoughts which, given the time when they were articulated – prior to the Amsterdam revision – were wholly feasible and certainly shared, but which nowadays have to be reconsidered in the light of the most recent developments in European integration.

the Community level of governance undertakes nowadays is – as we have seen – predominantly one of political and institutional co-ordination and less and less one of direct and prescriptive regulatory intervention.

The evocative image of 'polycentric and horizontal Europeanization' suggested in this connection by Streeck[14] offers useful interpretative clues for grasping some of the basic features of the phenomenon. The dynamics of Europeanization involve a complex and open process in which competition between the different national models coexists with the attempt to strengthen supranational channels of governance and sites of co-ordination and co-operation, possibly differentiated.[15]

The Community has, as a matter of policy, marginalized the model (which was in any case largely ineffective even during the years when it appeared to enjoy a majority consensus) of normatively imposing uniformity on national social systems via hard law. Particularly since the Treaty of Amsterdam was signed it has, however, developed new forms of response which – although leaving broad scope for differentiation – are also capable of re-unifying the composite Community order around reaffirmation of the central values of the European social model.[16]

The rebalancing of an economic constitution that had been biased in the direction of the clearly prevalent negative integration of national markets is at any rate following routes that are inevitably new and still in the course of construction.

The eminently procedural slant of the open co-ordination and reflexive harmonization strategy is still in search of the firmer anchorage, in full constitutionalization, of a mandatory core of Community fundamental social values and rights that will offset its indisputable elements of weakness. Social rights and policies are both ingredients needed in order to give substance to the re-balancing of European integration.[17]

In terms of normative content, the inevitable uncertainties and difficulties of the quest for a new and fair balance between the dictates of economic

[14] 'Il modello', p. 11.
[15] See also K. Dyson 'EMU As Europeanization: Convergence, Diversity and Contingency', *Journal of Common Market Studies* 2000, pp. 645ff., especially pp. 649–50, where Europeanization is seen as a process in which different discourses and logic systems coexist and which is constructed according to both 'bottom–up' (differentiation and competition) and 'top–down' (co-operation and convergence guided by the Community) thrusts.
[16] In this sense, albeit from different investigatory approaches, see M. Barbera, *Dopo Amsterdam. I nuovi confini del diritto sociale comunitario*, Brescia 2000, pp. 109ff., and I. Pernice, 'Multilevel Constitutionalism and the Treaty of Amsterdam: European Constitution-Making Revisited?', *Common Market Law Review* 1999, pp. 703ff., especially pp. 732 and 734.
[17] See T. Treu, 'Diritti sociali europei: dove siamo?', *Lavoro e Diritto* 2000, pp. 429ff., especially pp. 441ff.

efficiency and competitiveness, and the old and new demands of social protection, are reflected in the uneven and sometimes (at least apparently) contradictory nature of the 'messages' conveyed by the Employment Guidelines, as also by the goals that inspire the 2000 European Social Agenda. Deakin and Reed have described the guidelines as a 'curious mix of neo-liberal policy objectives, which stress deregulation and individual responsibility for training and labour market mobility, and neo-corporatist strategies, which envisage collective solutions to the reconciliation of flexibility and security'.[18]

A continuous and unresolved tension is clearly discernible between tendencies of a neoliberal stamp, which are inspired by an idea that Streeck has effectively described as 'competitive solidarity', and those which – sometimes regaining neo-Keynesian accents – assign a still central role to forms of 'distributive solidarity', in which they maintain the authentic fulcrum of social policy.[19]

The notion of employability, the original first pillar of the Employment Guidelines drawn up by the Council, and also those of 'active security' or 'flexicurity'[20] which in a sense serve as its background, give a clear indication of a tendency, albeit from profiles that are still uncertain and somewhat indeterminate,[21] towards the competitive reorientation of solidarity.

In this view of things, the focus of solidarity is tending to shift from forms of passive income redistribution, less and less effective and more and more constrained by rigid financial and economic constraints, to forms of employment-friendly activation of the abilities and opportunities of individuals for participating in the productive process. Supporting this logic, European social policy is tending to give way to employment policy, increasingly concentrated on reproducing the 'human capital' of

---

[18] S. Deakin and H. Reed, 'The Contested Meaning of Labour Market Flexibility: Economic Theory and the Discourse of European Integration', in J. Shaw (ed.), *Social Law and Policy in an Evolving European Union*, Oxford-Portland 2000, pp. 71ff., here p. 95.

[19] See Streeck, 'Il modello', pp. 13ff. The distinction between 'competitive' and 'redistributive' solidarity presents pronounced analogies with that between 'Schumpeterian' workfare and 'Fordist–Keynesian' welfare as put forward by B. Jessop, 'The Transition to Post-Fordism and the Schumpeterian Workfare State', in R. Burrows and B. Loader (eds.), *Towards a Post-Fordist Welfare State?*, London 1994, pp. 13ff.

[20] See Ferrera, Hemerijck and Rhodes, *Future*, pp. 46ff.

[21] And from implications that are sometimes decidedly problematic: see S. Giubboni, 'Flessibilità e diritto della previdenza sociale. Spunti ricostruttivi', *Rivista Giuridica del Lavoro e della Previdenza Sociale* 1999, pp. 569ff., especially pp. 584ff., for some critical comments on the ambiguous incidence of the 'employability' concept in strategies for the 'active' redesign of systems of social protection against unemployment.

subjects and equipping them with equal starting-points and hence equal chances of inclusion in an increasingly fragmented and, by the same token, competitive labour market, from a perspective that has been described as 'supply-side egalitarianism'.[22]

Alongside the emphasis on active strategies for the prevention of social need through the development of individual responsibility, however, there are also references to the more traditional dimensions of solidarity. One author has controversially read in the Nice Charter a return to 'a conception of static and redistributive solidarity of rights to a sharing-out of existing resources', with 'traces of statal dirigisme-labourism'.[23]

However much this statement may smack of polemic exaggeration and emphasize one-sidedly only one of the dimensions of solidarity embodied in the Charter, there is nevertheless no doubt that the latter reaffirms the central value and indispensability of strong and stable mechanisms of redistributive solidarity.[24] The role of these mechanisms features particularly significantly in strategies for combating social exclusion, where public intervention certainly cannot confine itself merely to action to correct market failures, in line with a purely competitive-solidarity approach, but – as specifically required by the Community – must also be directly aimed at guaranteeing everyone sufficient resources to ensure a decent existence, in a protective and redistributive logic.[25]

The idea which this albeit hesitant and problematic rediscovery of solidarity as a founding value of Community integration seems to share is that, far from being an obstacle to the dynamism of the economies of the Old Continent, a heightened European social element constitutes, on the contrary, one of the main factors of their long-term competitiveness and needs to be nurtured alike by effective employment policies and strong systems of social rights and guarantees. From this point of view it is very important that Article I-2 of the constitutional Treaty has affirmed the centrality of the Union's social values, in particular by pronouncing that European society is based on pluralism, non-discrimination, tolerance,

---

[22] J. Cohen and J. Rogers, 'Can Egalitarianism Survive Internationalization?', in W. Streeck (ed.), *Internationale Wirtschaft, nationale Demokratie. Herausforderungen für die Demokratietheorie*, Frankfurt am Main-New York 1998, pp. 175ff.

[23] A. Quadrio Curzio, 'Gli equivoci della solidarietà senza sviluppo e sussidiarietà', *Il Mulino* 2001, no. 1, pp. 40ff., here p. 42.

[24] For a more lengthy illustration of this aspect, see S. Giubboni, 'Solidarietà e sicurezza sociale nella Carta dei diritti fondamentali dell'Unione europea', *Giornale di Diritto del Lavoro e di Relazioni Industriali* 2001, pp. 617ff.

[25] Cf. A. Atkinson, 'Rischi della nuova economia e ruolo del welfare nell'inclusione sociale', *Quaderni Rassegna Sindacale* 2000, no. 4, pp. 37ff.

justice, solidarity and equality between men and women. Just as it is likewise important that its Article I-3 tends towards placing the Union's economic and social objectives on an equal footing by combining them in the balanced formula of 'a highly competitive social market economy'.

Hence, the stakes involved in the current redefinition of the European social model consist in not renouncing the ideals of emancipation and social inclusion that formed part of its founding mission, without threatening the international competitiveness of the European economies, and so making the high levels of cohesion and protection guaranteed – even if in new ways – by welfare the most important asset in meeting the challenge of global economic competition.

INDEX